Yenching University and Sino-Western
Relations, 1916–1952

Harvard East Asian Series 85
The East Asian Research Center at Harvard University administers
research projects designed to further scholarly understanding of
China, Japan, Korea, Vietnam, Inner Asia, and adjacent areas.

Yenching University and Sino-Western Relations, 1916–1952

Philip West

Harvard University Press, Cambridge, Massachusetts, and
London, England, 1976

Preparation of this volume has been aided by a grant from the
Ford Foundation.
Printed in the United States of America
Library of Congress Cataloging in Publication Data
West, Philip, 1938–
    Yenching University and Sino-Western relations,
1916–1952.
    (Harvard East Asian series; 85)
    Bibliography: p.
    Includes index.
    1. Yen-ching ta hsüeh, Peking. 2. Missions—China
3. China—Politics and government—1912–1949.
4. China—Politics and government—1949–   5. College
students—China—Political activity.   I. Title.
II. Series.
LG51.P95W47   320'.951'04   76–2564
ISBN 0–674–96569–8

To Lu-san

PREFACE

The most delightful part of my research for this book was the interviews with the Chinese and Western teachers and the alumni of Yenching University. The one I owe the first debt to is Grace M. Boynton. She gave me a "feel" for life in those days in Peking, and she allowed me to read her correspondence and journals kept over her thirty years of teaching English at Yenching. With her death in February 1970 I lost a friend.

Almost as extensive were my conversations with Philip Fugh, longtime personal secretary to Yenching president, John Leighton Stuart. The many hours of interviews with Fugh in Washington, D.C., were an invaluable source of information on the inner workings of the Yenching administration both in China and the United States.

Two of the most highly respected Yenching faculty living in the United States, William Hung and Mei-Yi-pao, also granted lengthy taped interviews, Hung in his study in the Harvard-Yenching Library and Mei in Iowa City.

The conversations with Yenching luminaries in the Philadelphia area were rich and valuable: with Randolph and Louise Sailer who worked closely in Yenching student affairs for some two decades; with Augusta Wagner and Margaret Speer, the latter letting me read the correspondence with her father and mother, Mr. and Mrs. Robert Speer, during her Yenching years; and with Ida Pruitt for tea and talk about her own radical critique of the Yenching experiment. My appreciation, too, to Abigail Hoffsomer of the United Board for Christian Higher Education in Asia, located in New York. She granted me access to the administrative papers and correspondence of the Yenching board of trustees, and for each of my many visits there she provided me with a desk and a typewriter in a room overlooking the Hudson River.

I went to Marlboro, Vermont, to see Mildred Raible and Dorothy MacArthur and talked with them about their father, Howard S. Galt. They kindly gave me a copy of his unpublished manuscript "Yenching University: Its Sources and Its History" (1939). Galt's study was the basis for much of Dwight Edwards' *Yenching University* (1959). Despite their partiality to the missionary enterprise, Galt's and Edwards' studies were valuable sources on the details of university life that fall outside the intercultural focus of this study.

I also went to Delaware, Ohio, for extended conversations with Bliss and Mildred Wiant about their two decades of teaching at Yenching; and to Elgin, Illinois, for a visit with Elizabeth Kirkpatrick who told me about her parents, Lucius and Lillian Porter, and let me read his diaries and their correspondence with her. While en route to Taiwan for a year of language study and research, I spent several hours with Stella Fisher Burgess, then 89, in Pomona. Her lengthy correspondence with me prior to her death in 1974 is scattered with nuggets of humor and biting insight on her experiences as an old China hand at Yenching and on her husband, John Stewart Burgess.

While in Taiwan and Hong Kong I interviewed some of the Yenching alumni. Among them special mention should be given to Liu T'ing-wei, for hours of conversation about his older brother, Liu T'ing-fang (T. T. Lew), to Wei Ching-meng for letters of introduction, and to Yeh Ch'u-sheng and Li Man-kuei for recalling their activities as student leaders on the Yenching campus in the 1920s and the 1930s. Among the Hong Kong alumni, I am grateful to T'an Jen-chiu, T'ien Hsing-chih, and Ma Meng for their personal recollections of student life and Yenching personalities and to Ch'en Li-sung who sent me the issues of the alumni bulletin, the *Yen-ta hsiao-yu t'ung-hsün,* of which he was the editor.

Beyond these American and Chinese contacts I was able to visit Nancy Lapwood in Cambridge, England. Ralph and Nancy Lapwood were the last full-time Western teachers to leave the Yenching campus in 1952. More recently, during a period of teaching in Japan the fall of 1974, I spent an afternoon with Ariga Tetsutarō of Dōshisha University in Kyoto. Ariga visited the Yenching campus as a guest lecturer in 1930, and he told of Dōshisha's valiant, but short-lived, efforts to strengthen ties with Yenching. My thanks, too, to Ikeda Kiyoko and

Yamamoto Sumiko of the International Christian University in Tokyo. They have shown a deep interest in my study and its parallel with their own work as educators and as scholars of intercultural relations between East Asia and the West. Professor Yamamoto's articles were the first source to alert me to the significance of Wu Lei-ch'uan, Yenching's first Chinese chancellor.

No less important have been my contacts in the academic community. With characteristic generosity, Eugene Wu of the Harvard-Yenching library reproduced microfilm copies of the Chinese language *Sheng-ming, Chen-li chou-k'an* and the *Chen-li yü sheng-ming,* used in documenting much of the Chinese side at the faculty level, and the *Yen-ta yüeh-k'an, Yen-ta chou-k'an, Yen-ching hsin-wen,* and *Hsin Yen-ching,* as major sources on the students. John T. Ma of the Hoover Library at Stanford was equally accommodating in making the vast resources of that library available to me. Glen Baxter provided a list of scholars who were connected one way or another with the Harvard-Yenching Institute over almost fifty years.

To friends and colleagues who have read all or part of the study I owe the largest debt: to Ezra Vogel, Paul Cohen, and John Fairbank who have read the complete manuscript in one of its various stages; to Stephen Levine, Madeline Levine, George M. Wilson, Teng Ssu-yü, Howard Boorman, Randolph Sailer, Stephen Tsai, Bliss Wiant, and M. Searle Bates, for their comments on parts of the study; to Charles Hayford, Donald Munro, Ross Terrill, and Hirano Kenichirō for stimulating comments on approaches and conceptualization; to Olive Holmes and Aida Donald for editorial assistance; and to Judith Berling and Sharon Mason for help in proofreading and indexing the manuscript.

Finally, I am grateful to the East Asian Research Center of Harvard University, especially to John Fairbank during his years as director, and to Indiana University for providing generous financial assistance over the past five years in preparing this study.

The views of informants and colleagues have had a definite influence in shaping this study of Yenching, but it goes without saying that the responsibilities for any factual errors and historical judgments are my own.

My first impression of Yenching University was that it represented a Western effort in China that I could respect, and I began by organizing the study around the theme of contributions, stressing the university's role in coeducation in China and in the development of sociology, journalism, and sinology. I was also aware of the large pool of Yenching graduates, more than three thousand of them, who went on to provide leadership in education, government, and business, on both sides of the civil conflict before and after the revolution. And then there was Yenching's role in diplomacy, with Stuart as the last American ambassador to China prior to the Communist Revolution and with two Yenching students of the 1930s playing key roles in Sino-Western relations in the 1970s, Huang Hua (Wang Ju-mei) as the People's Republic's first ambassador to the United Nations and James C. H. Shen (Shen Chien-hung) as the ambassador to Washington from the Republic of China.

I still appreciate these and other contributions, because of my strong respect for Yenching personalities. But upon closer investigation the theme of contributions appeared misplaced, especially so, as the study from beginning to end was carried out during the Indochina Wars. During those years my image of Yenching suffered, as the language used to justify the American effort in Vietnam sounded too much like the defense of missionary behavior in China. I have tried to avoid the pitfalls of present-mindedness, and yet there was no way to escape the idea that Western contributions in the modern history of East Asia were both positive and negative.

Yenching remained a meaningful subject for the study of Sino-Western relations, as my attention shifted away from contributions to the interactions between Chinese and Westerners. By examining the range in attitudes and behavior of individuals in one institution over more than thirty years, from the American businessmen who sat on the board of trustees in New York to radical students who would later become leaders in the Communist movement, I was able to appreciate the deep ambiguities in Sino-Western relations in the twentieth century. As the early years of Yenching's history were a testimony to intercultural cooperation, the last years became a study in the problems of the cold war in East Asia.

Contents

Illustrations (following page 88)

Courtesy of the United Board for Christian Higher Education in Asia
The department of Chinese at Yenching in 1928
The "Harvard Group" of the Yenching faculty in the late 1940s
Chancellor Lu Chih-wei and President John Leighton Stuart at the Yenching commencement in September 1936
The poet Hsieh Ping Hsin (Wan-ying) and Acting Dean of Women Ruth Stahl in the late 1940s
Christmas Eve 1949
Men's Fourth Dormitory at Yenching in the 1930s
John Stewart Burgess and Yenching sociology students in 1929
Chao Tzu-ch'en (T. C. Chao) in the late 1940s
A Yenching production of "Macbeth" in the early 1920s
Yenching women were the 1927 champions in the Peking Intercollegiate Ladies Basketball League
Peking University, March 1959, located on the former Yenching campus

Tables

Diagrams

Yenching University and Sino-Western
Relations, 1916–1952

1

Introduction

Prior to the nineteenth century Chinese history could be largely interpreted as an internal matter that had little to do with the West. Since then, however, Sino-Western relations have become an integral part of China's modern experience. With the penetration of Western military power into East Asian waters and China's defeat in the Opium War (1839–42) China was faced with an unprecedented foreign challenge from the sea. This Western penetration gathered momentum as China was forced into new wars with the West and in the aftermath of each was burdened with another treaty that increased the humiliation. Protected by gunboat diplomacy, treaty ports sprang up along the coastal and riverine areas, handling the huge volume of Sino-Western trade and producing the consciousness we associate with the rise of nationalism. When the Chinese Communist party fed and harnessed this nationalistic spirit more effectively than any other group and seized power in 1949, they removed first the overt expressions of American and European influence and a decade later those of the Russians. Nonetheless, the West continues to be an important part of Chinese history. Western values, such as the belief in progress, have now become internalized. The West also serves as a negative example, as Chinese leaders fashion a new order that is Western in some ways but also distinctly Chinese.

China has also been important to the West, especially to Americans, though this importance became evident somewhat later. The last three wars fought by the United States have taken place within the Chinese cultural area, the first as an ally of China against Japan, the second in Korea as Chinese and American soldiers engaged in full scale battles for the first time in history, and the third against Indochinese revolutionaries whose inspiration and models are linked closely with China's revolutionary experience. Each of these wars, especially the last, has had a large impact on American society. In suggesting the importance of these interrelationships, I do not mean to belittle the internal developments, which are certainly more significant in understanding the histories of both sides of the encounter. But the vacillations between mutual fear and friendship and the conflicts in collective self-images and national purposes throughout the twentieth century have had and continue to have far reaching consequences not only for both sides but also for the rest of the world.[1]

Trends in Interpretations

Despite the significance of Sino-Western relations a consensus of interpretation has not yet emerged. Subjective feelings and colored perceptions still dominate the analyses and the conclusions that scholars and other writers have tried to make. Unlike the many theoretical studies on development internally for both China and the various nations of the West, there is no commonly accepted understanding of relations between them. Sociologists have employed phrases such as interethnic stratification and cultural assimilation in their efforts to create a science of intercultural relations. But these studies are based largely on the patterns of adjustments of minority groups within a dominant culture, and the generalizations derived from them appear to be irrelevant to the problem of Sino-Western relations where cultural and political dominance remains an open question. Similarly, diplomatic scholars have presented interpretations of international relations, but too often their studies are limited to official relationships and are based largely on the documentation from the Western side. The configurations of diplomacy are very important in studies such as this, but diplomatic history is only one aspect of the intercultural relationship. The role of individuals who are not overly connected with diplomacy and the role of evolving myths and images may over the long run be an equally if not more important part of the relationship. In the area of unofficial relations the Chinese side remains largely unexplored.[2]

For many years the studies of Sino-Western relations were carried out by writers who were either connected with the missionary enterprise or endorsed the Western thrust into China. Kenneth Scott Latourette, in the preface to his monumental *History of Christian Missions in China* (1929), openly states how he is "thoroughly committed to the enterprise of Christian missions." One of the purposes of his study is to "interpret missionary activities in China more favorably than some who are not so committed." Tyler Dennett's *Americans in East Asia* (1922), has dominated later specialized writings and diplomatic histories dealing with East Asia, and his influence has reinforced the image of America's special relationship with China, one in which the Americans behaved more responsibly than their European counterparts.[3]

The breadth of Latourette's and Dennett's studies remains unsurpassed, but the Communist Revolution has stimulated scholars to question some of their assumptions and to reassess the nature of Sino-Western relations. In that reassessment two general trends can be found. The first one is the idea that contact with the West was a negative experience for China, in which the successive defeats in wars with Western nations and Japan for over a century were only the most obvious expression. More subtle, though no less damaging, were the effects of Western culture transmitted by missionaries, educators, traders, and businessmen, and by the thousands of Chinese students who went abroad to study. Y. C. Wang in *Chinese Intellectuals and the West,* 1872–1949 (1966) emphasizes the uselessness and alienating effects of this exposure. Western education, in Wang's words, produced an "elite unconnected with the life surrounding them." For the few who came to the cities from rural areas, Western education was a "process of urbanization, for once exposed the students never returned to their native places. The large use of foreign materials in the curriculum . . . perpetuated and further contributed to the alienation of the students from their native culture and surrounding life."[4] James C. Thomson sees the issue in *While China Faced West* (1969) as the failure of gradualism, that is the failure of reformist approaches, associated with Western influence, to respond effectively to the national problems that required bolder and broader solutions.[5] Wang's and Thomson's judgments are painful because many Chinese, as well as Westerners, had believed in the efficacy of Western influence and gradual reform for almost half a century. The tendency to dismiss China's past contact with the culture of Western Europe and the United States as cultural imperialism has become more broadly accepted in the West with the growing popularity of the writings and interpretations of Mao Tse-tung.[6]

A related theme within this first trend is the idea that Western efforts to help China were not only negative for China but futile from the start. Surveying sixteen Western advisers to China from the Jesuit missionaries working in the imperial court in the seventeenth century to the Russian experts working in China in the 1950s, Jonathan Spence in *The China Helpers* (1969) demonstrates how they all wanted to "bring improvement to China, either spiritual or material. Each adviser, in a way, had sought to control China's destiny." But in the end they were "used by the Chinese rather than using the Chinese" and were "swallowed by their own technique."[7] In Spence's interpretation their motives were reproachful and their efforts were misguided and naive.

A second general trend to emerge since the Communist Revolution is the idea that the direction of the impact in Sino-Western relations has shifted from China to the West. The roles have been reversed. The West not only has nothing more to teach China, but China in a sense has become a model for the West. The renowned British sinologist Joseph Needham has said, "The rest of the world needs to learn with all humility, not only from contemporary China but from the China of all time, for in Chinese wisdom and experience there are medicines for many diseases of the spirit." To Mark Selden, who echoes the sentiments of a new group of China scholars, the Chinese Revolution "offers inspiration" to and "addresses men and women everywhere who seek to create a society free from stifling oppression, arbitrary state power, and enslaving technology."[8] More recently leading China specialists in the United States have contributed essays to a volume entitled *China's Developmental Experience,* which is presented as a "unique contribution to American-Chinese understanding." It explores the "lessons, both positive and negative, that may be learned from China's developmental experience which might have a bearing on Western societies and on other developing nations."[9] The keenest area of Western interest in China is medicine, as can be seen in the hundreds of articles and many books on Chinese medicine appearing within the last few years. This turning toward China is not wholly new in the history of Sino-Western relations. Some two centuries ago many Western thinkers regarded China as a kind of model that gave support to their particular views of man and society.[10]

What is new, however, is the clear challenge to the assumption of the

West's dominance and superiority over China. For years modern history has been defined by the penetration of Western power and influence around the world. Some may still believe the West has something to offer China and that Western influence may continue to spread throughout the world. But for the Chinese, at least, the battle has been joined. The cycle, in Jonathan Spence's words, is over. Chinese advisers have "begun to compete in many areas with advisers from the West, seeking to prove the validity of a Chinese world view through the sophistication of Chinese expertise . . . China, which once surpassed the West, then almost succumbed to it, now offers to the world her own solutions."[11] Arnold Toynbee lends support to this perception when he writes, "It would not be surprising if the twenty-first century proved to be an East Asian century of human history."[12]

The possibility of China's dominance over the West may help to redress the previous imbalance and soften the sting of the appearance of Western superiority in the past, a prospect that may offend those who still support foreign missions, religious or otherwise. But others in the West now condemn any further expansion of Western influence. With this shift in perspectives, it is not uncommon to find among beginning students those who laud the demise of Western influence in China. They find it hard to believe that Chinese youth could once have been devotees of Dickens, Ibsen, Tolstoy, Tagore or be regular members of Bible study groups. One sure way to get a snicker in the classroom is to say that the YMCA, in fact, was once the most popular club on Chinese college campuses. Such disbelief is a measure of our own self-doubts.

Christianity and Chinese Culture

China's modern encounter with the West occurred largely in the areas of trade, missions, and diplomacy. Without suggesting that trade and diplomacy are any less important, I would like to focus on missions, especially Protestant missions, for they provide the more immediate background to this study. Protestant converts were always small in number compared to the Catholics, but the impact of Protestant missions in breaking down the Confucian order and in offering new ideas has been greater than that of Catholic missions. Mission stations were located in more than 1,500 of some 2,000 counties in all of China's provinces, but equally important was their broad system of schools and their political ties with the Chinese leadership during the late Ch'ing

(1644–1912) and the Republican (1912–49) years. The Protestant missionaries converted no more than a fraction of 1 percent of the Chinese people, and their influence in political circles rapidly diminished after Chiang K'ai-shek's rise to power in the late 1920s. This failure, though, was as dramatic as the apparent success in earlier times.

From the perspective of the Confucian value system the emphasis on the failure of Christian missions at the midpoint of the twentieth century is misleading, for the Communist success can be understood precisely in those areas where the missionaries were pioneers. The list of their pioneering efforts is extensive: the spread of literacy to ordinary people, the publication of journals and pamphlets in the vernacular, education and equality for women, the abolition of arranged child-marriages, the supremacy of public duty over filial obedience and family obligations, student organizations to promote physical recreation and moral guidance, and the acquisition and sinification of Western knowledge for use in remaking Chinese life.[13] These ideas were rather new in nineteenth century China, and they took hold first in the ideology of the great Taiping Rebellion (1851–64), later in the Hundred Day Reform program led by K'ang Yu-wei (1857–1927) in 1898, and still later in the broad programs of social reform in the first quarter of the twentieth century. Despite that success the missionaries and their converts failed to translate these ideas into enduring political forms. Their programs lacked the sharpness and comprehensiveness of Marxist analysis and the political relevance of Leninist principles of organization. And yet in the context of Chinese cultural history, this conflict between missionary anti-communism and the Communist condemnation of the missionaries, may be seen in some ways as a sectarian dispute. They differed in method but had similar purposes. André Malraux quoted Michael Borodin, the veteran Comintern agent, as saying: "You understand the behavior of the Protestant missionaries, don't you? Well, then, you understand mine!"[14]

One complication in evaluating the role of Christianity in China is the current scholarly aversion toward the religious underpinnings of the missionary enterprise. In a sense it is part of the ongoing conflict between religion and science that pervades twentieth century thought in both China and the West. Since the late nineteenth century Chinese leaders have denied the religious nature of their own thought and history. This denial was shared by key figures such as Yen Fu (1853–1921) Liang Ch'i-ch'ao (1873–1929), Hu Shih (1891–1962), and Ch'en Tu-hsiu (1879–1942), notwithstanding the great differences in their political ideas, confused loyalties to the past, and relationships with the West. Confronted with the West's overpowering strength, traditionalists sought to justify Chinese civilization in terms the Western world, which saw China as backward and inferior, could understand. And to the proponents of radical change, Western science offered the exciting vision of a new society and a powerful weapon in the education and mobilization of youth and the masses. In either case they were swept up in the tides of secularization which, in C. K. Yang's words, waved off religion with "defiance and even contempt."[15]

The controversy over science and religion gelled in the Republican years with the outbreak of the Anti-Christian movement beginning in 1922, and the Communist attack on religion down to the present day issues from this conflict as much as it does from the nationalistic irritation over the connection between missions and imperialism.[16] By the end of the 1920s the debate was so clearly won by science that the one error Chinese intellectuals, including Christians, have tried to avoid is the charge of being unscientific. Religious experience was justified by converts in scientific terms. Being scientific became linked with being patriotic.

This mistrust of religion also runs deep in Western thought, and it has come to influence both our interpretations of what is important in Chinese history and also the nature of Sino-Western relations. It shapes the kinds of questions asked and the kinds of materials employed in the craft of scholarship. This aversion, of course, was not so prevalent in earlier Western sinology, which grew largely out of the efforts of avowedly religious figures, like the German philosopher Leibniz and the European Jesuits who were part and parcel of the missionary enterprise itself. The controversy has sharpened in recent decades as the religious hold over the life of Western, especially American, colleges and universities, where much of the scholarship is done, has been associated with backward thinking and its decline with progress. This conflict became apparent in my study of Yenching, where the materials documenting the intercultural tie were often religious in nature. I had to cope with the doubts first within myself and then those of my colleagues that these kinds of evidence were too subjective to serve as valid bases for historical inquiry. This recent preference for so-called hard data and disdain for studying personalities and religious ideas has affected not only the study of Sino-Western relations but other areas of sinology as well. William T. deBary, for example, sees the tendency among Ming specialists to dismiss the religious experiences of individuals as conventional hagiography as a large obstacle to understanding the philosopher-states-man, Wang Yang-ming.[17] The judgments of those who claim to be more scientific may well be as value-laden and subjective as those who do not make such a claim. More than half a century ago William James noted that "scientific theories are organically conditioned just as much as religious emotions are; and if we only knew the facts intimately enough, we should doubtless see 'the liver' determining the dicta of the sturdy atheist as decisively as it does those of the Methodist under conviction anxious about his soul."[18]

One widely accepted explanation for Christianity's failure in China is the idea that the Chinese people did not understand concepts such as sin, guilt, and personal salvation. In *Missionaries, Chinese, and Diplomats* (1958) Paul Varg claims the Chinese people had no sense of sin. Un-like the West, Chinese society "created no inner struggle between the ideal and the actual, and consequently the Chinese had no sense of what the Christian termed sin or the love of God versus the love of self." As a result the "Christian church in China met no generally recognized needs" and "remained largely an esoteric enterprise without roots in the Chi-nese soil."[19] Varg's study is still the best survey of Protestant missions in China, but his interpretation is a facile one and ties in with another bit of conventional wisdom that the Chinese people, as Confucianists, did not understand religion because Confucianism was after all not a religion but a philosophy. This interpretation is frequently connected with the idea that Western religious ideas failed to take root because China was a shame oriented society in contrast to the guilt orientation of the West.

To be sure, there are important cultural differences between West-erners and Chinese, but do these differences explain the failure of Chris-tianity in China? I think not. Chinese culture was perhaps more pluralistic, even in times of greatest stability, than we are sometimes led to believe. Confucianism served well the interests of the imperial family, the aristocracy, and the gentry class for centuries, but not all members of the ruling elite regarded themselves as exclusively Confucianist. Shamanistic ideas such as the belief in ancestor worship predate the rise of Confucianism and coexisted with Confucian beliefs down to the pres-ent century. Buddhism was also very much a part of Chinese culture. It spread to all levels of society and brought with it an image of man and the universe replete with the ideas of sin and salvation. Twentieth century Chinese literature, furthermore, abounds with the themes of ghosts, spirits, and heavenly rewards and punishments. The pervasiveness of these ideas in the literature of the masses has been explored by Wolfram Eberhard in *Guilt and Sin in Traditional China* (1967).[20] Chinese notions of guilt and sin may not have been the same as those of Protestant fundamentalism, but it must be remembered that many missionaries and Chinese converts differed sharply among themselves in their understanding of these concepts.

The ways in which Buddhism and later Marxism became a part of Chinese life further reinforce the idea that Chinese culture cannot be simply equated with Confucian ideas and that Christianity as a set of ideas was not necessarily unintelligible to the Chinese people. On the face of it the Buddhist emphasis upon meditation and resignation from secular living, as seen in its rich monastic tradition, conflicts with the Confucian emphasis upon proper social relationships. Nevertheless, Buddhism succeeded not only in spreading throughout the whole of China but also in reshaping the new orthodoxy of neo-Confucianism in the twelfth century. And it did so despite the periodic persecutions and continuous rivalry with Confucianism over more than a thousand years of Chinese history. Traditionalists say that Chinese culture corrupted Buddhism, which may simply be another way of saying that Buddhism was not necessarily incompatible with Chinese culture. Indeed, to be Buddhist became for many people the mark of being Chinese.

Similarly it is hard to imagine more opposite images of man than the harmony orientation of neo-Confucianism and the struggle orientation of Marxism. In the early twentieth century who would have thought that Marxism would ever succeed in becoming accepted to the extent that it has by both rulers and ruled in China? But once Marxism achieved this measure of success, for whatever reasons, we find it as easy to see the continuities with the Confucian past as to point out the conflicts and discontinuities. In one sense to be Chinese today means to be Marxist.

When we look at the Chinese converts to Catholicism in the seventeenth century, we find among them high officials who converted to the Christian faith during their rise to prominence through the Confucian examination system and who rose even higher after their conversions. Coming down to the twentieth century, converts were made among those who as children and young students had studied the Confucian classics. It is true that there were among the converts those who were described as rice Christians, those who converted in return for a bowl of rice. But opportunism was certainly no monopoly of converts to Christianity in China, and the concept of rice Christianity may mislead more than it guides us in our efforts to understand the converts' side of Sino-Western relations. Christianity in China was received in a variety of ways. Its appeal was at times patriotic, at other times fundamentalistic. One Christian church, the Ye-su chia, or Jesus Family, which was sinified quite successfully, was very fundamentalistic and sectarian in outlook.[21]

This controversy over the relationship between Christianity and Chinese culture is enriched by comparisons with Japan. The popular Japanese writer Endō Shūsaku has written a novel, *Silence,* and a play, *The Golden Country,* which treat the persecutions of Christians in early seventeenth century Japan. In them he suggests that the Japanese people lacked the requisite concepts regarding the individual, sin, and God for Christianity to take root. Japan, in short, was a "mudswamp" which rotted all seeds from the outside. In the play, Lord Inoue, the official in charge of the bureau to investigate Christians, responds to the fact that some 200,000 Japanese had converted within the span of fifty years, by saying: "The plants were not growing. They only seemed to be. They didn't blossom. They only seemed to do so . . . No matter what shoots one tries to transplant here from another country, they all wither and die, or else bear a flower and fruit that only resemble the real ones."[22] Endō's thesis has been disputed by Japanese Christians who regard themselves as being fully Japanese and by others who refuse to equate Japanese culture with the values and political purposes of the samurai class and Tokugawa shogunate, which were responsible for the persecutions of the Christians.

The Politics of Sino-Western Relations

The suggestion that China was not culturally impervious to Western ideas does not imply that it was a carte blanche for those ideas. Quite the contrary, there was strong opposition to the systematic introduction of Christanity in the sixteenth century down to the present day. But it is important to understand the nature of the opposition. Who directed it? And how does it shape the larger interpretation of Sino-Western relations?

Paul Cohen in *China and Christianity* (1963) explores this official hostility toward "heterodox" ideas, beginning with attacks on Buddhism by Fu Yi (555–639) and Han Yü (768–824) and the Yung Cheng Emperor's (1723–35) sacred edicts and other proscriptions against

Christianity. This orthodox attack on heterodox ideas came to a head in the nineteenth century during the 1860s, the period of Cohen's study, when the Taiping rebels, whose ideology drew strongly upon Christian ideas, controlled the heartland of China and threatened to destroy the Ch'ing dynasty. By 1864 Chinese officials put down the rebellion and tried to stop any further spread of Christianity, but they were hampered in their efforts by the unequal treaties, which protected the spread of Christianity and which the officials, as employees of the central government, were legally bound to enforce. Despite this protection, hundreds of disputes, euphemistically referred to as missionary incidents, broke out over the last half century of Ch'ing rule.

These antimissionary incidents in Cohen's analysis were the result of the inevitable conflict between Chinese xenophobia and Western imperialism. It was a "cultural conflict" between the foreign missionary who took a "critical and often intolerant posture toward much of Chinese culture" and the Chinese intellectuals, whose responses "with very few exceptions, ranged from callous indifference to impassioned hatred."[23] Cohen's scholarly treatment of official hostility to Christianity in the late nineteenth century is an invaluable one, but his thesis raises several questions. For example, how far does the official xenophobia extend down into Chinese society? How might this history of heterodoxy be qualified if in addition to the Yung Cheng Emperor's edicts we included a discussion of his father's (the Kang Hsi Emperor, 1661–1722) edicts of toleration? And what generalizations can be made about Chinese culture from the writings of Chinese officials who are not just the bearers of cultural tradition but also pillars of a particular political structure?

These questions acquire an added significance when we turn from the official attacks on Christianity to the statistics on Chinese converts, first those of Catholicism beginning in the sixteenth century and then those of Protestantism beginning in the nineteenth century. Admittedly they lack precision, but definite trends do emerge. As a percentage of the population Christian converts were very few, but the trends within that small number may suggest something about the patterns of Sino-Western relations.

The first converts in the Chinese interior during the period of Jesuit missions were made in the last decades of the sixteenth century and increased to some 50,000 by the end of the Ming dynasty (1368–1644). Despite the changes in dynastic rule these conversions rapidly increased to an estimated 250,000 to 300,000 by 1700. This sevenfold increase in a little over a half century occurred under official tolerance and support which was given in exchange for the technical and scientific contributions of the Jesuit missionaries to the imperial court. The Jesuit success provoked jealousy among other Catholic orders working in China and culminated in the famous Rites Controversy in the eighteenth century which dealt a decisive blow against Jesuit efforts to adapt Christianity to Chinese culture. That controversy coupled with struggles for power surrounding the accession of the Yung Cheng Emperor to the throne and the jealousies of some officials toward the position of the Jesuits in the court brought an end to official tolerance followed by the proscription of the spread and even practice of Christianity. The eighteenth century persecutions of Christianity were led largely by officials and reduced the total number of converts by 1800 to an estimated 200,000. By then almost all foreign missionaries were forced to leave China. These persecutions, however, were sporadic and practically ceased in the early nineteenth century, even before the official proscription was lifted (partially in 1844 and completely in 1860). The number of converts again rose by 1850 to an estimated 300,000 and continued thereafter to rise to an all time high of some three and a half million a century later.[24]

The Protestant parallel to all this began later and was much smaller. By the time the first Protestant missionary arrived in China in 1807, the Catholic church was already well established in all of China's eighteen provinces and was led largely be a native clergy. The number of Protestant converts rose very slowly over the first half century of work, unless one includes the converts to Taiping ideology, in which case it may have numbered in the hundreds of thousands before the movement was crushed. By 1900 the total number rose to around 90,000 and over the next two decades increased some fourfold to over 350,000 and thereafter to an estimated half million by the late 1940s.[25] Since the Communist revolution in 1949 figures on the number of converts have been unavailable, but reports indicate that organized Christianity has been crushed, despite the constitutional guarantee of religious freedom.

What political factors help us understand these trends? To begin, there is an obvious correlation between the introduction of Christianity into China during periods of European political and economic expansion, first in the sixteenth century and then again more vigorously in the nineteenth and twentieth centuries. Similarly the decline of Christianity after 1949 correlates with the collapse of Western power and influence in China and the consolidation of the Communist power. These observations provide one of the parameters of Sino-Western relations, but do not fully explain the dynamics of intercultural history. The early Jesuit missionaries, for example, were brought to China in Portuguese carracks, but the establishment of their mission within China was quite unrelated to Portuguese military power, trade, or diplomacy. Their reception may have been political in the sense that the emperor and other high officials wanted first of all to use the Jesuit knowledge of mathematics and astronomy to strengthen the power of the imperial court through the more accurate prediction of eclipses and more precise calculations of the lunisolar calendar. These techniques were then used to demonstrate the emperor's superior understanding of the celestial order and thereby legitimize his claim to have the mandate of heaven. Important as these were, however, they do not explain why many other high officials, unconnected with these technological tasks in the central government, converted to Christianity and, more important, became evangelists themselves. Nor does it explain how Christianity spread as rapidly as it did in the seventeenth century throughout China to all levels of society.

What does appear clearly to be a political act are the official proscriptions and persecutions and the nineteenth century "incidents." Underlying themes in these attacks are the jealousies and rivalries within the ruling circles and the fear that the spread of the Christian faith, especially during the late nineteenth century period of dynastic decline, would destroy the social basis on which the political system rested. But those rivalries and fears were not shared by all the ruling elite in either the seventeenth or nineteenth centuries. In fact converts to Christianity in the earlier period occurred within the imperial household itself, while many officials and members of the gentry class tolerated Christianity even during periods of official proscription. By the end of the eighteenth century the Catholic church had declined in membership, but it was far from dead. Members of the literati class in the late nineteenth century supported Christianity even when the increase of missionary incidents was especially high. In the 1920s hostility again broke out in the Anti-Christian movement, as Marxist influence spread in student circles, providing converts to it a measure of cultural equivalence with the West by rejecting that part of the West more humiliating to China. But not unlike the earlier outbreaks of hostility, it too was in part an expression of rivalry among intellectual leaders competing for a following in student circles and among political parties trying to increase their own power.

In short the Christian experience in China defies simple categorization. Officials and peasants in Ming and Ch'ing times may have subscribed to common images of man that we label Confucian, but within that framework there was a rich diversity of thought and behavior. Some Confucian personalities turned to Christianity, not without some painful and humorous adjustments at times, to the requirements of monogamy, for example, but the fact is they did and without the sense that in doing so they were any less Chinese. These adjustments were easier to make within the flexible framework of Jesuit theology, but they were also made within the more rigid religious frameworks of the mendicant orders and of Protestant fundamentalism. We must also distinguish between the greater and the lesser traditions, that is, between the culture of the educated elite and the culture of the masses. In their poverty the masses may not have been as "blank" as Mao Tse-tung once suggested and as educational psychology in China today might indicate, but we can say with some certainty that they had a tradition of their own that was quite separate from, and at times in conflict with, the tradition of the literati.

The pluralism we must grant to' Chinese society also extends to the missionary enterprise, where differences among missionaries were sometimes greater than those between themselves and the Chinese people, as the Yenching episode so eloquently attests. There were in fact many faces of missions.[26] The historical record is scattered with instances of missionary arrogance, awkward communications, and misinterpretations. But a mutual relationship was unmistakably present in a way that qualifies the implications of the adage that "good intentions were not enough." The statistics and patterns of conversion indicate that the missionaries' claims to genuine reciprocity and community cannot be discounted. Could it be that the xenophobia, accompanying the missionary exodus in the early years after the Communist revolution, issued less from the resentments of the Chinese people than from the political designs of those who claimed to speak on their behalf? And that those spokesmen may have feared the actions not of the missionaries themselves so much as the actions of the nations whom the missionaries represented? Political considerations do set definite limits in our attempts to understand Sino-Western relations. But intercultural history is more than diplomacy and more than the side effect of the creation and diminution of political power on either side of the relationship. There is a realm of interaction that begins with the simple exchange of ideas and contacts between persons.

The excitement of a new idea, the influence of personalities, and the pressures of political realities are interdependent and can sometimes be explained in terms of the other. For example, the Christian's primary loyalty to God, as understood in the West, may threaten China's official efforts in the second half of the twentieth century to exact primary loyalties to the Communist party, just as that kind of religious loyalty may be seen as a threat to the interests of the ruling samurai class in seventeenth century Japan. Similarly, political pressures exerted by those in power produce real changes in the images Chinese and Westerners have of each other. But the attempt to explain intercultural relations primarily in political terms risks becoming little more than an apology for the group that is in power. Inquiries that seek only the antecedents for the Christian failure and the Marxist success in twentieth century China are too narrowly conceived. They miss the color of the Republican period, years when Yenching University was established and flourished and years when it was possible to hold many different views and still be Chinese.

2

The Search for an Exportable Christianity

Among the images Westerners had of China prior to the twentieth century, none was more enduring than that of a tranquil and unchanging society. The historical record shows, of course, that there was considerable change, even if it was within the framework of tradition. Confucian ideology dominated most learning all the way from the village schools to the examination system and occupied scholarly minds thereafter. But not all schoolboys and not all scholars rose through the examination system to become officials of the state. Nor were they merely concerned with Confucian ideas on the proper relationships within the family and the state. In their spare time scholars came together in small groups, known as *she* or *t'uan,* to engage in a variety of activities, from reading poetry to discussing large social and political questions. Political parties were officially banned by the emperor, but because a virtuous government was also a light one, there were large spaces within society.

These small groups became more numerous during periods of dynastic decline and especially so during the last years of the Ch'ing dynasty (1644–1912). China's defeat in the Sino-Japanese War of 1895 brought scholars and students together to discuss ways to save the nation, *chiu-kuo,* from the twin ills of decay from within and the threat of nations from without. The Confucian framework was crumbling.

New ideas had to be tried. By the end of the Ch'ing it is estimated that several hundred of these groups were formed in the large cities of China, and some of their ideas took political form.[1] Thus the famous reforms of 1898 led by K'ang Yu-wei and Liang Ch'i-ch'ao began as ideas discussed in two groups that had been studying the dissemination of Western ideas.[2] Two decades later the early Marxist study groups, which included Li Ta-chao, Ch'en Tu-hsiu, and Mao Tse-tung, soon led to the founding of the Chinese Communist party.[3]

The Life Fellowship: Sheng-ming she

Behind the vitality of Yenching University lay just such a group. It was called the Cheng-tao t'uan, or the Apologetic Group. It was formed in Peking in 1919, three years after the founding of the university, but the university's role within the missionary enterprise and its goals for Chinese society were articulated and refined within the discussions of the group. Unlike most such study groups, the membership included both Chinese and Westerners, who became the leading personalities in the early life of the university. Among them were John Leighton Stuart, president from 1919 to 1945; Lucius Chapin Porter, first dean of men and professor of philosophy; Howard S. Galt, professor of education and longtime administrative leader of the institution; John Stewart Burgess, leader in Yenching's social science program; and Luella Miner, first dean of the Yenching Women's College. Among the prominent Chinese members were Liu T'ing-fang (T. T. Lew), first distinguished Chinese returned student (returned from study abroad) to join the Yenching faculty in religion and psychology; Wu Lei-ch'uan, first Chinese chancellor and professor of religion and Chinese; Hsü Pao-ch'ien (P. C. Hsu), professor of religion and founder of the group; Chao Tzu-ch'en (T. C. Chao), professor of theology and longtime dean of the school of religion; and Hung Yeh (William Hung), first Chinese dean of men and distinguished sinologist.[4] Within a few years the group's name was changed to the Sheng-ming she or Life Fellowship.[5]

The members of the Life Fellowship were devout Christians whose common purpose was to "demonstrate the truth and merit of Christianity" and its relevance to China. They came together regularly to discuss "reform" and "indigenization" of the church in China. Their most important work was the publication of the *Sheng-ming,* or *Life Journal,* which appeared first as a quarterly in 1920 and later as a monthly. It was published in Chinese, with an occasional issue in English, and was financed out of the pockets of the group's membership to ensure independence in editorial policy. Their motto was to be "international, interdenominational, non-partisan in politics, independent of ecclesiastical control and scientific in outlook."[6] The editors of the journal firmly believed that Christianity had a role to play in China's national salvation.[7]

At its peak the journal reached a circulation of about 2,000 with mailings to 21 provinces, Japan, Indochina, and to Chinese communities in the United States. By no means did it speak for the whole of the Chinese Christian community, as there were at the time more than fifty Chinese language religious papers and periodicals for Protestants alone, some with much larger circulation than the *Sheng-ming*.[8] And yet in terms of the indigenization movement, and more specifically the intellectual thrust of Yenching University, it is especially revealing and authoritative.[9]

The articles in the publication were written as essays which were relatively new as a distinct literary form, and they were written in the vernacular (*pai-hua*), which had just come into vogue. Unlike the formality of earlier forms of Chinese prose, these essays were highly expressive of the personal opinions of the writer. One senses they were written hurriedly and edited only minimally. Their spontaneity seemed well suited to the purpose of spreading Christian ideas and the vitality of their religious experiences. This form of expression remained unchanged throughout the life of the publications.[10]

For the whole of the *Sheng-ming's* seven-year existence and the eleven years of its successor publication (*Chen-li yü sheng-ming,* or the *Truth and Life,* 1919–37), the editorship was held by professors at Yenching. Three special English-language issues appeared in 1922, 1925, and 1927, all of them edited by Lucius Porter. The topics discussed in the editorials often grew out of the regular meetings of the group, at least in the early years, and if not otherwise designated were assumed to represent the position of the whole group.[11] In addition to feature articles there were regular contributions on theological and biblical interpretations, devotional literature, book reviews, and literary pieces, including some of the early poetry of the writers Hsieh Ping-hsin (Hsieh Wan-ying) and Hsü Ti-shan, while students at Yenching. Management and publication were originally handled by the Young Men's Christian Association (YMCA) offices in Peking and later by the school of religion at Yenching.

The Search for an Exportable Christianity

In the Life Fellowship membership lists were kept, diaries indicate that regular meetings were held, and occasionally summaries of meetings were published.[12] And yet Western members rarely referred to it in their writings at the time, and Chinese members paid it only scant attention, even in autobiographical pieces discussing their "religious experiences." In the early years they met weekly, but by the late 1920s meetings were held infrequently. As their ideas became embodied in the growing university and as the members became involved in educational and religious work nationwide the Life Fellowship became a shadow organization. Its importance lay in the publications and the articulation of the university's position in Chinese society. If the university had a rationale in the early years, it was that of the Life Fellowship. But before exploring in greater detail the Western side of that rationale, I would like to discuss the context of its emergence: the Chinese setting; the lives of the major Western personalities at Yenching; and the founding of the university.

The Chinese Setting

The Western members of the Life Fellowship exuded an airy confidence which appears surprising in retrospect, but it followed from their reading of the trends within China in the first decades of this century. The Boxer Rebellion (1900) marked a definite watershed. Before then the number of converts to Protestantism was small. But it rapidly increased afterwards when China almost indiscriminately turned West and thousands of students flocked abroad for study. The number of converts to Protestant Christianity between 1911 and 1922 was about 200,000 or almost equal to the total number of the previous one hundred years of Protestant activity in China. By 1935 more than a half million Chinese belonged to one Protestant denomination or another. [13]

Within the Protestant effort itself, educational activities were the most promising. In 1889, 45 percent of the total number of Protestant communicants were students enrolled in mission schools. This percentage jumped to 64 percent in 1915.[14] Protestant mission schools were much sought after by young Chinese desiring to learn the English language and Western science, while Protestant missionaries exercised considerable influence over the Chinese press in its formative years. In the late nineteenth century Young J. Allen's *Review of the Times* (*Wan-kuo kung-pao*) was an important source of Western ideas; and the founders of the famous Commercial Press were trained by Protestant mission-aries.[15]

Commensurate with this rapid growth of converts was an increase in mission board money and personnel sent to China. Trailing far behind the Near East and India throughout the nineteenth century, China acquired its foremost position as a field for Protestant evangelization only in 1899, but it stayed ahead for the next half century.[16] By then Protestants enjoyed a distinct advantage in their ability to exploit China's new openness to Christianity. As Latourette has pointed out Great Britain and the United States, and within them the middle class, which benefited most from the accumulation of wealth during the Industrial Revolution, were predominantly Protestant. Great Britain, furthermore, was the largest trader in China; the British consul served as the most important foreign functionary in the treaty ports, and the English language was the medium of foreign commerce.[17] Meanwhile in the United States the agencies supplying many of the resources for this expanding field were the Young Men's and Young Women's Christian Association (YMCA and YWCA) and the Student Volunteer Movement. These organizations accounted for much of all voluntary activities on college campuses, and they trained a highly educated group of individuals for the mission fields.[18]

The YMCA, especially, set the pattern for the Life Fellowship's entry onto the Chinese scene.[19] Its well-known evangelists, Sherwood Eddy and John R. Mott, spoke to literally tens of thousands of curious city dwellers in the 1910s. At "warm-up" meetings held in 1913 prior to Mott's arrival in Peking, for example, more than 15,000 soldiers, students, officials, and merchants attended lectures conducted by YMCA staff members speaking on topics such as the wireless telegraph and the gyroscope.[20] The YMCA was conspicuously successful in the city of Peking. There over 60 percent of the population was male and included thousands of students and "expectant officials" who were cut off from their families and who were agonizing over the fate of their country, which they had been trained so long to serve. They formed a large group almost waiting to be organized.[21] One mark of YMCA success in 1913 was the enrollment of one third of the student body, or approximately one hundred students, in Bible study groups, at the American Indemnity College, later known as Tsinghua University.[22]

Regional and national YMCA conferences flourished. For the eighth national convention in Tientsin, April 1–5, 1920, a special train was provided from Shanghai to Tientsin with two first-class, three second-class, and five third-class cars. All of the 500 passengers were convention delegates with train tickets sold to them at half price. On the third day of the conference, Li Yüan-hung, President of the Republic, gave an official reception to all delegates at the convention.[23] By 1920 the YMCA had organized associations in more than twenty Chinese cities and two hundred schools, middle-level and above, including many government-operated schools.[24]

So respected were YMCA programs in China that by 1912 several provincial governors had requested branch associations in their respective capitals, while the provincial assembly of Kirin province asked that an association be organized in every district town of the province.[25] The coalition cabinet of the new Republican government, including Yüan Shih-k'ai, Ts'ai Yüan-p'ei, and T'ang Shao-yi, had also given its endorsement to YMCA activities.[26] By the 1920s and 1930s former YMCA secretaries had become prominent enough in the public eye that a list of their names resembled a "Who's Who in Republican China," especially among those public figures who were born after 1890.[27] In 1929 the cabinet of the Nanking government included ten ministers, six of them American educated, seven of them Christian, and two of them former YMCA secretaries.[28]

All Western and Chinese members of the Life Fellowship had worked closely with the YMCA.[29] John Leighton Stuart's work with the YMCA in Nanking in the early 1910s opened up for him a "whole new aspect of missionary effort," in which the Chinese "shared equally with the foreign secretaries in all matters of policy and finance."[30] In China the YMCA was the first Protestant organization to carry out a policy of Chinese control and support. In 1901, for example, there were seven foreign and three Chinese secretaries; in 1907 it was twenty-eight and sixteen; in 1912, seventy-five and eighty-five; and by 1934 there were only nineteen foreign secretaries (nine of them supported by the International Committee and ten of them locally) compared to 217 Chinese secretaries supported entirely with local funds.[31] Yenching university's efforts at sinification were an attempt to realize what was already being accomplished in the YMCA.

This confidence in the growth of Christianity was audaciously expressed in 1922 by the Protestant publication of *The Christian Occupation of China* edited by Milton Stauffer. This 468 page document—tabloid size with 110 pages of tables, diagrams, and charts appended—

was an impressive statistical account of the penetration of missionary activity into Chinese life. Its purpose was "speedier and more effective evangelization" by developing a "greater degree of efficiency, coordination, and balance in the work of all the [Protestant] missions throughout China." It surveyed in quantitative terms Protestant work with ethnic minority groups, students, the blind, rickshaw pullers, victims of leprosy, tuberculosis, and opium and the production of Christian literature in each province.[32] The repeated use of the word occupation was to many Chinese, including converts, sheer missionary arrogance. Also in 1922 another book, *Christian Education in China,* edited by Ernest D. Burton, was published. It was less arrogant in tone but similar in purpose. Burton's book called for greater cooperation among missionary educators in competing with the new national system of education. It may be no coincidence that the Anti-Christian movement began that same year.[33]

Missionary Educators

In their search for an exportable Christianity missionary educators dissociated themselves from the narrow proselytizing of their fundamentalist colleagues. Before the founding of Yenching each had been involved in education or social work representing the more liberal side of the Protestant church. They were part of two trends, one within missions in China, which stressed good works over evangelism, and the other within Protestantism, which emphasized the idea of Jesus as a social reformer, both a part of the broad movement known as the social gospel. In the latter half of the nineteenth century the Protestant church was prodded by Marxist accusations that religion had failed to address itself to the problems of social justice created by capitalism, but served merely as a tool of the ruling class. Its response was a theology and program of social reform, articulated for example in the work of the YMCA and YWCA. Protestant seminaries by the early twentieth century were adding courses on topics such as the scientific study of social problems. Together with secular socialism the social gospel movement played an important role in creating some of the nationwide programs for social reform in the West and to a smaller extent China.[34]

In retrospect we apply the labels liberal theology and social gospel to these missionary educators, but they did not define themselves as liberals at the time. Some would have resisted the label. Childhood experiences and the impact of China on their lives in those years preceding the May

Fourth period molded their definitions of mission as much as theological and ecclesiastical identities. Their coming together in the Life Fellowship with Chinese personalities was characteristic of the flux of Protestant Christianity as well as of Chinese thought and political events.

John Leighton Stuart (1876–1962). Stuart embodied the spirit of the Life Fellowship and Yenching University. He was also one of the best-known Protestant missionaries in China. Though coming from a dogmatic religious background, he became known for his theological flexibility and personal warmth. His fusion of religion, education, and diplomacy is an illuminating chapter in modern Sino-Western relations. His admirers among the Chinese were many.[35] His memoirs, *Fifty Years in China,* were translated immediately into Chinese, first in serial form and then in book form as *Ssu-t'u lei-teng hui-yi lu* (Taipei, 1954).[36]

Stuart's work in education was part of a long family tradition. His great-grandfather Robert Stuart (whose niece, Mary Todd, married Abraham Lincoln) served as one-time president of Transylvania College in Lexington, Kentucky. His father, John Linton Stuart, was one of the first three missionaries sent to China by the Southern Presbyterian Church, and he organized the earliest mission school in Hangchow. Stuart's mother, Mary Louisa Horton, was the daughter of Judge Gustavus Horton, mayor and prominent educator in Mobile, Alabama, and she founded a private school for girls in that city. After her arrival in China she started another girl's school in Hangchow.[37]

Stuart was born in Hangchow in a time when central China was still recovering from the devastation of the Taiping Rebellion and when the walls of mission compounds defined the parameters of foreign children's early existence. He was named after the executive secretary of the Southern Presbyterian mission board, John Leighton Wilson, and his childhood was strictly limited to contacts within his parents' mission. His Chinese playmates were "carefully selected" as was the choice of books—exclusively English—in his early home education. As a small boy Stuart enjoyed venturing out with his father on evangelistic trips into the countryside, but he later recalled "the curious questions of the 'listeners,' " and wondered even then "whether it was all worthwhile."[38] However distasteful, this missionary isolation was to him in his later years, Stuart nevertheless forged strong family and sectarian ties which he maintained to the end of his life.

Stuart's early questionings soon turned to "revulsion" when he began his formal education back in Mobile, Alabama, at the age of eleven. The newly arrived boy from Hangchow was extremely conscious of being different: his clothes were relics of British styles in Shanghai; his accent was that of "serious-minded elders who almost alone had been our acquaintances"; and he was "unbelievably ignorant of the language, habits, standards and juvenile meannesses of our American contemporaries." Most humiliating was the use his parents made of him and his younger brothers as part of their stock-in-trade to arouse popular interest in China as a mission field. They were made to "dress in costume, eat with chopsticks, sing hymns in Chinese—especially 'Jesus Loves Me, This I Know'—and otherwise furnish an exhibit."[39]

For fifteen years in American schools Stuart seemed eager to avoid all suspicion that he knew more about China than his peers. He wanted least of all to become a missionary. But the religious tides of the day would soon have great influence upon him. At the Pantops Academy in Charlottesville and then at the Hampden-Sydney College, between 1893 and 1896, in Richmond, Stuart became a leader in the popular activities of the YMCA and the Student Volunteer Movement. After college he decided on a teaching career and returned to Pantops to teach Latin and Greek. But religious pressures were too strong, and he succumbed by enrolling in the Union Theological Seminary in Richmond from 1899 to 1902. There he put his faith to the supreme test by volunteering for the mission field and what seemed to him like the inevitable return to China.

This decision to join the missionary cause came only after much inner anguish. He later wrote:

It is difficult to exaggerate the aversion I had developed against going to China as a missionary. It was not the country so much as what I conceived to be the nature of the life and work—haranguing crowds of idle, curious people in street chapels or temple fairs, selling tracts for almost nothing, being regarded with amused or angry contempt by the native population, physical discomforts or hardships, etc., no chance for intellectual or studious interests, a sort of living death or modern equivalent for retirement from the world.[40]

And yet there seemed no defense against the argument that if one were "really the follower of Jesus in the fullest sense he would be a foreign missionary unless prevented by external causes." Deciding to be a missionary was conclusive proof that Christianity was the "supreme value." After his decision he felt "contented, relieved, even enthusiastic."[41] He worked the next two years, 1903–04, traveling for the Student Volunteer Movement in the South and getting others to volunteer for the mission field. While in New Orleans he met Aline Todd, and after a double marriage ceremony with her sister and his best friend, Lacy Moffett, Stuart sailed for China with his new bride. He was then twenty-eight years old. After almost eighteen years absence, he returned to his birthplace and threw himself into language study and rural evangelism in Hangchow, following in the footsteps of his father.[42]

But the prospect of confinement to rural evangelism soon became unbearable, and Stuart's willingness to continue working with missions required a decisive redefinition of his outlook on China. That redefinition was essentially a twofold task, the first one being intellectual in nature. It meant turning away from the more narrowly defined faith of his father's generation. As a child he had grown up with that approach to religion, but his embarrassment over it as a schoolboy apparently never left him. His years in college and seminary had introduced him to new expressions of Christianity, such as liberal theology and the social gospel, which stressed man's goodness, not sinfulness, and the love, not the wrath, of God. In Stuart's words it meant separating the "theological concepts of a bygone age" from the "proven conclusion and clearly recognized trends of present-day scholarship."[43] Through his travels in the northern United States during his days in seminary and also through "some inner urge," he had discovered the conflicts between Southern Presbyterian orthodoxy and other "current trends." Given this exposure and his boyhood aversion it is surprising that Stuart returned to the work of his father for as long as he did, almost five years. Perhaps the conflict existed largely as ambivalence at the time and became clear only in retrospect. But after 1909 there was no turning back to the old ways.

Stuart's redefinition, however, did not make him a cynic or a rebel. To the end of his life he remained "at one" with his Southern Presbyterian colleges, realizing "with them, as was almost universally true in the South, loyalty to the past and its heritage was a primary virtue."[44] The task in redefinition was one of sorting out, not throwing away needlessly. "Scientific discoveries" and the "acids of modernity" had "cut deep into the teachings" of his upbringing, but in the end they failed to shatter or discredit the "enduring verities of the Christian faith." They merely "swept away obsolete accretions."[45] The theory of evolution had challenged the creation story in the book of Genesis and thereby weakened the hold of biblical literalism in his mind, but it did not destroy the authority of his own religious tradition. Over the span of his life "drastic changes" were encountered, but the "central core of the early faith" remained unchanged, which indicated that the "sources from which Religion draws its vitality are not apt to be seriously affected by extraneous or environmental factors."[46] In Stuart's mind Christianity which was not bound by Western culture held a universal message. Never for a moment did he doubt that it would have an appeal in China.

The second task in Stuart's redefinition was professional in nature. He soon left missionary preaching around Hangchow and returned to his earlier love of teaching. In 1909 he joined the faculty of the Nanking Theological Seminary, teaching Greek and New Testament theology. The Nanking years were perhaps his most pleasant ones. He loved his students and quickly identified with their patriotic feelings. There he also plunged into scholarly work, publishing in Chinese a book on the *Essentials of New Testament Greek* and a *Commentary on the Apocalypse*. He also compiled a *Greek-Chinese-English Dictionary of the New Testament*.[47] All his writings after that were limited to administrative and diplomatic correspondence and an occasional article.

Stuart remained at Nanking until 1919 when he went to Yenching as president. In 1918 the Yenching search committee was looking for someone to head the new institution, someone who was not embroiled in the rivalries among the constituent colleges in North China or any of the constituent mission boards representing England and the northern United States. As a missionary from South China and a Southern Presbyterian he qualified for both. The Yenching committee was impressed with Stuart's familiarity with the "Chinese point of view," his high esteem among both Chinese and missionary groups, his exceptional spoken Chinese, his scholarly attainments, and his appearance as an "unselfish man who more than most men reveals the spirit of Jesus."[48] Stuart later wrote that he decided to accept their offer "purely on religious grounds," but he did concede another factor in the decision, namely a "glimpse forming even then in my imagination of the potentialities of a Christian University, broadly conceived, in that historic city."[49]

In accepting the offer Stuart asked that he be spared the burden of raising money to finance the expansion of the institution. But ironically he plunged into fund raising, for which he possessed unusual skills, soon after his duties as president began in the late summer of 1919.

Yenching's ascendency from an obscure college at the time of his arrival to one of China's leading institutions of higher education within a decade must be regarded largely as the result of the talents Stuart brought to the post. As Dwight Edwards wrote, "Yenching University and Leighton Stuart are synonymous terms, or put in others words, when Peking University [one of the constituent colleges] called Leighton Stuart, Yenching University was brought into being."[50]

Stuart's redefinition of mission purposes away from evangelism and toward the social gospel was characteristic of Yenching Westerners generally. In 1926 he was praised in a leading English newspaper in North China for the "courageous realization and practice of the ideal that missions and imperialism have been, can, and should be divorced." Stuart, it claimed, had recaptured the vision and practice of the earliest missionaries who had spread Christianity in the Roman Empire not as conquerors but as a conquered people, had dispersed "without the least political backing," and had not been the "conscious or unconscious instruments of economic penetration."[51] Twenty years later when he was appointed American ambassador these qualities were again recognized by leading Chinese newspapers and even revolutionary leaders.[52]

Lucius Chapin Porter (1880–1958). Porter is the second most important Western figure in the Life Fellowship and Yenching University. He is the only figure in this study to have been with Yenching from its earliest beginnings until after the Communist takeover. Porter imparted to all a buoyant and optimistic spirit. His given name meant light, and he often signed it in the Latin from Lux. Many who knew him would certainly agree with these words spoken in memoriam: "He was a radiant person, vibrant with life as light is vibrant . . . At all times and places he was a welcome presence . . . He always lifted any moment to higher levels."[53] Hu Shih, who was one of the most highly respected thinkers in China in the Republican years, wrote these words after Porter's death: "He was an old and dear friend of mine ever since my first years in Peking . . . He was a good and liberal missionary educator who could tolerate my barbaric views on religion."[54]

Born into a family of educators and missionaries, Lucius Porter was a natural choice for Yenching University. His grandfather, Aaron Chapin of New England stock, had moved West and founded Beloit College in 1846. Beloit, Wisconsin, became the family home. It was there his parents would return on furlough and where Porter himself retired in 1949 until his death. His father, Henry Dwight Porter, was a missionary surgeon sent out by the American Board of Commissioners for Foreign Missions (Congregational), while aunts, uncles, and cousins pioneered in missionary education in North China. Porter was born in Tientsin and grew up in Shantung province in the small village of P'ang-chuang near the town of Te-chou. Like Stuart he received most of his early education at home before going to college in the United States. Reflecting on his formative years, Porter regarded himself as a "marginal man" living on the borders of three great cultures: the world of Chinese customs from boyhood days; the British ways of Tientsin, where he often visited, and Peking, where he later lived; and the American missionary culture of his home and formal education.[55] In his mind no one of these cultures "seemed superior to either of the others, all three were natural and good."[56]

After graduating from Beloit College in 1901 he taught and coached in the Beloit public schools. He then went on to Yale Divinity School (B.D., 1906) and spent a year of study in England and Germany on a Yale traveling fellowship. He returned to Brooklyn for a year as assistant pastor at the Clinton Avenue Congregational Church, working under Nehemiah Boynton, father of another Yenching luminary, Grace Boynton. He began work in China in 1909, teaching ethics, philosophy, and psychology, coaching sports, and directing the glee club (the first in North China) at the North China Union College in Tungchou. He taught there between 1909 and 1918, spending the last year as dean of the Tungchou division of the newly formed Yenching University.

Many alumni and colleagues at Yenching remember Porter as a physical fitness buff. Even at seventy-two he took great delight in suiting up and running the hurdles with members of the Beloit track team more than half a century younger than he.[57] His line-a-day diaries are scattered with comments on the weather, for running and physical exercise were a daily affair. Porter entered his work with the characteristic zest of a sports enthusiast. He seemed to thrive on adventure and became known as the general trouble shooter on the Yenching campus.

Porter spent the rest of his professional career at Yenching, interrupted only by visits to the United States and internment by the Japanese between December 1941 and September 1945. For two years, 1922–24, he was the Dean Lung Professor of Chinese at Columbia University, and for two years at Harvard University, 1928–29 and 1931–32, he was a lecturer in Chinese philosophy. Though he was not known for pioneering scholarly work, Porter played an important role in building the

Harvard-Yenching Institute, for which he served as executive secretary in China from 1928 to 1939, and in encouraging others in scholarship. He wrote for more general audiences on Chinese philosophy, but he also was at ease in scholarly discussions. Pursuing his scholarly interests he became an early member of the Far Eastern Association, formed in 1948, and when possible he attended its annual meetings and that of its successor organization, the Association for Asian Studies, until his death in 1958.[58]

Like Stuart, Porter seemed highly ambivalent in his feelings about the missionary enterprise. Just before his commissioning by the American Board he wrote that he had been fully expecting "not to be a missionary."[59] He had a strong distaste for dogmatism wherever it existed. He was "not bound by official theological conceptions of the nature of Christ or of Christianity." Following Christ, for him, was not to be "cribbed, cabined, and confined in a static world" of church dogma, rather it meant the "joyous freedom of mind and spirit."[60] In later years he saw himself becoming a "sort of double-ended missionary trying to carry Western Christianity, philosophy, and science to Chinese youth, and interpreting to Americans the richness of Chinese philosophy and outlook on life."[61] Porter's writings reveal a deep affection for both the Chinese people and their cultural heritage. He avoided the arrogance so crudely displayed by his father, who had praised the German soldiers as the "agents of God," in their carrying out punitive expeditions against Chinese villages around Peking after the Boxer Rebellion. His father had seen these acts not as a "matter of vengeance, but of simple justice," and regretted that "Providence discards the United States in favor of the Germans."[62]

In opposing these views of his father's generation, Porter seemed rarely self-righteous in doing so. Like Stuart he saw them as misguided but not evil. He openly acknowledged the family relationship to the Grafin von Waldersee, wife of the German commander who had led in this post-Boxer destruction of the Chinese villages, and he visited her once in 1908 during his year of study in Germany.[63] Porter also spent three months as a nurse to accompany back home a fellow Congregationalist, William S. Ament, who was one of the most vindictive Protestant missionary voices to be heard after the Boxer Rebellion.[64] Porter's widely circulated book, *China's Challenge to Christianity* (1924), was an articulate apology for liberal Christianity in China, and yet its liberal tone did not weaken his identification with the missionary enterprise.

Howard Spilman Galt (1872–1948). Galt was an early member of the Life Fellowship, and he played a major role in the formation of the university. For more than two decades he assumed large administrative responsibilities at Yenching. His life demonstrates further the Chinese influence in the evolving definition of mission at Yenching.

Galt grew up on an Iowa farm in a large "very religious" Congregational family with seven brothers and two half-sisters. With encouragement from his stepmother he went to Taber College in Iowa and later finished at the University of Chicago. During his college days he quickly absorbed the missionary zeal of the Student Volunteer Movement and, as typical of many such enthusiasts, pursued the beaten path to Hartford Theological Seminary.[65] There he met D. Z. Sheffield, a pioneer educator in North China, who urged him to go to China. Galt resisted the idea because he feared the language problem. But he soon overcame that fear and accepted the call. Ironically Galt was later known for his mastery of both spoken and written Chinese.

Arriving in China in 1899 on the eve of the Boxer War, Galt began his missionary career as an instructor in mathematics at the American Board's North China College. During that war Galt left China for Kobe in Japan where he taught for two years. He returned to the college to help in its reconstruction and served as its president between 1909 and 1912. Along with Porter he worked hard over the next five years to bring about the union of the small Protestant colleges which ultimately became Yenching University. It was Galt who represented the Yenching search committee in approaching Stuart in Nanking for the presidency.[66]

Throughout his career at Yenching Galt was especially interested in teacher training. He taught within and at times headed the department of education. Education, he thought, was truly the key to helping China, and he wanted his students above all to spread their learning and influence into the village schools. According to his daughters Galt regretted Yenching's remoteness from the Chinese rural scene, its high cost of tuition, and the urban orientation of most of the university's graduates. One of Galt's purposes in college teaching was to break the traditional hold of teachers over their students and the excessive deference of students in the classroom. The "democratic tendencies," Galt wrote, "should be expanded . . . developed and made habitual."[67] Though he was temperamentally stiff, he tried to "democratize" education at Yenching through coeducation and sports. His own specialties were tennis and baseball.[68]

Galt was more inclined to scholarship than either Stuart or Porter. In 1925 he went to Harvard and received the Ed.D. degree in 1927. Spared by the Japanese occupation from the time-consuming details of administration in the late 1930s, Galt doubled his scholarly efforts on the study of traditional education in China. That effort culminated in *The History of Chinese Educational Institutions,* which was published posthumously in 1951. Ending with the Six Dynasties period (222–589), his book is still regarded as a standard work in Chinese education. Galt wrote a second volume covering the rest of the premodern period, but the manuscript was only in rough form at the time of his death in 1948. The quality of that draft also appears to have suffered from his illness.[69]

For the first two decades of his work in China, Galt's attitudes toward the Chinese people reflected the trauma of the Boxer Rebellion. His daughters recall a certain severity and mistrust of the Chinese people while the family was still living in Tungchou. As a ten-year-old, Mildred, the oldest, once observed with "absolute horror" her father forcibly taking away a basket of sticks a Chinese neighbor woman had gathered for firewood from under the Galt hedge in the front yard. But Galt's daughters also noted a marked change in their father's attitude when the family moved to the Yenching campus, where intellectual ferment was strong. Galt in later years seems to have shed completely the vindictiveness of his earlier mentor, D. Z. Sheffield, who had justified the punitive campaigns of foreigners after the Boxer War not as "bloodthirstiness" but as an "understanding of Chinese character and conditions, and a realization that the policy of forgiveness means the loss of many valuable native and foreign lives."[70] In his daughters' words, Galt had begun his work in China with "well-meaning arrogance" but later moved away completely from "imposing American ways on the Chinese." During World War I Galt became a pacifist and a strong supporter of the Carnegie Peace Foundation. By the late 1930s scholarly interests overshadowed any remaining commitment to evangelism.

Galt's sympathies for China, though, did not translate into support for student political demonstrations. It was no secret that active Communist youth passed through the Yenching campus and sought out Stuart who seemed to encourage their radical tendencies. Galt "deplored" it and thought it "childish" of Stuart.[71] Galt was conservative. Steeped in midwestern piety, he rejected Pearl Buck's novels because they were too "erotic." He was attracted to Confucian uprightness which may help explain his apparently closer relationship, compared to Stuart, with the Chinese chancellor, Wu Lei-ch'uan. He frequently served as acting president while Stuart was away raising money, but their styles of administration were vastly different. Stuart was easy-going, while Galt was a stickler for protocol and for following the university's bylaws he labored so hard to write. Fortunately for Yenching the working relationships between the two never stretched to the breaking point. Stuart affectionately recalled Galt as the "constant safeguard against my more carelessly adventurous tendencies."[72] Galt was self-effacing. His manuscript history of Yenching barely suggests the importance of his administrative role and influence in the university.

John Stewart Burgess (1883–1949). Burgess worked at Yenching University only ten years, a much shorter time than many other old Yenching hands, and yet he is discussed here because of his prominent role in the Life Fellowship and in forging Yenching's ties with the YMCA in Peking and Princeton University.

Compared to the other three missionaries, John Burgess grew up in a more secular and urban environment. His father was an importer of crockery in New York City and once served as United States consul in England. But the family also had strong religious ties. Burgess's father was an elder in the Presbyterian Church, an active member of the YMCA, and a leader in prison reform in the state of New York. During his college years at Princeton John Burgess became active in the Student Volunteer Movement. After graduation in 1905 he studied briefly at Oberlin and Union Theological Seminaries, whereupon he went to Japan under the sponsorship of the Japanese government to teach English and work for the YMCA in Kyoto. In 1907 he went to Columbia University for further work in sociology (M.A., 1909; Ph.D., 1928) and returned in 1909 to East Asia as a YMCA secretary sponsored by Princeton students and alumni. This time, drawn by the "challenge of the awakening youth of China," he went to Peking. Burgess's connections with the missionary world were strengthened in 1905 when he married Stella Fisher (1881–1974), whose father Henry Day Fisher was a missionary in Japan.[73] Serving in various capacities with the Princeton-in-Peking Foundation and later the Princeton-Yenching Foundation, Burgess was a paradym of YMCA secretaries—disciplined, self-confident, optimistic, and committed to social progress and cross-cultural understanding.[74]

During his YMCA years in Peking in the 1910s, John Burgess organized a federation of community councils within the city, student social service clubs, and a maternity hospital, and he assisted in the work of welfare associations, a prisoner's aid association, and the China Famine Relief Committee.[75] Equally important was his contact with hundreds of students in Peking engaged in YMCA activities. His influence on Chinese personalities who became leaders of social welfare programs in China is unmistakable. One admiring student, Chang Hung-chün, has called Burgess the "father of social work in China."[76] Stella Burgess recalled James Y. C. Yen, who became famous for his work in mass education, as a frequent visitor in the Burgess home as far back as 1913. In her words Burgess's method with Yen, as with all his Chinese contacts, was the "John the Baptist method . . . He must increase, I must decrease."[77]

Burgess's contacts with Yenching were made through the Life Fellowship, and he began to teach sociology at the University in the school of religion, before organizing the department of sociology in the college. He pioneered in introducing field work into the study of sociology in China.[78] His younger colleagues at Yenching, Hsü Shih-lien (Leonard Hsü) and Wu Wen-tsao, who succeeded him as chairmen of the department, helped establish Yenching's reputation in sociology. So long as Burgess was the chairman social work and the study of sociology were combined, though the two fields of endeavor would soon separate, as the YMCA mystique weakened and the pressures for raising purely academic standards increased.[79]

In keeping with the religious orientation of Yenching in the early years, Burgess believed that scholarship should not be divorced from the practical and international purposes of the college. In the introduction to his most famous work, *The Guilds of Peking,* he hoped that familiarity with the social organizations of old China, such as the guilds, might be a "means of gaining a more fundamental understanding of the chaotic conditions incident to the transformation of this nation into a new economic and political unity. Such knowledge might also throw some light on how the inevitable fusion of Eastern and Western cultures might more harmoniously be brought about."[80] After years of social work in Peking Burgess concluded that Western sociology was too parochial in its conception and conclusions. As early as 1917 he wrote: "Most of the works on sociology ignore at least one-half of the human race in conclusions regarding the early field of social discovery."[81] Burgess helped another Princeton YMCA man and longtime Yenching trustee, Sidney

D. Gamble, in the first systematic survey of a Chinese city, *Peking: A Social Survey* (1922).[82]

Sickness among the children in 1926 forced the Burgesses back to the United States, where they spent the rest of their lives, save for John Burgess's one year return to Yenching in 1928–29. Teaching first as an assistant professor of sociology at Pomona College, 1930–33, Burgess then moved to Philadelphia where he became chairman of the department of sociology at Temple University and served as a professor there until his retirement in 1948. Noted for his imaginative lecturing, Burgess introduced courses in marriage and family and in the sociology of religion at Temple. In addition to work with students at Temple, he chaired the Wellesley Institute for Social Progress between 1938 and 1943, and founded the Philadelphia Adult Education Association and the Interracial YMCA in that city. He was also a member of the Americans for Democratic Action. Stella Burgess became a social worker in Philadelphia and regarded their work in adult education and with the race problem as a "continuation of Yenching drives."[83] Later on, the Burgesses became members of the Society of Friends.

The Founding of Yenching

Yenching University was composed of four schools and was formed between 1915 and 1920. The largest of the schools was the Methodist-run Peking University. It began as a college in 1890 and preceded by eight years the founding of the famous National Peking University, with which it was sometimes confused. It offered two courses of study, one in Chinese for instruction in the Chinese classics, science, and mathematics, and the other in English for all subjects other than the classics. By 1915 English became the dominant medium of instruction as the college reflected the growing demand for foreign language competence in government and business circles.[84]

The second largest school was the North China Union College located in Tungchou, thirteen miles east of Peking. It was organized as a liberal arts men's college in 1903 by the American Board of Commissioners for Foreign Missions (Congregational), the Presbyterian Mission, and the London Missionary Society. The purpose was to consolidate their educational work following the complete destruction of their schools around Peking during the Boxer War. Before the war the site of the Union College was occupied by the North China College, which, unlike Peking University, did not "aim to fit men for the many newly opening avenues of profitable employment under government control." Rather it bent all "energies to the training of a band of young men so thoroughly Christian in spirit that they cannot but give their services . . . to the church."[85] To ensure protection against students seeking these "secular" jobs upon graduation, the medium of instruction was exclusively Chinese.[86] The downfall of the Boxers and the growing popularity of Western ideas suggested to both the Peking and the Tungchou schools the desirability of exploiting pro-Western sentiment among prominent Chinese for the benefit of the missionary enterprise.[87]

The third school was the North China Union College for Women in Peking. Known originally as the Bridgman Academy, after its founder Mrs. Eliza J. Bridgman, it was later managed by two relatives of Lucius Porter: Mary H. Porter and Jennie Chapin. The Bridgman Academy was also completely destroyed by the Boxer War, which took the lives of a third of the students.[88] The school became the North China Union College for Women in 1907, with Luella Miner as its first president. In 1920, after several years of negotiation, it officially merged with Yenching University.

The fourth school was the school of theology, which was a union of the theological seminary of the North China Educational Union and two Methodist theological schools in Peking. It was in fact the first of the schools within the university to achieve union, in 1915.

The merger of the two men's colleges was accomplished over two years. Both the bylaws of the board of trustees and the Certificate of Incorporation of Peking University were revised in December 1915 to include all four Protestant mission boards. The reorganization of the board of trustees took place the next spring, followed by the formation of a new board of managers in Peking in the fall of 1916. But the union of the student bodies of the three schools did not take place until the fall of 1918 when the students at Tungchou moved inside the city walls to the K'uei-chia-ch'ang campus of Peking University. Even after union with the men's college in 1920, the women's college continued operation on the American Board compound at Teng-shih-k'ou located more than two miles north and west of the main campus. It maintained only minimal contact with the students and teachers of the men's college until the whole university moved to the new site five miles northwest of Peking in 1926. It is convenient to date the founding of Yenching from 1916 when the boards of trustees in New York and managers in Peking were formed.

One of the most troublesome snags in the union effort was the selection of a name for the new university. According to Howard Galt, H. H. Lowry, president of Peking University for twenty-five years from 1894 to 1919, had serious misgivings about merger with the various schools of the North China Educational Union because they were infiltrated by missionaries with "dangerously liberal ideas." Lowry, however, held the trump. If Protestant mission schools were to exploit effectively the growing receptivity to Christianity in the nation's capital, then the Peking University campus had to be the site. The non-Methodist educators acquiesced temporarily in Lowry's insistence that the English name be Peking University, but the alumni of the two men's colleges were adamant in their unwillingness to accept the Chinese names of the other, Hui-wen ta-hsüeh for Peking University and Hsieh-ho ta-hsüeh for the Union College.

Resolution of the name controversy came only with the board's acceptance of a recommendation by a committee of Chinese educators, including Ts' ai Yüan-p'ei and Hu Shih of National Peking University and Wu Lei-ch'uan, then of the Peking Board of Education. They recommended Yenching, the literary name for Peking. The official English name, Peking University, was used until 1925 because from the promotional point of view, "it was much easier to interest prospective donors in America in an institution with the name . . . which was immediately understood, than to use a name like Yenching, which had to be explained." As Howard Galt pointed out, "Confucius, and some other people in the world, have at times regarded the significance of names as of grave importance."[89]

A second thorny issue was the selection of a president. Early in the merger negotiations, Lowry let it be known in no uncertain terms that he was to be the president of the new university. The trustees in New York, no doubt with some proddings from others in the field, recognized that Lowry's narrow sectarianism would only impede the development of the new enterprise and by the spring of 1917 had appointed him president emeritus and acting president. After more than a year of looking, the Yenching board of managers approached Stuart.

Stuart was reluctant to accept at first because of the sectarian bickering and the sharp antagonism between the partisans of the two men's colleges. Furthermore, the capital investments by the four mission boards had been exhausted in purchasing additional land adjacent to the campus, leaving nothing for buildings. The budget, though pitifully small, was twice the current income. The hundred or so students, Stuart thought, were "not the sort one would have thought of as promising college material"; while the foreign faculty were even more unpromising. Only two Chinese teachers were on the faculty, and no plans had been made to secure additional funds. He was also unfamiliar with the North China scene and his prospective associates. But he soon overcame these reservations and began to give shape to the dream he had in mind.[90]

The third major issue confronting the new university was the question of location. The K'uei-chia-ch'ang campus was simply too small to accommodate university expansion. Located just inside the walls of the southeast corner of the northern or Manchu part of Peking, the campus was bordered by a road along which camel caravans carried coal into the city. These unpaved roads became dusty in winter and muddy in summer. In addition, all the buildings were overcrowded, and the site lacked adequate sewage facilities. Prior to Stuart's arrival the board of managers had initiated the search for a new site, but their efforts proved to be useless. After devoting much time to the search, the board finally decided upon the purchase of a sixty-acre piece of land located five miles northwest of the city wall near the town of Haitien just a mile away from what later became the Tsinghua University campus. The land site, the Jui Wang garden, was one among many other summer gardens owned by former Manchu princes and was within a few hundred yards of the ruins of the famous Yüan Ming Yüan, the great imperial summer palace which had been destroyed by the British and French in 1860. These former gardens had the distinct advantage of being relatively cheap, because that part of Peking was largely inhabited by impoverished Manchu communities. It was a beautiful location, as the imperial families had recognized centuries before, midway between the city walls and the picturesque Western Hills. The main portion of the site had originally been developed by Ho Shen, the powerful courtier of the Ch'ien-lung Emperor (1736–95), but a century and a quarter later it lay largely in ruins. The landscaped artificial hills, lakes, and islands remained, and the waterways were constantly fed with clear water from the famous Jade Fountain further to the West.[91] The memories of Yenching alumni, writing decades later, often focus on the physical beauty and historic significance of the Haitien campus.

Building on the new site began in the fall of 1921 and the first structure to be started was Ninde Hall for the school of religion. Over the next two years money continued to pour into the building programs, largely due to the efforts of Vice-President Henry W. Luce working in New York. University authorities anticipated moving to the new campus in the fall of 1923, but constant civil strife in the area among rival warlord armies, unexpected problems with the power plant, and a slow-down in the financial campaign in the United States postponed moving out until 1926.[92]

The image of the university was closely tied to its physical setting, its suburban location, and its fine set of buildings. The architectural style was chosen by the board at a time when the Chinese faculty were pre-occupied with their Western experiences and the missionaries favored preserving the "best" of the Chinese cultural tradition. It was a time of mutual admiration for both cultural groups working in the business of higher education. The prevailing view was held by the Westerners, who dismissed the economy and utility of Western architecture. Their fasci-nation for things Chinese was also shared by wealthy philanthropists in the United States.[93] Henry W. Luce saw an advantage in being able to show designs of buildings in the Chinese style to prospective American donors. Those who argued for a Western style of architecture cited the prevailing trend in styles used for government and public buildings. For the school of religion Liu T'ing-fang argued that the Gothic style ex-pressed the spirit of Christianity better.[94] Apparently his many years in the environs of Broadway and 120th Street in New York had left their mark.

The case for the Chinese style of architecture received further support from Henry Killam Murphy who designed the new campus. For some years Murphy had been studying and experimenting with the Chinese style in a number of buildings he had designed for mission colleges in Nanking and Foochow. In 1914 he visited the Forbidden City of Peking and was completely captivated by that "finest group of buildings in the world," and he determined that "so magnificent a style of architecture should not be allowed to die."[95] Murphy also loved the garden setting of the new site. With the solid endorsement of the Western-dominated board of managers he adopted the design and proportions of the palace style and created a campus that became known as one of the most beautiful in existence in the world at the time. But the Chinese-style buildings were highly inefficient. The library was characterized as "an architect's dream and a librarian's nightmare," and the huge attics of all buildings were practically useless because of a lack of ventilation. These spaces were used as extra rooming facilities for poorer students. For the Yenching authorities, however, architectural inefficiency was more than offset by the advantages gained in "proclaiming to all comers that Westerners were interested in preserving the best in Chinese culture."[96]

Exportable Christianity

This pride in Yenching's architectural design and auspicious location reinforced the missionary educators' belief that they could have the best of the old and the new. In advocating their cause to patriotic Chinese they acknowledged the difficulties created by Christianity's association with the destructiveness of the West's penetration into China. In 1917 Stuart admitted how much the "impact of our Western civilization" had produced "materialistic agnosticism," the rejection of all Chinese religions as "superstition inconsistent with modern culture," and an "increase of cosmopolitan vices and the fading away of the nobler Chinese moralities." Into the "welter of crumbling beliefs . . . and shattered standards," Stuart candidly wrote, "Christianity had intruded itself, unwelcomed, misunderstood, an Anglo-Saxon aggression, an irritating anachronism." How can the "foreign evangel," he asked, "adapt his message to such a situation?" The task for Stuart and his colleagues was to find an exportable faith which would be "accepted alike by scholars and patriots and toiling masses, re-interpreted in Chinese terms and revivifying Chinese traditions."[97] Stuart's thinking was part of the larger trend in Protestant missions. It was a movement away from individual salvation toward good works.[98] But to regard this shift as merely a secular trend would be misleading for liberal theology was no less rooted in religious enthusiasm than fundamentalism. Dwight L. Moody, a national leader of the American YMCA, was also the most popular evangelist of his day. Faith and works to these liberal Protestants were inseparable.

Rarely did Yenching's missionary educators attempt to make any systematic statement of their religious faith. Nor was the original appeal of Christianity to their Chinese colleagues made in such a way. Rather they presented Christianity in ways that would appeal to Chinese intellectuals, in terms of the immanence of God, the humanity of Jesus, and the idea that China had a contribution to make to Western society.

Immanence of God. The prevalent theology of Stuart's parents' generation, as well as of the nineteenth century Protestant effort in China generally, had portrayed a God who was revealed exclusively through a divine Christ who in turn could be discerned only through the strictest application of biblical literalism. In their view the nature of man was basically evil. Salvation was strenuous enough for those who had heard and followed the word. But for those who hadn't, the gospel must be spread with the greatest urgency. In the words of Hudson Taylor, founder of the largest mission in China, the China Inland Mission, and a speaker to a gathering of Student Volunteers in Detroit in 1894, the Chinese people "are passing away. Every day, every day, oh how they sweep over! . . . There is a great Niagara of souls passing into the dark in China. Every day, every week, every month they are passing away! A million a month in China are dying without God!"[99] The Western members of the Life Fellowship reversed this pessimistic view of life and presented an immanent and loving God who was revealed not only through the intercession of the Christ figure but also through a wide range of religious experiences. Man's nature in their view was basically good, and man was quite capable of bettering his earthly life. China was not dark, nor were Chinese souls passing away.

With that kind of theological flexibility they were well suited to handle the challenge of science, which threatened their more fundamentalist colleagues. To them the revelations of science, including the theory of evolution, were just one more expression of the immanence of God. One member of the Life Fellowship, J. B. Tayler of the London Missionary Society, employed the images of science in building up his own view of God. For Tayler, the force of gravity, amazing in its own right, was far short of the "incredible energies" that would be released from the breaking up of the atom. But even those forces were weak when compared to the bonds holding men together in society. It was still more profound to "enter within the veil where the soul holds converse, more intimate than human fellowship, with the Divine. In that inner sanctuary dwells the Presence which creates all spiritual energy, and from it are sent out, whenever the love that is willing to give its own life is found to release them, messengers clad in light to create new forms of higher social life."[100] So long as the wonders of science were understood within the realm of God's immanence, these missionaries had no quarrel.

Within those bounds they believed science could become a tool of Christian social work. By sponsoring such work, the missionaries could make a direct appeal to the growing number of Chinese students who linked patriotic feeling with being scientific. Already in the late nineteenth century Chinese leaders had made associations between mission schools, modern education, Western learning, science, and mathematics. And in a very simple way YMCA evangelists had recognized this connection in patriotic minds when they exploited scientific gadgetry in attracting crowds to evangelistic services in the 1910s. Yenching University and other Christian colleges in China carried this theme further in their stress upon the teaching of the natural and social sciences.[101] They would train students to be scientific in their thinking and would also pioneer in scientific research. Burgess lamented in 1917 the *ch'a-pu-to* (fairly good is good enough) mentality among his Chinese contacts and the "absence of the habit of careful analysis and inductive study of fact." He believed that scientific surveys were the necessary first step in the systematic and Christian betterment of Chinese society. Christian work would translate into "technical social service" and the application of "modern scientific principles."[102] Science for Howard Galt was the science of education. He wanted to exploit "all the knowledge and all the experience bound up in the modern science of education, as well as all of the devotion and self-sacrifice of our Christian faith."[103] These missionary educators were more comfortable with science thus defined than they were with the fundamentalistic attacks on science.

This cooperation with science, however, did not mean Yenching was merely becoming secular. Original religious purposes were challenged by students within and governmental pressures without, but in the minds of the missionary educators they remained primary to the end and served as the university's reason for existence. It is not just a coincidence that the top Chinese administrators at Yenching were largely members of the Life Fellowship and the school of religion. Internationalist purposes, furthermore, were defined first and foremost within the framework of the church and the missionary enterprise, even when the university's financial base in the late 1920s became more and more secular. These missionary educators openly supported the patriotic search for national salvation, but in their minds salvation was more than just a technical or secular task. It always carried spiritual connotations. For them, and also for the Chinese members of the Life Fellowship, the *chiu* of religious salvation (*te-chiu*) was connected with the *chiu* of national salvation (*chiu-kuo*).

If the concept of the immanence of God could allow Christianity to serve as a handmaiden for scientific advancement in China, no less could it provide the power and "dynamic" in the task of national salvation. In

Stuart's words great powers would be released "through the indwelling Spirit of God," from which China would find new strength as a nation in its efforts to overcome both the internal and the external humiliations of the recent past. The "essential issue," Stuart wrote in 1917, was "one of power. The Church has not very much to add to the moral or even to the philosophic ideas of the Chinese. But so pragmatic a people will be quick to discern the vital energy in the Gospel as they have ever been conscious of this lack in themselves. Our doctrines should be taught to them as descriptions of function." The simple acquaintance with the personality of Jesus Christ was one means of discovering this secret of power. The discovery, furthermore, was not limited to the intellectuals. Lucius Porter claimed that when the rural masses, "gripped by the heavy bondage of crass ignorance and fearsome superstitions," had responded to the "story of Jesus and the impact of His personality," a new kind of man was created "more radiant and inspiring than anything seen in the rural products of the past." Personal and social salvation were essentially two sides of the same coin. In Porter's words, "The personal repentance and rebirth necessary for entering the Kingdom of God found . . . expression in the sacrificial love and service within the social community."[104]

Such a functional interpretation of Christianity was bound to create enemies at home in the West where conflicts among the modernists and fundamentalists crossed sectarian lines and divided Christian bodies throughout the world. Liberalism was charged with spreading the doctrine that a "God without wrath brought men without sin into a kingdom without judgment through the ministrations of a Christ without a Cross."[105] In 1921 Stuart was bitterly attacked by Griffith Thomas in the *Princeton Theological Review*. The attack was focused on a series of lectures Stuart had delivered in 1919 at a YMCA secretarial conference on the world basis of Christianity. Thomas's agitation gave Stuart a "notoriety that has caused me keenest pain and humiliation," and he feared he would be "branded with a stigma" that would "injure the cause to which I am giving all that I have to give." Stuart insisted he was "proud to be a minister of the Southern Presbyterian Church," and he was "ready at any time to receive admonition or reproof from the constituted authorities of my Church or to be called to account by them." He had "never been interested in labelling myself or others as conservative or liberal and (except as a victim) am now making my entry into such discussions." He concluded, "I welcome all enlargement of human knowledge in other fields without fear that it will injure religious faith, however it may compel changes in the intellectual conception of such faith. If such convictions brand a man as liberal, then here I stand. I cannot do otherwise."[106]

The controversy over Stuart's religious credentials covered the years when the theory of evolution was hotly debated among religious and political leaders in the United States and was climaxed by the Scopes trial in Dayton, Tennessee, in 1925. Stuart put an end to it in 1926 only by voluntarily subjecting himself to a thorough examination (during one of his money-raising trips to the United States) of his theological views by the East Hanover Presbytery of the Southern Presbyterian Church in Virginia, under which he had received his ordination. In his defense Stuart used the phraseology familiar to "these conservative southerners—all of whom know me as a fellow student or younger colleague from earlier associations." He received a "unanimous rising vote" of endorsement. At the end of the hearing one "tall lanky brother" suggested the meeting register its disapproval of the "secret methods used by those northern people" who had denounced Stuart and charge them with behaving contrary to the "code of gentlemen, to say nothing of being unChristian." The attack had been directed from Philadelphia and Princeton. Stuart was further exonerated in 1926 in an editorial of the *Presbyterian of the South,* which was certainly no stronghold of liberal thought. In the end he emerged from the scuffle with renewed faith that "Christian workers of differing theological interpretations can work together happily and harmoniously if there is . . . a common purpose to reveal the spirit of Christ in all human relationships."[107] Throughout his adult years in China, Stuart could be as flexible in administrative relationships as in theological issues, a quality most advantageous to Yenching, whose constituency ranged from church executives of the Southern Presbyterian church to radical Chinese students.

The Humanity of Jesus. These missionaries interpreted Jesus as a compassionate figure who provided the inspiration for social reform in China. In 1918 Burgess noted the major role Protestant Christianity had played in the social progress of Meiji Japan, in terms of education, prison reform, industrial welfare programs, and anti-vice and corruption campaigns. Though some steps behind its achievements in Japan, it was also playing a role, Burgess claimed, in the social welfare movement within China.[108] Social reform indeed had been a major concern of patriotic Chinese since the turn of the century. It was not the desirability of change over which patriotic Chinese differed, rather it was the direction, the speed, and the agents of that change.

In presenting Jesus as a social reformer to the Chinese people the Western members of the Life Fellowship were echoing a major tenet of the social gospel movement. They believed that Christian social reform would earn the respect of Chinese leaders. Within Confucianism Stuart found an "ethical passion" and an "unquenchable conviction of the essential goodness of human nature and the supreme worth of man's moral struggle." But, he argued, Confucius had "no sympathy with progress" and had emphasized ritual to such an extent that the ethical dimensions of his thought had degenerated into a morality of externals." It had died because it had failed to "touch the deeper springs of life." It "looked backward" and thus provided no "motive to progress nor the means of readjustment to the new conditions of world contact."[109] Nevertheless the "strong appreciation of ethical values" among Chinese intellectuals was seen as fertile ground for the social gospel. They would respond to the "positive quality of Christian love . . . as broad and as deep as the wants of men, knowing no other limits, rejoicing in the hardship and even in the humble nature of the service." It was a "dynamic doctrine which will cure—if aught can cure them—the woes of existence and the corruptions of organized society. The surpassing moral beauty of the character of Jesus has a winsomely cogent appeal." In its "more modern statement in terms of immanence and personality," the Christian message would "awaken their enthusiastic allegiance and fit in with their own conceptions."[110] In Howard Galt's eyes Christian education was the most significant form of social activity and it provided the "guiding power and the dynamic force" not just for the redemption of individuals but for the "penetration . . . of Christian ideals and the Christian spirit" throughout the whole of Chinese society.[111]

From these interpretations of the power of God, the humanity of Jesus, and the goodness of human nature, there sprang up within the Life Fellowship a grand optimism about the future of Christianity in China that seemed almost unquenchable. The missionary educators perceived that the problems China faced were largely obstacles that could be overcome with the application of a little more effort. Only rarely did their understanding of China's situation suggest to them that their earlier purposes might be misconceived or that their methods were unworkable. At times their optimism seemed to blind them to harsher realities, and it gave the Yenching experiment a touch of unreality amid the nationalistic tides and China's social disorder. They remained wedded for more than thirty years to a belief in the efficacy of gradual social change along western lines and in the indispensability of western help in carrying out social reform.

Edgar Snow, reflecting on his two years of teaching at Yenching from 1934 to 1936, connected this sense of unreality with the life styles and political immunity of foreigners generally: "All this was but a pleasant mirage, on the surface of which the foreigner lived so agreeably on his favourable exchange rate, his extraterritoriality, and illusions that China would never change. Behind it an old society boiled and fermented toward an agonizing turnover of total revolution."[112] In the early 1920s Stella Burgess captured this disparity between Chinese and foreign living in her poem, "Afternoon Tea in Peking." It was a gathering of foreigners, of "well-nourished men" and "over-nourished wives" eating "dulcet cakes of tireless artistry" and leisurely conversing in "gay voices flooding through the ambrosial whiffs of pungent tea." But she could not forget the other scene:

I wonder if he's at it yet,
That old man I saw as I rode here
Propelled by human brawn?
His toil-warped hands caressed the willows
Growing by the City's moat,
While, furtively, his fumbling fingers
Clutched the tenderest twigs and tucked
Them in the gunny-sack beneath his arm.
Willow leaves, you know,
Boiled with the bark of elm—
In a discarded tin—
Can ease that gnawing, grinding pain,
And add a little fuel
To the flickering embers of an old man's life.

ANOTHER CUP? YES, TWO LUMPS, PLEASE.
ANOTHER SLICE OF CAKE—YOU'VE ONLY JUST BEGUN.[113]

Yenching's style of living was indeed comfortable in many respects. Lucius Porter's line-a-day diaries in the early 1920s are dotted with conversations and meetings with famous personalities such as Ts'ai Yüan-p'ei, Hu Shih, and Chiang Mon-lin, and also with John Dewey and Bertrand Russell during their visits to China. Despite their heavy teaching loads they seem to have had time for the joys of the intimate college life, such as religious celebrations, intramural sports events, theatrical and musical performances, and much entertaining.[114]

Snow's and Burgess's comments, though, may reflect more the egalitarian outlook of both religious and secular reformers among the foreigners working in China than it did the prevailing Chinese views on the matter. The social gospel was a constant reminder to remember the poor, and yet foreigners in the past had always been given special privileges and had been expected to live apart from the masses. The favored position of missionary educators in the Republican years was not really that different from the treatment given to foreign residents since the revolution in 1949.

Yenching Westerners, furthermore, were by no means spared from great personal suffering, though it may have been smaller compared to that of the nineteenth century Protestant missionaries. The families of all the figures considered here seemed unusually burdened by childhood diseases and deaths, and many of them underwent great personal hardship during the Japanese occupation period, either as refugees in West China or as prisoners in Japanese internment camps.[115] Edgar Snow's assertion, in short, is misleading. The Westerners' optimism seemed rooted not just in the amenities of foreign existence in Peking during the Republican years. It seemed to be more rooted in the nature of their Christian faith.

Yenching missionary educators were not unmindful of the huge problems confronting China. They acknowledged the political chaos caused by warlordism and the "economic exploitation and political aggression of Western powers in China." They also recognized the prevalence of "dense ignorance," the "superstitions," and the "shocks" to the old standards of morality that came with the "invasions of modern ideas" and the "craving after material prosperity." But characteristically they remained optimistic. They sensed a "fundamental and essential unity among the people," the "beating of a strong pulse." In fact they perceived China to be in an age of "great renaissance" which was "changing the people's general attitude toward life." It was the "culmination of a long process of intellectual revolution which has been going on ever since China came into contact with the West." They concluded there was "no time more critical and yet more full of promise." They spoke of Christians contributing to the "salvation of the nation—a nation which includes one fourth of the human race."[116] Out of the current chaos a new and better order seemed about to arise. Large problems loomed, but the Christian faith always gave the promise of hope.

On the question of hope liberal Protestants and Marxists had something in common. But the bases of their hope differed profoundly. The difference lay not in the desire for fundamental change, but in the method of producing that change. It was the choice between social reform and social revolution, between nonviolence and class struggle. To be sure, Protestant reformers would use the term social revolution on occasion to describe their efforts, but they meant by it the gradual changes that YMCA programs and Western education were already producing. Liberal Protestants and Marxists also converged in their condemnation of capitalism both in the West and in its emerging forms in China. In 1923 Yenching missionaries wrote several articles for an issue of the *World Tomorrow*, a "Journal Looking Toward a Social Order Based on the Principles of Jesus," in which they decried the capitalist and "industrial invasion of China."[117]

Beyond these two points, though, they diverged sharply over the whole question of political power. The word power was often used by the missionary educators, but it was commonly used in reference to the power of ideas in religion and education. The struggles involved in the creation of political power were clearly secondary. Yenching missionaries sided with whatever government—warlord, Nationalist, or Communist—was in control. They were above all accommodators to political power. Their picture of China did not ignore social injustice but relegated it to second place. The primary attention remained focused on religious matters. Salvation meant unity with a merciful God and with all fellowmen, including the just and the unjust. The realization of social justice, or the coming of the Kingdom of God, was inevitable, and therein lay the roots of their optimism. But most likely it would be slow in getting here. Man's role in change was important, but it remained secondary to God's. The kingdom, after all, was God's, not man's.

How one interpreted the teachings of Jesus on the question of social justice had a bearing on the understanding of two key words, which are found again and again in the writings of patriotic Chinese and which were no less the concern of the missionary educators at Yenching. Those words were service and self-sacrifice. In the Life Fellowship they were associated with the Christian idea of stewardship and its most exalted form, philanthropy. Laudable as these concepts were, they were essentially individualistic in meaning and had little to say about the theological implications of the growth of commerce, the industrial revolution, and the accumulation of wealth. Rather than turn their backs on economic progress by taking seriously Jesus' clear condemnation of wealth, they chose to emphasize the parable of the faithful steward who had used wisely—and profitably—the money entrusted to him.[118] Western members of the Life Fellowship would speak in abstract terms about avoiding the evils of capitalist society in the West, but rarely did they condemn the institution of private property. Service and self-sacrifice were understood as partial, not total, commitments and were not to be used in the overthrow of existing institutions.

The ideal of service was enshrined in Yenching's school motto, "freedom through truth for service" (yin chen-li te tzu-yu yi fu-wu), which was chosen by Stuart. But it clearly meant work within the given social order, however unstable or problematic it might be. And sacrifice meant working more diligently than the graduates of government schools in the jobs of teaching, business, and politics. There were "social service" activities attending the life of the university, but these amounted to little more than relief programs, for which major responsibility was borne by faculty wives.[119] These projects were essentially auxiliary in nature. All the money spent on them was only a fraction of a percent of the annual budget for the university as a whole. The university through its graduates would define service in terms of the existing order, with few questions asked. In the ongoing debate in China in the 1920s over "problems" and "isms," that is, between reformers and revolutionaries, between those who advocated incremental "bit by bit" solutions to discrete problems and those who wanted sweeping changes, these missionary educators were decidedly with Hu Shih, the Deweyite gradualist, rather than with Li Ta-chao, the Marxist revolutionary.[120]

China's Contribution. Unlike the previous generations of Protestant missionaries generally, but very much like the Jesuits of the late Ming and early Ch'ing periods, the missionary educators at Yenching were above all cultural relativists. They presented themselves as such ardent accommodators to the Chinese scene, that to have gone any further would have defined them out of a job. They had become critical of the missionary enterprise of their parents' generation, but they remained within it because it provided the means to serve as cultural mediators between East and West. The relationship was a mutual one. Yenching

University suggested the means for a Christian role in China's national salvation, but China also had a contribution to make, through the university, to the West.

The writings of these Western figures are filled with words like world culture, spiritual and human exchanges, and internationalism, a vocabulary which expressed in cross-cultural terms the imperatives of Christian love. Their vision of an international Christian community in China was marred over the years, but it did not die until later events eliminated any Western role there. Given the close association of the missionary enterprise with China's modern century of humiliation by the West, it has been argued that this spirit of altruism was little more than a front for cultural imperialism or a subtle means of exploitation. In Jonathan Spence's words there was in missionary work that "indefinable realm where altruism and exploitation meet."[121] However true this may be, Yenching must be seen as something of an exception, as the Chinese record clearly shows.

When Western members of the Life Fellowship spoke of learning from the Chinese, they are to be taken seriously. In his book *China's Challenge to Christianity* Lucius Porter argued that the Chinese people had a "real contribution" to make to the "human understanding of Christ and of God." To Porter "the spirit of the Eastern Chinese may yet understand more fully than Westerners do the Christ who came from the East."[122] The view of the "intimacy of man with nature" as suggested by Chinese painting and poetry was a basis for the "spiritual and human naturalism" that served as a corrective to the "naturalism of the West which tends, under the influence of the exact sciences, towards mechanistic interpretations." The "fund of human interest stored in China's traditions" could be drawn upon to strengthen the "forces working in the West to make human values foremost in industrial processes in place of selfish gain." Finally, the "industry and cheerfulness of the Chinese, their practical habits and reasonableness, their fine courtesy and appreciation of human relationship" were qualities from which Westerners had much to learn.[123]

The corollary of China's contributions, Porter argued in a lecture at the Yale Divinity School, was the abandonment of the "white man's burden . . . interpreted as the responsibility of the white race for the orderly organization of other people." That "unjust sense of responsibility" had laid "intolerable burdens . . . upon the races of darker pigment." It was necessary to distinguish between "real Christianity and

Westernism . . . We ourselves need a fresh understanding of Christ
. . . The West has taken the Christ from the East. The West needs
the help of the East to reinterpret Him." The cultural exchanges between China and the West would hasten the day of a "united humanity." For Christians there should be no "strong nations imposing on
ignorant and reluctant peoples, but earnest souls in every race, convinced
of the spiritual equality of men, developing more of mutual respect and
understanding."[124] Combining Christianity's role in the national salvation of China with the Chinese contributions to Christianity and the
West, Porter articulated a credo of internationalism which became a
basic rationale for the university.

For Stuart, Yenching University was at the heart of that international
vision. While imprisoned by the Japanese in World War Two he reflected on more than two decades as president and saw Yenching as the
"realization of dreams which have in part come true." The "only practical guarantee against recurrent and ever more disastrous wars" was the
"sublimation of patriotism in an all-inclusive world-citizenship" and the
establishment of a world state. Stuart disclaimed any knowledge of the
stages involved or the final form such a world citizenship would take,
but the Christian church with its "loyalty that transcends all national
boundaries" and its worldwide organization was faced with a "heavy
responsibility and a superlative opportunity" in generating the "popular
endorsement of such an aim." The Christian colleges in China were part
of the church's cosmopolitan mission. Stuart hoped Yenching would be
pervaded with a "certain atmosphere . . . making the students interna-
tionally minded, almost unconsciously, and bringing together like-
minded persons from several countries into a community fellowship that
would enrich and broaden the whole life of the campus." It was especially appropriate that such an experiment should be made in China, for
the "moral philosophy of no other country has had a broader more
inclusive outlook." Such internationalism did not necessarily conflict
with the "recently intensified nationalistic trends" in China, unless the
students became "convinced by unhappy experiences that narrow patriotic loyalty is their only hope for national survival." Even in the great
uncertainty that Yenching would be reestablished in postwar China,
Stuart "passionately" hoped that it would be "one more testimony" for
those who see the "need of a more inclusive cosmic patriotism and who
are willing to strive and suffer for its realization."[125]

In more practical terms this appreciation of China's contribution

meant indigenization of the Christian enterprise, in which Yenching
personalities played a leading role. In the university itself it was phrased
as "making Yenching Chinese." But support for indigenization never
was intended to exclude the actual participation of Westerners in
China's national salvation. Internationalism would be a dead letter if
Westerners were gone. For Stuart, Yenching, while becoming "Chinese
in a more thoroughgoing sense," would also become "more widely and
avowedly international." The university's role in "generating dynamic
energies" and in "demonstrating the feasibility of friendly intercourse
among those of all countries," seemed not too "chimerical an aspira-
tion." Its foreign origin would then become not a "historical necessity to
be gradually forgotten, but a permanent advantage."[126]

For John Burgess Yenching's international mission was rooted in
China's need for the "experience and training of social thinkers of
America" as it tried to "master the process of modern life." The leaders
of these new movements "must be Chinese," but those who "advise and
inspire may be Americans." If these Western figures were in "close
touch" and were sympathetic to the Chinese people there was no
"nationality that is more warmly welcomed or that has a greater influence with the Chinese than the Americans."[127] Lucius Porter insisted
that China "must work out her political salvation alone. No one can
help her from without by any sort of direct influence." But he also
maintained that through education and the encouragement of social service the "friends of China can offer much help that will have indirect
but significant bearing on the political situation."[128]

In their search for an exportable Christianity the Western members of
the Life Fellowship may have had more in common with the early
Jesuits in China than they did with many fellow Protestant or Catholic
missionaries of their own generation.[129] To be sure, Stuart and his
Western colleagues may not have achieved the intellectual stature of
Matteo Ricci (1552–1610) and his followers. Nor did Ricci's message
stress the "social dynamic" of Christianity or "national salvation." Official China in 1600, after all, did not face the same problems it did in
1900. But in other ways they were strikingly similar: they worked from
the top down; Ricci dealt with officials, Stuart primarily with students.
Both spoke Chinese fluently—though none of the Western members in
the Life Fellowship could claim Ricci's mastery of publication in the
language—and they had great respect for Chinese philosophy. Further-

more, they recognized that interpretations of the meaning of Jesus' life and teaching had to transcend any doctrine or dogma produced by the Western church, and they followed Chinese customs—Stuart was not opposed to ancestor worship and Ricci performed the *kowtow*. They both exploited science in appealing to the intellectually curious. Finally, they both attempted to build a world culture (Ricci spoke of a Sino-Christian civilization).[130] Both Ricci and Stuart emphasized personal diplomacy in furthering the Christian message, and they succeeded so well that both earned a reputation for being as Chinese as they were Western.[131]

One notices also the similar role played by opposing missionary groups and the current behavior of Western nations in undermining the early Jesuit and liberal Protestant work in China. Both Ricci and Stuart fully acknowledged a natural Chinese skepticism toward Christianity.[132] But to them neither Chinese culture nor the Chinese people were inherently anti-Christian. The first strong wave of anti-Christian sentiment during Ricci's work occurred largely in response to Spanish massacres of Chinese residents in Manila in 1603. And Ricci's successors were expelled from China as a result of the Rites Controversy, which was forced less by Ch'ing officialdom than by the Pope in deference to mendicant orders competing with the Jesuits.[133] Similarly, opposition to Stuart's mission was as much Western in origin as it was Chinese. Fundamentalist colleagues undermined Yenching purposes both in China and the United States. More important was the role of the Western powers, such as in the mid-1920s and later the American intervention in the Chinese civil war in the late 1940s and the 1950s, in fueling the spirit of ultranationalism that ultimately brought Yenching's experiment in internationalism to an end.

Yenching University carried no single purpose, rather it reflected many, sometimes conflicting, purposes. Though it later became most famous as an institution of higher learning, its founders did not define their work exclusively in terms of education. Upon assuming the presidency of Yenching in 1919, Stuart carried few illusions about Yenching's ability to compete with other institutions such as Peking National University (Peita). Compared to Yenching's 35 teachers and 160 students, Peita had 305 teachers and 2,248 students. The government institution published one daily paper, fourteen periodicals, and three series of book publications, while Yenching was just struggling to put out decent catalogues and bulletins. Yenching's budget in the early years was pitifully small compared to Peita's lavish support.[134]

In the early years Yenching educators were riding the crest of Chinese enthusiasm for the ideas of John Dewey, who lectured widely in China, but they never settled for his secularism. When the Deweys visited China between May 1919 and July 1921, they were in close touch with Yenching. They stayed for a few weeks in the home of Dwight Edwards, a YMCA man on the Yenching board of managers; Alice Dewey taught an English class at the women's college; the Porters and the Burgesses entertained them frequently during the two-year visit; and the Porters renewed the contacts in 1923 when Porter taught at Columbia.[135] These missionary educators admired Dewey as an educator, but they parted ways when it came to the question of religious experience.[136] In turn, Dewey brooked no sympathy for evangelism in education and regarded mission schools as merely one vehicle for the spreading of his ideas.[137] Stuart never conceded the conflict between religion and education and he saw Yenching as a demonstration of the advantages of religious belief and a protest against the antireligionists. The "rise of great non-religious and anti-religious colleges," he wrote in 1921, "may be turned to advantage by furnishing the contrast in moral output. But it is an acid test."[138]

The one area where missionary educators could agree with their secular colleagues was the importance of the students. Receptive to new ideas at the time of Yenching's founding, the students became the focus of these missionaries' hopes. Rising nationalism would prevent Western evangelists from ever making China Christian on their own, but if Christianity could unite with the patriotic tide, the task might be performed more effectively anyway. The students were also the key to China's national salvation. "The leaders in China," Burgess wrote in 1917, "more than those of any other nation, are young men." The destiny of China rested on the "shoulders of these college men." They were "intensely patriotic and deeply interested in fundamental questions." But they were also "often confused and disorganized," and Western teachers could help them out.[139] Though educational purposes remained vague, Yenching was propelled forward by the strong leadership of John Leighton Stuart, as his colleagues and Yenching alumni have so often claimed. When Yenching was conceived, it was only one among some twenty Christian colleges, and one of the lesser known at that. Its location in Peking was certainly auspicious, but location itself was no guarantee of eminence.

Stuart delivered his first commencement sermon at Yenching on June 16, 1919, with not a single student present. The few who were not imprisoned in the wake of the May Fourth demonstrations had gone to watch and welcome their comrades being released that day by the government police. This patriotic movement, he wrote friends back home, began with the students, wherein lay the "one hope for this distracted country. And it is a great hope. They are now effecting a nation-wide, permanent organization which will be a powerful weapon against foreign aggression and official treason." In the June demonstrations the Christian students had "come into a recognition all out of proportion to their numbers, accentuating immensely the importance of Christian leadership." These students, he wrote,

must have the highest ideals of service and sacrifice, a patriotism that can be patient and can suffer heavy losses, the living power to live and inspire others to live according to the demands of duty under these new conditions. Only the Christian gospel can produce this spirit and steady men into selfless devotion to the country's needs. The Christian movement will save not only individual Chinese but China . . . And as go the students, China will follow with all its vast population.[140]

Before long, student tides would challenge Stuart's fond hopes. And yet throughout the missionaries' work at Yenching, religious experience, cosmopolitanism, education, and patriotism all seemed to converge in their minds. It was a vision that died hard.

3

The Chinese Rationale

Though it included Western members, the Life Fellowship was very much a Chinese organization. It was convened originally by Hsü Pao-ch'ien. Its publications were in Chinese and were edited for almost twenty years by Chinese. Yenching University was indelibly stamped with Western influence, more so than the Life Fellowship, and yet it too had a Chinese rationale which was articulated by the Chinese members in the Life Fellowship.

Christianity in the New Culture Movement

Since the New Culture movement, roughly 1915 to 1922, liberals and Marxists, reformers and revolutionaries have competed for the claim of heir to the meaning of that movement. Within Yenching University itself students and professors would later dispute its significance. The hardening of political lines since then have blurred the open spirit of that time. Both the Life Fellowship and Yenching University were founded in that period, and the confidence they displayed derives from perceptions then that Christianity and Western liberal arts education could be rooted in Chinese society. The Chinese members of the Life Fellowship spoke of a Christian New Thought Tide (*Chi-tu-chiao hsin-ssu-ch'ao*), while the Western members spoke of a Chinese Christian Renaissance.

The leaders of the New Culture movement did not concentrate their attack on religion in the late 1910s. Rather than abolish religion they argued for religious freedom.[1] In fact the members of the Life Fellowship were on quite friendly terms with these leaders. On March 14, 1920, Hsü Pao-ch'ien called a weekend conference at the Temple of the Sleeping Buddha, Wo-fo-ssu, in the Western hills near Peking and invited them to attend. They accepted. Among the non-Christians attending were Ts'ai Yüan-p'ei, Hu Shih, Li Ta-chao, and Chiang Mon-lin, all from Peita, while among the Christians present (heavily representing Yenching) were Stuart, as chairman of the conference, Porter, Burgess, Galt, Charles H. Corbett in physics, and Dwight Edwards. The meetings began with testimonies from the Christians followed by presentations from the non-Christians outlining their social concerns. It is doubtful the conference had any serious effect on the non-Christian participants, but it demonstrated the openness toward Christianity.[2]

The New Culture leaders gave other visible evidence of their support to the purposes of the Life Fellowship. Hu Shih, the illustrious professor from Peita who led in the movement to popularize the use of the vernacular in Chinese literature, was certainly no Christian convert. And yet when the Anti-Christian movement began in the spring of 1922, he openly defended the influence Christian morality might have on the nation.[3] He endorsed Yenching's cosmopolitan goals through his friendship with Stuart, his frequent appearances in Yenching classes and assembly meetings, and his intercession in the 1930s in securing money for Yenching from the central government.

Chou Tso-jen was one of the most popular literary figures in the New Culture period and the brother of Lu Hsun, and he openly endorsed Christian ideas. For over seventeen years, beginning in 1922, he offered courses in Chinese literature at Yenching. Though never a professing Christian himself, he attributed the "source of the humanistic ideas of modern literature," especially in the works of Tolstoy and Dostoyevsky, to the sermon on the mount.[4] Most of the Chinese people, he argued, had "religious needs" but were not able to meet them through the substitutes of science or social service. Christianity at its best could incorporate the "scientific spirit" in the overthrow of the present "cruel and barbarous religions of China." But it also had to be dissociated from the gods of the older Chinese religions, lest it become merely a Chinese god in foreign costume. Chou warned against creating any religious dogma that would obstruct freedom of thought.[5]

The strongest verbal endorsement of Christianity came from Ch'en

Tu-hsiu, "Mr. Renaissance" himself, and later the first secretary to the Chinese Communist Party. In 1917 Ch'en responded to an inquiry from a reader of *Hsin ch'ing-nien* (New youth) asking why the editors of this influential periodical had not taken a stand against Christianity. He replied the "value of a religion was in direct proportion to the extent of its benefit to society." Though not a Christian, he believed Christianity could meet the needs of the Chinese people, now that Confucianism was on the decline.[6] But he also saw a political value. On the eve of the May Fourth demonstrations in 1919, Ch'en acknowledged the role of Christian students in Korea for their leadership in the demonstrations and he urged Chinese youth to emulate the courage of the Korean Christians and refrain from looking "condescendingly on Christianity."[7]

A year later in 1920 Ch'en expressed his deep admiration for the figure of Jesus in a lengthy article "Christianity and the Chinese People," published in the *Hsin ching-nien*. In it he denounced the growing hostility to Christianity as a distinct weakness of the Chinese people, a "blundering attitude" which he hoped the intellectuals would overcome. In his opinion the proper rational attitude was to treat Christianity as an issue of social significance. Christianity, he conceded, had antagonized the Chinese because of the insincerity of its followers, the diplomatic troubles caused by the missionary enterprise, its rejection of ancestor worship, and the mystical practices of the Catholic church. But antiforeign hostility was a wrong attitude to have.

Christianity's contribution to China, Ch'en argued, was its dynamism and moral force. Confucianism was rich in its ethical teachings, but it lacked driving force. It had been too closely tied to the interests of the rulers in China. By contrast Jesus had worked with the common people. Ch'en's attraction to the figure of Jesus was very personal: "We should try to cultivate the lofty and majestic character of Jesus and fill our blood with his warm sympathetic spirit. In this way we shall be saved from the pit of chilly indifference, darkness, and filth into which we have fallen."[8] Jesus would inspire a spirit of sacrifice, which the Chinese people needed if China were to be saved. Jesus' teachings on wealth also supported Ch'en's dislike of capitalist society and values. Ch'en warned against the rice Christians (*ch'ih-chiao-t'u*), and the misuse of Christianity by politicians in China for their own ends.[9] In his apology Ch'en quoted the New Testament extensively and his statement was cited widely by missionaries and Chinese Christians over the next two decades.

Within a few months after writing this praise of Christianity Ch'en turned to Marxism and the Russian Revolution and began work with the Socialist Youth Corps in Shanghai which spearheaded the Anti-Christian movement. But even as the general secretary to the newly founded Chinese Communist Party, Ch'en refused to accept unquestioningly the attacks on Christianity. He distinguished between Christian doctrine and the Christian church. Belief in the virgin birth, the miracles and the resurrection of Christ was only a "small shortcoming in the larger body of Christian doctrine," but the evils of the church throughout history could be piled as "high as a mountain." Especially disgraceful was the complicity of the Christian churches in the recent world war. Christian altruism and self-sacrifice were still worthy of respect, but under the oppression of "imperialist aggression and capitalism" one had to ask "sacrifice for what and love for whom?"[10]

The endorsement of Christianity was not limited to these popular leaders in Peking. There were officials in the succeeding governments during the Republican period who were converts to Christianity. In 1918 the Christian National Salvation Association (Chi-tu-chiao chiu-kuo chu-yi hui) was founded in Shanghai by the colorful Hsü Ch'ien, a scholar of the highest rank (*hanlin*), who served in high positions under the Ch'ing court, the warlord Feng Yü-hsiang, and Sun Yat-sen. Hsü's organization was open to all people regardless of nationality or creed, and it espoused a faith that provided at once the basis for China's national salvation, and for the destruction of private property, the "source of all evil and international wars."[11] This national salvation society was more loosely organized than the Life Fellowship, and it is not clear how many of Hsü's political colleagues may have been influenced by it.[12] Hsü's daughter later attended Yenching University.

Chinese Christian Educators

Even without the support of the New Culture leaders, the Chinese members of the Life Fellowship would have promoted Christianity. They had converted prior to that period and they believed in the validity of those experiences long after Christianity had come under attack. Here we will focus on the family backgrounds and personalities of five important members of the Life Fellowship who may be regarded as the cultural counterparts to the missionary educators. All taught in the school of religion at Yenching and exerted a great influence on the life of the university, especially in the formative 1920s.

These five Chinese figures became well known in the small circles of Protestant effort in China, while their missionary colleagues remained relatively small fish in the larger pond of Protestantism in the West. Conversion to Christianity in China seemed to create greater discontinuities with the past than the decision to become a missionary in the West. The Chinese members seemed more self-conscious than their Western colleagues. They wrote more and on a wider variety of topics, and there is more biographical information available on Yenching Chinese, even in the United States, than there is on Yenching Westerners. The sketches of these personalities appearing in biographical dictionaries of the Republican period emphasize their careers, while those in the pages of Life Fellowship publications dwell more on the formative influence of their conversion to Christianity. One can hardly understand the nature of the Chinese commitment to Yenching University without fully appreciating these earlier experiences.[13]

Liu T'ing-fang (T. T. Lew, 1891–1947). Liu was the first editor-in-chief of the *Sheng-ming* (while he was still a student in New York), the first prominent returned student to join the Yenching faculty, and the Chinese personality with perhaps the greatest influence on Stuart in the early 1920s. Not quite five feet tall and plagued throughout his adult life with headaches and respiratory disorders, Liu nevertheless was an imposing figure. Stuart once observed that if Liu had ever taken the often advised vacation "his brain would spin like a ship's propeller out of water." Liu's influence in the Life Fellowship and at Yenching declined in the early 1930s, but over the previous decade his work had extended far outside university circles into the larger Protestant community and the world of higher education.[14]

Liu was born in Wenchow, Chekiang, into a prominent family who had become wealthy in the late nineteenth century from the importing of Swiss dye stuff along the China coast. The Liu clan property at one time had included more than one third of all the real estate along the main north-south street in Wenchow. One event, though, broke Liu's line of succession to this wealth, and that was the conversion of his grandmother to Christianity. His wealthy grandfather had turned to a life of debauchery and opium smoking from which he soon died. In her bereaved condition, Liu's grandmother would visit the gravesite of her husband just outside the city walls, occasionally stopping to rest at the Liu clan pavilion alongside the road. One day, Liu's younger brother recounted, a China Inland missionary passed by the pavilion and noticed the widow in her sorrow. He stopped to console her and left with her a copy of the Bible. The Liu family had staunchly opposed the spreading of Christian influence in Wenchow, but moved by the missionary's gesture, she took the Bible, read it, found comfort in it, and professed belief in Christianity.

The family elders were enraged by her decision and demanded that she publicly renounce Christianity by bowing down in the clan hall before the ancestral tablets. She went to the hall, but instead of bowing down, she defiantly picked her son up in her arms, turned her back on the tablets, and with her face turned upward prayed out loud. She was quickly banished from the Liu clan with only 100 mou of land and a few family documents. Because she was literate, Liu's grandmother was asked to become the head of the mission's school for girls. His father later married one of the girls in the school. Like the grandmother, Liu's mother was also widowed by the untimely death of her husband and also later became the principal of the Wenchow Girls' School. Thus began the Liu family's Christian connections and service in education.

Liu came up through the ranks of the missionary schools first in Wenchow and later in Shanghai, but he was also given a solid training in the Chinese classics.[15] He attended St. John's preparatory school and college in Shanghai for three years where he took all the scholastic and oratorical honors, but he became so critical of the school's policy of education that he left.[16] In 1913, at twenty-two, he went to the United States where he began study at the University of Georgia and then transferred to Columbia University, graduating Phi Beta Kappa in 1914. In 1918 he completed the B.D. degree at Yale and then returned to Columbia where he received the Ph.D. degree in psychology and education in 1920. While at Columbia he was president of the Chinese Student Christian Association and an associate editor of the popular *Chinese Students' Monthly*. During his graduate years he married Wu Chang-sheng (Katherine Wu) who later lectured at Yenching in education and from 1921 to 1927 was the dean of women at the Peking Normal University. Liu's wife had previously studied in Georgia at La Grange College where she became close friends with Soong Mei-ling, later Madame Chiang Kai-shek. Prior to his return home, Liu taught religious education at Union Theological Seminary and was the first Chinese ever to teach any subject other than Chinese in an American theological school.[17]

Years before the founding of Yenching, Stuart and Liu had developed strong personal ties. As a student at St. John's School Liu had written critical articles in church publications which impressed Stuart, who contacted Liu in person and offered to finance his education abroad.[18] From these early contacts Liu acquired a deep feeling of loyalty to Stuart, and when Stuart began to upgrade the faculty at Yenching, he turned first to Liu, then a newly returned Ph.D. from Columbia University with extensive contacts among other prominent Chinese students. Stuart later wrote, "His assistance at this initial stage both in the selecting and then in securing desirable Chinese for the faculty has had a very large part in the direction given to Yenching policy."[19] Stuart turned to Liu, more than to other Chinese, for advice in handling the problems of political unrest on campus in the 1920s. He valued Liu's "remarkable intuition" and "incisive appreciation of the larger movements and their significance. Again and again I have longed for him to turn to in trying to form judgments in these baffling perplexities."[20] In a more personal vein Liu became for Stuart a bridge by which he passed over from superiority feelings characterizing his earlier missionary work to "another region in the land of friendship" and racial equality.[21] Liu felt the mutuality of the relationship and reportedly requested Stuart to rid Yenching of all the "bad missionaries" as a condition of his teaching there.[22] Others, though, saw in Liu's behavior the mark of a sycophant. If this was true, Stuart never accepted it. He explained Liu's behavior as the legitimate expression of the complexities surrounding his life.[23]

Upon his return from the United States in 1920 Liu accepted simultaneously the deanship of the graduate school of education at Peking Normal University, a lectureship in psychology at Peking National University, and a professorship in theology at Yenching's school of religion, where he became the dean the following year. In 1924 he ended his teaching responsibilities at the government institutions. Liu was a prolific writer. In addition to editing and writing for the Life Fellowship's publications, he was associate editor of the *Journal of New Education* (*Hsin chiao-yü*), 1922–25. He translated vast quantities of Western Christian writings into Chinese, including the early works of Kahlil Gibran which appeared in *Chen-li yü sheng-ming*. Between 1932 and 1934 he published more than sixty books and articles on psychology, education, Christianity, and philosophy, in both Chinese and English. His sermons and services of worship were popular among Christian communities throughout China, and he bore major editing responsibilities for the publication in 1936 of the widely used *Sung-chu sheng-shih* (Hymns of universal praise).[24]

In the early 1920s Liu was Yenching's bright Chinese star on the horizon, and there was talk of him succeeding Stuart as president. But Liu's personality antagonized his colleagues, and he became quite unpopular with students.[25] By the mid 1930s hostility toward him mounted to the point where even Stuart's intercessions no longer counted. Conveniently he was asked by the Nanking government to serve as a member of the Legislative Yuan, and he moved his family to Shanghai where he continued writing.[26] In 1942 Liu went to the United States to seek relief from his chronic illnesses, and he died of tuberculosis in 1947 at the Southwest Presbyterian Sanitorium in Albuquerque at the age of fifty-six, surely an unhappy man.

Wu Lei-ch'uan (1870–1944). Perhaps the most intriguing member of the Life Fellowship was Wu Lei-ch'uan. He had achieved the highest distinction and honor as a *hanlin* scholar under the traditional examination system and later served as the first Chinese vice-president and later Chinese chancellor of Yenching University, 1926–34. Colleagues and alumni have differed widely in their evaluation of his role in the university. And yet all remember him with fond affection. In Mei Yi-pao's words he was a man of "complete wisdom, great experience, and integrity. Everybody trusted him. He could not be mean. He was a father confessor and an advisor."[27] Grace Boynton, Wu's neighbor for some years in the Lang Jun Yüan faculty residence compound, also stressed Wu's sage-like qualities, his garden home, his diet of rice and vegetables, his dress in somber gray or black, his long hours with books and writing brush, and his quiet conversations with friends out on the stone terrace sipping rice wine under the moon.[28] Some Yenching figures have suggested that Wu's role was to legitimize the university in Chinese eyes, at a time when westernization came under attack.[29] Wu did symbolize a certain continuity with the past, as he neither read nor spoke any foreign language and never traveled abroad.

Wu Lei-ch'uan (Chen-ch'un) was born in Hsü-chou, Kiangsu, though his family's native place was in Hangchow, which was also Stuart's birthplace. With no railroad, telegraph, or postal service, Hsü-chou had very little contact with the outside world. Even the *Shen-pao* (the *Shanghai News*), founded in 1872, rarely reached the town walls. Wu spent the first seventeen years of his life in this isolated world. Western penetration along the Chinese coast seemed far away. His grandfather had served as a district magistrate in Hsü-chou for many years, and his father, a minor local official, worked and later resided in Ch'ing-chiang, Kiangsu. Despite official rank the Wu family with five children and many relatives living in the same household was quite poor. In Wu's boyhood days the family often ate only vegetables and the clothes he wore were handed down. Wu's mother taught all her children to be frugal and willing to endure hardship and these became qualities which characterized Wu to the end of his life.[30]

Wu began the study of the four books and five classics at the age of six (seven *sui*) with the teacher hired to tutor his older brothers, and most of his boyhood energies were spent in preparing for the periodic tests in the traditional examination system. Concentrating on book learning, character writing, and practice in the "eight-legged essays," Wu had little idea of China's national troubles, and he later regretted the narrowness and irrelevance of this long period of tedious training. Nevertheless, at the age of sixteen (seventeen *sui*) he took the first level examination and received the degree of *hsiu-ts'ai*, in Hangchow, but not until he was twenty-three in 1893 did he succeed in passing the provincial examination with the title of *chü-jen* after three previously unsuccessful attempts. He reached the summit of his scholarly career in 1898 when he passed the metropolitan and imperial examinations in Peking with the title of *chin-shih* and soon thereafter was honored with membership in the Hanlin Academy.[31]

Despite this greatest honor, Wu failed in the turmoil of the abortive 1898 reforms and the Boxer Rebellion to receive official appointment. As the third son he was required by his older brothers, who had received appointments, to care for the ailing father. Thus he lived for the next six years in Ch'ing-chiang attending to his filial duties while studying Chinese history and the classics and pursuing further training in the writing of official documents. These years were later described by Wu as a time of "indescribable sadness." His father had taken up opium smoking and acquired a second wife who disliked Wu's wife and forced her to leave. The family income was also inadequate and Wu had to use some of his scholarship money to meet family needs. Even as a *hanlin* he lived in a small hut made of reeds and pounded earth near his father's house.

After Wu's father died in 1905 and his mother a year later, he strictly observed the periods of mourning and refrained over the next four years from seeking official appointment. He did, however, turn his attention to education, serving first as headmaster of the Chekiang Provincial College (Chiang-pei kao-teng hsüeh-t'ang), from 1905 to 1909, then in 1909 a year with the Chin-shih kuan, a training program for *chin-shih* title holders without official appointments, and finally in 1910 in Hangchow as headmaster of a middle school. There he also became active in the newly formed provincial assembly. When Hangchow declared independence from the imperial government in 1911 Wu was appointed civil magistrate of the city, but he lost this position in the ensuing chaos. In 1912 he began work for the Chekiang Provincial Board of Education and later that year went to Peking to serve as head of the secretariat in the board of education from 1912 to 1925 with the title of senior assistant (*ts'an-shih*).

The link between Wu's Confucian background and his career at Yenching was his conversion to Christianity in 1914. Soon after his arrival in Peking he began to despair over the meaninglessness of his own life and the fate of China.[32] His life as an official in the bureau of education merely followed the "daily tide, partaking only in the joys of drinking and eating." Two close friends were attending the nearby Anglican church on *Tung t-ai-p'ing* street and urged him to consider Christianity. Never having seen a copy of the New Testament before, Wu bought one, quickly read it through, and soon accompanied his friends to the Sunday worship services. He was moved by the solemnity of the service and the sincerity of the Chinese preacher, who stressed the theme of serving the people (*wei-jen fu-wu*). The appeal of Christianity then must have been strong indeed, for he soon enrolled in a baptism class where the intellectual level among the ten members was so low that one member wanted to set up a business selling baptismal robes. He was perplexed by the theological arguments and disputes he soon encountered, but he set them aside for a time because Christianity had brought to him a "peace of mind" he had not known in a long time.[33] After baptism he plunged into church work, writing articles in religious newspapers, leading baptism classes for the growing number of intellectuals coming into the church, and preaching. He also conducted weekly prayer groups and participated in the church's YMCA activities. Soon after conversion his wife and one child died, and he was forced to live alone. Coping with his suffering from these losses was made easier by his intense involvement in church work.[34]

The first eight years after Wu's conversion are marked by a rather uncritical acceptance of Christianity. But the Anti-Christian movement shook his confidence. He followed closely the debates on religion in the current literature and sought ways to preserve his faith.[35] But the attack on religion forced Wu to confront the foreignness of Christianity. As a result Wu partially separated himself from the Life Fellowship and formed another group known as the Chen-li she or Truth Society, which published the *Chen-li chou-k'an* (Truth weekly) for three years from 1923 to 1926, largely under Wu's leadership. Other Chinese members of the Life Fellowship were asked to join, but Westerners were expressly prohibited from participation. In 1926 the weekly merged with the Life Fellowship's monthly, but the Truth Society continued to meet separately from Westerners.[36]

In the late 1920s Wu's religious faith was marked by a return of self-confidence, and he labored hard to create an indigenous Christianity in China. Wu dissociated himself further from the Western church, though he still attended worship services and read widely (in translation) on theology and church history. Wu wrote regularly for the publications of the Life Fellowship, but it was not until the late 1920s that his ideas acquired clearer form. His first systematic statement was *Chi-tu-chiao yü Chung-kuo wen-hua* (Christianity and Chinese culture), which was published in 1936. In it he tried to fuse elements of the Confucian past with Christianity and a politically radical interpretation of national salvation. His second book, *Chi-tu-t'u ti hsi-wang* (The Christian's hope, 1939), was more devotional in nature and restated Wu's defense of Christianity as a basis of hope during the despair of the Japanese occupation in North China. His third book, *Mo Ti yü Yeh-su* (Mo Tzu and Jesus, 1940), tried to strengthen the appeal of Christianity by comparing it with the philosophy of Mo Tzu. All three books were published by the YMCA Press in Shanghai, and all reveal Wu's most serious efforts to create an indigenous Christian philosophy.

Wu began teaching at Yenching in 1922 first as a part time lecturer in the school of religion and in 1925 full time in the department of Chinese. He was appointed Yenching's first Chinese vice-president in 1926 and chancellor in 1929. For nine months in 1928–29 he served as vice-minister of education in Nanking under Chiang Mon-lin, who had attended the Chekiang Provincial College when Wu was headmaster there. Wu experienced frustration in asserting his influence as chancellor over the life of the university and resigned in 1934. After that, with periodic returns to his native Hangchow, he continued teaching in the department of Chinese and living in a kind of semi-retirement. All

Yenching colleagues and alumni interviewed remember Wu only for his scholarly quiet and religious piety during these years. Indeed in appearance he projected such an image. But his later writings show him to be the most politically radical member of the Life Fellowship. After the Japanese attack on Pearl Harbor in December 1941 the university was closed, and Wu moved inside the city walls. There he spent the next three years in the Sung-p'o Library in Pei-hai Park, doing copy work for others and selling pieces of his calligraphy. It was a skill he had acquired through long years of preparation for the traditional examinations, taught as "documentary Chinese" to Yenching students in the mid-1930s and used in making small gifts for friends throughout his years at Yenching. In his last years he put it to practical use in eking out a living.[37] He died on October 26, 1944.

Hsü Pao-ch'ien (1892–1944). Hsü Pao-ch'ien taught at Yenching a shorter time and carried fewer administrative responsibilities than the other Chinese figures discussed in this section. But he deserves mention because of his leading role in the Life Fellowship, as the founder of the group, later editor of its publications, and frequent contributor.[38] He also exerted considerable influence at Yenching faculty meetings, where according to Mei Yi-pao, Hsü was a member of the "loyal opposition" and carried weight through the exercise of the "sheer brilliance and analytic sharpness of his mind."[39] Hsü was less well known than Liu and Chao in Chinese circles, and yet the odyssey of his own thought illuminates the larger problems of Chinese Christian intellectuals.[40]

Born in Shang-yü, Chekiang, Hsü grew up with a strong Confucian background. His grandfather had been a scholarly physician (*ju-yi*), and his father's older brother (who had considerable influence on the boy) was a *hsiu-ts'ai* and an avid Confucian scholar. As a boy Hsü attended Confucian temple ceremonies each month and the ancestral rites twice a year, but his childhood was not limited to the Confucian world. His mother and grandmother were devout Buddhists, and he would frequently go with them to the temples and help them in the reading of Buddhist scriptures.

Hsü was a child prodigy. He began study of the Confucian classics at home with his uncle and family tutors. He claimed the ability to recognize 1,000 characters at the age of three (four *sui*), a year later upon entering private school to read T'ang poetry and the *Classic on Filial Piety,* and soon thereafter to recite the four Books and three of the five Classics. Though saturated with this classical literature, he recalled that

Confucianism did not come alive until some years later in his early teens when he studied the neo-Confucian literature of the Sung and Ming periods while attending the Shao-hsing Prefectural Middle School (Shao-hsing fu-li chung-hsüeh). In 1910 he enrolled at the Customs College (Shui-wu hsüeh-hsiao) in Peking and graduated from there in 1915, second in his class.[41]

Hsü's family had always been hostile to Christianity. His uncle had supported the Boxer Rebellion in North China and enjoined the boy on entering middle school in Shao-hsing not to enter any foreign church. The uncle had also forbidden young Hsü not to associate with the revolutionary party of Sun Yat Sen or cut off his queue. But within a few years Hsü had done all three. In 1912 he followed closely the establishment of the new Republican government, replacing the imperial dynasty, but he became disillusioned with the "magic of republicanism" and the corruption of the new rulers. He concluded that China's national salvation (*chiu-kuo*) had to begin at a more basic level by changing first the lives of the people and creating a group of men devoted "unselfishly to the good of the country and the people." For awhile he turned to the works of the neo-Confucianists, especially those of Chang Ts'ai and Wang Yang-ming, for direction in this fundamental task, and he joined the Confucian Society (K'ung chiao-hui) in Peking. But he soon left in discouragement because of its formalism and inability to generate the unselfish spirit.[42]

Out of disillusionment as a student at the Customs College Hsü turned to the newly founded YMCA in Peking, attending first some of its public lectures. Then in 1912 he began study of the Bible, by himself lest anyone unduly influence him for or against it. After a half year of study he came to two conclusions: that through the inspiration of Jesus' personality the Chinese people would become less selfish; and that Christianity deserved further serious study because it united thought and action. Lectures by Sherwood Eddy and John R. Mott in Peking also strengthened his interest. But Hsü had difficulty resolving the questions of the miracles, the divinity of Jesus, and the conflict between the creation story in the Old Testament and the theory of evolution. A year later at the annual summer conference at Wo-fo-ssu, sponsored by the Princeton-in-Peking YMCA secretaries, Hsü found some answers. He discovered that modern science and the theory of evolution had not invalidated, but in fact enriched, the creation story in the Bible.[43]

The biggest obstacle was the divinity of Christ, and he overcame it with the help of John Stewart Burgess when the two went for a hike one day. Hsü's account of the event in his autobiography appears extraordinary, and yet it characterizes the nature of religious conversion in China during those years. Hsü asked how Jesus could be regarded as the son of God, to which Burgess replied, Jesus may be God's son, but so is everyone. From that moment Hsü claimed, he decided to become a Christian. That obstacle seems like such a small one, and the conversation with Burgess suggests that Hsü was well on his way to conversion before the conference. He was content to let the miracles take care of themselves. He told others that conversion for him in no way meant abandoning his belief in Confucianism. The two faiths were complementary and would unite in helping China to achieve national salvation. Confucianism would continue to serve as the cultural basis for the Chinese people, and Christianity would fill in the gaps and inadequacies (*pu-tsu*). Hsü described his conversion as a moment of great happiness, and coming down from the conference center he recalled, like St. Francis in another time and place, how the "weeping willows and the flying birds were all laughing with me."[44]

Following his conversion Hsü pursued religious work with a crusading zeal. He became impatient because the church made so few demands on him. In the fall of 1914 Hsü started with Burgess the Social Service Club (She-hui shih-chin hui), which organized playground activities, night education classes, social surveys (beginning notably with the rickshaw coolies), lectures on public health, and a small relief program in the city. In 1915 Hsü became chairman of the club with a membership of 600 students. He claimed it was the "one great organizing force for social work among the 8,000 college men of the city." Ch'ü Ch'iu-po, later secretary to the Chinese Communist Party, was one devoted member of the group who joined in the activities with an "unbelievable fury," before his conversion to Marxism and journey to the Soviet Union. Hsü also organized many Bible study groups and took credit for abolishing gambling in one of the dorms of the Customs College.[45]

Upon graduation from the college in the spring of 1915 Hsü was forced to decide upon his career. Working with the Customs Service seemed like a dead end, for there was little chance that the Chinese would ever gain control of the customs revenue. Such bureaucratic work was also ill-suited to the service orientation of his Christian faith. After much consideration he turned his back on this prestigious line of work and chose instead to become a student secretary of a new YMCA branch, which had been recently organized by Burgess on the west side of Peking. The salary was almost half that of the government job and was offered with no promise of advancement. In the course of his work over the next six years, Hsü organized YMCA chapters in almost every government and private middle school and college in Peking. He believed that many students held mistaken ideas about Christianity but would be receptive if it were carefully explained.[46] With this thought in mind Hsü and another close YMCA friend, Hu Hsüeh-ch'eng, organized the Cheng-tao t'uan, which was the forerunner of the Life Fellowship.

A year after his conversion Hsü returned to Shang-yü to see his family. His father seemed unbothered with Hsü's new ideas, but his uncle remained adamant, especially over the issue of Christian opposition to ancestor worship. Hsü mollified his uncle with the argument that Christians too were supposed to honor their parents and that all patriotic Chinese were opposed to the more superstitious aspects of ancestor worship. After considerable effort Hsü converted his wife and younger brother to Christianity, and he took them to Peking to live with him when he began YMCA work in 1915. By then the uncle's defenses had crumbled, and he too converted and accepted a more fundamentalistic version of the faith which included a belief in the miracles. The uncle's earlier exclusiveness had found new form. But any religious conflicts within the family were subsumed to the common commitment to the Christian faith. Hsü founded a church in his home town which provided an outlet for his uncle's religious enthusiasm. The uncle turned his home into a village school and would invite Hsü back home to lecture on "public health, democracy, and Christianity."[47]

In 1921 Hsü went to the United States for two and a half years of study at the Union Theological Seminary in New York and Columbia University. He was extremely busy with extracurricular activities among Chinese students there and spoke more than a hundred times to American church groups on Chinese culture and the Chinese Christian movement. Hsü visited the West a second time in 1930, spending one year as a special secretary of the World Student Christian Federation traveling mostly in Europe and then another year back at Columbia University where he received the Ph.D. degree in 1933. His dissertation was published that year at Yenching as *Ethical Realism in Neo-Confucian*

Thought. This book marked the high point of Hsü's scholarly work and reveals his preoccupation with the effort to link Christianity with Chinese thought.

During his first visit to the United States Hsü became intimately acquainted with Japanese students in the dormitory at Union and was converted to pacifism. Later he joined the Chinese Fellowship of Reconciliation (Wei-ai-she), serving as its national chairman in 1928, and he maintained contact with his Japanese friends well into the 1930s. In 1938 he met Mahatma Gandhi at the Madras World Christian Conference and returned to China to organize ashrams along Gandhian lines.[48] Hsü's forthrightness and independence of thought, so often remembered by his friends, were no more evident than in his leadership in these kinds of activities at a time when anti-Japanese feeling among patriots made pacifism highly unpopular.

Hsü's tenure at Yenching was shorter than that of his four colleagues discussed here. When he returned to China in 1924 he became a part time lecturer in religion and philosophy in the Yenching School of Religion, while serving concurrently as the administrative secretary to the Peking Christian Student Union (Chi-tu-chiao hsüeh-sheng shih-yeh hui). During the period of full time teaching at Yenching, from 1926 to 1935, Hsü wrote extensively for the *Sheng-ming* and *Chen-li yü sheng-ming* and became a leading figure in Christian activity on the Yenching campus. From 1932 to 1934 he was the acting dean of the school of religion.[49] He left Yenching in 1935 because of the budget squeeze and went to Li-ch'uan, Kiangsi, to become the general secretary for two years of the government-sponsored rural reconstruction project. He returned to academic life at Shanghai University until the Japanese invasion there and later took a position with the Christian Literature Society (Chung-hua Chi-tu-chiao wen-she) in Chengtu, a position he held till his death in a truck accident in 1944. Just before his death he was in the midst of translating William Ernest Hocking's *Meaning of God in Human Experience.*[50]

Chao Tzu-ch'en (1888–). Chao is clearly one of the great Chinese Christian leaders of the twentieth century.[51] His books on the life of Jesus and St. Paul and on New Testament theology were still published in Hong Kong and in use in Protestant seminaries in Taiwan long after the Communist revolution. Though Chao was the last of these five Chinese figures to begin teaching at Yenching and was simply not present at the early meetings of the Life Fellowship in Peking, he nevertheless became a powerful influence in both. He had been on the editorial board of the *Sheng-ming* from the beginning, and he later served as editor of the *Chen-li yü sheng-ming*. He was dean of the school of religion at Yenching for more than twenty years from 1928 until after the revolution. Yenching University and Chinese Protestant Christianity have often been associated with his name. Chao's childhood and early training further demonstrate the varieties of social backgrounds the Chinese members brought to the Life Fellowship.

Like Stuart, Liu, Wu and Hsü, Chao was a Chekiang man. He was born in the town of Te-ch'ing. As his family were devout Buddhists, Chao once considered becoming a Buddhist monk, and he later described his childhood as a world of spirits and apparitions. Every reality, from the sounds of the rustling leaves of the trees to the horror he felt looking at the Buddhist pictures of hell at his aunt's funeral, was seen as the work of spirits. As a boy he saw himself as physically weak and timid, though in later years he grew to be quite tall physically and was known for his self-assurance. Chao recalled being sensitive to the frailties of others and would insist his mother give generous alms to the beggars, despite the family poverty. The story of the sorrows of the Buddhist figure, Liu Hsiang-an, were so moving that as he read it his mother would cry. But Chao's remorse would last into the following day, long after the others in the family had dried their tears. So well known was Chao for his guilelessness that friends of his would later tease him, pointing out the superfluousness of becoming a Christian, since he would have behaved like one, even as a Buddhist.[52]

Chao's parents sacrificed heavily—at one time selling a small piece of land—for the young boy to receive a good education in the classics. His teachers, though, were not narrow Confucianists, and he was heavily exposed to Chinese poets and other non-Confucian literature. At thirteen (fourteen *sui*) he had to decide which direction to pursue in further education, Chinese studies in Hangchow or Western studies in Soochow, Kiangsu. In trying to make up his mind he drew lots using bamboo slips in front of idols at the local Buddhist temple, with the resulting instruction to go to Hangchow. But for the first time in his life he experienced a conflict between his own desires and the direction suggested to him by the spirit world, and he took the unprecedented step of rejecting the latter. At fourteen he entered the preparatory school at the missionary Soochow University (Tung-wu ta-hsueh), graduating from the college there in 1910.[53]

Chao's religious conversion occurred in two stages. His earliest contact with Christianity was made during childhood when his grandmother had taken him once to attend a worship service in a nearby church. Members of the Chao household could also hear singing every Sunday morning coming from that church, and when he considered the possibilities of Western studies, he consulted a teacher acquaintance who happened to be Christian. But it was not until his arrival in Soochow that Chao faced the stronger religious pressures through contact with missionary personalities and student converts. At Soochow University students were required every Sunday to attend services and memorize scriptural passages without missing a word. Chao was a native of Chekiang and found this exercise particularly irritating because it had to be done in the Soochow dialect. The students were constantly lectured on "heaven, the church, hell, spiritual salvation, Jesus' precious blood, and other doctrines" until Chao's "heart burned like fire" and he sought release through conversion. He returned home and with the zealousness of a new convert he trampled on the ancestral tablets and Buddhist idols and was stopped only by his mother's crying. A close friend took him aside and urged him to reconsider his decision.[54]

Chao stayed out of school for awhile, but he returned to Soochow University to get the Western learning he thought all youth needed if they wanted to make a contribution to China. Religiously, though, he reversed himself and became a leader in the antireligious attack on campus. The sight of students praying would infuriate him, and he upbraided them for their betrayal of Chinese culture. His hostility also expressed itself as antiforeignism, and at one meeting he publicly announced, "When we are powerful enough, we will kill all the foreigners."[55] But this opposition to Christianity was short-lived and weakened in the face of economic difficulties at home and the trials of working out an arranged marriage.

Despite Chao's overt hostility, the teachers of the school, notably its president, D. L. Anderson, took a special interest in him, which Chao later claimed began his second conversion experience. John R. Mott of the YMCA was also on the Soochow campus during Chao's personal crisis and gave a series of lectures which deeply impressed him. He returned to reading the Bible and regular worship and asked to be baptized. This second conversion lifted him out of his despair, and he joined in the popular Christian activities on campus. At the time, his classmate and lifelong friend Lu Chih-wei—later chancellor and then president of Yenching—was also converted. Chao prayed fervently, and threw himself into every available form of Christian work. He was the first president of the campus YMCA. After persistent efforts he convinced his mother and wife of the limitations of Buddhism and converted them to Christianity. Upon graduating from Soochow College in 1910, Chao stayed on to teach Chinese, English, mathematics, and the Bible and influenced many students to convert to Christianity.[56]

In the summer of 1914 Chao was sent by the Southern Methodist church in China to the General Conference of the Methodist Episcopal Church South in Oklahoma. That fall he entered graduate school at Vanderbilt University in Nashville, where he earned the M.A. degree in 1916 and the B.D. degree in 1917. Following his study he traveled to England, Europe, and the Middle East, and he returned to Soochow University to teach sociology and religion and became the first Chinese dean of the college in 1922. That same year he was invited by Stuart to teach at Yenching, but he did not leave his job at Soochow until 1925. At Yenching he continued his extremely busy schedule of teaching, administrative work, writing, and translating Christian literature—poems, hymns, worship aids, articles and books—all in the attempt to strengthen the indigenous church movement. Chao became widely known in international Protestant circles, and in 1948 was elected one of the six vice-presidents of the World Council of Churches at its first general assembly in Amsterdam.[57]

Over a period of some forty years Chao's thought swung back and forth between evangelism and social action, conservative and liberal theology, indigenization and ecumenicity. The evolution of his thought shows how difficult it is to describe the Life Fellowship in conventional terms. In recalling the literature out of the past that influenced his decision to become a Christian, he mentioned the figure of Chu-ko Liang and the writings of the early poets, T'ao Ch'ien and Tu Fu, the Sung scholar-patriot, Wen T'ien-hsiang, and the Ming philosopher-statesman, Wang Yang-ming. He would later use quotations from or about each of these figures as epigrams for his writings on Christianity. In his efforts to convert other students at Soochow, Chao freely used the Christian concepts of sin, personal salvation, heaven, and hell. But after his study in the United States and closer identification with the patriotic tides of the New Culture movement Chao's thinking changed. It became more "scientific" and "ethical" and less "mystical"; more a "social" and less a "personal" religion; and more concerned with the present world and less with the "hereafter."[58] The Protestant church movement in China was strongly linked to Chao's leadership, and the publication of his *Yeh-su chuan* (Life of Jesus, 1935), was an early attempt to adapt Christianity to the Chinese setting. But later in the 1930s, when North China was occupied by Japan, Chao became discouraged. He turned inward, indigenization diminished in importance, and he articulated a more Pauline-oriented theology. This conservative trend was reinforced by his cruel experience in a Japanese prison during World War Two and it carried into the late 1940s. Then again, on the eve of the Communist revolution, the pendulum swung back, and Chao led the drive to bring the Chinese Protestant church into line with the new government directives on religion.[59]

Hung Yeh (1893–   ). Commonly known by his first name as William or Wei-lien, Hung was less active in the Life Fellowship than the others discussed in this section, though he occasionally served on the editorial board of the group's publications. As the second distinguished returned student (after Liu T'ing-fang) to join the Yenching faculty, he became prominent as the first Chinese dean of the college from 1924 to 1927. Later he excelled in scholarship, for which his editorship of the *Harvard-Yenching Sinological Index Series* (1930–1946) and his writings on the poet Tu Fu are perhaps the most famous. He played an important role in the Harvard-Yenching Institute in China and contributed to the institute's various publications over more than four decades. A partial listing of Hung's scholarly publications is interspersed with articles of a more religious nature.[60] Hung's combining of religious and scholarly purposes lay at the heart of the Yenching dream.

Hung was born in Foochow, Fukien, his family's native place. But he spent his early years in Shantung province where his father was a district magistrate at the end of the Ch'ing dynasty. As the oldest of six sons, Hung was given a good education at home in the Confucian classics, tutored often by his own father.[61] His conversion to Christianity occurred in 1912 while he was attending the Methodist-run Anglo-Chinese College in Foochow. As a new student there Hung took it upon himself to dissuade the students from their belief in Christianity, and to enhance his chances of victory he offered extra sacrifices at the ancestral graves. He would stage public debates with his Christian teachers and created a sensation by citing the "worst parts" of the Bible and the "best parts" of the classics. So disruptive was Hung that the faculty considered expelling him. But there was one who counseled patience, Mrs. John Gowdy, wife of the schoolmaster.[62]

Toward the end of these attacks on Christianity Hung's father died, leaving the boy deeply shaken. Mrs. Gowdy sent for him and comforted him by pointing out the parallel between Jesus' early death and that of the boy's father. She assured him that his father, having been upright, would be with Christ. Hung recalls how surprised he was by this liberal interpretation, for he had been told that all non-Christians would go to hell. She replied, "God would not be so unfair!" And then she urged him to consider the good things of the Bible, such as the teaching about meekness, and asked him to apply it to his own life. Hung was so moved by her compassion that he decided to be baptized immediately. Publicly he renounced all that he had said against Christianity and asked to be forgiven by the school community. Like the figure of St. Paul he championed the Christian cause with the same enthusiasm with which he had previously attacked it. He joined the local Salvation Army band and brought his whole family into the Methodist church.

Another Western figure, Edwin C. Jones, a bachelor chemistry teacher and later president of Fukien Christian University, 1916 to 1923, left a strong imprint on Hung. In 1914 he offered Hung the chance for further education in the United States. The decision was difficult to make. Hung's grandfather and mother preferred that he work with the Customs Service which would ensure an adequate income for the family, and they feared he might be forced to become an American citizen. But they consented when they discovered that such a condition was not part of the offer. Hung went to the United States, graduating Phi Beta Kappa from Ohio Wesleyan University in 1917, and later received the M.A. degree in history from Columbia in 1919 and the B.D. degree from Union Theological Seminary in 1920. During these years Hung participated in student gospel teams and became an articulate spokesman for China in church and student circles. He was asked to return to China to teach at Yenching in 1921, but the board of trustees requested Stuart to allow them to use Hung's services in raising money for the university. Hung's years in America were so formative in shaping his view of life that it became as easy for him to think in English as in Chinese. His list of publications shows that his religious writings are largely in English, while the majority of his scholarly writings are in Chinese.

When Hung went to Yenching in 1922 as a part time lecturer in history, he also served as the Chinese pastor in a Methodist mission to Fukien students residing in Peking. The next year he began teaching full time in the history department and served as the acting head. As dean of the college between 1924 and 1927, Hung dedicated himself to raising Yenching's academic standing to "make it the peer of Peita." Upgrading meant antagonizing colleagues and students: in Stuart's words, he had to bear the "the brunt of our efforts to raise our standards and then to maintain them rigidly."[63] During Hung's deanship Yenching became known as one of the leading universities in North China. After 1927 Hung continued to carry committee responsibilities and played an especially crucial role in library administration, but he changed his focus and turned to the world of scholarship. He went to Harvard as a visiting lecturer in 1928–30, where he studied with the famous sinologist Paul Pelliot and worked at the Harvard-Yenching Institute. He was imprisoned for five months in Peking during the war with Japan, and later returned to Yenching for one year after the war. He left China in 1946 to lecture at the University of Hawaii and the following year at Harvard, where he has worked ever since, consulting with members of the Harvard-Yenching Institute and continuing his scholarly pursuits.[64]

The Intercultural Connection

These biographical sketches suggest that early twentieth century Chinese intellectuals were not immune to the appeals of Christianity. The hope of the missionary educators in finding an indigenous leadership, equal in its commitment to the Christian faith, became a reality. As a group the converts were not as prominent as their non-Christian counterparts in institutions such as Peking National University. Nor were they as prominent as their religious counterparts in another time, the so-called "three pillars" of the late Ming period, Hsü Kuang-ch'i, Li Chih-tsao, and Yang T'ing-yün.[65] But there was no question in their minds, nor in the minds of their Western colleagues, of their legitimate place in the Chinese scene. Before the Republican period they were deeply rooted in the classical tradition, and after that they were as full blown in their patriotism as any of their contemporaries. Their ties with the missionary enterprise were strengthened by a common outlook and converged around the three issues of religious experience, China's national salvation, and a commitment to the internationalist idea.

The Chinese members of the Life Fellowship were not unmindful of

China's past contacts with Christianity and the presence of a definite thread of hostility related perhaps to an understandable suspicion of things foreign and official mistrust of heterodox ideas. Their own conversions to Christianity in the late Ch'ing and early Republican years, coinciding with a rapid increase of conversion generally, were a sign that this hostility, however pervasive it might have been before, had definitely weakened. But they also recognized that even in these years of openness to foreign ideas, they could not escape the feeling that conversion raised questions about their feelings of being Chinese. It touched all their personal relationships. The observance of church regulations, for example, conflicted with the practice of ancestor worship.[66] It was a conflict they had known well in their younger years, but one that also rapidly disappeared once Confucianism itself came under attack in student circles in the 1910s.

In the 1920s a new kind of defensiveness emerged as a response to the attacks made on Christianity in educational and literary circles, and the defense was often begun by a return to the validity of their earliest religious experiences. Indeed, when the Chinese members of the Life Fellowship wrote about themselves the titles of their writings often included the phrase religious experience (tsung-chiao ching-yen). In 1934 Hsü Pao-ch'ien edited for the YMCA Press a collection of eighteen such autobiographical sketches, including his own and those of Wu Lei-ch'uan and Chao Tzu-ch'en.[67] Both Wu and Chao had published earlier versions of their religious experiences in the Sheng-ming ten years before, while Hsü's lengthier account of his "twenty year religious experience" appeared in serial form in the Chen-li yü sheng-ming in 1933 and 1934 when he served as editor. One common theme in all these short pieces is the description of a period prior to conversion of intense personal crisis and after conversion a new peace of mind. When doubts about the Christian faith arose in Wu Lei-ch'uan's mind, he seemed to return to the vivid reality of that earlier experience in the Anglican church in Peking.[68] Chao Tzu-ch'en underwent even more drastic shifts in thought over almost fifty years, and yet the clarity of his earliest religious experience seems to have diminished very little, if at all.[69] Protestant Christianity for these converts had become the anchor in a time of personal despair. The Christian hope would weaken in the face of antireligious tides in the 1920s, but they failed to destroy the validity of that earliest experience.

The Chinese members of the Life Fellowship had a didactic purpose in publishing these religious testimonies. They hoped the readership, especially students, would be inspired and that the word would spread and through some sort of chain reaction would gradually affect the whole of China. But they also published these testimonies simply to edify themselves. After all, the Life Fellowship publications never reached a circulation of more than 2,000, and it is questionable what proportion of the readership were potential prospects for conversion.[70] They wrote, as they so often said and as the name of the Cheng-tao t'uan suggests, to witness to the truth or the way.[71] These Chinese figures were religious stalwarts. Making Yenching University "more Chinese" to them may have meant altering religious regulations, but it did not mean abandoning religious purposes.

There has been a longstanding argument, from the earliest Catholic missionaries in the thirteenth century to the present day, whether or not the Chinese people have understood the concept of sin.[72] One of the problems, of course, is defining the term. Some members of the Life Fellowship may have subscribed, at an earlier time in their religious experience, to a view of original sin stressing man's depravity, but for most of them the more optimistic view of human nature won out. Even within the liberal framework though, there was still a profound sense of things having gone wrong, which was due not simply to the calamities of the modern period. The missionary educators and their Chinese counterparts would still use the word sin in their English writings, though it was by no means their prime concern. Various terms in Chinese were used to describe this lack within their own lives and within China as a whole, terms like *tsui, fan-tsui, tsui-e,* and so on, all approximating the meaning of sin. Wu once spoke of man's indolent nature (*tuo-hsing*).[73] These terms may not capture the notion of original sin as understood by the fundamentalists, but the missionary educators did not hold to such a view either. They believed that no matter how good man's nature might be, there was still the necessity of religious experience to pull the Chinese people through their trauma of modern times. Chao Tzu-ch'en wrote, "We are like lost sheep wandering in the mountains. Wild animals are all around us and the cold is piercing our skin. We have nothing to eat, nor do we have any shelter . . . We dash around aimlessly, but still we cannot find our way home. We struggle with nature and we struggle with the wild beasts. We think that this is life, that this is the only kind of life. Sometimes we become extremely tired and we call out in despair, but from the distant mountains we can only hear the echo of our cries."[74] Other religious terms such as repentance (*hui-kai*) and salvation (*te-chiu*) were also frequently used in their writings, suggesting further that the religious vocabulary of the missionary educators was not necessarily a problem for these Chinese converts.

They saw sin as selfishness (*tzu-ssu*) and gave it an interpretation which resembles earlier Chinese (both Confucian and Taoist) views of self and society.[75] Wu Lei-ch'uan had difficulty comprehending the concept of original sin, which he encountered in Bible study classes, but he resolved the problem by equating the term with selfishness. The selfish spirit was perhaps more the result of the bad social customs than it was innate to man, but that did not diminish its need of correction.[76] "In man's search for happiness," Chao Tzu-ch'en wrote, "he only thought of himself and became indifferent to other people. Thus love was gone . . . Without love, man became separated from God, and this is sin. Man's selfishness is sin."[77] If selfishness was man's sinfulness, then salvation was the overcoming of the selfish spirit, which was possible when one turned his attention to the figure of Jesus. Jesus was, in Hsü Pao-ch'ien's words, the "unrivaled expression of the unselfish person." The rules and regulations of Christianity, he wrote, would change with time, but the unselfish spirit (*pu-tzu-ssu ti ching-shen*) was undiminished by the changing customs of society. Salvation for Wu was not "attaining eternal life after death, but removing from oneself the evil of selfishness so that one could then sacrifice himself to society." In a time when great Chinese figures of the past were being cast off as irrelevant, Jesus would become, they argued, the new exemplar, the teacher, the master. Overcoming selfishness was a rigorous task. Christianity was not cheap grace. One had to strive in cultivating the unselfish spirit, which for them was often described in the terms of *hsiu-yang,* or Confucian moral self-cultivation.[78]

In defending the validity of religious experience they plunged directly into the controversy over science and religion in China in the 1920s. Previously all Chinese members of the Life Fellowship had identified with the rationalism of the New Culture movement. Indeed, one is impressed how often the articles in the *Sheng-ming* appealed to science, reason, and the investigative and critical spirit in making their apologies for Christianity. We recall that the original purpose of the Life Fellowship was to present Christianity as a rational approach to the problems of the day. Furthermore in the name of reason, these leaders of the sinification movement would attack both the superstitious and arbitrary elements of the Western church, while warding off the unscientific attacks of the anti-Christian forces. They insisted that science did not invalidate religious experience.[79] They supported Chang Chün-mai (Carsun Chang) in his spirited defense of religion, and they clashed with Hu Shih and other advocates of the "scientific philosophy of life," who slighted religious experience.[80] In the 1920s Hu Shih's standing in student circles was high, and the debate with him became complicated, for he was at the same time one of Yenching's more ardent non-Christian supporters.

They articulated their defense of religion in a variety of ways. In the fall of 1919, before a student gathering in Taiyüan, Shansi, Hsü Pao-ch'ien acknowledged how much the New Culture movement had benefited Christianity by encouraging students to keep open minds. But it had also failed to provide them with any criteria for selecting from among all the new ideas presented to them. Without such a standard, confusion and cynicism would result. Christianity, Hsü argued, was eminently compatible with the spirit of criticism, but it went a step further in offering "constructive criticism." It also protected youth from the dangers of purely academic discussions, for the figure of Jesus was a constant reminder that any talk of social reform had to begin with oneself.[81]

Over the next two decades Hsü was haunted by the continuing attacks on religion by the advocates of scientific thought, but he never conceded their argument. In his search for replies to critics of religion he found support in neo-Confucian philosophy, which he had studied in school as a young boy, abandoned for almost two decades, and then rediscovered. By exposing the "unscientific" and "unscholarly" attacks by Hu Shih on the "quiet sitting" and "mind culture" of the Ch'eng-Chu school of philosophy, he hoped thereby to vindicate the spiritual side of Christianity. To Hu Shih "utilitarian and scientific considerations" exhausted "all values," but to Hsü Pao-ch'ien "metaphysical speculation and cultivation of the inner life have their inherent and independent value."[82] Buttressing his defense of religious experience by citing the major tenets of neo-Confucian philosophy. Hsü argued that even in the age of science there was an order in the universe; that this order was ethical; that this life and the world we live in were not dreams but real; that there was something of the sage in every person; and that through education and self-cultivation everyone could realize his sagehood. Such a deeply rooted philosophy of life, Hsü insisted, was still tenable and could not be "easily dislodged even by the combined attack of such theories as mechanistic evolutionism, positivism, materialism, and behaviorism."[83]

Chao Tzu-ch'en, early on, had recognized that Christianity would appeal to Chinese intellectuals only when it could be argued on the basis of "reason and faith not contradictory to reason." He also agreed it was necessary to eradicate vestiges of the old society which prevented the full development of personality. But like Hsü he decried the New Culture's destruction of the "ethical spirit."[84] Having "satisfied our demand for liberation," it had not "provided us with the sustaining power for the building up of life." In fact it had increased immorality and selfishness. Mission schools like Yenching would avoid the pitfalls of government schools like Peita where "hot headed, one-sided, unscientific youths have not yet shaken off the smell of their mother's milk."[85] Therein lay one of the clearest purposes of Yenching, namely character building. Liu T'ing-fang claimed in 1924 that some of the "cleanest and most outstanding figures in the sordid political environment in China" and the pioneers in social welfare were products of the Christian colleges.[86] Christianity, they thought, would make its contribution to China in ways similar to those in earlier periods of Chinese history when the revivals of Confucianism were supposed to correct moral decay and political corruption.

Hung Yeh employed still another tactic in discrediting the rationalists' attack on religion. He explored the tenacious hold of the heaven concept (t'ien) in Chinese life. As an ideograph it could be found everywhere in popular writings and ornamentation, and as a word it occurred frequently in conversation. As an idea representing the emperor, the spirit world, the universe, or simply nature, with much of the ambiguity and comprehensiveness that the word heaven suggested in English, Hung noted how it had "given considerable embarrassment to scholars who attempt to define it according to the requirements of logic."[87]

The role of tradition in defending religion here is illuminating. There had been a time when Confucianism for Hsü, Wu, Chao, and Hung was a major point of departure. But the Confucian world was crumbling, and troubled minds in troubled times turned to Christianity for peace of mind. Hsü Pao-ch'ien wrote that on the eve of his conversion he believed that "what China needed was an unselfish people concerned

about the nation." Such a spirit could be found in Confucian personalities, but now they were gone. What was needed was the revival of the
Confucian spirit, and Christianity would help produce it.[88] When religion was attacked in the circles of students they wanted most to reach,
they returned to Confucianism, not as the previous frame of reference
but as one means of defending the legitimacy of their own conversion
experiences. They cited the classics endlessly to buttress their arguments.
This use of tradition was important not only in their debates with the
voices of antireligion but also as a reassurance to themselves, when
others accused, that conversion had made them no less Chinese.[89]

National Salvation. The attack of science on religion represented only
a small part of the New Culture movement, compared to the overriding
concern with national salvation. For the Chinese members of the Life
Fellowship, too, national salvation was of first importance, and they
presented Christianity as one help in the task. Salvation which met only
individual needs may have attracted them at the moment of conversion
but by the time of the founding of the Life Fellowship, salvation which
failed to address the larger problems of society was to them no salvation
at all. One of Hsü Pao-ch'ien's motives for studying Christianity was to
find solutions to the "political difficulties of the time." Later Wu Lei-
ch'uan affirmed that "individual salvation and social reform" were one
and the same. True conversion to Wu meant discovering the imperative
to deny oneself and devote all for the sake of social reform. The first
question in Liu T'ing-fang's mind in 1924 was "How can China be
saved?. . . Can the gospel which saved the soul of individuals also
save the soul of the nation? Can the teaching of Jesus be really put into
practice and create a new Christian social order?" Christianity for Liu
would help create "new political leadership to deliver the country out of
disorder and corruption." Chao Tzu-ch'en claimed that Christianity
would become the basis for the "social reconstruction of China."[90] This
preoccupation with the practical contributions of Christianity overshadowed the theological disputes that were then so important in the
West. God, for them, was broadly understood as truth, nature, high
principle, and so on, while they preferred seeing Jesus as human, rather
than divine.[91] "When I speak of Jesus," Wu wrote, "I mean only Jesus
as a man." The Western emphasis upon the divinity of Jesus, Wu
thought, distorted the real meaning of his personality (*jen-ko*); "How
can we who are human and not divine imitate a Jesus who is divine and
not human?"[92] Wu's understanding of religious faith became closely

linked with national salvation in a way reminiscent of Confucian pre-scriptions for social harmony. The goal was political stability. In order to achieve it society had first to be transformed, but that transformation in turn required attention to the spiritual problems of life. Political, social, and spiritual matters, were interconnected in such a way that inattention to any one would be harmful to the other two.

To Chao Tzu-ch'en in the 1920s Jesus was only a man, though to be sure the greatest man in history. Other great men, Confucius, Mo Tzu, Socrates, and Plato, had also known God, but none had reached the height of Jesus' moral excellence. The understanding of Jesus as only "one among many saviors," in no way diminished in Chao's mind the value of Christian salvation.[93] The greatness of Jesus' personality alone justified imitation and worship. Jesus became the inspiration for sacri-fice and service to society. In Hsü Pao-ch'ien's words, Jesus would lead youth to give of their "love and service" and "sacrifice themselves in unselfish living."[94]

They frequently spoke of the kingdom of God (*t'ien-kuo*), as under-stood in the social gospel movement in the West at the time. This heavenly kingdom, as Wu put it, was not "in some other world; even less is it the place where people go after death." Rather heaven was the "destruction of all the hatred and injustice in this world and the fulfill-ment of the love and justice of God." In the words of the day, it was the "reform of the old society and changing it into a new one." Later Wu would equate it with socialism.[95] This connection between the Christian faith and the new society would weaken during the Japanese occupation, especially in the case of Chao Tzu-ch'en. But it was firmly established in the thinking of the Life Fellowship before then and was renewed with the coming of the Communist Revolution.[96]

All agreed that following Jesus meant carrying out social reform, but they would later disagree on how the change would come about. How would the problem of justice, which figures so prominently in the social gospel understanding of the kingdom of God, be realized? The question was not academic. It was discussed with students who continually re-minded these professors that national salvation was an immediate and practical issue. How should social change come about, gradually within the given political order, or through work outside of it, including at-tempts to overthrow it as represented by the increasingly popular posi-tion of the revolutionaries? The implications for the purposes within the university were far reaching. The ideal of service to society was enshrined in the university motto, but how was service to be rendered? The question plunged to the heart of career preparation and employment upon graduation. What values would teachers try to impart to students in their understanding of national salvation? And how might Yenching's Western connection influence Chinese answers to these questions?

These kinds of questions were already discussed within the Life Fellowship in the earliest years, but they acquired greater urgency by the early 1930s. In 1920 Liu T'ing-fang saw Jesus transcending the reformist-revolutionary conflict and argued that his teachings could be used to support contradictory positions. Jesus fit into the established order of his day by being baptized, by observing the sabbath, and by telling people to pay their taxes. But there were times, Liu pointed out, when Jesus offended the customs by gathering wheat on the Sabbath, breaking eating taboos, and mixing with people of questionable repute. Liu also saw Jesus chasing the moneychangers out of the temple with a whip as an example of violent confrontation with established practices. Jesus had equivocated. He said he had come to fulfill the law but later claimed he had not brought peace but a sword. On balance Liu concluded Jesus spent more time opposing the law but always short of political revolution. The highest form of revolution, after all, was spiritual.[97]

But rising national consciousness would not allow Liu and his colleagues to rest with this definition of the Christian imperative. The prospects for establishing the kingdom of Heaven in the Chinese context seemed to recede further and further in the distance. Student protest would remind them that the gradualist formula for national salvation was too limited. As patriots they were forced to address themselves to questions of creating new forms of political power. China's weak position in the international realm throughout this period was also telling evidence that the issue was far from settled. The hope that liberal democracy would work and that the liberal West would help China faded. In addition they had to confront the reality of Japanese imperialism.

Student leaders at Yenching soon came to speak of national salvation in terms of struggle and violence. But in the early understanding of the Life Fellowship Jesus was still the prince of peace and could not be used to justify the violence of revolution. The conflict was never completely resolved in their own minds. Chao Tzu-ch'en wrote in 1935: "Two things are constantly struggling in my mind. The one is thorough-going social revolution, and the other thorough-going compassion. And I have decided to be revolutionary in spirit, and follow the course of gradual change in action."[98] Christianity for all members of the Life Fellowship meant power, a power to aid in national salvation. They saw Jesus as a spiritual revolutionary, at times as a social revolutionary, but they consistently skirted the issue of political power.

Internationalism. The Christian doctrine of love, which lay at the heart of religious belief in the Life Fellowship, clearly meant reconciliation whatever the differences among nations. The subject of internationalism (or cosmopolitanism) was discussed endlessly in the pages of the *Sheng-ming* and the *Chen-li yü sheng-ming.* Antireligious and antiwestern pressure forced a constant reaffirmation of this belief, as Chinese educators insisted they were both patriots and Christians.[99]

They agreed with most of their contemporaries that China had much to learn from the West, but they never subscribed to complete westernization. They were more optimistic about the capitalist West than their Marxist contemporaries were. In the West they saw forces such as the social gospel movement that were blunting the evils of competition and doing it short of revolution. They wished to strike a middle position, in Hsü Pao-ch'ien's words, one of "cultural synthesis rather than surrender or victory."[100] Liu T'ing-fang stated the position a bit more flamboyantly in 1924: if the "higher institutions of the world," meaning the colleges and universities, did not help solve the problems of international conflict, "then let Chin Shih Wang rise from the grave and apply torches to the educational work of the world in the same wholesale fashion as he did to the scholars and literature of China centuries before Christ." Yenching for Liu was a "laboratory exercise for international comity."[101] In 1925 Chao Tzu-ch'en wrote, "We are here to create a universal homogeneous consciousness, in order that the ideal social order called the Kingdom of God, or the brotherhood of man, may be realized among us and that international living may be maintained without further brutality and bloody conflict."[102] They quickly acknowledged how the mistakes of the Western church and the missionaries had weakened the Christian appeal in China, but the figure of Jesus kept alive for them the vision of a new cosmopolitanism, even in the midst of current international realities degrading to China.

One of the roots of this commitment to internationalism was earlier Chinese experience with foreigners. Missionaries had helped shape religious experiences: Stuart with Liu in Shanghai; Burgess with Hsü at Wo-fo-ssu and in YMCA work in Peking; Gowdy and Jones with Hung at the Anglo-Chinese college at Foochow; and Anderson with Chao at Soochow College. The popular evangelists, John R. Mott and Sherwood Eddy, who had addressed thousands of Chinese youth in the 1910s, were also inspiring figures. It was only natural, Liu T'ing-fang argued, for Chinese people who had learned from childhood the importance of reciprocity (*pao*) to respond to these Western initiatives in times of personal distress and find within that experience a basis for internationalism.[103]

Educational experiences, furthermore, reinforced their favorable views of the West. Of the first three decades of his life Chao Tzu-ch'en regarded his three and a half years of study in the United States as the happiest. He admitted in 1923 that his religious experience had thus been unavoidably Americanized (*Mei-kuo hua*). But he felt no shame in the admission.[104] So formative were Hung Yeh's years at Ohio Wesleyan and Columbia that upon his return to China in 1921 he did "most of his thinking in English." He was proud to be "marginal," a "Chinese-American," a "hybrid," a "union of diversities."[105] Upon returning to China they were fluent in English, and the quality of their writing in it at times surpassed that of their Western colleagues. The pleasantness of the foreign experience was no doubt associated with the vast improvement in social status which education in America brought to returned students in the Republican years, but self-serving alone seems to be an insufficient basis for understanding their commitment to internationalism.

Wu Lei-ch'uan's views of the Western tie were somewhat different from those of the other Chinese members of the Life Fellowship. In accounts of his religious experience he made no mention of any Western figure, and he never indicated interest in going abroad. In any case he knew no English. It has been suggested that he was jealous of those who did, though one does not find evidence for this in his writings. In pointing to Wu's differences with Westerners in the Life Fellowship, as demonstrated by his founding of the Truth Society in 1923, one should not conclude he was opposed to all things Western. On the contrary, he seemed unbothered by the idea that Christianity had been introduced from the West, and he frequently quoted Western thinkers whose works were translated into Chinese. However quaint in appearance or traditional in his training, Wu had no desire to return to the days of the past. Out of the social revolution he espoused would emerge a new China hardly recognizable to his father's generation or for that matter to most of his own. He later spoke of the impending world tide that would sweep away the evil and the selfishness in all societies, both in China and the West.[106] Christianity for him clearly transcended national differences.

Rising national consciousness, though, never allowed these Chinese figures to rest secure in their international connections. Furthermore they were disappointed in their efforts to spread the Christian faith among intellectuals. And yet they believed they might purify the faith of its Western accretions. If so the figure of Jesus would become more attractive. Upon returning to China after his first term of study in the United States, Hsü Pao-ch'ien concluded that the church in America failed to represent the "true spirit of Christianity." He doubted the church there could survive the onslaught of American materialism. Christians in East Asia thus had a large responsibility in discovering and then preserving the true faith.[107]

Internationalism at Yenching meant borrowing, even copying, from the West. To the question, "Why copy the West?" Hung answered in 1931, "What else to do?" Students and intellectuals had "simply found the old ideas and ideals unworkable under new conditions." The Chinese ship was sinking. It was a question of swim or be drowned. But the West was beginning to "free itself from the strain and stress that it has created." Hung perceived then (he had just spent two years at Harvard) a "growing desire for leisure," a "return to the bosom of Nature and receiving again those caresses which the machine does not give," and a "widening sympathy that is beginning to promote cooperation and harmony among groups hitherto bent upon the impulse of competition and strife." The Western ship itself might not be so seaworthy. Hung thought China would "abbreviate some of the new patterns to be copied" but also "save some of the old patterns to be discarded." Very much in the tone of Lucius Porter, Hung concluded: the time may come when "East and West may cease to be antithesis in human thinking. The best that each has will be shared by both. And a writer in the distant future, musing over the life of mankind as a whole may yet visualize a picture wherein man sits, not perhaps with a bowl and chopsticks, but still at the foot of a towering *tien* [heaven] that has kept on leveling, balancing, and harmonizing."[108] The prospect of the West's learning something of value out of the Chinese past softened the sting of copying the West too uncritically.

In all the writings of the Life Fellowship, it is difficult to find a clear statement on educational philosophy. Such clarity came hard in the cross-currents and fast moving tides of those years—waves of conversions in the 1910s, the craze to study in America, the New Culture movement, and the multitude of formulas for national salvation. Writings in those years are filled with anxieties about the future and hasty searches for the imperatives (*shih-ming*) suggested by each new crisis. Nothing seemed to stand still. Still, the Chinese members of the Life Fellowship were serious in their commitment to higher education. Yenching University was a place where they could try to put their ideals, as outlined above, into practice. It was a place where youth were, and youth were seen as the hope of the future.[109] As with science, there was a magic quality about education, especially Western education. The magic promised prestige and good jobs. But it would also help save the nation (*chiao-yü chiu-kuo*). Liu T'ing-fang believed a price had to be paid to create national unity. It was the "blood of the race, poured before the altar of unselfish service, and the most important of all forms of service is education."[110]

If the missionary educators were serious about sinification, they could not have found a better group to take over responsibility for the running of the university while maintaining earlier purposes. Other Chinese faculty may not have shared the degree of their commitment to Christianity. But neither were the Chinese faculty outside the Life Fellowship hostile to their kind of Christianity.[111] Commitment to the importance of religious experience, to character building, to service and self-sacrifice, to national salvation through education, and to internationalism, then, suggest the parameters within which educated Chinese gave their loyalty to Yenching University.

Top *Men's Fourth Dormitory at Yenching in the 1930s.*
Bottom *Yenching women were the 1927 champions in the Peking Intercollegiate Ladies Basketball League.*

Top *A Yenching production of "Macbeth" in the early 1920s. These amateur performances drew large audiences in Peking, and the proceeds went to studen[t] activities.*

Left *Chancellor Lu Chih-wei and President John Leighton Stuart at the Yenching commencement in September 1936. Commencement was delayed into the fall because of the interruption of the December Ninth Movement in 1935.*

Right *John Stewart Burgess and Yenching sociology students in 1929.*

Facing Page

Top *The "Harvard Group" of the Yenching faculty in the late 1940s. From left to right: Ch'i Ssu-ho, Weng Tu-chien, Lin Yüeh-hua, and Chou Yi-liang, who is currently the chairman of the history department at Peking University.*

Middle *The department of Chinese at Yenching in 1928. From left to right: Shen Shih-yüan, Ma Meng, Hsü Ti-shan, Feng Yu-lan, Wu Lei-ch'uan, Chou Tso-jen, Jung Keng, Kuo Shao-yü, and Huang Tse-t'ung.*

Bottom *The poet Hsieh Ping Hsin (Wan-ying) and Acting Dean of Women Ruth Stahl in the late 1940s. Miss Hsieh was a graduate of Yenching in 1923 and later taught there along with her husband Wu Wen-tsao, who was chairman of the department of sociology.*

Right *Chao Tzu-ch'en (T. C. Chao) in the late 1940s. Chao was the major Chinese link in the life of the university from beginning to end, as an editor of Life Fellowship publications, longtime dean of the school of religion, and a leader in Yenching's transition to the revolutionary order.*

Top *Christmas Eve 1949, a year after the turnover, with 150 Yenching carollers.
Bliss Wiant is playing the reed organ strapped to a donkey cart.*

Bottom *Peking University, March 1959, located on the former Yenching campus. The
building in the center was Bashford Hall, named after Methodist Bishop James Bashford
who was instrumental in the founding of Yenching University.*

4

Organizing a Bicultural University

The Life Fellowship articulated some of Yenching University's broadest purposes, and it helps explain what appears in retrospect to be the unlikely convergence between Chinese patriots and mission boards in the West. But Yenching was much more than the Life Fellowship, and by the early 1930s many Yenching students may not have known of the Life Fellowship. For them the university held an attraction of its own quite apart from previous connections with the Life Fellowship.

One of the greatest attractions about Yenching was its location. Peking, the "northern capital," was the home of the imperial family and the capital of Ch'ing dynasty. It continued to be the seat of the various Republican governments until 1927 when Chiang Kai-shek moved the central government to Nanking, the "southern capital" and Peking became Peiping, or "northern peace." Peking was also the center of literary activity. The faculty of the National Peking University were the leaders of the New Culture movement, and Yenching students had easy access to this intellectual excitement plus that of the May Fourth and subsequent political demonstrations during the first ten years of the university's existence on the K'uei Chia Ch'ang campus located just inside the city walls.

This excitement was more than personal. The students were an elite. They saw themselves as the heirs to the Confucian literati of the past whose positions in society were destroyed with the abolishment of the examination system in 1905. They were to be the shapers of China's new political consciousness. The special sense of mission among Chinese youth in higher education was reinforced by their small numerical size. In the Republican years they represented less than 0.01 percent (around 40,000) of the whole population (400,000,000). Less than one out of every 10,000 Chinese attended college or university. And as an excellent liberal arts college located in Peking, Yenching students were an elite within the elite.

This sense of importance was not diminished by the university's move in 1926 to the Haitien campus some five miles northwest of the city walls. The loss of proximity to the city itself was offset by a regular bus service and by the closeness to Tsinghua University, whose prestigious faculty and student body were located only a mile from the Yenching campus. It was also offset by the exquisiteness of the new buildings and the peaceful surroundings of the former imperial gardens. Yenching's private status and distance from the city walls may have encouraged, in John Israel's words, the "free-thinking, socially conscious, politically active undergraduates," to pursue their patriotic activities in the early 1930s in ways other state-controlled universities, including Tsinghua, couldn't.[1] The famous December Ninth movement (1935), which is comparable in importance to the May Fourth movement, began on the Yenching campus.

Yenching produced and attracted many famous personalities. The writers Hsieh Ping-hsin (1900–   ), Hsü Ti-shan (1893–1941), and the playwright Hsiung Fo-hsi (1900–65) are important in the history of modern Chinese literature, and they were all graduates of Yenching University in the early 1920s. They became well known patriots, and much to the satisfaction of the members of the Life Fellowship, they all happened to be Christians. After their graduation they went to the United States for further study and later returned to teach on the Yenching campus. In the late 1920s other famous intellectuals came to Yenching to work, among them the historian Ku Chieh-kang (1895–   ), known as the father of folklore studies in China, and the philosopher Chang Tung-sun (1886–   ), a famous interpreter of Western philosophy in China. These well-known individuals spent much of their time in literary activity outside the university. But they brought prestige to the institution and cooperated with other Yenching personalities, like Lu Chih-wei (psychology), Hsü Shu-hsi (political science), and Wu

Wen-tsao (sociology), who along with members of the Life Fellowship bore major responsibility for the ongoing job of running the university. Their contributions as scholars and teachers and the standards they exacted from their students were part of the Yenching excitement.

Yenching students were expected to become bilingual, as required courses were offered in both Chinese and English. In the Republican years a premium was put on English competence in political, economic, and intellectual circles, and Yenching became known for its excellent training in the language. But it became equally famous for its program in Chinese studies and the scholarly publications in Chinese of the Harvard-Yenching Institute. Its undergraduate curriculum over thirty years resembled its Western liberal arts model, with requirements in both Chinese and Western literature, philosophy, history, and the natural and social sciences. As a haven of liberal arts, Yenching stressed general competence, character building, and moral discipline. These were qualities celebrated in the Confucian ideal and may help account for the large number of Yenching students coming from prominent families, which reportedly included seventeen great grandchildren of the nineteenth century statesman, Tseng Kuo-fan (1811–72), and five grandchildren of Liang Ch'i-ch'ao (1873–1929), as well as the children of many prominent families of the Republican period. In a sense Yenching had it both ways. It projected an image of idealism and service that appealed to patriotic sentiment but it also appealed to the elitist impulses. It never suffered for lack of applicants, which ran as high as twelve for every new position in the freshman class.

The new campus had a dreamlike quality about it. A large wall was built around it in 1927 as a possible protection from the outside world. It became a kind of refuge from the emotional strain and turbulence of the Republican years. In interviews and their writings Yenching alumni frequently refer to this secure environment of the campus. Homesickness (the Yenching students came from all over China), the confusion over whether or not to participate in student demonstrations, the new freedoms of thought and social interaction, and the doubts about the future were all part of an anxiety ridden college life.[2] Yenching students were members of a generation seeking liberation from the bonds of tradition, but "the power of darkness," to quote Lu Hsun, still hung over them as the new thought raised as many questions as it answered.[3] The Yenching faculty seemed ready to help. They opened their homes to students, especially at Christmas and Easter times, and Christians and non-Christians alike accepted the invitations. Everyone seemed busy and involved. The group excursions into the beautiful Western Hills, two modern gymnasiums and tennis courts, and the artificial lake on the campus were enjoyed by everyone in the campus community. Physical exercise was emphasized, and the intramural track meets were major university events. President Stuart and Chinese deans shared the responsibilities for starting and judging the events. The yearbooks for the 1930s show page after page of snapshots of healthy and well-dressed youth, smiling, laughing, hiking, swimming, skating, competing, and carrying out practical jokes, much like the stereotype of college life in America at the time.

The Yenching spirit often mentioned by the faculty and alumni was the expression of some or all of these qualities of campus life. The stimulating and supportive environment were taken for granted by most Yenching students, especially during the "golden" years on the new campus from 1926 to 1937 before the Japanese occupation of North China. But to Stuart and his colleagues this atmosphere could not be assumed. It had to be created. The differences between evangelists sitting on the board of trustees and student radicals were serious and required constant attention. The differences had existed from the start, but they became acute in the early 1920s with the rise of the Anti-Christian movement.

The Anti-Christian Movement

The almost indiscriminate receptivity to Western ideas in the early years of the New Culture movement soon come to an end, and it was replaced by a more narrowly defined nationalistic sentiment which affected Yenching in the form of the Anti-Christian movement (*fan-Chi-tu-chiao yün-tung*).[4] This movement began formally in 1922 and was stimulated by the growing impact of the Russian Revolution in 1917, China's humiliation in the Treaty of Versailles in 1919, and the general iconoclasm of the New Thought. It is difficult to know just what constitutes a movement (*yün-tung*) or what it meant for one to be a participant in it. The actual number of active participants may have been quite small. But the movement had considerable impact on Sino-Western relations because it combined antireligious and antiforeign sentiment.

The Anti-Christian movement may be conveniently divided into four stages. It began with the sudden appearance of articles, broadsides, posters, and the convening of students in major cities throughout China to protest the upcoming World Student Christian Federation conference scheduled to be held at Tsinghua University in April 1922. This conference was sponsored by the YMCA and marked the high point of Christian influence among students in both private and public schools. The YMCA and the conference were denounced by the leaders in the Anti-Christian movement for helping the "property-holders who eat without working . . . rob and oppress . . . the property-less who work but can't eat" and for "training running dogs of capitalism."[5] The second stage was the Movement to Restore Educational Rights (Shou-hui chiao-yü ch'üan yün-tung), which in 1923 opposed the independent status of mission schools and advocated a unified system of national education.[6] In 1924 it succeeded in getting the National Association for the Advancement of Education (Chung-kuo chiao-yü kai-chin she) to pass a resolution at its annual meeting requiring all mission schools to register with the central government.[7]

The third phase of the Anti-Christian movement began with the famous May Thirtieth incident in 1925 when British officered police killed twelve students demonstrating on behalf of mistreated Chinese workers in Japanese owned cotton mills in Shanghai. This incident provoked a series of strikes and boycotts among students, merchants, and Chinese citizens, which crippled British trade in South China for more than a year and closed many Christian institutions in central China.[8] A fourth phase was the Northern Expedition led by Kuomintang armies beginning in July 1926. In January 1927 representatives from the mission schools went to the city of Wuhan and asked Michael Borodin, the Comintern adviser to the new government, about the future of their schools. He could not guarantee protection to anyone who was "neutral to the revolution" or did not have the "right attitude." When they pressed him for clarification Brodin replied, "Do you look to the treaties for protection?"[9] This last phase was climaxed by the killing of six missionaries in Nanking in March 1927, and it forced the temporary exodus of more than 5,000 of the 8,000 plus Protestant missionaries from China.[10]

This devastating effect on missions was partially offset by the defense of Christianity and religious freedom from prominent non-Christian figures such as Chou Tso-jen, Liang Ch'i-ch'ao, Ts'ai Yüan-p'ei, and Hu Shih.[11] Moreover the sensationalism of the attack belied actual strength. Many members of the National Association for the Advancement of Education were themselves either trained or employed in mission schools, and they prevented the antiforeign forces from eliminating Christians from membership in the association.[12]

Even before the attack tensions had existed at Yenching between the missionary educators in the field and the trustees in New York over administrative policies and the evangelical purposes of mission education. The Anti-Christian movement brought those conflicts out into the open. Before the attack Yenching Westerners supported sinification efforts in mission schools and the Chinese church but the attack forced them to reconsider their roles as missionaries even further. In September 1923 the Western faculty of the men's college voted unanimously to abandon compulsory chapel in favor of a weekly voluntary religious service. A year later religious requirements were reduced to a two-hour per week freshman course, though even then most faculty favored making all religious courses elective. This last requirement came to an end in 1927.[13]

In 1924 Stuart saw the attack on Christianity as a "revolt against the white race in China," and he admitted that foreign domination of the church in China was possible only because "foreign countries have military power to maintain the unequal treaties and the Chinese government can't do anything about it."[14] After the May Thirtieth incident Lucius Porter said missionaries needed to "confess our own sins and the sins of our Governments towards the Chinese." They needed to be "penitent and loving" and to attack "with all our strength . . . the conditions in Western contacts with China that have led the Chinese to feel as they now feel."[15] The marked decline in student interest in religious activity was cause for alarm, Stuart thought, only on the assumption that "foreign missions existed to enroll members in churches that are replicas of Western ecclesiastical units." Religion to Stuart was "too sacred and precious to be enforced by regulations upon mature students, especially when it was associated with racial antagonisms."[16]

In their new awareness Yenching Westerners acted boldly in ways not usually associated with the missionary enterprise. Stuart led a delegation of missionaries to see American Ambassador MacMurray and protest the American involvement in the Taku Bar incident of 1926. In that incident eleven Western nations, including the United States, had invoked the Boxer Protocol of 1901 and forced their way through a Chinese blockade which was cutting them off from access to the city of Tientsin.[17] To show his support for the politics of the Left Kuomintang in 1927 Lucius Porter came to the rescue of Fanny Borodin, wife of Michael Borodin, when she was jailed in Peking in the wake of Chiang Kai-shek's rise to power, and he aided in her escape back to Russia.[18] As a result of these activities and the Yenching students' leadership in strikes and demonstrations after the May Thirtieth incident, the university became known as a hotbed of communism. H. G. W. Woodhead, British editor of the Peking and Tientsin *Times* and the *China Yearbook,* had Yenching in mind when he castigated those Americans who come from a "country which has shown itself so unwaveringly opposed to Bolshevik propaganda" and then "expose themselves, and not without some grounds, to the charge that many of their schools and colleges offer the most fertile soil for the spread of Bolshevik propaganda."[19] At the high point of antiforeign hostility during the Northern Expedition the trustees advised the Western faculty to leave China. But Stuart replied with characteristic optimism, that the "Chinese and foreign teachers and students are working together" and their sense of unity was only "strengthened by the present disturbances." The crisis provided just one more "splendid opportunity . . . to practice international fellowship and Christian principles."[20] No one left.

As a result of the Anti-Christian movement mission schools were forced to register with the central government. Yenching's Western faculty had voted to register with the Peking Board of Education in 1921, but the government failed to follow through.[21] The Peking government in 1925 and the newly organized Wuhan government in November 1926 issued registration requirements that forced mission schools to rethink their purposes. The regulations in 1925 forbade the propagation of religion and the teaching of religious courses, and it required the president (or vice-president if a foreigner was already head) and a majority of the local board of managers to be Chinese. The 1926 regulations were stronger, requiring the head in all schools to be Chinese and demanding strict conformity with curriculum standards set by the government.[22] Schools that did not comply faced possible government action. Yenching authorities began immediately to institute the necessary changes. Within a few years registered schools, in the name of party education (*tang-hua chiao-yü*), were also required to organize military training programs for men students, weekly memorial services for Sun Yat-sen, and compulsory courses in party doctrine. Yenching readily complied in all three areas.

The Anti-Christian movement ended any lingering thought that the university existed to convert Chinese students to Christianity. In Stuart's words, "Government registration and other subtle forces have swept the university out of the placid seclusion of a somewhat self-contained foreign propagandist society into the swirling currents of Chinese national life." The fruits of the past resulting from "required religious instruction," he admitted, were "gained more than is generally recognized by an administrative authority due to treaty rights and financial resources or to the masterful and single-minded missionaries working upon docile plastic youth."[23] With the passing of the hope of making China Christian in any comprehensive or meaningful way—with the removal of the "white man's burden"—Stuart and his colleagues were freed to devote all energies to making Yenching academically more respectable and "more Chinese."

The Chinese members of the Life Fellowship had little difficulty agreeing with many of the charges leveled by the Anti-Christian movement. Antedating the movement itself, they had some exceedingly caustic things to say about Western influence in the church and mission schools. The abandonment of proselytizing purposes, increased Chinese control over these institutions, registration with the government, and more emphasis on things Chinese in the curriculum presented no problems.[24] The attack, in fact, signaled new opportunities to assert themselves.

In more personal terms, though, the attack produced considerable anxiety. Wu Lei-ch'uan never recovered the clarity of his earlier faith, and he was saddened in realizing that the church, which was to lead society, was now associated with backwardness.[25] Hsü Pao-ch'ien was so depressed that he suffered insomnia for six months.[26] They feared that Christianity would be seen as invalid among the students whom they hoped most to reach. In Liu T'ing-fang's eyes the student disruptions connected with the attack on Christianity were "crude, clumsy, and full of mistakes." But rather than oppose them, Christian educators, Liu believed, should recognize that the students were merely putting into practice the values they had been taught in the mission schools, namely to be "independent in thinking," and "interested in national salvation, national welfare, and practical citizenship."[27] The Life Fellowship had hoped to lead while the students followed. But the Anti-Christian movement started to reverse those roles.

The weakening of the Christian cause was also due to the behavior of Western missionaries and their connections with the unequal treaties of the nineteenth century. Early converts were not unmindful of this connection, but it became especially irritating with the spreading influence of the Anti-Christian movement. Wu Lei-ch'uan became angered by missionary condescension and because they "despised" the Chinese as a "wild people without a culture" as in Australia and Africa. After the May Thirtieth incident he was angered by the missionaries' silence generally on the matter, by their refusal to pressure their governments to apologize to China, and by their "slavish support of the separation between church and state." Any future attempts to seek military protection from Western governments for their work, he warned, would signal the "end of the Christian church in China."[28]

Wu and his colleagues were also sensitive to the anti-Christian charge of denationalization, or the loss of national character (*kuo-min-hsing*) that came with conversion. The charge had been leveled against converts before, but it did not assume threatening proportions until 1922. In addition to the familiar "rice Christians" (*fan-wan ti Chi-tu-t'u* or *ch'ih-chiao-t'u*), converts were also labeled foreign slaves (*yang-nu*) and half-foreign (*pan-fan*).[29] Yenching Chinese admitted that in some cases conversion and attending mission schools may have weakened patriotic feeling. These schools, after all, remained outside the mainstream of Chinese life, were controlled by foreigners, ignored government orders, and overwhelmed their students with Western subjects to the extent that some students were unable to tell the general outline of Chinese history and geography.[30] Furthermore, converts were asked to join a church that was isolated from Chinese society. In so doing, Wu felt, they learned to respect foreigners while looking down on their own country.[31]

However much the Chinese members of the Life Fellowship agreed with anti-Christian arguments, they remained committed to the Christian faith. But from then on it would be a more sinified (*Chung-kuo-hua*), an indigenous (*pen-se*), faith. Furthermore, not all missionaries in their eyes were bad. The Western faculty at Yenching, for example, had "used every opportunity," even before the May Thirtieth incident, to "help their fellow countrymen understand Chinese patriotic sentiment," and had "stood fearlessly by the Chinese."[32] Yenching Chinese were also unhappy with the implied illegitimacy of the label rice Christianity. Many converts to Christianity were poor people who merely responded to acts of mercy. Only the missionaries pitied them, Liu T'ing-fang wrote, while "in our society we won't move a hair to help a compatriot. How can we curse the missionaries when they do what we are supposed to do?"[33] Nor did attendance at mission schools, as such, preclude the budding of patriotic feeling among students, at least at Yenching. Liu came up with his own analysis of student strikes following the May Thirtieth incident and concluded that most strike leaders, including those in public schools, had previously received from a half to ten years of instruction at mission schools. Some of these leaders in the mission schools, furthermore, were themselves active Christians who were studying theology and had even received scholarships from churches both in China and the West.[34]

They also objected to the anti-Christian argument that the spirit of internationalism and patriotic feeling were incompatible. Wu maintained that patriotic Chinese did not "need to hate" the foreigners. Rather, with "patriotism as the premise," the task was to "draw nearer to Christ's nature . . . attain his peace of mind," and support "both nationalism and internationalism." Liu argued that "just as we cannot be hated because we are Chinese, so too we cannot hate foreigners because we are Chinese." Hsü Pao-ch'ien saw the benefits of rising nationalism, such as "waking the masses up out of their thousand years of sleep, and forcing them to rise up and save themselves." But he also warned against the "dangers which lie ahead" of following the path of "narrow nationalism."[35]

Because the Anti-Christian movement was politically embodied in the registration requirements of the central government, there was no way Yenching administrators could avoid the issue. In the early years before the enforcement of governmental regulations, the control of the university was effectively in the hands of the mission boards. In the last years just before Yenching's closing in 1952 this control shifted largely to the Chinese government. But in the thirty years in between the ideals of cultural and racial equality were translated into institutional form. The task was defined as "making Yenching more Chinese."

To most Yenching profssors the task of sinification was largely one of creating a racial balance in the composition of the faculty, the university committees, and the local board of managers. More nationalistic groups within the Chinese faculty also wanted to transfer ultimate financial and administrative authority over the life of the university from Western hands to Chinese hands. Still others, including some student leaders, questioned the possibility of making the university Chinese enough, so long as the Western tie remained strong. These three ways of looking at sinification—as a problem of control, authority, or identity—were not necessarily exclusive of each other. And yet the emphasis on one and the ignoring of another had important implications for the intercultural relationship. Those who were unconcerned with institutional authority and identity followed President Stuart's leadership with relative ease. But more militant voices at times wanted to sever all ties with the West, even at the risk of closing the university.

The Trustees and the Managers

Stuart and his colleagues concluded that the survival of the university required as a minimum that the board of trustees in New York relinquish some of their power and authority to the board of managers in Peking. Yenching University had originally derived its legal status through incorporation of the board of trustees in the state of New York. Even after completing registration with the Chinese government in 1928 the Yenching administration faithfully submitted its annual report, certified by the American consulate in Peking, to the regents of the University of the State of New York until 1949.[36]

Like most boards of trustees in American church colleges the Yenching board was nonsalaried and nonprofessional. It was composed largely of mission board executives, philanthropists, and New York businessmen with a keen interest in the church enterprise. It usually numbered about twenty-five members. After the union of the men's and women's colleges in 1920 the board included women, first by co-option and later through regular election, though the women kept their separate committee to the end.

Table 1 is a listing of the trustees for 1945 and reflects the composition of the various boards throughout the university's history. Their professional backgrounds and their associations with China say something about their views on education and on the role of Yenching in Sino-Western relations. First of all they had a high level of education and an almost exclusively urban orientation, as most resided along the North Atlantic coast, particularly in New York City. A majority had strong YMCA or YWCA affiliations, reflecting a social reformist approach to problems in China. The board in 1945 was relatively old (the average age was sixty-five) and their contacts with China went back largely to the earlier phases of the missionary enterprise before the impact of the Anti-Christian movement. Furthermore they were closely affiliated with American big business and the Chinese government, three having received awards of merit from the Nationalist government in the 1940s. Finally, only half of the board had working experience in China

Table 1. List of Yenching Trustees, 1945–46 (incomplete)

Name	Profession	Experience in China	Education	Associations and distinctions
Corbett, Mrs. Charles H.	Lay church leader	Missionary	Hunter (AB)	Beirut College for Women, trustee; YWCA
Corbett, Mr. Charles H.	Professor (Yenching, Union, Oberlin); church executive	Missionary educator		YMCA; United Board for Christian Higher Education in Asia
Danforth, William H.	Business (founder Ralston Purina Co.); banker; philanthropist		Washington University (ME)	YMCA; author: I Dare You, etc.
Davis, Arthur V.	Business (president, Aluminum Company of America)		Amherst (AB)	Chinese Order of Jade (1940) Chairman of Yenching Board of Trustees 1939–45
Finley, Mrs. John H.	Lay church leader; husband, editor of New York Times			YWCA; trustee Yenching Women's College for thirty years
Gamble, Sidney D.	Church executive; scholar; relief worker	YMCA; research	Princeton (AB) Berkeley	YMCA; author: Peking: A Social Survey, Institute of Pacific Relations; Current Chairman of the trustees
Gamewell, Francis D.	Church executive	Missionary educator	Cornell (AB) Columbia (PhD)	Chief of fortifications during seige of Peking, 1900
Jones, Rufus M.	Professor; author; relief worker	Hocking Commission	Haverford (AB) Harvard (PhD)	Founder American Friends Service Committee; author, fifty books
Lowry, Howard F.	College president (Caroll, Oberlin); author		Wooster (AB) Yale Pittsburgh (PhD)	

Table 1 (Continued)

Name	Profession	Experience in China	Education	Associations and distinctions
Luce, Henry R.	Business; editor philanthropist	Born in Shantung	Yale (AB)	Founder, Time-Life-Fortune; United China Relief (1940); Chinese Order of Auspicious Star (1947); Yenching trustee, 1935–51
McBrier, Edwin H.	Business (partner, F. W. Woolworth); banker; philanthropist	China Inland Mission		YMCA; Chinese Order of Jade; Yenching trustee, 1919–50
Moore, Elizabeth Luce	Writer; philanthropist	Born in Shantung	Wellesley (AB)	YWCA (National chairman 1944–64; Asia Foundation (Director); Wellesley (trustee)
Pfeiffer, Mrs. Timothy	Welfare worker		Rye Seminary	New York City Mission Society (work in Harlem)
Rounds, Leslie R.	Banker, pastor		Skidmore	
Rathbone, Josephine	Educator (Pratt Institute Library School)		Michigan (AB) New York State Library School (PhD)	American Library Association (President)
Slade, Mrs. F. Louis	Philanthropist, husband (prominent manufacturer)		Bryn Mawr	YWCA and women's suffrage; Institute of Pacific Relations (trustee); YU Board of Trustees, 1935–48
Van Dusen, Henry P.	Seminary president (Union Theological Seminary); author		Princeton (AB) Edinburgh (PhD)	YMCA; Rockefeller Foundation trustee; Council on Foreign Relations

Sources: "Members of the Board of Trustees of Yenching University," June 5, 1929, AP:BT; minute, December 6, 1945, AP:BT; *Who's Who of American Women; Who Was Who in America; National Cyclopedia of American Biography;* and *New York Times,* obituary columns, in which twelve of the seventeen members were featured.

and most of these within the missionary framework. They were liberal in outlook for the most part, and yet they were quite removed from the spirit of Chinese nationalism, which was forcing basic changes in the field.[37] They agreed with the spirit of indigenization, but as a board they were also committed to evangelical purposes within the missionary enterprise. All the English-language constitutions for Yenching, including key sections of the original charter of Peking University in 1915 and the last English revision of 1928, stated the purpose of the corporation as follows: "to establish and maintain . . . a university, founded and conducted on strictly Christian and evangelical, but not sectarian principles." The word evangelical is significant, for it often appeared in the board's minutes and indicated its reluctance to dilute the proselytizing function of the university.[38]

The trustees wielded their power over the university primarily in two ways: through appointment of the faculty and administration; and approval of the annual budget. Until the spring of 1928 they exercised final authority over appointments of all staff and faculty with the rank or equivalent of associate professor and above to ensure that all appointees would be Christian of "evangelical faith." But after the Nationalist government had ordered all private schools to register, the board's appointive powers were reduced to the presidency and the deanship in the women's college, while all other powers of appointment passed on to the board of managers. The revised constitution of 1928 retained the loyalty clause to the Christian evangelical faith, but the power to waive it was given to the board of managers.[39] The initiative for amending the constitution could come from Peking, but the ratification of any amendments required a majority vote by the trustees and by three out of four constituent mission boards. No amendments or revisions in the English-language constitution were made after 1928, and final authority over the annual budget never left the trustees' hands. As a concession to pressure from the field the constitution of 1928 deleted the clause that threatened the withholding of annual payments if the university departed from the "strictly Christian and evangelical" principles, and yet the trustees' financial authority was in no way diminished.[40] (See Diagram 1.)

The board of managers originally served the twofold purpose of ensuring the strong influence of mission-board representatives over the university and of lending prestige to the college by the selection of dignitaries within China but not connected directly to the college itself.[41]

Diagram 1 Organizational Chart of Yenching University, 1925

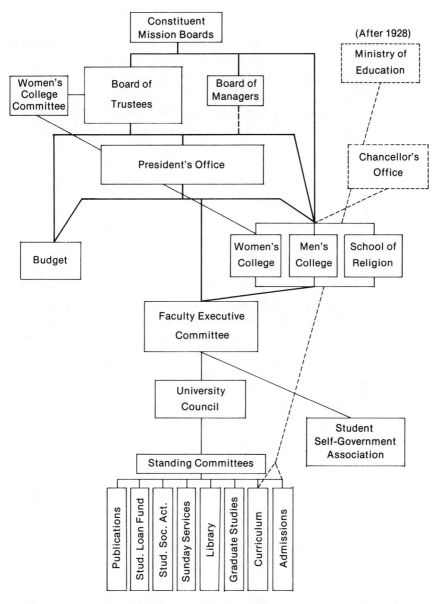

Note: The power of the president's office was enhanced by the president's serving simultaneously as the chairman of the faculty executive committee (which met in his home), the university council, and ex-officio of the board of managers.
Source: Yenching University Bulletin, 8.25:12-22 (October 1925), AP.

In the early years it was composed exclusively of Westerners, but in response to nationalistic demands a majority by 1926 and two thirds by 1930 had become Chinese. Changes in composition also reflected a decrease in representation from mission-board appointees, so that by 1935 only four of the fifteen were elected by the four constituent boards, while the remaining eleven were elected from among the faculty, the alumni, and the larger Chinese community. Like the trustees, the managers, as reflected in the membership list for 1935–36 in Table 2, were strongly affiliated with the YMCA. All members, for whom information is available, had received a liberal arts education in the West. Furthermore, leading figures on the board were prominent officials in the Nationalist government and two others were selected, it appears, because of their family connections with other officials.[42] No information has been found to indicate that any member of the board challenged Yenching's liberal arts and American orientation. As late as 1928 all the Yenching managers, excluding the three selected from among the faculty, were named by the trustees, but they were in effect Stuart's appointees. Even after Stuart became ambassador in 1946, they remained in outlook his appointees. Their meetings in the late 1940s were held in Shanghai or Nanking with Stuart as chairman.[43]

The basic administrative changes that occurred under the slogan of "making Yenching Chinese" were carried out by Stuart. He carefully reassured the trustees that registration with the Nationalist government in 1928 would not erode original purposes. But his correspondence and visits to New York reflected the bind the university was in. He respected the trustees for the power they held and for serving as the Western anchor in the intercultural relationship. But he was also in sympathy with the demands for a greater Chinese voice in university administration. Not the least of his concerns was preserving his own position in an institution he had done so much to create. The attempt to harmonize all these considerations challenged to the utmost his skills in diplomacy, sometimes in amusing ways. In July 1927, for example, fearing the new regulations of the Kuomintang government would seriously conflict with the existing constitution, he hastily asked the trustees to establish the "final authority of the board of managers in matters affecting administration." He reassured them that in actual practice the trustees "always have and doubtless always will follow the recommendations of the managers" and that the "ceding of authority is more apparent than real."[44]

A few months later in December he stood before the trustees in New

York and argued the necessity of "making adjustments . . . with Chinese nationalism . . . so that the institution may survive" and expressed his conviction that the "nationalist movement is thoroughly reasonable and its demands only those which any self-respecting people have a right to make." He suggested the following changes: the board of trustees should, like those of Lingnan University, reconstitute itself as the "American or Anglo-American Foundation," and should lease or entrust its property in Peking to the board of managers though it would still retain control over the annual budget; it should relinquish all appointive powers over the staff, except that of president; and the board of managers should be completely Chinese, not because terms for government registration required it, but because conducting its meetings in Chinese would help "decrease the consciousness of the masterfulness of the Westerners," and would also help develop a sense of responsibility among the Chinese members and prepare them for the time when they would be completely in control. Stuart reminded the trustees that they would still have ultimate control over the property.[45] Lest the trustees think Stuart was speaking lightly, he said it was conceivable that a time would come when a Chinese board of managers might prefer to "sacrifice all support . . . rather than conform to the wishes of the Trustees, in which case the Trustees would have lost the institution completely anyway."[46] The breaking away of Chinese faculty and students from St. John's University in Shanghai to establish the independent and Chinese controlled Kwanghua University just after the May Thirtieth incident was an ever present reminder that Stuart was not imagining things.

The questions raised by the trustees following Stuart's presentation reflected their basic skepticism. They asked, if the power to elect all teachers lay in the hands of the Chinese, would there not be a tendency to elect fewer Westerners? (Stuart reassured them that there was no desire to get rid of the foreign staff if it was willing to comply with registration requirements.) Would not field control over the selection and dismissal of faculty create difficulties for constituent mission boards operating through New York? (Yes, but that adjustment had to be made.) How could the Christian character of the institution be maintained under Stuart's proposed plan? (He reassured them that Christian requirements in the selection of faculty would remain the same.) Would an increase in Chinese staff mean the university could operate on a smaller budget? (Stuart replied there would be little saving in view of increased salaries being paid to the Chinese, which would be equal to

Table 2. List of Yenching Managers, 1935–36 (incomplete)

Name	Profession	Education	Other associations
K'ung Hsiang-hsi (H. H. Kung), chairman	Minister of finance (Nanking)	North China Union College; Oberlin (AB) Yale (MA)	Married to Sung Ai-ling (sister to Mme. Chiang Kai-shek); many prominent positions in the Nanking government and Kuomintang Party; board of managers, 1929–49; titular chancellor, Yenching, 1937–46
Yen Hui-ch'ing (W. W. Yen), vice-chairman	Ambassador to USSR	St. John's; T'ung-wen Kuan; Virginia (BA '00); Peita	Minister of foreign affairs, 1920–22; prime minister, 1922; ambassador to European countries, 1913–20; minister to United States, 1931–32; board of managers, 1923–50
Chou Yi-ch'un (Y. T. Tsur)	Vice-minister of industry (Nanking)	Yale (BA '09); Wisconsin (MA)	Former president, Tsinghua University; acting chancellor, Yenching 1933–34; China Foundation for Promotion of Education and Culture, 1924–28; Minister of agriculture, 1945–47; minister of health, 1947–48; board of managers, 1932–50
Ch'üan Shao-wen (S. J. Chuan)	Banker, Kincheng Bank (Peiping)	Peita ('10); Yale (BA '17)	YMCA; Chinese labor battalions in France 1918–21; president's assistant, Yenching, 1926–29; comptroller, 1930–31; board of managers, 1932–50
Sun K'o (Sun Fo)	President of legislative yuan (Nanking)	California ('16); Columbia (MA)	Son of Sun Yat-sen; minister of finance, 1927–38; minister of railways, 1928–31; board of managers, 1934–37
Huang Yung-liang	Retired official (Tientsin)	University of Nanking ('96) Drew Seminary; Columbia	Diplomatic service, 1903–10; ministry of foreign affairs, 1914–17; YMCA national committee 1900; board of managers, 1934–37
Ch'en Ch'ung-shou, Mrs.			Board of managers, 1935–37

Table 2 (Continued)

Name	Profession	Education	Other associations
Wang Cheng-fu, Mrs. (information is on husband)	Mining engineer	Peiyang University; Columbia (1910–15)	Chinese Student Christian Association (New York); YMCA secretary, Peking, 1915–16; brother to Wang Cheng-t'ing (Kuomintang official and minister of foreign affairs, 1928–31); board of managers, 1934–37 (Mrs.)
Lin Chi-chun, Mrs. (information is on husband)	Ceramics engineer	Tsinghua (1911–16); Iowa State; Ohio State	Board of managers, 1930–37 (Mrs.)
Wang Hsi-chih (S. T. Wang)	Superintendent of Peking Union Medical College		Nephew of Wang Cheng-t'ing; board of managers, 1930–37
Edwards, Dwight W.	Relief worker; church executive	Princeton (BA '04)	Representative of Princeton-in-Peking; forty plus years YMCA secretary, Peking; board of managers, 1918–48; author, Yenching University
Cross, Rowland M.	Missionary educator		American Board Yü Ying Middle School in Peking
Gleysteen, William H.	Missionary educator	Michigan (BA); Columbia (MA); Union (1904)	Board of managers 1918–36; Peking American School; Truth Hall, boys school, Peking, principal 1907–27
Krause, O. J.	Missionary; mission board executive		Former businessman in Salisbury, Md; Treasurer of Methodist mission in Peking
Baxter, Alexander	Missionary		London Missionary Society

Sources: Yenching University, Faculty Directory, 2.15:21 (October 1935); "List of Yenching Board of Managers," February 26, 1949, AP:BM; Who's Who in Republican China (Shanghai, 1936); Howard Boorman, ed., Biographical Dictionary of Republican China; Princeton Yenching Gazette, December 1938, AP; Stuart to Garside, June 25, 1934, AC:JLS.

those of the Western faculty within a year.)[47] The board was doubtful if prospective American donors would give money to an institution in China over which they had no control.[48]

By the late 1920s the clash between Western control and Chinese nationalism had produced an anomaly in administrative organization. For twenty years the trustees and managers tolerated the existence of two separate constitutions—one English and the other Chinese—which flatly contradicted each other. The Chinese version was drawn up during Stuart's absence in the United States in 1927–28, when Wu Lei-ch'uan and a faculty committee produced a Chinese constitution which was subsequently adopted by a general meeting of the faculty on May 28, 1928.[49] That constitution, which is the first available Chinese version, was revised in 1929, 1931, and 1934, but none of the revisions significantly altered the original. The English revision of 1928 had ceded to the managers complete power of appointment over the faculty, but the Chinese draft of 1928 went much further by granting the managers the power to approve or revise the constitution (not the board of trustees and the four constituent mission boards). In it the managers also appointed all administrative officers of the university including the president and the dean of women (not just the chancellor and the dean of men). Finally it gave the managers final approval of the annual budget (not the board of trustees). The only mention made of the trustees in the Chinese constitution was in reference to property and endowments: "The board of managers (*tung-shih-hui*) is commissioned by and on behalf of the founders (*she-li-che*) to guarantee the security of property and endowments." Nowhere is the old term for the board of trustees, *t'uo-shih-pu,* used.[50]

The minutes of the board of managers reveal several half-hearted attempts to resolve the contradictions between the two constitutions by naming the English version as the authoritative interpretation and as the "working document for the guidance of the constituent bodies of the university," while the Chinese version was reserved for registration of the university with the Nationalist government.[51] Repeatedly, but without result, Chancellor Wu Lei-ch'uan reminded the managers that registration with the government required the university to comply with the Chinese version. Stuart did not seem to be bothered by this anomalous situation perhaps because he perceived himself as indispensable in coordinating relations effectively between the field and New York. Without the trustees' support the university could not function financially, but without the managers the university could not function politically.

Broadening Yenching's Financial Base

In financial terms the practical result of making Yenching Chinese meant shifting the base from one dominated by the constituent mission boards to a more secular one, and broadening it to include contributions from Chinese sources.[52] In December 1916 when final consolidation arrangements were made, the four mission boards contributed an initial capital sum amounting to a total of US $350,000.[53] In addition each mission contributed to the annual budget, and the staff, which was almost entirely Western, were largely mission board appointees. The Chinese staff was small, the building program nil, and class facilities a bare minimum. The university budget for academic year 1917–18 was only about US $35,000. Of that amount 87 percent came from mission-board sources, while nothing came from secular or private sources either in America or China.[54] By 1936–37 the total figure increased almost seven times (twelve times in local currency) to approximately US $215,000. Of that amount 14 percent came from mission boards, 55 percent from private sources in America, and almost 10 percent from private and public sources in China.[55] (The actual amount available in local currency varied widely depending on the rates of exchange which fluctuated from approximately 1:1 when the university was founded, to 2:1 in the late twenties, to more than 4:1 in the mid-thirties, 16:1 in the late thirties, and several thousand to one by late 1948).

Stuart's success in raising money from private American foundations was impressive, especially with the Hall Estate and the Rockefeller Foundation. Charles Martin Hall, who discovered the electrolytic process for separating aluminum from bauxite, had amassed a huge fortune, and his will stipulated that one third of his estate (which in 1928 amounted to $14,000,000) should be used for educational projects. The categories of institutions that could benefit from his estate were those involved in "education in foreign lands, to wit, Japan, continental Asia, Turkey and the Balkan States in Europe." The will included two conditions which required that the funds be managed by boards composed of Americans or British and could not be used for instruction in theology.[56] In seeking the money Stuart exploited personal connections with the trustees of the Hall Estate. He was so effective that he not only got the money but also the support of Arthur V. Davis, president of the

Yenching University and Sino-Western Relations

Aluminum Company of America, who served as chairman of the Yenching trustee board from 1939 ot 1945. By 1936–37 the money from the Hall estate (see Table 3) composed 68 percent of the total university endowment and 31 percent of the annual budget.

Table 3. Major Secular Sources of Income for Yenching University Prior to 1937

Source	Year	Endowment (US$)	Plant (US$)	Annual appropriations (LC$)
Hall	1921	50,000[a] HE		5,000[a] HE
	1926		248,500[a] HE	
	1928	1,000,000[a] HE 500,000[a] HYI		
	1928–37			HYI[c] varying from 41,630[c] (1926–2 to high of 128,7 (1930–31)
Rockefeller				
	1921		50,000[a] RF 90,000[a] CMB	
	1922			22,656[c] CMB
	1925–30			28,000[c] CMB (yearly)
	1928–36			US $140,000[b] LSR (over 7 years)
	1932	250,000[a] RF		
	1934–37			206,300[c] NCCRR (over 3 years)
Chinese				
	1923			5,000[f] PI
	1924			11,000[e] PI
	1927	LC $320,000[a] MDC		
	1929		Dorm (LC $50,000), wall, and gate[a] PI	
	1934–37			c. 60,000[ade] MOE (yearly)
	1934–37			15,000[a] CFPEC (yearly)

Interpretation: Hall and Rockefeller sources amounted to 68 and 11 percent, respectiv of the total 1936–37 university endowment.[a] Combined endowment income and annual propriations from Hall, Rockefeller, and Chinese sources amounted to 31, 21, and 10 per respectively, of the 1936–37 budget.[c]

Organizing a Bicultural University

Organizing a Bicultural University

Key to abbreviations:

	Hall Estate	HYI	Harvard-Yenching Institute
	Rockefeller Foundation	CMB	China Medical Board (Peking)
)E	Ministry of Education	PI	Private Individuals
	(Nanking)	LSR	Laura Spelman Rockefeller
)C	Million Dollar Campaign		Fund
CRR	North China Council for		
	Rural Reconstruction		
PEC	China Foundation for the		
	Promotion of Education and		
	Culture (American Boxer		
	Indemnity)		

Sources:

a. Edwards, pp. 174–75, 228–30; b. Galt, pp. 211–15, 223, 391; c. AP BT, May 8, 1922; y 7, 1926; July 15, 1927; March 13, 1928; April 10, 1929; April 11, 1930; April 7, 1932; cember 19, 1934; December 2, 1935; February 17, 1936; October 2, 1936; d. PSYTI, 1931, 335; e. Stuart to Miss Deborah Haines, September 26, 1924, AC:JLS; f. Phillip Fugh, rview, May 1, 1968.

The other major secular source of financial support in the West was the Rockefeller Foundation whose gifts amounted to 11 percent of total endowment and 21 percent of the annual budget for 1936–37. Whereas the Hall Estate money was used primarily in the humanities, the Rockefeller funds were concentrated in the sciences. The China Medical Board, which administered Rockefeller Foundation money in Peking, underwrote the major expenses for Yenching's natural science program, while money from the Laura Spelman Rockfeller Fund covered more than half the operating costs of Yenching's social science program between 1928 and 1936. The North China Council for Rural Reconstruction, also Rockefeller money, financed Yenching's program of instruction in rural problems between 1934 and 1937.[57]

Stuart's efforts to create a Chinese financial base met with constant frustration. He was careful not to promote an unpopular cause among prospective donors during the Anti-Christian movement in the hope that its influence would subside. Furthermore by the late twenties his fund-raising success in the United States reduced the incentive to work within the Chinese community. Nevertheless throughout the 1920s and 1930s he worked with Philip Fu (Fu Ch'ing-po), his private secretary during his years as president and also later as ambassador, to make Yenching financially Chinese. Philip Fu came from a distinguished Manchu family with a long line of officials in and outside the imperial court.[58] In

Stuart's words Fu had a "political acumen from his ancestors" and an "instinct for dealing with the Mandarin psychology," which would help Stuart in his contacts with Chinese officials.[59] For almost twenty years Fu worked with Stuart but received no salary from Yenching. As Stuart's private secretary he became the target of much criticism from both Westerners and Chinese and was accused of utilizing Stuart for his own political advantage. But Stuart dismissed the criticism and insisted that Fu used his own contacts "in order to help me get in touch with important people difficult for me to reach."[60]

Stuart had intended to begin the promotional program in Peking, but Fu suggested starting in other cities where the risk of failure would have a less adverse effect on the university. A gift of LC (local currency) $5,000 from Chang Tso-lin, the Manchurian warlord, following a visit by Stuart and Fu to Mukden in 1923 was encouraging. A year later Stuart secured a few individual gifts from other prominent officials, LC $3,000 from Tuan Ch'i-jui, former premier of China, 1916–18, and provisional chief executive, 1924–26, and LC $7,000 from General Feng Yü-hsiang. At a luncheon given in Stuart's honor in November 1926 at the Grand Hotel de Pékin, wider public endorsement was given to Yenching in speeches by Ku Wei-chun (Wellington Koo), acting premier, Liang Ch'i-ch'ao, and others. Such support was particularly auspicious because most schools and businesses in the city were closed at the time because of warlord strife. In 1927 LC $50,000 was raised for the building of a dormitory from private Chinese sources. Also in 1927 prominent Shanghai bankers and officials, led by Yü Hsia-ch'ing, who was chairman of the Chinese Chamber of Commerce, formed a committee for the promotion of the Yenching cause. One other notable contact was Wang Ching-wei, political associate of Sun Yat-sen and later head of the Japanese sponsored government in Nanking, 1940, who promoted a financial drive for Yenching in Shanghai in 1935.[61] Stuart maintained friendships with all prospective donors, regardless of the size of their contributions, and he encouraged them to send their children to Yenching.

In 1933 Stuart launched the Million Dollar Campaign for endowment funds in China. It began auspiciously with the Yenching faculty pledging LC $90,000, but the campaign lost momentum when students pledged only LC $27,000. Yenching alumni also contributed to the campaign, but after four years it reached only a third of its goal or LC $320,000.[62] This weak response among students and alumni reflected

China's uncertain future in the face of increased Japanese military pressures. In 1934 the Ministry of Education granted Yenching over LC $60,000 ($63,048 in 1935–36 and $65,117 in 1936–37) with no restrictions.[63] Despite these encouraging signs, the proportion of funds from Chinese sources in the university's annual budget never amounted to more than about 10 percent.

One very sizable contribution from a wealthy banker almost wound up in the hands of the university authorities in 1929, but it hit a snag which triggered a serious conflict between the field and the trustees over the question of investments in China. On June 1, 1929, the Rockefeller Foundation notified the trustees of its decision to grant US $250,000 to Yenching as an endowment for the natural sciences on the condition that the university authorities match the grant with an equal amount.[64] In anticipating the grant Stuart had already organized a nucleus of prominent Chinese personalities in Peiping. Within a few months after the announcement from New York he informed the board he had received a pledge of an equivalent amount, or LC $625,000, from Chou Tso-min, who was the managing director of the Kincheng Banking Corporation and a political leader in North China. There were conditions attached to the pledge which stipulated that the aggregate amount of US $500,000 must be deposited in Chou's bank. Chou would then invest these funds in China until enough was earned to cover the bank's share, at which time the whole amount would be turned back to the trustees. Stuart estimated that even with a conservative rate of interest on investments in China at the time the return could be made within four years.[65]

The trustees objected at first and cited the constitution which allowed them only to invest, not deposit, any funds raised. They also objected to investing funds outside the United States and said their policy would be the same were a similar offer made by a German or a French banker.[66] But Stuart traveled to New York and temporarily disarmed the board. On the basis of his assurances they went to the Rockefeller authorities who initially accepted Chou Tso-min's pledge and turned the quarter of a million dollars over to the Yenching trustees. The only problem remaining was the final arrangement with Chou. New York's procedure was to set up a Special Committee on Investment, which was asked to investigate the situation in China. If it unanimously found the proposal satisfactory, it was to proceed with Chou's arrangement.[67]

After the investigation one member of the committee concluded that Chou Tso-min's offer was merely a pledge and not a cash gift. The trustees took this objection as a lack of unanimity and decided against Stuart. Chou lost face. In Stuart's words, the "long protracted delay in reaching the decision deeply offended" Chou and "produced a questioning as to my sincerity and our confidence in him." In averting the risk of Chinese investments the trustees were about to lose the "active help and goodwill of a man who had intended to help in raising money in China."[68] Despite the turn of events Stuart continued pressing for investments in China and for Chou Tso-min's support. He proposed in August 1930 that the board ask the Rockefeller trustees to revise the terms of the original grant. If they agreed, he would then request the board to remit the quarter million to China to be invested not under the special committee but under the finance committee of the board of managers.[69] As the problem simmered Stuart became concerned not just with Chou, whose offer he felt could be reactivated, but also with the managers, who also wanted the trustees to transfer funds to China.

The trustees responded by offering to send a mission to Peking to reassure him of their support. But Stuart took their offer as an insult. He suspected the cost of the trip would come out of the field budget, and he thought the opinions of the managers (mostly Chinese now) ought to carry more weight than those of the trustees. Exasperated by the dangling of a quarter million Rockefeller dollars and his and the trustees' inability to snatch it, he threatened to resign. Rather than approach the Rockefeller Foundation themselves the trustees asked Stuart to visit the States in the spring of 1931 to do the begging once again. Stuart overcame his own protestations and headed for America. He finally won Franklin Warner, former chairman of the board, to his side. But the trustees grew tired of pressure from the field and brought an end to the investments controversy in December 1933. They decided that all investments had to be in the hands of the trustees as a condition of the implied agreement with the American donors, that Western donors would be more willing to contribute in the future if they knew all funds were in the hands of the board, and most importantly that the "responsibility for the custody and investment of endowment funds . . . secured is one of the factors making for the interest, activity, and permanence of the Board of Trustees." Their decision: "Funds secured through the Board of Trustees should be held and invested by them, and those funds secured in China through the efforts of the Board of Managers should be held and invested by them"[70]

In the end the trustees barely succeeded in meeting the extended deadline for the Rockefeller grant. They finally pulled together the requisite amount with a generous US $50,000 loan from the Harvard-Yenching Institute and an even more generous acceptance of the arrangement by the Rockefeller trustees as meeting the terms of the original grant.

Stuart reluctantly let the issue die. Certainly the major obstacle to investing funds in China was not legal, for the trustees could have changed the English constitution as swiftly as they did in 1928 with regard to administrative authority. When faced with the problem of Yenching's registration with the Nanking Ministry of Education in 1928, the trustees asked a court in Niagara Falls whether they could grant any more funds to Yenching in view of Hall's stipulation that beneficiary institutions be substantially controlled by Americans or British. The court ruled that Hall's statement was merely "prefatory" and not an "obligatory limitation."[71] Furthermore, the Rockefeller Foundation might have been willing to have their grant invested in China had the issue been pressed by the trustees, for one of its main purposes was to promote self-reliance among the beneficiaries. When Stuart went to see the Rockefeller trustees in December 1929 just after his arrival in the United States, they were so enthusiastic over the announcement of Chou Tso-min's offer that they quickly made another US $250,000 grant. But they soon withdrew it upon learning of the reluctance of the Yenching trustees.[72] A less hesitant response from the trustees might have induced Chou to be more flexible in his terms, as Stuart consistently maintained.

Those in the field also argued that endowment funds could be invested in gold bonds of the Chinese government, which were actively traded in Hong Kong and London.[73] Income from the investment of endowment funds in China during the 1930s would have produced several times the amount produced in America, but the trustees feared China's political instability. They had had a bad experience investing securities at higher rates of interest in the late twenties and did not find the arguments from the field persuasive.[74] Minds preoccupied with the security of trust funds were not very interested in the nationalistic feelings of their colleagues in China.

The trustees also used their control over funds to forestall any further weakening of Yenching's ties with evangelical Christianity. In June 1929 E. M. McBrier, treasurer of the board of trustees, donated $100,000 to a fund known as the McBrier Foundation for Biblical

Instruction and Christian Work. Earlier he had given $100,000 for the building of a recitation hall. According to the conditions of the McBrier fund the money was to be used outside the regular budget items to promote Christian work in leading students into a "personal experience of faith in and obedience to Jesus Christ as their Savior and Lord."[75] The way Stuart matched these conditions with the program he had in mind reveals his amazing flexibility, bordering on administrative slipperyness. In a personal note to Mr. McBrier he agreed with the evangelical concern: "This institution is in danger of being lost to the Christian cause in ways you realize quite acutely and others of which I am more conscious than you." He asked McBrier to trust him "both in reference to my judgment and in my earnestness of purpose to be your co-worker in putting this fund into effective use."[76] Effective use for Stuart meant support for publication of the *Chen-li yü sheng-ming;* scholarships to several dozen students coming from poor homes, which he argued would "transform the whole religious tone on our campus"; salary support for Hsü Pao-ch'ien in the school of religion; and support for Mr. and Mrs. Harry B. Price, teaching respectively social economics and religious education. Despite the impossibility of matching the McBrier funds to any good purpose within the university, an average annual sum of approximately US $1,500 was sent to the field in the late thirties and forties to support the frills of evangelism.[77] But its potential resources were never tapped by the field.

Making the Faculty More Chinese

Sinification at Yenching meant fundamental changes in the composition and recruitment policies of the faculty. In both areas missionary influence declined while the power of the Chinese faculty members increased. In 1919 the teaching staff was composed of twenty-five Westerners and four Chinese, and in keeping with evangelical purposes all of them were appointed and paid directly by the four constituent mission boards. Like the faculty of many church related colleges in America at the time, most of these Western teachers had received little or no specialized Western training. Before 1920 Stuart alone at Yenching possessed a doctorate degree, and that was in theology.[78] But the Anti-Christian movement quickly reversed these patterns, so that by 1927 Chinese members of the faculty dominated the Westerners by about two to one, a ratio that was roughly maintained over the next two decades.[79]

In addition to these shifts in racial balance changes occurred in the religious composition of the faculty. Few as were the Chinese on the faculty in the early years they were all Christian.[80] But by 1928 the percentage of Christians among some forty full time Chinese teachers had dropped to 65 percent and still further by 1930 to 53 percent.[81] A similar shift took place in the religious affiliations of the Western faculty. By 1928 exactly half, or fourteen out of twenty-eight fulltime members, had no direct missionary connections and were paid directly out of the university budget, which Stuart effectively determined.[82] The number employed as missionaries and appointed directly by the constituent mission boards had dropped from a high of twenty-five a decade earlier to fourteen. By 1928 the trustees had largely come around to Stuart's thinking on the matter. But before then, in 1922 for example, when he had asked each mission board to give up its powers of direct appointment and contribute a pro-rated fixed sum to be used at the university's discretion in securing faculty members, the trustees not only refused to comply but tried to bring the few existing university appointees more directly under mission board influence. They argued then that the university was an integral part of the missionary enterprise, and they asked that each foreign member of the faculty, not representing any mission board, be accepted by one of the boards as an affiliated member, in order to "stimulate their foreign missionary consciousness."[83] But faced with antiforeign pressures in the field, Stuart was in no position to accede to this request, and the trustees let the issue drop.

As the Chinese faculty outnumbered the Western faculty the conflicts between evangelical and academic purposes and between generalists and specialists sharpened. The majority of the Chinese faculty in the late 1920s were still Christians and did not advocate abandoning religious purposes altogether. Furthermore they believed in the generalist nature of liberal arts training. But they wanted to increase Yenching's prestige, which they regarded as a matter of raising the academic qualifications for faculty recruitment. Their standards were based largely on the model of American graduate education. This process began with the arrival of Liu T'ing-fang, the first Chinese Ph.D. on the faculty, in 1921. Liu was particularly sensitive, as he had just received his Ph.D. from Columbia University.[84] Stuart agreed with Liu's request and proceeded with the upgrading of the faculty, recognizing that academic excellence, where necessary, would take precedence over religious qualifications. Over the first years many heads rolled and there were bitter feelings.[85]

Liu continued to influence recruitment patterns through his associations with other Chinese students at Columbia and through family connections. He came to know them through the activities of the Chinese Student Christian Association (in New York) and through YMCA related activities both in China and the United States.[86] In 1930 twenty-six of the ninety-eight full time and part time Chinese faculty and thirteen of some forty full time and part time Western faculty had studied at Columbia University. Another common connection among the Chinese faculty, which Liu symbolized, was the YMCA. In 1930 twelve of the senior Chinese faculty had served as YMCA officers or secretaries, while many more than that had been longtime participants in YMCA activities.[87] Finally, Liu's family connections were important in two key appointments. Hsü Shu-shi (professor of political science, onetime national secretary to the YMCA in China and ambassador of the Republic of China to Canada, 1962–67) and Lu Chih-wei (professor of psychology and later president of Yenching) married sisters of Liu and joined the Yenching faculty after the marriage, which was performed in a double ring ceremony by Stuart in 1921.[88]

By the time the university moved to the Haitien campus in 1926 Yenching's academic reputation was high. It was known as one of the top three universities in North China. Its prestige was not as high as Peita and Tsinghua overall, and yet in the early 1930s more research grants were awarded by the ministry of education to Yenching than to those from any other university in China, including Tsinghua and National Central (Nanking) universities, both with much larger student enrollments.[89] In addition to academic excellence and intellectual excitement, Yenching offered job security and academic freedom. In 1925 eight national universities, including Peita, suffered drastic cuts in their budgets because of warlord rivalries and factional disputes within the central government. The salaries of professors in these institutions were six months in arrears.[90]

After 1928 the Nanking government nationalized Tsinghua University and strengthened political control over the national universities that threatened academic freedom. As a private university Yenching was spared this degree of political interference. In this context two Peita professors, Ku Chieh-kang and Chang Tung-sun, came to Yenching respectively in 1929 and 1930 and taught there for almost twenty years. In the late 1930s and 1940s, Yenching increasingly employed its own graduates after they completed further study abroad.

Beyond increasing the ratio of Chinese members on the faculty, the goal of making Yenching more Chinese was measured in terms of racial equality in salaries and housing. It was a question of overcoming the legacy of missionary work in China in which the foreigners were given preferential treatment over their Chinese co-workers. The question of treatment (*tai-yü*) became especially sensitive. Early on, Stuart had promoted the idea of equal treatment, and the arrival of Liu T'ing-fang in 1921 and Hung Yeh in 1922 on the faculty provided him with his first opportunity to put his words into action.[91] Hung insisted that the trustees pay him a salary equal to that of a missionary of the Methodist church, of which he was a member. One trustee warned that acceding to Hung's request might "cause embarrassment and perhaps lack of harmony in personal relationships" with Chinese colleagues at Yenching. But Hung persisted, and even without the trustees' approval Stuart arranged for Hung to begin teaching at Yenching while serving as a Methodist missionary for Fukien residents in Peking, at the going missionary rate.[92] Liu's salary was not a question, as he taught simultaneously in two other institutions until 1924.

One problem in establishing racial equality in salaries lay in the differing conceptions of teaching. In the early years mission boards regarded missionaries not as employees but as volunteers, and mission salaries were not so much a payment for services rendered as an allowance to cover living expenses. Mission boards furthermore regarded the financial needs of all missionaries as basically the same with only minimal recognition of time served on the field. In contrast the financial support of university-appointed Chinese was calculated on a graduated salary scale based on the professional qualifications of training, teaching experience, and publication and research. A highly trained Chinese appointee starting with a lecturer's salary based on the graduated scale resented the higher fixed salary of a new missionary appointee with less training. In 1920 the highest paid Western mission-board appointee received LC $3,000, while the highest paid Chinese received LC $1,800. Both received university housing. In 1927 the highest paid Chinese faculty in 1928, Liu T'ing-fang, made a total of LC $4,875, or almost LC $3,000 less than the highest paid Westerner.[93]

In 1930 a special faculty committee composed of younger Chinese members asked the university to adopt a single salary schedule for all members of the staff. Their request was supported by the university-appointed Western faculty whose salaries lagged behind those of mission-board appointees. Within a year the trustees approved a uniform salary schedule that was based solely on merit and applied to all university appointees.[94] At the same time a uniform table of academic ranks was adopted with promotion criteria that were the same for both Westerners and Chinese. Any faculty member could apply for one year's leave with salary after six years continuous service. A similar graduated scale was worked out for administrative staff members classified into four ranks to which graded salary amounts were assigned. The economic benefits enjoyed by all full time teachers and administrators included housing, medical and dental allowances, travel in China on university business, tuition scholarship for one child at Yenching upon the completion of three years teaching, and annuity benefits. Special consideration was given to the Western faculty in only two areas, children's education and travel to and from the home country.[95] After the war with Japan the question of salaries again divided the faculty as ruinous inflation discriminated in favor of Westerners who had access to higher rates of exchange.[96]

The establishment of racial equality in housing was difficult because some Chinese did not want the expense of modern conveniences such as heat, light, and plumbing. They preferred instead to receive a housing allowance, live more simply off campus, and use the savings for other things. But Stuart feared that unless complete equality in housing were established the students would infer that foreigners were "given preferential treatment and the Chinese relegated to inferior accommodations."[97] A few faculty members like Wu Lei-ch'uan and Grace Boynton preferred not to comply with this principle. The more expensive Western housing, they thought, separated them "necessarily from the pervading poverty of Chinese life around them" Nor did the trustees share Stuart's commitment to equality in housing. When he requested more money in 1929 to build more houses for the Chinese faculty, they refused to send it. So Stuart took out a private loan in his own name.[98] By the early 1930s racial discrimination in housing came to an end. In fact the largest university house appeared to be occupied by the family of Chao Tzu-ch'en.[99]

Liu T'ing-fang made a biting analysis of the question of treatment in 1936 in the Yen-ta yu-sheng, the alumni bulletin. Despite the establishment of racial equality in salaries and housing, Liu continued to resent the "masterfulness" of the foreigners. He believed that a certain feeling of superiority remained among the liberal missionary educators and that the original desire to convert Chinese still lingered on. He also resented their standards of professional training, which he thought were generally inferior to those of their Chinese colleagues.[100] But Liu's sharpest attack was reserved for his Chinese colleagues, who suffered from what he called a "psychology of dependence" (*yi-lai hsin-li*), which was rooted in their years spent at mission schools, long educational experiences in Western countries, and then work at Yenching. Defending his less Westernized colleagues, who occasionally refused to turn in grades as a protest to the Westerner's preoccupation with efficient evaluation of students, he attacked his more Westernized colleagues for failing to stand up to foreigners. Ironically Liu himself seemed to demonstrate as well as anyone this spirit of dependence. Inconsistently, he excused Stuart, who had been like a father to him since boyhood, from all the charges made against Westerners.[101]

Chinese Studies and Vocational Education

One direct effect of the Anti-Christian movement on the Yenching curriculum was to reduce the importance of the school of religion in the life of the university and simultaneously to strengthen the program of Chinese studies. From the beginning Stuart had a special interest in religious courses at Yenching. The first two returned students to be recruited, Liu and Hung, first taught in the school of religion. Ninde Hall, which housed the dorm, classrooms, and offices of the school, was the first building to be started and completed on the new campus. And after government regulations in 1927 required the school to separate from the rest of the university, Ninde Hall continued to function as the center for the school, while its students still participated actively in student affairs throughout the 1930s and 1940s and even after the Communist takeover for three years.[102] Nonetheless the pressures of the antireligious drives could not be ignored, and the school in other ways was forced from the center to the periphery of university life, while Chinese studies increased in importance.

In 1917–18 more than one fourth, or twelve out of forty-four, of the total faculty were employed by the school of religion, while by 1925–26 the fraction dropped to less than one fifth and by 1930–31 less than one tenth. The opposite trend occurred in the number of faculty employed in the teaching of Chinese and related subjects. In 1917–18 only two of the total forty-four faculty taught Chinese, while by 1930–31 almost one fifth, or twice the number in religion, were teachers in Chinese studies. This reversal of roles may also be found in the changes in the relative size of budget allocations over almost three decades. In 1923 16 percent of the total budget was spent on the school of religion, compared to 3 percent in Chinese studies. But by 1930 the percentages were reversed and remained roughly the same over the next twenty years.[103] In 1927 Hung Yeh, then dean of the college, proudly claimed that Yenching no longer needed to "share the disgrace of inferior Chinese courses, a charge so frequently made against missionary education institutions."[104] After 1930 the balance between religious studies and Chinese studies remained relatively constant, as the Anti-Christian movement had effectively waned by then.

The school of religion also suffered a sharp decline in applications, enrollments, and graduates. For the first five years graduates from the school composed more than one sixth of the total, but in the five year period between 1927 and 1931 they amounted to less than one twelfth of the total university graduates. And of the fifty-three graduates from the school of religion in the latter five year period only three had received the bachelor of divinity degree, the others receiving short course certificates often representing no more than one year of study.[105] The attrition rate among those enrolled in the school of religion in the 1920s was high, the number of applications to the school dwindled, and the requirements for admission were lowered.[106] Stuart attributed this declining interest in religion to the absorption of students in nationalistic endeavors and to an antiforeignism, making the Chinese students "unwilling to give their services to organizations thought of by the Chinese as essentially foreign or controlled by the West."[107] In 1932 Chao Tzuch'en, then dean of the school, admitted that most students wanted to have nothing to do with the church and were more interested in experiments with primitive communism and forays into the countryside to arouse the masses.[108]

The Anti-Christian movement did have the effect of making the curriculum of the school of religion somewhat more Chinese through the addition of courses on the history of Chinese Christianity, Christianity and social questions, and courses on Taoism and Buddhism. But these changes were small compared to the overall purposes and organization of the school, which clung almost slavishly to the Western model. Even after the total enrollment had dropped to a low of twelve, the school still listed over forty courses, parroting largely the course offerings of Protestant seminaries in the West.[109] Nor did the attack on Christianity result in any serious reconsideration of the kinds of jobs graduates should be trained for and expect to find. In 1930 Dean Chao Tzu-ch'en saw the major employment problem as one of finding jobs with salaries large enough to "cover [the graduates'] necessary expenses, amplified by their numerous wants."[110] He conceded that as "ministers of the word of God" they had to "face hardships" and be "prepared for self-sacrifice," but the demands of "modern Chinese society" and the thoroughly Western curriculum made such ideals hard to realize.[111] By the 1930s the desire to increase academic prestige, measured according to Western standards, had turned the school of religion into an institution that seemed far removed from the spirit and early goals of the Life Fellowship.

The Anti-Christian movement also appeared to have little effect on the basic liberal arts curriculum. The course requirements and academic program of the Yenching students throughout the 1930s and 1940s were not that different from those in the early 1920s. The students would graduate with concentrated study either in literature (wen-hsüeh), the natural sciences (li-hsüeh), or the social sciences (fa-hsüeh, often translated as public affairs), but beyond that all were expected to have basic training in Chinese, to be proficient in English, and to be exposed to course work in all three areas. Yenching leaders recognized the problem of job suitability in a country as poor as China for students trained in liberal arts, by experimenting with vocational education. This experimentation began with Stuart's acceptance of the presidency in 1919. He recognized then the tendency of mission school education to "train students for professions for which there are few callings." A broad range of technical courses, he argued, ought to enable each student to find a career of "larger social and economic value to the nation" and to the Christian cause.[112] The four-year college course, he asserted, ought to consist of two years general preparation followed by two more in specialized work, which would effectively abolish the old American conception of a liberal arts course, which was a "luxury China cannot now afford."[113]

Experimentation in vocational education took several forms. The first was the school of animal husbandry, founded in 1920 in cooperation with Ch'iu Jen-ch'u, a wealthy businessman in Peking. The school aimed to "assist public-spirited Chinese in an endeavor to improve the economic conditions of China's poor." In 1921 Ch'iu fell into financial ruin, but the school was able to continue for the next ten years with funds left over from the China International Famine Relief Agency. In

1928 the department was transferred to the school of agriculture and forestry of the University of Nanking, although the experimental farm located near the campus continued in cooperation with Yenching's department of chemistry.[114] The second vocational experiment was the department of leather manufacturing set up by Joseph Bailie. In 1923 the department provided training to eleven of General Feng Yü-hsiang's officers who became foremen in various branches of the leather industry. Leather tanning was discontinued as an independent unit after 1926, although courses related to tanning were continued in the department of chemistry.[115] A third experiment was the Bureau of Industry and Labor, whose purpose was to collect and disseminate statistics and information regarding trade conditions and industrial needs to Chinese and Western businessmen. Stuart eyed this project as a possible source of income, but the trustees refused to authorize its establishment.[116]

Other experiments were tried in home economics, which offered courses into the 1930s, and in pre-engineering.[117] All these efforts in vocational education appeared half-hearted compared to the basic commitment to liberal arts. The enrollments in vocational courses at Yenching reached a peak in 1927–28 when they accounted for 26 percent of the total student body. But in 1930 it amounted to only 10 percent of in 1936–37 only 1 percent of the total.[118] One explanation for the small interest in some of the vocational programs was the disdain among educated Chinese toward physical labor, which was articulated in Mencius' distinction between those who worked with their minds and those who worked with the hands and which became deeply implanted in traditional education. Yenching educators challenged this assumption by emphasizing physical education, intramural sports, and student employment in physical work on the campus. But its effects lingered on, more perhaps within the faculty than in the student body itself. In terms of prestige liberal arts had become a kind of twentieth century substitute for the Confucian classics. Yenching's four year degree program always seemed to carry more status than any short course or two year program in vocational education. In moments of patriotic enthusiasm Yenching students would set aside their concern for status, but the concern reappeared with the passing of the patriotic tide. Reinforcing these tendencies were the guidelines from the ministry of education of the Nationalist government between 1927 and 1949. Most of its ministers were educated in the United States and looked to the liberal arts model in America in designing a system of higher education for China. They only seemed to toy with vocational education. In the face of sustained student disinterest and governmental indifference Stuart dropped the issue of vocational education after the mid 1930s.

The department of journalism was one exception to this otherwise unsuccessful experiment in vocational education. Founded in 1919, the department established a close affiliation through Vernon Nash with the University of Missouri School of Journalism in the 1920s. In the 1930s newspaper publishers in China added their support. The trustees assumed financial responsibility reluctantly. Under the leadership of Nash and his successor, Liang Shih-ch'un (Hubert Liang), the department experimented with various bilingual newspaper publications, notably the *Yenching Gazette,* 1931–32, the *P'ing-hsi pao* (West of Peiping journal) in the spring of 1932, and the *Yenching News* (*Yen-ching hsin-wen*), published irregularly by the department from September 1934 on. Many of China's leading journalists in the thirties and forties graduated from this department. By 1936 journalism had become the fourth most popular department in the college with sixty-three undergraduate majors (behind biology, economics, and sociology).[119] Some well-known American journalists in China such as Edgar Snow, Nym Wales, and F. McCracken (Mac) Fisher worked with the department in the 1930s.

As with the liberal arts curriculum generally, graduate education at Yenching further illustrates the problem of fitting Western educational forms into the Chinese setting. By virtue of its leading position Yenching was singled out in the various attempts at correlation among the Christian colleges in China to become a major center for graduate education. It offered the first M.A. degree in 1922 and ten years later provided graduate training in twelve departments to 120 students or a little more than one sixth of the total enrollment. Government regulations in 1933 restricted Yenching to graduate training in four departments and forced graduate enrollments down to only forty-nine for 1936–37.[120] Yenching administrators discussed offering the Ph.D degree, but it never got beyond the planning stage. Even Peita ceased all graduate training after 1933.

The Yenta Christian Fellowship

Two other measures of the influence of the Anti-Christian movement were the declining percentage of students professing belief in Christianity and the organization of the Yenta Christian Fellowship. Figures on the Christian affiliation among Yenching students, as indicated in Table 4 and Diagram 2, were published only between 1924 and 1935, and they show a marked drop from a high of 88 percent of the total student enrollment in 1924 to 31 percent in 1935. These figures were gathered each fall at registration when students voluntarily indicated their religious affiliation, if any. Because of the growing unpopularity of Christianity by then and possible noncompliance with the question, the fig-

Table 4. Student Enrollment and Christian Membership at Yenching, 1917–1951

Year	Number of Students	Number of Christians	Year	Number of Students	Number of Christians
1917	106		1935	884	273
1918	88		1936	826	
1919	94		1937	588	
1920	137		1938	942	
1921	142		1939	982	450[a]
1922	298		1940	1,086	
1923	332		1941	1,156	
1924	438	385	1942	342	
1925	552	336	1943	380	
1926	616	330	1944	408	
1927	633		1945	816	
1928	700	337	1946	781	
1929	747		1947	921	360[a]
1930	808	296	1948	800	
1931	811	359	1949	990	
1932	788	297	1950	1,148	
1933	815	287	1951	1,600	130[a]
1934	800	272			

Sources: Enrollment figures are for fall semester of each academic year and for 1917–23 are from Earl H. Cressy, Christian Higher Education in China (Shanghai, 1928), 27; 1924–35 from PSYTI (1937), 182; 1936–49 from "Enrollment Figures of Christian Colleges in China under Protestant Auspices," handwritten chart in United Board archives, AC:UB; 1950 from "Incomplete Report on Student Enrollment, 1st Semester 1950" in GMB:PC; and 1951 from Ralph Lapwood letters, July 31, 1951. The number of Christians for years 1924 to 1935 are from irregular bulletins published by the China Christian Education Association in Shanghai, nos. 8, 14, 22, 26, 28, 29, 30, 33, 35 and 38; figures for 1939, 1948, and 1951 are from letters written by John Leighton Stuart, September 9, 1939, Lucius Porter, December 12, 1948, and Ralph Lapwood, November 15, 1950, respectively, and are estimates based on the assumption that each of the small groups in the Yenta Christian Fellowship was composed of approximately twenty members each, and that approximately three fourths of the total were students, the rest being faculty and workers.

[a] Rough estimate.

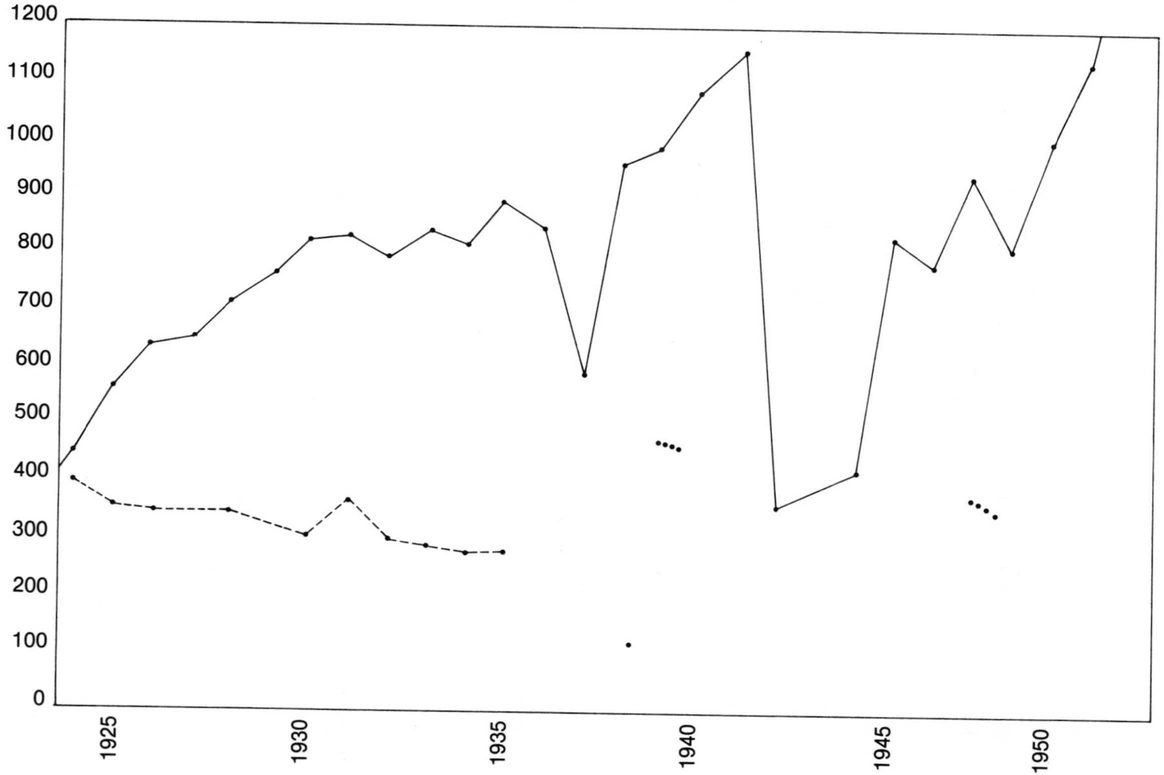

Diagram 2 Student Enrollment (solid line) and Christian Membership (dotted line) at Yenching University, 1924-51

ures are likely deflated. Percentage figures for earlier years may well have run higher than 88 percent. The figures for 1939, 1947, and 1951 are approximate and represent membership in the Yenta Christian Fellowship. The relative lack of figures after the mid-1930s reflects the university's declining interest in the religious affiliations of students and changes in admissions policies, as more graduates of non-Christian middle schools were encouraged to apply.

Despite the effects of the Anti-Christian movement Christianity still held an appeal to a large number of students. Worship services and religious activities helped soften the pressures of academic life, the separation from families, and the personal problems characteristic of many youth in the Republican years. In fact there was some resurgence of interest in Christianity in student circles. Between 1934 and 1936 the YMCA evangelist, Sherwood Eddy, addressed almost three hundred and fifty thousand people in China and secured more than 10,000 decisions. He was reportedly given especially warm receptions at government schools.[121] During the great uncertainty pervading the years of the Japanese occupation of North China religious interest at Yenching again increased, reaching an all time high for the 1930s. One student in the school of religion, Wei Chao-ch'i, converted to Christianity in 1928. In the 1920s he had attended missionary schools in Peking, but then he became an advocate of revolutionary violence, which included his readiness to "kill the traitors" in helping China down the road to national salvation. Before long, though, personal despair and thoughts of suicide turned his attention back to the Christian faith because it offered hope. Whenever he spoke of death, darkness and destruction, his Christian friends would answer with life, light, and truth. In 1932 he converted his whole family and other friends to Christianity and enrolled in the Yenching School of Religion to prepare for the Christian ministry. He later supported the Christian rural reconstruction project at Li-ch'uan, Kiangsi.[122] Wei's conversion suggests that devastating as the Anti-Christian movement may have been in the 1920s, Christianity had not lost completely its appeal among students. Some of the Yenching alumni interviewed in Taiwan and Hong Kong in the late 1960s claimed the Anti-Christian movement was never a serious force to contend with. Others acknowledged its damage to the Christian cause but refused to accept the validity of the accusations.[123]

The Yenta Christian Fellowship was organized in 1926 at Stuart's initiative to meet the continuing religious interest of students on the new campus, where the relative isolation in the Western suburbs broke down the established loyalties on the old campus to particular churches within the city walls. It was hailed as a model for the indigenous church. Wu Lei-ch'uan praised it for serving believers, not missionaries, for transcending denominational lines which had always confounded converts in China, and for stressing a living spirit and not the hollow form of a Western transplant. The only requirement for joining was to sign the original statement of purpose: "to grow in the knowledge of our Lord Jesus Christ and to live according to the way that he taught and lived."[124]

After the government regulations in 1926 prohibited the administration from performing any official role in religious life, the Yenta Christian Fellowship assumed responsibility for all religious activities on campus. Among them were short chapel services, held four times weekly in the late 1920s and reduced to twice weekly in the 1930s. Sandwiched into fifteen minute sessions between the first and second morning class periods, these services drew attendances rarely exceeding more than a few dozen, and yet they were continued into the early 1950s.[125] Other activities included three Sunday services each week, one of them being the highly liturgical service of the Anglican church, and campus wide celebration services at Christmas and Easter. Government regulations prohibited special Christian holidays but did permit a "founder's day," which Yenching celebrated on December 25. Attendance at these Christmas services remained high throughout the 1930s and 1940s and included many who were not regular members of the fellowship.

The President and the Chancellor

Like college presidents in America at the time Stuart played the pivotal role in the life of the university. As an administrator he coordinated the disparate groups within the institution, deftly interpreting the pressure of events on the field to the trustees and securing their tacit and frequently reluctant approval of needed changes. With equal skill he persuaded the dissatisfied members in the field, especially students, not to abandon ship, despite questions about its seaworthiness. Even as an educator he demanded high standards and established flexible policies not often associated with the missionary enterprise. Yenching and non-Yenching sources alike attest repeatedly to his magnetic personality.

To be sure, not everyone was pleased with Stuart's presidency. The deans of the women's college, for example, found it difficult to forgive him for his slighting of women in establishing coeducation at Yenching. Even Grace Boynton, who was known for her loyalty to Stuart, saw the union as a "bitter experience" for the women. Luella Miner, the first dean under the union, was "forced to resign." Alice Frame, the next dean, suffered a nervous breakdown in her "effort to get Leighton to observe the conditions of the merger," while Boynton saw herself as the "only member of the women's college faculty who did not feel bitter." Margaret Speer described the union as a "swallowing up."[126] Chinese figures often vied for his favor and found themselves divided among those on the fringe and those in the inner circle of Stuart's contacts.

Nevertheless, with charisma and unusual administrative skills Stuart was at the center of making Yenching Chinese. He was instrumental in increasing the power of the managers, such that it was, over that of the trustees. And in deference to the Chinese faculty and students he effectively ended all proselytizing functions while dramatically improving Yenching's professional image. He firmly believed it was possible for Yenching to be equally cosmopolitan and Chinese.

But sinification for Stuart did not mean diminishing his own role in university life. It soon became clear that he and the Chinese chancellors approached the issue of racial equality in administration quite differently. In defining his position as the president Stuart relied on the English version (1928) of the university's constitution, which clearly placed Stuart above the chancellors, and flaunted the Chinese version (1929). According to the Chinese constitution Stuart's position as president (*hsiao-wu-chang*) was to be filled through nomination by the managers and appointment by the chancellor (*hsiao-chang*). Stuart's responsibilities were to help (*hsieh-chu*) the chancellor, substitute for him when he was gone, and raise money.[127] In the Chinese version, Stuart's position was clearly below the chancellor's.

Chancellor Wu Lei-ch'uan was the first to confront this ambiguity in job definitions. It appears that Stuart wanted only an honorary chancellor or a figurehead when government regulations in 1928 forced Yenching to fill the new position. Wu was Stuart's third choice for the job, after Yen Hui-ch'ing, long time diplomat, and Wang Ch'ung-hui, then minister of justice in Nanking. In all of Stuart's correspondence with the trustees during Wu's four year tenure as chancellor from 1929 to 1933, Wu is mentioned only rarely. Some of the alumni and teachers have remembered Wu as a weak administrator and quite accepting of the secondary role forced upon him.[128] Stuart was indeed a more commanding figure, and while alumni publications are filled with memorials to Stuart, Wu is recalled only rarely. But others had high regard for Wu's abilities. Howard Galt regarded Wu in the early years of his chancellorship as a "veritable tower of strength in all administrative matters."[129] And Chiang Mon-lin certainly would not have asked Wu to serve as his vice minister of education in 1928 without concurring in large measure with Galt's assessment. In any case Wu took the job seriously. He informed the managers in his first meeting with them that the Chinese constitution would serve as the legal basis for university administration, and he hoped Nanking would enforce its terms.[130]

Stuart perhaps feared as much, until he was reassured in 1928 that the Nanking government would not enforce the Chinese constitution. By then the Nationalist government abandoned any pretense of revolutionary politics and turned to Western nations, especially the United States, for support. Stuart, in fact, became a useful ally in the Western community in North China where Chiang Kai-shek's control was tenuous at best. In 1928 the government appointed him the trustee of two prestigious government institutions. Stuart openly acknowledged his "anomalous predicament," having been appointed first to the China Foundation for the Promotion of Culture and Education and then to the Tsinghua University board of trustees by a "government whose regulations I am flagrantly violating by continuing, although a foreigner, as president of an institution of learning on Chinese soil."[131] Stuart's liberal arts pattern of higher education fit well into the political order of the Nationalist government.

But Chancellor Wu Lei-ch'uan did not perceive higher education in Stuart's terms. The Anti-Christian movement had forced him to recognize that his and the Life Fellowship's previous prescriptions for national salvation were now inadequate. National salvation through study (*tu-shu chiu-kuo*) simply ignored the urgency of China's political situation. Salvation through moral example (*jen-ko chiu-kuo*) which had served in 1924 as the theme of the national YMCA conference, appeared to have little effect, and no one talked about it anymore. So too with the theory of salvation through better men in government, *jen-ts'ai chiu-kuo*. Wu was now attracted to a fourth approach, namely saving the nation through struggle and sacrifice (*fen-tou hsi-sheng yi chiu-kuo*), which he had heard articulated earlier by a student urging others to disregard the question of food, abandon their families, do away with the pleasures of life, and "turn our faces to the 400,000,000 compatriots."

Wu liked this spirit of determination and courage, but before youth
could take up the struggle, they had to go through a period of moral self-
cultivation (*hsiu-yang*).[132]

Why self-cultivation? Youth lacked experience and wisdom. Their
patriotic goals were commendable, but their methods were often ineffec-
tive. They needed to cultivate a correct sense of purpose and above all
maintain the capacity for total self-sacrifice, even at the expense of
reputation and family, which Wu recognized as being especially difficult
for Chinese. By imitating Jesus, students would understand the meaning
of "bearing the cross" and "complete self-sacrifice." Study, character-
building, and the training of talent—earlier rationales—would contribute to the task of national salvation only in the sense of preparing youth
for the inevitable struggle ahead.[133]

More than Stuart, Wu Lei-ch'uan appeared concerned about the
plight of poorer students, and he reportedly used part of his own salary
to give them financial aid. He once tried to divert a large American
donation, designated to build a chapel, to the scholarship fund. When
the donor heard of Wu's proposal, he threatened to withdraw the funds.
But Stuart assured him the scholarship fund was "merely the suggestion
of our Chinese Chancellor" and would not be taken seriously.[134] Wu's
attempts to redefine a philosophy of education for Yenching never
seemed to satisfy. It was as if the only way to fuse his earlier commitment to Christianity with China's situation was to move in a politically
radical direction that negated the basic assumptions of liberal arts education.

Wu's emphasis on struggle and sacrifice had implications that would
have disturbed Yenching's political connections both in New York and
Nanking. But meanwhile Stuart enjoyed the confidence of the central
government and most of the faculty, and he contented himself with
establishing Wu's nominal position in university administration. The
English letterheads on university stationery placed Wu's name above
Stuart's, and on formal occasions, such as commencement, Stuart followed behind Wu in the procession. In Wu's conception of administrative organization the chancellor's office (*hsiao-chang pan-kung ch'u*)
distinctly headed all other administrative bodies.[135] But Wu's office
and the size of his staff were always smaller than Stuart's. To anyone
passing through Bashford Hall, Stuart's quarters were obviously the
center of administrative activity.

Wu stopped attending the managers' meetings, which were held in

Stuart's house. Howard Galt once informed Wu that he was "really wanted as an active head of the institution," but Wu became so discouraged that he submitted a letter of resignation in May 1931 after only two years in the chancellorship. When the managers refused to accept it, he consented to serve two more years on the condition that he would handle only the official correspondence with Nanking. During these years he greatly reduced his involvement in university life, limiting himself to the correspondence, occasional chapel appearances, and teaching Chinese. He successfully resigned in May 1934 and retreated to his native Hangchow to write.[136]

When Wu returned to Yenching in 1937 he continued teaching documentary Chinese and advanced composition, and he resumed active participation in the Yenta Christian Fellowship. But his name was conspicuously lacking from the list of faculty homes open to students during the Christmas celebration. On his seventieth birthday in 1940 members of the Chinese faculty set up the Wu Lei-ch'uan scholarship fund, amounting to LC $6,000, and prepared to honor him through publication of a special edition of the *Yenching News*. But Wu declined the invitation in view of the political situation.[137]

Lu Chih-wei's experience as chancellor at Yenching further illustrates Stuart's ambivalence on the question of Chinese control. Lu was highly respected among his colleagues for his scholarship, and he appears to have accepted top administrative responsibilities only reluctantly.[138] Lu began as the acting chancellor from 1934 to 1937 (after Wu's resignation and another interim year under Chou Yi-ch'un), but he stepped aside during the Japanese occupation in North China to allow Stuart to exploit his extraterritorial position as an American citizen to protect the university. After the war with Japan Stuart was asked to help restore the university. Meanwhile K'ung Hsiang-hsi (H. H. Kung), longtime finance minister of the Nationalist government, had gladly accepted the purely nominal position as the Chinese chancellor between 1937 and 1945 to allow Stuart full reign. (Mei Yi-pao was acting president and acting chancellor of the refugee university in Chengtu from 1942 to 1946.) But K'ung's reputation had become so questionable that Stuart was forced to sever his own personal ties with the man and withdraw support of him as chancellor.[139] Stuart's appointment as ambassador in July 1946 brought about his and K'ung's resignations and reopened the question of who would head the university.

An administrative committee with Lu Chih-wei as chairman took charge in 1946, but both the trustees and faculty pressed for finding a full time replacement. Previously the trustees were opposed to following the Chinese constitution, but in 1947, in response to suggestions from the field, they recommended Lu as their first choice for the chancellorship. Furthermore they agreed to abide by the Chinese definition of the position. But when Stuart balked at the possibility of Lu's selection, the trustees deemed it wise not to "go into technicalities at this time." Instead they approved Stuart's recommendation of William Adolph, professor of chemistry, as acting president. Lu's position for the next two years remained anomalous. During Adolph's presidency he even stopped attending meetings of the faculty executive committee.[140] When Adolph resigned in July 1948, an administrative committee again took over, with Lu as chairman and Dwight Edwards (who moved into Stuart's house) as executive secretary.

Stuart's ambivalence on the Chinese leadership continued throughout the 1940s and came to an end only with the Communist takeover. Outwardly, he told the trustees he was reluctant to continue advising the Yenching group from his ambassadorial post in Nanking because he feared his influence interfered with "those who are carrying on" and prevented their "accepting responsibility for what they ought to be doing themselves." In 1948, when he fully expected that President Truman would lose the election and that he would be replaced as ambassador, he spoke of returning to America to help in the financial campaign for the China colleges with no intention of returning to Yenching for fear that he would "simply be in the way."[141] But inwardly he felt that the institution had been largely his own creation, and that a strong Western leadership was a witness to the university's international character. Stuart appeared suspicious of entrusting the real headship to any Chinese person, at least to anyone not of his own choosing. Whenever Lu's candidacy for the headship arose, Stuart readily recognized him as an obvious choice. But each time, Stuart also pointed out Lu's weaknesses, such as his "whimsical, temperamental disposition" and, even as late as March 1949, his lack of fitness for routine administration and money raising qualifications.[142]

Despite Stuart's reservations many faculty and students regarded Lu as the head of the university after the war.[143] After the Communist takeover the question of the authority for Lu's appointment again arose. In February 1949 the managers took it upon themselves to appoint him head (hsiao-chang), with no English equivalent.[144] The trustees were then asked to confirm the appointment but they pointed out that the managers' action followed the Chinese constitution and thereby rendered superfluous any action in New York. In the end they decided to concur in Lu's election.[145] Lu himself refused to regard the managers' appointment as authoritative and waited instead for authorization from the new government. His headship after 1949 was received with wide acclaim by all Chinese and Westerners.[146] Stuart finally relinquished the presidency in his own mind only after Lu had already served for several months. He indicated this in handwritten postscript appended to his last official communication to the trustees regarding the administration of Yenching. The postscript read, "I have urged that C. W. Luh be called 'President' as the English equivalent of *hsiao-chang* and that the term 'Chancellor' be discontinued."[147]

In September 1929 at the formal opening of Yenching University, Franklin H. Warner, chairman of the trustees, presented to Chancellor Wu Lei-ch'uan a golden key. Wu interpreted the ceremony to mean the "university was now to be the responsibility and under the control of the Chinese."[148] But Dwight Edwards, then a member of the board of managers, gave a quite different interpretation of the exchange, saying it merely symbolized the "formal opening of the buildings for university purposes."[149] Howard Galt's version of the ceremony was more ambiguous, saying the key ceremony "symbolized the transfer of the buildings, constructed largely through the efforts of the Trustees in securing the funds, to the academic head [meaning only Wu] of the university, and the buildings were declared formally open for the purposes of the university."[150] For the next twenty years, largely under Stuart's dominating influence, the trustees' final authority in financial and administrative matters was hardly challenged. The ambiguities over the meaning of making Yenching Chinese remained largely unresolved. But soon after the Communists came to power the ambiguities were erased, and the idea of being Chinese was absorbed into Mao Tse-tung's emerging views on education and intercultural relations. Western interpretations of the issue soon became irrelevant.

5

The Radicalization of a
Student Elite

The students legitimated the university. They were its reason for existence. Through them Christianity and liberal arts would spread and
contribute to China's national salvation. After providing them with the
tools of a college education and inspiring them with the ideals of service
and self-sacrifice, the faculty hoped the students would then fan out into
society, apply their skills and inspire patriotic feeling and the spirit of
sacrifice among the Chinese people. The students were the voice of
nationalism, which Yenching as a Western style institution could
ignore only at its peril. It was student openness to Christianity in the
years of the New Culture movement that inspired the Life Fellowship to
believe it was possible to pursue evangelical purposes and academic
excellence at the same time. It was the sharpening of militant nationalism during and after the Anti-Christian movement that forced Stuart
and his colleagues to see that evangelical purposes were no longer possible. Furthermore student protest in the 1930s, expressed as anti-Japanese nationalism, forced Yenching leaders to see that academic excellence was not enough, that education's contribution to national salvation
(*chiao-yü chiu-kuo*) was much smaller than the university's founders
had earlier believed. Finally, after World War Two, the students articulated the appeal and rationale of the emerging Communist movement

that forced Yenching educators to alter drastically their whole understanding of Sino-Western relations.

As with the student movement nationally, student protest at Yenching
varied widely in expression, from mild editorial attacks on the university
or the government to the more extreme forms of student strikes which
disrupted all of university life for weeks on end.[1] One can chart this
evolving protest as it passed through three major phases: from anti-
Japanese hostility beginning with the May Fourth movement (1919);
to the more radical critique of political movements in the December
Ninth movement (1935); to the post World War Two dissatisfaction
that was fired as much with anti-American sentiment as the fear of a
rehabilitated Japan. Behind these changing phases of protest, however,
are questions about the students that illustrate Yenching's position in
Chinese society during the Republican years. First, what were the socio-
economic origins of the students, and what about the "aristocratic" atmosphere of the campus? How did these factors affect patriotic consciousness? Second, what about student employment after graduation? What
about job suitability and the problems the students faced in applying
liberal arts training to their perceived needs of the Republican years?
Third, what were the themes in organized student protest, and how did
they influence student attitudes toward the university and Sino-Western
relations? Finally, what were the faculty responses to student protest?
What effect did it have on their attitudes toward the university?

Student Origins and the Aristocratic Image

One common criticism of Yenching, especially after its move to the
new campus in 1926, was its aristocratic image. Critics both inside and
outside the university sometimes referred to it as a "school for the
aristocracy" (*kuei-tus hsüeh-hsiao*). This image was tied to the beautiful
campus and to its location in the gardens of former imperial rulers. It
was also connected with the social backgrounds of the students, the high
cost of tuition, and a certain exclusiveness in terms of the predominantly
Christian middle schools from which they came.

At the formal dedication of the new campus in 1929 Yen Hui-ch'ing,
chairman of the board of managers, opened the ceremonies by comparing Yenching's experience to that of Cinderella. After having passed
through seven years of poverty on the K'uei-chia-ch'ang campus just
inside the city walls, Yenching had by then experienced three years of

palatial life with its magnificent set of buildings on the Haitien campus. Chang Po-ling, president of Nankai University in Tientsin and close friend of Stuart, seized the metaphor in his otherwise congratulatory comments and reminded those attending the dedication ceremonies that princes and princesses like Cinderella "live in luxury without any regard for the common people." He warned, "May that never be true of those who live in these palaces."[2] Faculty and student sensitivity to this warning was keen because if the university became only a school for the elite, then the goal of training students to serve and identify with the common people was in jeopardy. Wealth and elitism ran counter to the whole spirit of twentieth century patriotism in a country as poor as China, to say nothing of the spirit of the social gospel in the Life Fellowship. This sensitivity to the charge may also be due to their belief that Yenching was not that much different from other Chinese colleges and universities, whose students also faced insoluble problems in translating their patriotic ideals into practical contributions. In Yenching eyes the critics had no monopoly on patriotic virtues. To a certain extent both were right.

Figures on the social origins of students (Table 5) show that roughly one third of the student body in the 1930s came from families whose fathers were businessmen of one sort or another. By contrast less than one tenth of the students came from working class families. But the proportion of Yenching students with business and working class backgrounds differed little from the average of the other thirty-nine colleges in China as a whole in 1933.[3] Yenching students may have come largely from comparatively wealthy families, but such was the case for most college students all over China.

Yenching's high cost of tuition may be a more accurate basis for the image of the university as an aristocratic school. From 1927 to 1937 tuition more than doubled from $50.00 to $110.00 per year. Over the same period dormitory fees stayed the same, $40.00.[4] By comparison with other universities, Yenching's fees were generally higher. In 1930, for example, tuition at Peita was $40.00 and at Tsinghua $20.00. During the inflationary crisis after the war tuition fees climbed in December 1947 to LC $2,500,000 and total expenses to more than LC $4,500,000. Such an increase, of course, affected all students, regardless of wealth, but it bore down particularly hard on those from poorer homes.[5] Yenching's yearly cost per student was also high. In 1929 it was LC $1,212. Though not as high as Peking Union Medical College (reportedly

Table 5. Origins of Yenching Students According to Parental Vocations

Category	1923[a] Number	Per cent		1930[b] Number	Per cent		1936[c] Number	Per cent
Business		26.8			34.8			31.8
Business	22		Commerce	255		Commerce	222	
			Banking	16		Banking	28	
			Industry	12		Industry	13	
Professional		30.9			24.8			23.3
Education	10		Education	102		Education	86	
Medicine	6		Medicine	38		Medicine	54	
Ministers	8		Church	26		Church	17	
Other church workers	1		Social Service	13		Social Service	6	
Editors	1		Communications	22		Communications	22	
						Law	6	
						Journalism	4	
Government		18.3			12.8			18.1
Government	14		Government	95		Government	121	
Military	1		Military	9		Postal	10	
						Military	17	
Working class		8.5			9.4			7.9
Agriculture	7		Agriculture	67		Agriculture	42	
			Workers	9		Workers	23	
Other	12	15.5			18.2			18.9
			Retired	20		Retired	41	
			Deceased	5		Deceased	38	
			No report	120		No report	79	
Total	82			809			826	

Note: Main categories on left of table represent clusters of professions from the various sources to provide a basis for meaningful comparison. Other subcategories represent the actual terms used in the original source.

[a] Report of Stuart to the Board of Trustees, April 13, 1923, AP. These figures are for the eighty-two members of the freshman class in the men's college.
[b] PSYTI (1931), 330.
[c] PSYTI (1937), 186.

$20,741), Fukien United College ($2,385), Tsinghua ($1,742), or Sun Yat-sen University ($1,319), it was nevertheless considerably higher than the average for the other Christian colleges and almost twice the $693 average for all institutions of higher learning.[6]

To offset this high cost the university organized financial aid programs, but their effect on the accessibility of poorer students to the university varied over time. One student claimed in 1935 that during his four years of college he had received no help from his parents, but like many others in his situation he was able to graduate through a combination of scholarships, student work programs, and special room accommodations for poor students in the attics of dormitories.[7] Other reports indicate that financial aid programs were more limited. In 1923, for example, only six out of eighty-two applicants were granted some form of scholarship aid. That year a work study program was organized for teaching in primary and middle schools near the university. Teaching Chinese to foreigners, typing, copying, working in the student cooperative store and library, and serving as gardeners, household servants, messengers, and as shopping guides for foreigners were also forms of employment. But precise figures are lacking on the number of students availing themselves of these opportunities. In the early years on the new site the huge job of landscaping provided more student employment, but by 1930 that job was completed. In 1928 only twelve out of a total student enrollment of 700 had received scholarships. Student loans were also available but were limited to sophomores and above.[8] In 1939 Stuart increased financial aid to students cut off from their homes due to the Japanese occupation. He persuaded the trustees to finance a scholarship program that benefited more than 300 students.[9] During four years as a refugee university at Chengtu, 1942–1946, most students were without financial sources of their own, and Mei Yi-pao, acting president, adopted the principle of "seeing the student through college as long as he or she deserved a college education." Scholarships and relief came from the university itself, the International Student Relief Committee, and the ministry of education in Chungking which provided the costs of food for all students from occupied territory.[10]

After the war university authorities strengthened the student aid program. The war had destroyed the livelihood of many students' families, with near poverty often the result, and the effects on study were potentially crippling. Of the 436 students enrolled on the Yenching campus at Haitien in 1946, sixty-nine received outright grants, though forty-two of them were tuition only. In addition, work study programs provided jobs for 108 students in repair work, staffing, and service jobs. Some students worked as much as forty hours per week.[11] Drawn together by their common hardship, Yenching students in 1947 organized the Poor

Students Self-Help Association to find jobs and provide direct aid, however small, to the neediest cases. In December 1948 the university itself administered scholarships and loans benefiting 45 percent of the total student body.[12] After 1949 up to 50 percent of student food costs were borne by the new government, though tuition was rising even then. In short, efforts to provide student aid to offset the high costs of tuition before the late 1940s were meager and sporadic, and it was hard to dismiss the charges of aristocracy.

The aristocratic image was also connected with Yenching's low student-faculty ratios. Low ratios were seen as marks of quality education in America, and Yenching, eager to use American standards, set an average ratio of about 3:1. This ratio remained stable from the 1920s until the war with Japan. In fat years the trustees were as proud of the ratio as was the university, but after the war when funds were tight, they criticized Yenching administrators for such low ratios. Requests from the field for more money to buy coal for winter heating were hardly justified, the trustees pointed out, when Yenching's student-faculty ratio was 2.9:1, compared to Nanking University's 4.3:1 and the average for all Christian colleges 6.5:1.[13]

Reinforcing this elitist image was the kind of schools from which the entering freshman class was selected. Here the discrimination was more religious than economic. Applicants were solicited from three major sources, the university's own preparatory school (yü-k'e), whose checkered existence came to an end in 1929, specially accredited Christian middle schools, and public secondary schools. The accredited schools originally were limited to those managed by the four constituent mission boards of the university, but they later included other Christian schools and even some private schools. In 1933 Yenching recognized thirty-eight such schools located in nine different provinces in China and one in Java.[14] Prior to Yenching's registration with the government in 1928, graduates from the accredited schools were exempt from taking entrance examinations and were admitted solely on recommendation. But even after registration students from these schools were tested in only two subjects, Chinese and English. All other students had to take the lengthy comprehensive examinations given in major cities throughout China.[15] Religious discrimination in admissions became more serious after 1930 when entrance to Yenching had become extremely competitive. For the academic year 1935–36, for example, only 295 students were admitted to the freshman class out of a total number of

1,487 candidates. The percentage figures for the incoming freshman class from the accredited middle schools were 81 percent in 1925, 86 percent in 1928, 68 percent in 1931, and 64 percent in 1936. Similar figures for those coming from government schools were 5 percent in 1926, 3.5 percent in 1928, 8.2 percent in 1931, and 13.0 percent in 1936.[16] This shift favoring students from nonaccredited schools was small and did little to weaken Yenching's exclusive and aristocratic image.

What many faculty and alumni have approvingly referred to as the "Yenching spirit" became for others, including some on campus, a kind of cliquishness, which may also be related to the aristocratic image. Recalling her years as a student at Yenching in the 1930s, Han Su-yin disliked the so-called Yenching spirit because she mistrusted the missionaries and the university's religious purposes. But she also felt discriminated against by her fellow students because of differences in wealth and race. She was relatively poor. She was also Eurasian and was once rudely attacked in the student weekly for dating Americans in Peiping.[17] Similarly, two of Ida Pruitt's adopted daughters attending Yenching felt snubbed because of their lower class backgrounds and regarded many of the Yenching students as elitist snobs.[18]

Employment and National Salvation

The aristocratic image based on student origins was somewhat offset by the employment patterns of Yenching graduates. Patriotic feeling and Yenching idealism steered a large number of them away from family backgrounds in commerce, banking, and industry to careers in teaching, which were hardly avenues to wealth (Table 6). While roughly one third of them came from these wealthier homes, only about one tenth chose business careers upon graduation. And while about 10 percent of them came from homes whose fathers were in education, roughly 40 percent pursued careers in teaching. This departure from the career patterns of their parents reveals the belief in the efficacy of education and the influence of Yenching educators.

That 50 percent which did not go into business or education, found jobs in other areas such as government work, religious and social work, and research and advanced study. Compared to the national average Yenching's success in placing graduates was excellent.[19] In the mid 1930s unemployment and job suitability were the big worries of college educators.[20] Surveys done by the ministry of education in 1936 indi-

The Radicalization of a Student Elite

Table 6. Vocations of Yenching Graduates

Vocation	1888–21[a]		1917–31[b]		1934–36[c]	
	Number	Percent	Number	Percent	Number	Percent
Education	133	29	490	39	–	39
Politics	19	4	113	9	–	16
Research or advanced study	41	9	154	12	–	15
Religious and social work	108	26	155	12	–	14
Business	18	4	110	9	–	8
Medicine	37	8	15	1	–	2
Journalism	–	–	15	1	–	2
Agriculture	1	–	17	1	–	–
Other	113	20	143	14	–	4
Total	449		1248		475[d]	

Sources:

[a] Sidney D. Gamble and John S. Burgess, *Peking: A Social Survey* (New York, 1921), 382. (Figures from 1888 to 1916 are for Yenching's Methodist constituent Peking University).

[b] Figures are for the vocations of all graduates from 1917 to 1931 including graduates of the college, graduate division, school of religion, short courses, and special courses. *Alumni Directory, II* December 1931, 113.

[c] Figures are only for graduates of the college and graduate school. Galt, 327.

[d] PSYTI (1937), 183.

cated that more than half of all college level graduates of 1933 and 1934, or more than 10,000 students, were still "tramping the sidewalks, unemployed, downhearted, and hopeless." And among 2,630 prospective graduates surveyed in May 1935, fewer than 600 had either found jobs or intended to continue study, leaving more than 2,000 unprovided for.[21]

But Yenching's numerical success masked deeper problems. Forty percent of the graduates may have turned to education, but questions began to arise about the efficacy of education itself. A Nanking University student phrased the problem in 1924, by asking how education could contribute to China's national salvation. How could such a small number of Chinese citizens, the students, generate political power to meet the challenges of China's external and internal humiliations? Faith in education appeared to be misplaced. Noting that middle school teachers aimed to prepare students for university education, the student asked, why university education? Answer, to get a diploma. Why a diploma? Answer, to become a middle school teacher. "Thus men revolve around education, generation after generation. Can such a merry-go-round save the country?"[22] Fu Ssu-nien, onetime chancellor of Peita, also used the circular image in 1932. Without better education there was little hope for improvement in the political situation. But bad politics in turn prevented the development of a good system of education, "on and on like a circle with no way to break out."[23]

Stuart acknowledged the difficulties facing college educators in connecting their work to the original goals of service, self-sacrifice, and national salvation. In 1936 he criticized the growth in the educational system that favored colleges at the expense of elementary and secondary education. He noted that between 1915 and 1925 the number of institutions, overall expenditures, and student enrollments for higher education had increased twenty, forty, and one hundred fold respectively. Corresponding increases for secondary schools were only five, thirteen, and eight fold, and for elementary schools the increases were a mere three, five, and four fold. Stuart saw this lopsided development as the result of "too imitative acceptance of Western models."[24] And yet he excused Yenching from this general pattern by citing the university's impressive employment record. He also felt Yenching graduates had a special contribution to make because of their idealism and sense of responsibility, the qualities he associated with the character-building purposes of the university. He was especially impressed with their performances during the war of resistance against Japan in the "primitive spot" of Yunnan Province where sixty or seventy "Yenchingians" were exhibiting the "true spirit of service."[25]

Others at Yenching, however, were less sanguine than Stuart. Mei Yi-pao doubted that Yenching had any edge on other colleges when it came to "sterling character and integrity."[26] Liu T'ing-fang, furthermore, did not take Yenching's employment record as evidence of superior education because many graduates had received their employment through "pull" and family connections, not the regular channels. Their success had little to do with the suitability of their preparation. At best, education meant service to society, but Liu noted most Yenching graduates going into teaching took jobs in Christian middle schools, which were as isolated from Chinese society as the colleges themselves.[27] Chu Yu-kuang, who taught at Yenching in 1936, was one of the few who attempted to analyze in depth the relationship between graduates of schools like Yenching and the larger problem of service to society. "Modern education," he wrote in 1932, "tends to educate men out of their native environment." By instilling a desire for "new comforts" and "new ways of living," it cultivates a "thorough disgust of existing conditions in their homes and communities," and results in a "flocking to the 'high life' in big cities." Chu argued that just as there existed a "social barrier between the educated classes and the common masses in old China, so modern education has widened the social distance between them."[28]

From Stuart's perspective the war with Japan provided Yenching graduates with one more opportunity to reveal their training and character, but other Westerners on the faculty saw the arrangements so skillfully worked out by Stuart with the Japanese authorities as reminders of the special privileges which they associated with higher education generally. In 1939 Presbyterian missionary educators at Yenching asked searchingly: "Are we encouraging [the students] to live in a dream world, to take the easy way, to escape from the struggle?" Is Christianity "becoming an unreal belief that 'God's in his Heaven all's right with the world' in the spirit of Pollyanna?" They feared that the "bitter needs" of the graduates' families would drive most of them into a "pot-boiling struggle for the greatest salaries possible" and away from the "positions of the greatest social usefulness." They ended, "Are we training builders of the New China, or a lost generation who will have no real place in the future?"[29]

Patterns of Protest

Between their arrivals on campus and their departures upon graduation the students spent an average of four years at Yenching. No four year period during the whole of Yenching's existence passed by without major political disturbances outside, which was reflected in student agitation on the inside. Each one of these tides, as they were called, created considerable anxiety at the time, but they occurred so frequently that Yenching educators, Western and Chinese alike, learned to take them in stride.

In the evolution of student protest two themes stand out. One is the resilience of the university itself to withstand the tides and quickly make up lost classes and exams in an effort to maintain academic standards and to preserve faith in the institution when the tides appeared to threaten its reason for existence. The other theme is the cumulative effect of student disruptions. It never seemed possible to return to the status quo ante. Rather than reaffirm earlier purposes after each new protest, the university leaders searched for new ones. Reflecting these seemingly contradictory trends Yenching in the late 1940s on the eve of the Communist takeover was still a flourishing institution, and yet when the revolution forced it to change its whole outlook on Sino-Western relations, most students and faculty seemed not too surprised.

Radicalization itself held different meanings at different times. During the May Fourth period it could be expressed as an attack on tradition, and in that context the Life Fellowship was radical. Being radical then was more cultural than political. But by the late 1920s, especially after the May Thirtieth incident (1925), being culturally radical was not enough. Patriotic feeling, which all students claimed to have, required political form. The belief in the efficacy of education was no longer a simple one to make, and the desire to learn from the West was no longer a unitary feeling. It was not enough to be merely an advocate of change. Questions had to be refined: which pattern of change, reform or revolution; which model, socialist Russia or capitalist America; which ideology, Marxism or Christian liberalism; whom to serve, the government in power or revolutionary movements; which national leader, Chiang Kai-shek or someone else. If the students at Yenching appear to have moved in a direction that is identified with revolutionary thought it is because they were forced to raise these kinds of questions. And the answers, in the context of liberal arts education and the political order which sustained it, did not come easily.

It was no secret among YMCA workers and Chinese educators in mission schools that radical thought had made large inroads into student circles by the early 1930s. As with intellectuals and writers generally students were searching, in Wu Yao-tsung's (an early member of the Life Fellowship and later national secretary for the YMCA) analysis, for more "comprehensive solutions to the problems of Japanese imperialism, political decay, and social and economic stagnation." In the 1920s students had been intensely interested in such social problems as "family and sex relations, illiteracy, narcotics, and the reform of certain time-worn customs." But in the 1930s the emphasis shifted to the fundamental reconstruction of society and to changes of the "whole social structure, rather than minor changes within the old framework."[30] Kiang Wen-han, YMCA secretary in Shanghai, concluded in 1937 that the attitudes of students attending Christian colleges had changed: from the "outcry for individual development" to one for a "collective struggle"; from the "worship of idealism and liberalism" to "sheer realism and authority"; and from concern for an "individual way out" to an "actual identification with the masses."[31] Students in the 1930s, in John Israel's study of student nationalism, rejected Hu Shih's—and the YMCA's—"bit by bit, drop by drop" approach to national salvation. Instead they "sought an all embracing doctrine" that would analyze China's "backwardness, ubiquitous injustice, and submission to imperialism," place them in a theoretical framework, and "prescribe a revolutionary course of action."[32] Such a trend in thought, Liu T'ing-fang noted, was inimical to the whole process of liberal arts education.[33]

When Stuart addressed the Yenching students at the opening convocation in September 1932, he was concerned with only one issue, the threat to "democratic thinking." He saw the threat coming from both the left and the right. He warned the students to be vigilant, lest both the university and "progress" in China be destroyed. By then Kuomintang agents had worked their way into student circles, but of greater concern to Stuart was the growing influence of radical thought.[34] To Stuart the popular controversies over facism and communism in the 1930s were less significant than the conflicting issues of freedom and centralism, individualism and collectivism, reform and revolution, idealism and realism. The increasing influence of radical thought in Stuart's eyes might ultimately sustain either the far left or the far right. But it could not sustain the liberal arc in the circles of intellectual debate.

Like all students in China, Yenching students were in the forefront of the patriotic tides, but their fear of being overly influenced by foreign ideas, especially after the Anti-Christian movement, may have been an added incentive for their activity.[35] Margaret Speer, dean of the women in the mid 1930s, thought that the "burden of proof rests with our students to show that they are patriotic and are not the slaves of foreigners."[36] One Yenching student served as a representative of the Peking Student Union to the national committee coordinating the nationwide strike in June 1919 following the May Fourth demonstrations. In 1920 the vice-president of the general affairs committee of the Peking Student Union and in 1921 an elected member of the executvive committee of the National Student Union were Yenching students.[37] Throughout the 1920s Yenching students participated in all patriotic activity in Peking. The December Ninth movement of 1935 was largely organized by Yenching student leaders.[38] And during the revolutionary takeover of North China in 1948–49 Yenching students received the new leadership with as much patriotic enthusiasm as the students on any other university campus.

Political outbursts on campus would ebb and flow in an adverse relationship with the effective control exercised by the government over a thirty year period. In the early 1930s when Kuomintang control over North China was at its peak, and later in that decade during the Japanese occupation, there was very little protest activity. Similarly the mid 1920s, the mid 1930s and the late 1940s were times of weak political control, when students could protest with minimal consequences. For the two academic years beginning in 1946 and 1947 at least six different strikes lasting two days or more occurred on the Yenching campus.[39] Student protest at Yenching avoided repression in part because of the university's foreign connection.

The question arises, how many Yenching students actually participated in student strikes. The number, of course, varied according to the issues and risks involved. Two very popular strikes, Patriotic Week in December 1931 protesting the Manchurian Incident and the three day "leave of absence" protesting poverty and economic chaos in November 1948, received nearly unanimous support from the student, and in the case of the former, from most of the faculty. Other strikes such as those in March and April 1936 just after the lengthy December Ninth protest, attracted only a minority and were in fact opposed by large segments of the student body who wished to return to their studies. Still other protests were somewhere in between and commanded the participation of several hundred persons. Four hundred and thirty-one students, or more than half of the total enrollment, joined a strike protesting the Japanese takeover of Suiyuan in November 1936, and three hundred students marched to Peiping protesting political repression in November 1947.[40]

The nature of Yenching student participation in protest activities can be further seen in the December Ninth movement in 1935. Outraged by Nanking's passivity and compliance in Japanese efforts to gain control over North China, more than half of the 850 students at Yenching marched to the walls of Peiping on December 9 to protest. The police prevented them from joining the demonstration with other students inside, so they returned to campus and called a university wide strike the next day. That strike lasted almost two months. Patriotic sentiment was so high that even the most timid struck class and joined student surveillance activities against expected police arrests on campus. Only a few students stole time off for study. Gradually, though, anger subsided and half the student body left campus within three weeks. Among the half that stayed, fifty joined propaganda teams that went out into the countryside. The rest maintained strike discipline on campus in accord with orders from the Peiping Student Union.[41]

In their general analyses of student protest, two Yenching historians, Dwight Edwards and Howard Galt, have emphasized the leadership role of the Communist students. But their interpretations are misleading. It appears that a small group of Communists had been active on campus since the late 1920s, but none of the December Ninth strike leaders were Communist.[42] Chang Chao-lin, president of the student body, Ch'en Han-po, editor of the weekly, and Wang Ju-mei (Huang Hua), chairman of the executive committee of the student government, were all Manchurian refugees and prior to December 1935 apparently had very little contact, if any, with the Communist underground. Prominent women leaders in the strike, Li Min and the sisters Kung P'u-sheng and Kung Wei-hang (Kung P'eng), came from established Christian homes and were still largely involved in YWCA types of activities.[43] In time, to be sure, all of them would become closely tied to the Communist movement, but that was after the strike was over.

Strikes were the most dramatic but not the only expression of student unrest. In their weekly newspaper student leaders published attacks on the university, after which the administration would occasionally threaten to withdraw the university's subsidy for the paper.[44] The big character poster (ta-tzu pao), which consumed hundreds of square feet of paper and had the advantage of sparing both students and faculty the risk of losing face in a direct verbal confrontation, was another popular form of protest. Finally, there were numerous little campaigns to raise money and supplies, and even to make steel helmets, in support of Chinese military resistance to Japan in the 1930s. Each one of these combined careful coordination, which the students handled with a flourish, and a sense of personal sacrifice in joining the masses and soldiers in the cause of anti-Japanese patriotism. Money for these campaigns was raised by personal contributions, fasting, and the selling of personal belongings.[45]

Any attempt to assess the changing political attitudes of Yenching students based on their weekly (Yen-ta chou-k'an) and monthly (Yen-ta yüeh-k'an) publications must be interpreted with caution.[46] Student moods changed from year to year and defy easy generalization. Yet these publications may be regarded as important indicators of student opinion because of the connections between the editorial boards, the student government (*hsüeh-sheng tzu-chih hui*), and readership tastes. The editors of the weekly and the monthly were appointed by the student executive committee, which in turn was elected by the student body in the annual spring elections. One may debate how seriously the majority of students regarded the elections, but one cannot deny a certain degree of representation, especially since election rules were scrupulously observed.[47] Kuomintang agents on campus, especially in the early 1930s and the late 1940s, provided a check on attempts by radical leaders to gain control and vice versa. Any blatant violation of their sensibilities would in the course of time become self-defeating for any particular editorial policy. The radicalization of student thinking, as seen in student publications, clusters around four issues: the role of intellectuals in national salvation; their changing perceptions of the masses; their growing resentment of foreign influence; and the question of civil rights.

The Role of Intellectuals. Both students and faculty at Yenching were transitional and marginal figures, standing "in between" the end of the imperial Confucian and the beginning of the Communist political orders. The University was seeded and nourished in this fluid environment, but it grew only so long as its Chinese members turned to the West for their ideas and inspiration. Indeed Western education marked them as a special kind of elite and threatened to make them "rootless cosmopolitans," alienated and separated from the masses and society whom their education was training them to serve. As Joseph Levenson has stated, "In the old society there was just the natural distance (divisive, but domestic) between literate and peasants." But now on the "two sides of the great divide, there was the Western(ized) and Chinese."[48] Self-conscious of their privileged status, Yenching students tried to root themselves more firmly in their Chinese context. It was an elusive task.

In the 1920s students and faculty converged in their political assessments. Both gave the patriotic movements of these years their open support, and both believed for the most part that their greatest contribution to national salvation was first to educate themselves properly in an institution such as Yenching before fanning out into society. By the mid 1930s, however, this consensus had begun to fall apart. Student writings stress repeatedly the necessity of replacing not just "improving" the social order.[49] The imperative, one student wrote in the monthly in 1930, was to "abolish the present system and bring in a new social system. This is the only way out."[50]

At the end of the December Ninth strike student articles in the weekly were especially hostile to the faculty's insistence on returning to classes as usual. At the Monday morning Sun Yat-sen assembly gathering of all faculty and students in early February, Acting Chancellor Lu Chih-wei merely announced classes would resume and refused to give any consideration to "crisis education," which student leaders wanted in place of the regular courses.[51] After the resumption of classes the issue of "crisis education" had become such a hot issue that even the faculty talked very little about anything else. When another foreign professor opened his class without a word about the strike, announced the date of the final exam to be made up, and then proceeded to lecture as if nothing had happened, the student editors of the weekly were furious. Another Chinese professor provoked their wrath when he dismissed "crisis education" as nothing more than a student's dream. Professor Liu Chieh in the department of Chinese was severely reprimanded by the weekly for insisting that General Sung Che-yüan had not intentionally helped the Japanese in North China and for urging students to quietly return to their studies.[52] One Yenching student attacked his classmates who planned for careers in government or in business upon graduation. They ignored the fundamental need to liberate the masses and only added to China's deeper colonization. He sneered at those seeking work as writers, whose works the "colonizers" would be more than willing to distribute.[53]

In ignoring these student leaders' demands the faculty may have reflected considerable sentiment among other students. Margaret Speer saw the demand for emergency training as "merely a maneuver to try and keep us from getting back to work. I don't believe there are two dozen Yenching students who want to follow these particular leaders, but they are very clever politicians."[54] One Yenching alumnus saw these demands as meaningless jabs at an educational pattern which the radicals were as much a part of as the more conservative students. They would spend a "night, crowded in freight trains like sardines in tins, on their way to petition the government on national problems in the name of patriotism," but upon graduation would refuse to render "useful service in the interior," preferring instead to reside in the large cities, even if it meant unemployment.[55]

However hypocritical student protest may have appeared to some students and faculty in the 1920s and early 1930s, it does seem clear that the December Ninth movement created a definite watershed in thinking on the campus. After that the growing separation between the political sentiments among student leaders and the basic assumptions of senior faculty and university administrators increased. This separation was portrayed in a short piece entitled "The Professor's Tragedy" appearing in the weekly. In the sketch the professor was seen as being extremely well informed on subjects ranging from Chuang-tzu's natural philosophy to Hegel's arguments on idealism, to new inventions in earth moving. He was also fluent in four languages, and so erudite—"his learning is a library room encompassing the 10,000 things"—that a recent visit to the Soviet Union was to him nothing more than a "small ship on a big ocean." Having attained the dream of his youth ("learning is power") the professor, nonetheless, was a lonely figure because of his separation from the "realities of Chinese life." In the heat of the December Ninth movement, according to the article, the professor had momentarily identified with the students, but he was unable to join them in their actions. His explanation: "The truth is, all things that exist have their reason. Resistance would be a waste of effort. We can't take things too seriously."

Recalling his own patriotic activities at the time of the Shantung question in 1919, the professor expressed sympathy with the students clustered about him, but he also warned, "Everyone's objectives must be pure and not excessive . . . I hope you won't be used by the party." A student objected, "No one can be used by another. If the objective is the same everyone can rise up and proceed together! As for May Four destroying the old customs and teachings, no one today regards that to be a mistake, outside of a few older ones." The professor's face got red, but trained in patience, he merely lifted his pipe, puffed on it, and then said, "Of course, I understand very well. Perhaps our interpretations aren't the same just now." Whereupon a student quickly joined in, "That's right, professor! Our interpretations aren't the same. The professor has a family, his position in society, and he is older." At this the professor appeared injured as if from an electric shock. "Really?" he asked, "has my blood become completely cold?" The article ended, "After giving the student's doubt a twist in his own mind, he got up nervously. But his manner was set and cold, and on the surface he gave not the slightest trace of suffering. In fact he gave a little laugh. But from his laugh we sense the kind of tragedy that comes with the passing of an age."[56]

The generation gap found further expression in the late 1940s in articles commemorating the May Fourth movement. Both faculty and students could agree that the movement had been a major turning point in Chinese history. But student writers drew sharp lines between the "old" and the "new" May Four. The old May Four generation, represented by Mei Yi-pao of the administration, largely reminisced and concluded the "results were very satisfactory."[57] A younger faculty member, Yen Ching-yüeh ('28), was no less appreciative of May Four and the successive student movements that kept alive the goals of national salvation. Formal education since May Four had helped students to sort through the contradictions between the new ideas and the old values, between their experiences as youth and the continuing ties with their families. It made them self-conscious and self-confident at the same time. But the kind of education linked with the May Fourth movement also generated confusion because it led to problems in unemployment and misemployment. There was too much emphasis, Yen thought, on book learning and the seeking of high status jobs, which the spirit of the new May Four would help to correct.[58] The apologists for the new May Four resolved to carry out the "promises which the old May Four failed to fulfill." The old May Four had merely replaced tradition with "foreign capitalism and civilization," which led only to confusion in attempts to create a new system of thought. With capitalism had come individualism, whose adherents refused to cooperate with the masses. The new May Four generation would avoid those errors by uniting thought with action, by abandoning individualism for collectivism, and by trying to stop the civil war then raging between the Communists and Nationalists.[59] In the eyes of Yenching radicals, Hu Shih, the epitome of the old May Four, behaved "like a man with a Chinese body but an American brain" when he criticized student radicals at Peita in the late 1940s.[60] The lesson for Yenching professors, who were identified with Hu, was clear.

This growing conflict over the role intellectuals should play in society was also evident in the kinds of heroes the youth were expected to emulate. The writer-poet Hsieh Ping Hsin ('23), was a product of the May Fourth period and by the mid 1930s a respected member of the Yenching faculty, but she chose a radical figure as the heroine in a short story entitled "My Student," presumably a Yenching student. The woman in the story had abandoned her wealthy background to take up a life of toil and sacrifice in Southwest China. Born in Shanghai, raised in Australia where her father was ambassador, educated in a college and married to a classmate, the heroine had moved to Yunnan during the war, bore a family of three children, learned to work with her hands, and in a moment of crisis had donated large quantities of her own blood to a friend. Her depleted supply in turn weakened her body and she contracted an incurable disease, from which she died while pregnant with the fourth child.[61] The significance here is that the heroine had become the revolutionary figure capable of living in spartan austerity, and not the successful professional breathing into the government or business or even education system the breath of Christian influence, which it was hoped would somehow benefit China.

It is impossible to draw hard and fast lines between these generations at Yenching. Early graduates like social worker Chang Hung-chün ('20), the playwright Hsiung Fo-hsi ('23), and mass education worker Ch'ü Shih-ying ('22), alternated between teaching at Yenching and working with rural reconstruction projects in the 1930s. But these were a minority of the faculty. Most of the faculty of the May Fourth generation were reluctant to rethink seriously their commitment to education or to consider leaving the security of their jobs. And yet when pressured to do so after the Communist takeover, they apparently offered little resistance.

A brief look at another group, the board of managers, shows more clearly than the faculty, how student leadership after the mid 1920s departed from what the founders had hoped the university would help produce. The managers, to be sure, were not intellectuals in the sense the Yenching faculty were, and yet they did embody a Christian ideal that Stuart especially had in mind for the students. As a group they were older than the faculty and more closely bound to the political order in which the university was conceived and in which Sino-Western relations flourished most easily. Not inclined to intellectual debates, these men and women projected a kind of Christian activist ideal. Among them were prominent officials in the Nationalist government. The Chinese managers were cosmopolitan, fluent in English (in which they conducted their meetings), and comfortable with Westerners. They seemed almost as much at home in New York, where some retired after 1949, as in Peiping or Nanking. Most of them had strong ties with the YMCA and YWCA and were the kinds of Christians featured in missionary literature. They practiced a pious and individualistic Chirstianity which probed social questions no more deeply than Chiang K'ai-shek's hollow New Life movement (1934–37). One could observe their lives and scarcely know that the Anti-Christian movement had occurred or that Christianity had by the mid 1930s lost most of its social appeal. As patriots they joined Stuart in wresting greater control over the university from the trustees in New York. But even a Chinese controlled Yenching still followed the Western model. Making Yenching Chinese for them was predominantly a racial and geographical, not a political, problem. The managers were ill equipped to handle the concept of revolution, and they had much to lose when it did occur. To Yenching student leaders in the 1930s and 1940s the board epitomized the bankruptcy of the gradualist approach to national salvation.

The students found it difficult to translate political ideals into establishment careers. They had, as John Israel states, become "psychologically and socially displaced persons." In the words of Ma Chi-wei, the hero in *Season of the Stranger* by Stephen Becker (who taught English at Yenching and Tsinghua 1947–49), the students were known as troublemakers and young radicals in college days, but after graduation they became the "bankers and engineers and customs officials, the teachers and the merchants . . . who think only of the troubles of their group." Wen I-to, the famous poet who had taught at Yenching, and who was murdered by Nationalist police in 1946, was one of the few, in Ma's eyes, who represented more than "his profession and more than himself. Wen I-to is dead for that reason. There will be no more like him. It is too late. One way or another, the teachers have had to make the decision, and they have all decided. I do not judge them harshly. But there will be no heroes among your [teacher] colleagues."[62]

The Discovery of the Masses. Yenching student writings from the early 1920s to 1948, and then of course after the turnover, paid steady attention to the Chinese masses. But their perceptions changed from one of benevolence to one of respect for the role the masses could play in China's national salvation.

From the very beginning Yenching students were involved in projects with the masses. Swept up in the enthusiasm of the May Fourth activities in the summer of 1919, students in the men's college conducted an open air school in the shade of trees. With the onset of winter they began to build their own school for the masses (*p'ing-min hsüeh-hsiao*). By 1921 they had raised LC $1,500, which was equivalent to

about forty annual tuition payments, and constructed a building on the
Yenching campus. A staff of twenty organized the school, complete with
president, vice-president, treasurer, publicity chairman, dean of the faculty, and teachers. Classes included the teaching of the phonetic alpha-
bet, health, math, writing, drawing, manual work, and singing. Peak
enrollment for the school was seventy. Future plans called for enlargement of the school rooms, a popular library aimed primarily at students'
parents, a course in manual training, and a course in Chinese military
techniques.[63]

Students in the women's college also sponsored mass education projects. In addition to operating a half-day school in 1921, they opened up
a refuge near Paotingfu, southwest of Peking, for 218 girl victims of
famine. The district magistrate and the local gentry made two temples
available, while the refuge was managed by two women students, Chang
Yün-yü and Lan Jui-hsien, with assistance from other students who
came in shifts every two weeks. The girls were given food, shelter, and
oral instruction in the Bible, geography, arithmetic, and hygiene. They
were also taught the phonetic script, singing, games, and sewing. The
project lasted from January to August. Funds were raised in the college
with proceeds from dramatic productions, followed by larger donations
from American friends, including a gift of $250 from Wellesley
College.[64] Student interest in similar educational projects over the next
thirty years was channeled through special subcommittees of the student
government and the Yenta Christian Fellowship.

The university administration also had an interest in the countryside.
Protestant missionaries had worked in villages for several decades in
medicine and education. Unlike the Bible thumping evangelist who saw
rural China only as a sea of unsaved souls, they recognized fundamental
problems that required more than religious solutions. One of Stuart's first
moves as Yenching's new president in 1919 was to establish a department of agriculture. But agriculture never was a successful subject at
Yenching. Most students in the department enrolled in the short course
program and often failed to complete even one year of study. They were
never more than a small fraction of the total student body. In 1931 only
seventeen alumni were listed for the department for the whole of its
existence. Other agricultural programs at Nanking and Lingnan were
more impressive, but even there vast discrepancies existed between the
content of agricultural education and the realities of rural life. Chang Fu-
liang, who was a leading figure in rural reconstruction in the 1930s,

claimed that students trained in Western techniques and measured by Western standards were simply unprepared for work in the countryside.[65]

The department of sociology at Yenching also organized an experiment station in the nearby town of Ch'ing-ho in 1928. It provided an opportunity for onsite training in rural problems. It also experimented with new varieties of seeds, the improvement of crop cultivation, new techniques for wool weaving, rural cooperatives, and mass education. In the area of public health it started a program of disease prevention, undertook a program of midwifery, and later operated a dispensary service with resident nurses and a part time physician.[66]

In 1935 Ch'ing-ho was eclipsed by Yenching's involvement in the North China Council for Rural Reconstruction, organized by Stuart, among others, and financed largely by the Rockefeller Foundation. By that time Yenching had, in Galt's words, gone rural minded. Stuart hoped this "awakening concern over rural reconstruction" would improve the "moral and spiritual welfare of our students" and that the "spirit which has inspired the Mass Education Movement" would "permeate all of our academic life and give dynamic quality to the concept of service which is enshrined in our motto."[67] Combining field work with theoretical training, the Rural Reconstruction Institute at Yenching sent students and professors to observe, to research, and to help in the administration of projects at Wen-shang hsien and Tsining in Shantung and at Ting-hsien in Hopei between 1934 and 1937. It also added courses in rural education, rural sociology, rural cooperatives, the rural economy in modern Europe, comparative rural movements, and local government to the curriculum in the college of public affairs. In September 1936 the college reported that forty students and faculty from Yenching were either serving permanently on project staffs (14), collecting thesis materials (8), training in field work (7), or had visited the projects (11). Though the number involved in all projects at any one time amounted to only a small fraction of the total student body and graduates, the spirit of rural reconstruction appeared to give university administrators a new, if brief, sense of direction.[68] But in all these manifestations of rural consciousness the masses were still seen largely as the objects of philanthropy.

Another group turned to the masses out of their search for cultural identity. This effort was headed by Ku Chieh-kang, who taught history at Yenching and was famous for his pioneering work in Chinese folklore. Ku was quite popular among radical students and was known in the 1920s for his support of the various "go to the people" movements, which had begun soon after the May Fourth movement. Having rejected the Confucian tradition, Ku Chieh-kang turned to the masses in his attempts to reconstruct a past, "consistent with his will to retain a Chinese identity for twentieth century China." He believed that if "Good Men wish to do their best, then they ought to leave the filthy, righteous world of Peking, and go to the people, organizing education . . . Society has no hope of being reformed unless . . . everyone desires to go into each and every village to wear the villagers' simple clothing, eat their coarse food, and make special efforts to educate the people." But Ku never joined in rural reconstruction projects, nor did he give more than lip service to mass education. The masses to him were an inspiration, but his interest remained largely academic and patronizing. In the 1930s Ku was criticized for regarding the masses as objects of study, of nostalgia and sentimentalism, and for overlooking the "cruel aspects of an old society which ultimately had to be acknowledged as one's own source of origin." Unlike Lu Hsun who found tragedy and pathos in which he himself was deeply involved, Ku Chieh-kang and his students, the critics charged, found only data.[69] Despite these shortcomings Ku's works later became useful to the Communists.

Nearer home, one student presented a lengthy eulogy of one of Yenching's laborers, Lao Chang, a janitor of the Wang Residence Hall. The student reported a conversation with the forgotten old man lying on his deathbed. Lao Chang had held the lowest position, received the lowest pay, and yet had worked the longest of any person in the university. His wife was a servant for one of the faculty. Both were resigned to their inferior positions in society, but toward the end of the conversation the student asked him about the future, to which the dying man replied, "It is too late for me, but my son will certainly not let them make him into a slave! Certainly not!"[70] The exchange reported here is contrived and the student's attitude patronizing, but unlike the rural reconstructionists, the fate of the masses is viewed with mounting anger.

In addition to the views of the philanthropists and folklorists, there emerged a third approach, which was articulated by Yenching student writers in the 1930s and was similar to Mao Tse-tung's view of the masses as the basis of revolutionary change. These students dismissed the social activism of the rural reconstructionists and stressed the importance of revolutionary politics. During the December Ninth strike a group of about fifty Yenching students went to the town of Ku-an some thirty miles south of Peking for training in mass mobilization. The "fragments" of their experiences were printed in the weekly testifying to the "spirit of warmth and resolve" of the liberation movement, to the "opening of one's eyes and facing the dark reality," and to the realization that the "village . . . hid and held great power." The students had taken a "sacred oath," which read, "We deeply resolve to spread propaganda, to fear no obstacle, to spare no sacrifice, and to train and organize the masses. Until we reach our objective we swear not to return to school." Their resolve was slightly marred by the fact that most of the countryside venturers were back in school a month later.[71]

Student leaders launched an active campaign in the weekly in the spring of 1936 to discredit rural reconstruction. They approached the subject with an analytic rigor that surpassed the university's official reports on the subject. Their major objections were the snail-like pace of reconstruction, the government's obstructive tactics, the threat from Japan, which could quickly wipe out all the progress made thus far, and the superficiality of the reconstruction concept. Nothing less than China's physical and spiritual existence was at stake. The problem of mass education, they argued, was not the removal of illiteracy, which might only strengthen the hands of those who had "the power and money to maintain the social order." Rather it was making the masses understand the "reasons for their lack of food and clothing" and the nature of the economic relationships that were holding the villages together. The student critics were incensed by the reconstructionists' faith in the Rockefeller Foundation, which got its money from the selling of products in China. They insisted on "beginning from the beginning" with a set of questions that no one could ignore in the discussion of rural China. What about the unequal distribution of land and wealth; the corruption of the Nanking government; its dependence on landlord support; and its attempts to destroy the Communists? Taking these realities into consideration, one simply could not talk about reconstruction. Rural reconstruction, they concluded, was simply a dead end road.[72]

Yenching students remained interested in the masses during and after the Japanese occupation, but apart from the few who joined guerrilla activity against the Japanese or went directly to Yenan to work, their interest remained largely academic.[73] Many undergraduate and master's theses were written on rural problems in the college of public affairs in the late 1920s and the 1930s.[74] But after the war rural reconstruction projects were at a standstill, and any interest in rural problems was largely confined to the various relief efforts in the impoverished communities around the campus. Increasingly the concern with the masses came to mean support for the Communist side in the civil war.

Resentment of Foreign Influence. Japan was the central focus of student nationalism for more than a quarter of a century after the May Fourth period, and Yenching was no exception. The hostility directed against Japan was an expression of defensiveness the students felt about China's political impotence. Any nation daily reminding patriotic Chinese after World War One of their helplessness could have served as the object of attack equally well. Whether Chinese students possessed peculiar weaknesses and social inhibitions which made them prone to antiforeign outbursts, as Stuart once suggested, is a moot question.[75] Antiforeign hostility was discriminating and was not necessarily the mark of being radical. In fact foreign ideas, through the spread of Marxism-Leninism, could help articulate radical sentiments, and Westerners like the journalist Edgar Snow would become personal friends of Mao Tse-tung. Yenching was increasingly resented in the minds of student leaders because its Western associations were identified with those parts of the Western presence that were hurtful to China.

These changing attitudes among student leaders can be traced in their writings about Stuart and the growing American association in the 1930s and 1940s with the Nationalist government, especially after Stuart became ambassador. In the early years Yenching students deferred to him in almost every area of university life. He touched deeply the lives of hundreds of students through performing baptisms and marriage ceremonies, through personal counseling, and through helping them secure scholarships, find jobs, and escape the police. Even in 1936 the executive committee of the student government, which had just conducted the most threatening strike in Yenching's history, praised Stuart on his sixtieth birthday as a model for students to imitate.[76]

But support for Stuart and for his kind of internationalism waned after that. After 1937 Stuart clamped down on student protest activity in his painstaking efforts to protect Yenching's delicate relations with the Japanese authorities. Many complied, others simply left to join resistance movements, but a few openly defied Stuart's efforts. In 1939 two Yenching freshmen attempted to assassinate Chou Tso-jen because of his cooperation with the Japanese occupation.[77] And after the war several prominent Yenching families, including Ch'en Ch'i-tien

(Gideon Ch'en), former dean of the college of public affairs, were ostracized by Yenching students because of collaboration with the Japanese during the war.[78] Their hostility toward Stuart increased after the war when he became the American ambassador. They resented his sponsoring of Christmas dinners which were served on campus and paid for by the American embassy. For them the food was not a gift. During one of his visits to the campus in June 1948 a student reportedly threatened Stuart's life just after he had defended the current American policy of strengthening Japan.[79]

Apart from their feelings about Stuart, students were sensitive to the pervasiveness of American influence. Even before the Anti-Christian movement of 1922 had made antiforeign attacks popular, student apologists for Yenching expressed hope that the university finances would soon be handled by Chinese and not by the "people who founded the university and have no relationship with the Chinese people."[80] In 1930 the student weekly carried an article, "The Reconstruction of Yenching University," that lashed out at Western influence and charged the university with: lowering the academic standards by employing missionaries as teachers; introducing religious bias in admission policies; reducing the Chinese chancellor and deans to mere puppets of Western personalities; and discriminating against poorer students by raising tuition fees. Many such articles, according to Howard Galt, were carried by the weekly in the late 1920s and 1930s.[81]

Anti-American sentiment reached its height after the war when American marines were stationed in North China to help in the repatriation of Japanese. Though small in number, their presence and their behavior toward the Chinese people reminded the students of China's century long humiliation by the West. The most serious incident was the Peiping Rape Case of Christmas Eve 1946. In response to it Yenching students petitioned the university administration to suspend accommodations for returning American professors and their families on campus, until after the case was settled. In January they formed the Yen-ta k'ang-Mei hui, or the Yenta Resist America Society. In March and April 1947, just as the marines were preparing their departure from Peiping, a rash of incidents broke out. In one case Yenching students collected a condolence fund for the family of a boy who while playing near the West air field in Peiping was shot to death by an American soldier. In other incidents a rickshaw puller was stabbed to death by two marines in a dispute over the fare; three children were killed when a shell, thought to be a dud, exploded; and Chinese newspapermen, reporting on the departure of the marines, were ejected from the Peiping railway station by American military police. These incidents, combined with the shift in American policy toward the reconstruction of Japan and the emerging Truman Doctrine, which favored a stronger American role in the civil war, united students of varying political persuasions. They marked a turning point in Sino-Western relations at Yenching, for they showed that hostility to Americans did exist among the students, and that it could be organized.[82]

These expressions of antiforeign feeling, whether directed against Japan or the United States, were unwelcome to those who hoped Christian influence would instill the spirit of internationalism. A study done in 1933 on the correlation between exposure to Christian influences and the strengthening of international and interracial attitudes among students in the Christian colleges, including Yenching, showed little positive effect. Conducted under the auspices of the Institute of Pacific Relations, the study indicated a slight change, but nothing more than the "natural improvement due to ordinary education and maturity," and concluded that friendly contact with foreign teachers did not necessarily improve international attitudes.[83] It would be wrong to overemphasize these expressions of antiforeign sentiment among Yenching students over the years. But it would be equally mistaken to conclude that the internationalist purposes of the Life Fellowship were uppermost in their minds. When the political order sustained relations with the West, or if there appeared to be no alternative, the intercultural connection was affirmed. But when the prospect of a new political order emerged, the commitment to internationalism weakened rapidly, even among many of the Chinese faculty.

The Demand for Civil Rights. Another issue that drew student fire was the freedom to write, speak, organize, and protest without university, local police, or government interference. Many protests from the 1920s to the 1940s arose over the ill treatment and occasional death of students, both inside and outside Yenching: the sympathetic strike over the imprisonment of hundreds of students in June 1919; a strike over the death of Wei Shih-yi, a woman student at Yenching who was killed by police during the March Eighteenth (1926) demonstration; the three-day strike in March 1936 protesting the arrest of seven Yenching students for their participation in a memorial service honoring a Peiping student who had died in jail; and a sympathetic protest in 1948, coordinated with Tsinghua University and attended by an estimated 4,000 students, over the arrest of a student from T'ung Chi University (Shanghai) who was charged with attempting to injure the mayor of Shanghai.[84] Others could be mentioned. During periods of political repression Yenching students would organize vigilante groups to thwart police efforts in rounding up political suspects.

No doubt the commitment to civil rights, which was quite alien to Chinese thought in the past, had become a reality on the Yenching campus in the Republican years. And yet student protest advocating civil rights also tended to reinforce Yenching's aristocratic image. Especially was this apparent when Yenching students in March 1948 demanded that the Nanking government guarantee them the protection of civil rights, while at the same time they asked the government to pay all student fees and decrease student academic loads.[85] The demand for financial security on top of more civil rights went against the spirit of sacrifice, personal and collective, that underlay student radicalization. In the context of Chinese poverty and the increasing identification with the masses, the insistence upon having it both ways appeared hypocritical. In the end the issue of civil rights turned out to be a rather minor one, for when the Communists took over the campus in December 1948 most of the students quickly brought themselves in line with the new political guidelines, which they knew would deny them the rights they had earlier demanded.

What emerges from this limited survey of student writings is the impression of general dissatisfaction with Nationalist politics and liberal arts education. Not one article in the monthly, *Yenta yüeh-k'an,* could be interpreted as supportive of Nationalist politics, while five or six major articles in the June 1931 issue alone were supportive of revolutionary politics.[86] In the area of education only once did available issues of the *Yen-ching hsin-wen* in the 1940s carry an article explicitly defending liberal arts education, and that was by Chancellor Lu Chih-wei.[87] A survey of these student writings show a widespread usage after the late 1920s of such terms as capitalism, imperialism, social system, liberation, masses, struggle, and so on, which were used to justify revolutionary politics. At the same time there was a corresponding decrease in the use of such terms as freedom, equality, service, mutual help, adaptation, and so on, terms that Hsü Pao-ch'ien had used to capture the liberal spirit of the Life Fellowship in 1920.[88] The slogan "national salvation through study" in one student writer's eyes in the mid 1930s had become debased.[89] Despite these currents of disaffection most students continued to study hard and get along well with the faculty and administration. As late as 1947 many freshman compositions in English classes revealed a great attachment to Yenching.[90] Even the politically disaffected were not immune to the lure of the beautiful campus, warm human relationships, and the spirit of hard work and lofty idealism. Their disaffection was real but not strong enough for more than a few to leave school.

Faculty Responses

The Yenching faculty were understandably upset with the interruptions created by student protest. And yet they sympathized with the students. The recurring irony is the role of extraterritoriality, an issue which irritated students again and again but which provided the faculty with a power used repeatedly to protect political suspects and secure the release of those arrested. Lucius Porter listed the trips to the police station to free students with about as much nonchalance as quips about the weather in his line-a-day diaries. Out of sympathy more than a dozen faculty, Chinese and Western, followed the December Ninth marchers to the walls of Peiping with university vehicles to help the "most footsore and weary" return to campus after the day's twenty-mile walk in ten degree weather. The women's college faculty used their Wellesley contacts with Mme. Chiang Kai-shek, to secure the release of Yu Ju-ch'i, who was imprisoned after a march in Peking March 1947, and Lucius Porter interceded in July 1947 on behalf of students who met opposition from the local defense corps organized by the Kuomintang authorities in a village near the campus. In the latter case, as with other instances, an appreciation for face saved the day—the students were released if they kept silent while the militia shouted out their slogan, "Down with bad Communist sympathizer students."[91]

The Chinese chancellors were especially supportive. Despite the distance in temperament and age, Wu Lei-ch'uan alongside John Leighton Stuart, had led a parade of 700 to 800 students, faculty, and university officials in December 1931, after the Manchurian Incident. They marched through the principal streets of neighboring Hai-tien and Ch'eng-fu and along the main highway eastward to Tsinghua University.[92] Before then Wu had defended student protest by comparing it to the "hollow words and futile actions of their elders." By their actions, he wrote in 1927, they had destroyed the naive faith in that sort of education that understood only the "accomplishments of reading books" but which failed to "attack the problems at hand." To Wu the students' cries and actions were the "vitality of the nation," and he criticized those who would scoff at their patriotic outbursts.[93]

During the December Ninth movement Lu Chih-wei said he could not "handle the students in a detached way. I am quite in sympathy with their actions. When a pig is slaughtered, it is natural that there be some squeaking, though perfectly useless. The students are the only people that can do the squeaking." Lu's stand against periodic searches by Kuomintang police for students suspected of Communist sympathies in the late 1940s had earned for him wide respect in student circles.[94] Younger Chinese faculty who were graduates of Yenching also sided with students in the late 1940s. Hou Jen-chih, history, actually donated LC $50,000 to the Yenta Resist American Society in 1947.[95] Even the American faculty members were sympathetic to the student strike protesting the presence of American troops in China in 1947.[96]

But the faculty could also deal harshly with the students. Its executive committee reprimanded the students in January 1933 because holding mass meetings during exam time, sending threatening letters to the faculty, and picketing the deans' offices "were acts they considered to be subversive of university administration and order." They required all students registering for the next semester to "assent to the simple principle that no action passed by any organization within the University which is contrary to its administrative authority or regulations can be regarded as valid."[97] The requirement was of little use, and the faculty continued to vascillate between sympathy and anger over student protest. Occasionally outright bitterness was expressed over the trials of dealing with student protest. Margaret Speer, dean of women during the disruptive December Ninth strike, despaired in 1936 over the "yawning psychological gulf" separating the East and the West, a gulf "so deep that it can never be filled up, so wide in parts that one cannot get over it all, and almost always so wide that half one's energy is used up in bridging it."[98]

Stuart's responses to student protest were also ambiguous. He changed over time depending on how he perceived the political situation and the status of Sino-Western relations. The students furnished him with a "highly sensitized instrument with which to register the swelling intensity of Chinese nationalism."[99] When they struck over the Manchurian Incident in 1931, he joined them fully in one week of organized protest activity. He was away in the United States raising money during the traumatic two-month long December Ninth strike, and yet he followed it closely in the *New York Times*. Fearful that the strike activity might jeopardize donations to Yenching, he urged American supporters to set aside their doubts and read revolutionary history, which records that "British military officers said that if they could only suppress the students in Princeton, Yale, and Harvard, they could soon put down the revolution."[100]

Upon his return to Yenching in March 1936 Stuart attempted to reunite the faculty and students in those tense days in the wake of the strike, urging them all "not to suppress the old loyalties, but to become absorbingly interested in something so great" (such as the Japanese crisis) that the "less important things cease to dominate our minds." With characteristic diplomacy he first conceded a point to the faculty, by noting the "crudities and excesses of inexperienced, volatile, self-important youth, and the debasing of their energies to trivial or improper uses." But then he nodded approval to the students, who had "revealed a lofty idealism and a passionate loyalty to their country's cause which stands out as one of the most hopeful happenings in contemporary life." He added that "sneering at schoolboys who ought to be studying their lessons instead of meddling with national affairs becomes gratuitous when one remembers the internal disorders and external dangers which have been menacing the very life of the country and the moral and material incapacity of each rapidly shifting governmental group to remedy the situation."[101] More than one student was excused from discipline by the faculty through Stuart's intercession.[102]

The pervasive optimism of the missionary educators had for the most part succeeded in straddling the larger political issues, but occasionally it would falter. In February 1937, pressed between December Ninth and imminent Japanese control over all of North China, Stuart asked with "harassing insistence," why, apart from "sentimental attachments, plant investment, and providing a livelihood for teachers," should not the Christian colleges in China be closed? His faith in the students had carried him, almost cheerfully, through the many crises of the 1920s and early 1930s, but the weight of student dissatisfaction, combined with the failure to put Yenching on a Chinese financial base, almost shattered that faith. Desperately he asked: "Will the creative energies ever latent in the Christian faith organize—as life always does—into forms and functions adapted to the altered environment and awaken in Chinese intellectuals an equivalent for what had been achieved in earlier stages through missionary zeal?"[103] Thanks to the diversions and the new challenges of the Japanese occupation, and the internment, then the rebuilding of Yenching, and finally the ambassadorship, Stuart was spared from answering his own question for a long time. Indeed no one at Yenching after the mid 1930s could reply easily in the affirmative.

The Chinese faculty's responses to the radicalization of Yenching students ran parallel to their growing perplexity over the relationship of liberal Christianity to the political order. In the 1920s they had believed that Christianity would "contribute" to national salvation by creating a new morality. But that vision rapidly faded. In 1927 Hung Yeh wrote there "must have been thousands of Christian men and women who have lived a Christlike life of the highest standard." But these "moral and spiritual contributions have not made their mark on Chinese civilization to any degree capable of verbal presentation."[104] Liu T'ing-fang was even more discouraged. Even within the Chinese church, he decried, the ethical behavior of its members had nothing to do with Christianity. Rather it was rooted in the traditional concepts of Chinese society. When Chinese Christians repeated "Jesus loves me" and "God is love" and then pursued "selfishness and profit seeking in their affairs with men" they earned for the church the contempt of outsiders.[105] Hsü Pao-ch'ien was dismayed by the bickering and lack of commitment of the Christian students working with rural reconstruction in Li-ch'uan.[106] Reflecting on character building in the mission schools, Mei Yi-pao thought the people at Yenching were as prone to opportunism and selfishness as those in government institutions.[107]

Yenching Christians believed in service to the government and took extended leaves of absence to work for the Nationalist government: Hsü Shu-hsi, political science, as adviser to the ministry of foreign affairs; Hsü Shih-lien, sociology, as technical adviser to the ministry of industries and vice-director of the national bureau of rural reconstruction; Chang Hung-chün, social work, and others, serving as local officials in rural reconstruction efforts; and Wu Wen-tsao, sociology, Chinese adviser and member of the Allied Council in Japan in the late 1940s.[108] But Nationalist politics become so corrupt as to make their contributions appear to be highly problematic. In 1932 Wu Lei-ch'uan accused the Nationalist leadership of increasing the burden of the people, wasting millions of tax dollars in trying to destroy the Communists, who alone were concerned with arousing the masses, and alienating the intellectuals. The central government knew only how to cheat the masses.[109] Liu T'ing-fang expressed his political disaffection in a responsive reading used as part of a worship service. In the text the leader stated China's problems in these specific terms: "slothfulness, indecision . . . and love of selfish comfort"; "indifference to a policy that suppresses public opinion and curtails the liberty of the common people"; "toleration of a political regime that emphasizes external show but neglects real service"; "internecine wars that have been fought for selfish gains and have depleted our nation's resources"; and "lips that do not agree with hearts and conduct that betrays speech." For all these qualities, characterizing the current political leadership, the congregation was asked to respond, "Forgive us, people of China."[110]

The Chinese members of the Life Fellowship remained steadfast in their commitment to Christianity, even in their disaffection, but the consensus of the 1920s gave way to fundamental disagreements in the 1930s. Wu Lei-ch'uan began to move in a more radical direction, while Chao Tzu-ch'en, despite strong emphasis on Jesus as a social reformer (as seen in his famous *Yeh-su chuan,* 1935), rejected the revolutionary approach outright and insisted that the Christian faith could endorse only a gradualist approach to the problems facing China.[111] The trend in Wu's thinking coincided with his own frustrating experiences as an administrator at Yenching. His *Chi-tu-chiao yü Chung-kuo wen-hua* (1936), culminated a decade of anxiety over the question of Christian patriotism and became a popular interpretation of the Christian faith in Protestant circles in China in the late 1930s.[112]

Wu came to believe that the Christian faith and revolution, contrary to the popular mind, were complementary. Jesus Christ, he claimed, was a revolutionary, and the church should not be a defender of the status quo. Wu failed to understand the Jesus Christ concept until he put it in the context of national salvation of the Jews.[113] Jesus became Christ to the Jews because he was the one who promised to restore them as an independent nation from the oppression of Roman imperialism. His refusing to become their king did not mean rejection of this political issue. Rather Jesus believed that the restoration of the nation could be achieved only after the injustices within society were first corrected. The analogy to China's situation in the 1930s was obvious, namely the need for a fundamental change in the social order.[114] The only political force that defined national salvation in these terms, Wu concluded, was the Communist party. Its intellectual framework and political program suggested a viable alternative for patriotic Christians.

Wu conceded that some would insist that communism and Christianity were diametrically opposed, as seen in the conflict between the materialistic and spiritual views of life. But Wu believed the contradiction was not basic. After all, the concept of the kingdom of God, which was so prominent in the thinking of the Life Fellowship from the beginning, was understood essentially as the physical betterment of life on this earth and the removal of social injustices. He urged Chinese Christians to recognize two important facts: first that China was moving in a revolutionary direction anyway; and second that Christianity in China had ceased to grow. If it were to survive at all, it would have to make accommodations to the revolutionary cause. Wu still thought the "national revolution needed the spirit of Christianity," but if Christianity was not "infused with revolutionary qualities, it could not exist in a revolutionary period."[115]

How could one possibly amalgamate communism's stress on struggle, centralism, and the use of military force with the values of "freedom, equality and love," which had become so closely associated with Christianity? Wu answered by saying the Christian was first and foremost concerned with truth. Jesus, after all, had said, "You shall know the truth and the truth will make you free" (John 8:32), making freedom conditional to truth and not the other way around. Furthermore one's understanding of the truth changed with the conditions of the times. Thus "If centralism and dictatorship are the truths of the times, then our concepts of freedom and equality should temporarily be abandoned for the sake of truth. This is the spirit of Christianity." The only way to change society in meaningful terms was social revolution, and that necessarily meant the use of force. Wu could respect the pacifists who insisted that "Christianity could never serve military power and the cause of revolution," but a realistic understanding of China's situation showed that "social change could only be gained through political power which in turn required the use of military force." In the Second Coming, Jesus had spoken about "fighting, killing, and calamitous difficulties," and his early followers had felt that these fearful things would become a reality. Jesus had already anticipated what many Christians feared most.[116]

The clinching argument in Wu's view was Jesus' views on property and economic justice. Wu believed it was imperative for all Christians to oppose the system of private property. He cited the parable in which the rich man asked Jesus how to get to heaven and Jesus told him to sell all that he had and give it to the poor. "Seeking first the kingdom" meant to Wu seeking economic justice.[117] Only the Communists were seriously addressing themselves to this problem and were prepared to end the system of private property. Social reform might endorse the idea of economic justice, but it was incapable of carrying it out in any meaningful way. Revolution was the only answer.

Chao Tzu-ch'en rejected Wu's synthesis of religion and revolutionary politics. Chao dismissed Wu's interpretation as being both theologically and historically inaccurate, and by destroying this trunk of the argument "all the other branches of the tree would fall." Social justice was one of Jesus' concerns, but not the most important one. Chao rejected Wu's tampering with materialism and argued, with the force of extensive quotations from the New Testament, that it was absolutely impossible to compromise Jesus' teachings about the spirit with the marxists' concern for the economic basis of life. Communism and Christianity, to Chao, were irreconcilable.[118] By the late 1930s Chao, too, had become disillusioned with the political order, but he responded by rejecting all of politics. Christians had to avoid the temptation to "make compromises and identify Christianity . . . with schemes and plans for social and economic reconstruction." The Christian faith was opposed to all the "evils, the wrong and the injustice, the falsehood and the destructive methods with which a scheme of revolution or reconstruction may be in identification." Christians also believed that "the poor are always with you and that under whatever a regime a people live, there are always pain, suffering, and sorrow and consequnetly always the need for our little bits of philanthropic work and love and friendliness."[119]

At first glance Wu and Chao appear to hold opposing views on the Christian role in national salvation. But a closer look shows that they shared a common rejection of the Life Fellowship's earlier, almost naive, faith in the efficacy of gradual social reform. Wu rejected it because it was too slow. Chao dismissed it because the liberals' "naturalism and humanism" have "created in the Chinese youth and . . . thoughtful Chinese Christians a skeptical attitude toward all conceptions of God."[120] Disillusioned by his experience in a Japanese prison in the early 1940s Chao condemned the "free atmosphere" of Yenching University. Liberal Christianity had become meaningless to him. The students and faculty had not drawn close to God, but only "emphasized fellowship and talked in superficialities." He criticized Yenching's attempt to synthesize Christianity and Confucianism without realizing the fundamental contradiction between Christianity and Chinese culture.[121] A decade earlier he had been a leader in that synthesizing effort.

When Hsü Pao-ch'ien left Yenching in 1935 he also had some harsh words to say. The university's liberal atmosphere, beautiful campus and excellent learning facilities were "perfect for study, teaching, and writing," he conceded, but he despaired over the separation between the masses of China, whose lives were getting worse, and the Yenching community, whose lives were getting better. In such an environment it became impossible to teach students to "sacrifice their lives in service to the masses." The only way to serve society, he concluded, was to leave the easy life of the university and "merge with the lives of the masses."[122] Wu Yao-tsung, also an early member of the Life Fellowship and a national leader in the Chinese YMCA, rejected the "shallow idealism" of social reform in these terms: "Our schools may be producing students who know nothing except to uphold the status quo"; "Our philanthropy may be an unconscious means of perpetuating existing evils"; and "Even our rural work may only help to build up a magnificent system that in the end will have to be pulled down again."[123]

Words aside, perhaps the most eloquent testimony to the weakening of liberal Christianity was the demise of the Life Fellowship itself. Its membership had expanded and diluted to sixty-five, including a large share of the Yenching faculty, while the *Chen-li yü sheng-ming* ceased publication after June 1937.[124] The group had failed to lay the intellectual foundation through which Christianity would aid in the task of national salvation. Key personalities who had helped shape Yenching's policies in the 1920s became on the eve of the Japanese occupation a dillusioned band united neither in purpose nor in action. Liu T'ing-fang at the age of forty-six left Yenching in the summer of 1936 and went to Shanghai to continue some writing, while serving as a member in the Legislative Yuan. Wu Lei-ch'uan at sixty-six was the oldest of the five and had returned to Yenching from a two-year retreat in Hangchow. He continued writing and teaching Chinese, but he withdrew from active involvement in university life. Hung Yeh at forty-four had left high level administrative work and since 1930 was devoting his energies mostly to work within the Harvard-Yenching Institute. Hsü Pao-ch'ien at forty-five left Li-ch'uan in 1937, disillusioned with rural reconstruction, and went to teach at the University of Shanghai (Hu-chiang ta-hsüeh). Chao Tzu-ch'en at forty-nine was dean of the school of religion, which by 1937 had dwindled to a staff of eight, only three of them Chinese, and he turned his attention almost exclusively to religious work at Yenching and to writing. Those still at Yenching continued to work together harmoniously within the Yenta Christian Fellowship, but their efforts were confined largely to spiritual fellowship and small acts of philanthropy. The vision of Christian social reconstruction was all but gone.

6

The Cosmopolitan Ideal and Politics in the Republican Years

Politics forced Yenching educators constantly to reexamine basic purposes. The Anti-Christian movement had largely invalidated evangelical purposes, and by the mid 1930s it was no longer clear how much relevance Yenching had to the patriotic idea of national salvation through education (*chiao-yü chiu-kuo*). In the late 1910s studying and teaching at Yenching were very patriotic things to do, but twenty years later China appeared almost to be passing the university by. One purpose Stuart and his colleagues continued to affirm, however, was the cosmopolitan ideal. The affirmation was not an easy one to make amidst the ground-swell of anti-Japanese nationalism. Ideally even Japan could be included, but the realities of the Japanese occupation only strengthened the particular commitment to the Sino-Western friendship side of the world community.

Coping with Japanese Imperialism

More than any other Chinese member of the Life Fellowship, Hsü Pao-ch'ien clung tenaciously to the belief that Christian love should transcend the spirit of anti-Japanese nationalism in China. In the early 1930s he tried to set up an exchange program with Dōshisha University in Kyoto, the most famous Christian university in Japan. His contact there was Ariga Tetsutarō, a roommate of Hsü's from seminary days in

New York and a professor of religion at Dōshisha. After very careful preparations were made Ariga managed to spend one month on the Yenching campus in November and December of 1930. Speaking in English he gave more than a dozen lectures on campus and was once warmly received by 130 Yenching students at a meeting sponsored by the student government.[1]

If the suspicions between China and Japan made Ariga's visit in 1930 difficult, the Manchurian Incident of September 1931 made any further visits well nigh impossible. Nevertheless Hsü continued to buck the waves of anti-Japanese nationalism, and with his help six members of the Yenta Christian Fellowship maintained contact with students from Dōshisha even after the incident. In one of their letters the Dōshisha students spoke of shaking off the "lethargy of professional patriotism" and receiving the "great love of Jesus Christ for humanity." Hsü and his students publicized this correspondence and reminded the Yenching student body that while they had a firm duty to resist aggression, they also were compelled as Christians to transcend nationalism, to oppose militarism wherever it appeared, and to be "sympathetic with Japanese youth . . . in their fight for peace and against militarism."[2] As late as 1935 Hsü tried to arrange a return visit for himself to Dōshisha, but by then communications had broken down on both sides.[3]

Confronted by the growing pressure from Japan, Hsü's pacifism weakened. During his two years with the Li-ch'uan rural reconstruction project he was saddened by the "passivity and inertia of the Chinese peasants." Reluctantly he concluded that the only way to make them politically conscious was to give them military training and discipline. Hsü never abandoned completely the pacifist ideal, but he came to believe that a "nation has the right to fight for its existence." He became upset over indiscreet Western inquiries into the activities of the Chinese Fellowship of Reconciliation, which by 1937 had practically ceased to exist.[4] By then most Chinese members of the Life Fellowship had serious doubts about the Christian doctrine of love and its applicability to the reality of Japanese imperialism. Before long many Westerners at Yenching had also begun to identify strongly with the Chinese resistance.[5]

Hsü Pao-ch'ien's efforts at reconciliation, though, were small compared to those of John Leighton Stuart between 1937 and 1941. Stuart's motives, to be sure, were mixed. In all of his extensive contacts with the

Japanese a primary purpose was to "get Yenching known and established in the consciousness of the [Japanese] leaders—both for the sake
of the university and the students." Stuart was convinced that trying to
bring about real friendship between the Japanese and Chiang Kai-shek
was the best protection for the university.[6] His contacts with Japanese
officials were complex, reflecting the very nature of the Japanese occupation itself. One group was represented by General Itagaki Seishiro, who
was minister of war in the Konoye cabinet in 1938, had served in 1939
as the chief of staff of the Japanese army in Nanking, and was regarded
generally as a proponent of nonexpansion in China. The contact with
Itagaki was made with the help of Paul Liu ('32), who was a teacher in
Manchuria and was forced to work for the Japanese. Another group was
headed by Ugaki Kazushige, former war minister in the 1920s and
Japan's foreign minister in the Konoye cabinet. Ugaki was also known
as a voice of moderation in Tokyo on China policy.[7] Stuart's contact
with Ugaki was made through the Japanese Presbyterian Elder Tagawa,
a "nice old man," who thought war was evil and wanted friendship
with the United States. Tagawa traveled back and forth trying to find a
way to end the war. He was put in a detention camp by his opponents
for his efforts, but was released in April 1941, when he resumed contact
with Stuart through Shanghai. Another important close contact was with
Wang K'o-min, who was a friend of Stuart (same age and also born in
Hangchow) and who served as the head of the puppet government in
North China.[8]

Because of these contacts with the Japanese and his close personal
friendship with Chiang Kai-shek Stuart was uniquely suited for the
negotiation attempts. He made at least four extensive visits to the wartime capital of Chungking, bearing messages and inquiries from the
Japanese authorities, and upon his return reporting Chiang's responses.
These four trips were made in April 1939, July 1939, April 1940, and
April 1941. Each lasted several weeks due to the difficulties of travel
between Peiping and Chungking.[9] Stuart was highly ambivalent. He
helped the students escape to the resistance areas, and he sided openly
with the Chinese resistance in his lengthy confidential reports to the
trustees over these years.[10] He spoke frequently of the hope that North
China would, before long, be reunited with free China, and he made it
clear to the Japanese that any negotiations with the Nationalist government were conditioned by the independence of China. But these senti-

ments, as his reports amply show, did not preclude reconciliation efforts. As late as the spring of 1941 Stuart took his mediating role seriously and believed it possible to avoid all-out war.

In addition to his work with the Japanese occupation outside the university, Stuart used the new alignment of forces to broaden Yenching's international base within. His first "venture in Christian idealism" was to invite Dr. Torii Ryūzō, a well-known Japanese archeologist, to teach at Yenching in 1937. With the help of his wife and two daughters, Torii "steadily broke down the prejudice against having any Japanese among us and actually came to be on friendly terms with many individual members of the faculty."[11] Stuart also used his Japanese contacts to establish communication with Berlin, resulting in small annual grants to the department of Western languages which were cheerfully accepted, the last one being made in the autumn of 1941. Similarly the Italian government granted Yenching eight fellowships in 1937 for which eight students were selected. Only acute international tensions prevented them from sailing. As late as September 1941, at the opening university assembly of the new academic year, Stuart continued to affirm his faith in this kind of internationalism.[12]

Stuart hoped that China would not resort to war in confronting the Japanese threat to China's political and territorial integrity. In 1937 he perceived there were "large numbers in Japan itself who do not now understand and would not approve their own militarists." Relying on these moral forces in the present struggle between China and Japan "may well provide an experiment" in the settlement of international conflict. "More positively, and indulging in prophetic hopes," Stuart concluded, "China may point the way toward saner and less brutally coercive methods for the betterment of humanity than have been achieved elsewhere." He wanted China to follow a type of higher nationalism that would improve the life of the people while helping fashion a "peaceful international order, that might also include Japan."[13] Hindsight indicates that Stuart's ideal was little more than an indulgence of prophetic hopes. Certainly by the late 1930s Stuart's ideas found little support among the Yenching students.

Stated in such vague terms Stuart's hopes did indeed seem awfully naive in the midst of virulent anti-Japanese nationalism. The sporadic efforts to make contact with Japanese students by the Yenta Christian Fellowship and the presence on the campus of the Torii family were little more than token gestures. China in the 1930s and early 1940s was simply too preoccupied with national survival. Furthermore, Stuart's insistence on cooperation with the Japanese in the name of Christian reconciliation was possible because he was acting as an American. The few Chinese students and faculty at Yenching who collaborated with the Japanese, with motives similar to Stuart's, would be condemned as traitors (*han-chien*) and ostracized by the Chinese community after the war. The bitter experience of war had forced a choice that all members of the Life Fellowship had been reluctant to make. For most members of the Yenching community nationalism by then was simply irreconcilable with an internationalism that included the Japanese. The Christian ideal shattered in the face of Chinese realities. And yet if one can avoid concluding that the war with Japan was inevitable or if one considers the staggering human costs of World War Two Stuart's efforts appear to be more convincing. Stuart may not have been deluding himself or deceiving others. The conflict between his Christian convictions and sympathy for anti-Japanese patriotism was unavoidable, and he simply handled it in a way different from most of his contemporaries at Yenching. It was a question of priorities.[14]

Yenching and the Kuomintang Government

As with the Japanese, Stuart's motives for establishing ties with the Kuomintang leadership were idealistic and political in nature. He regarded Kuomintang personalities as an anchor to the Chinese side of the intercultural relationship, but he also knew that accommodation to the Nationalist political order was necessary to Yenching's survival. In addition there was the ideological attraction of Chiang's opposition to communism. Unlike other Yenching personalities Stuart was quickly impressed with Chiang's religious piety, especially so after Christianity was on the decline among Yenching students.

Stuart practiced personal diplomacy with prominent political figures in the 1920s in his efforts to broaden Yenching's base of support in China. With similar motives in mind he made his first formal contact with the Kuomintang leadership. Before 1927 he had feared the Russian influence on the southern leadership, with which Chiang was associated. But he quickly changed his assessment when Chiang turned on the left Kuomintang leadership, forced the Communists underground, and sought Western aid and recognition for the new Nationalist government.[15] After the revolutionary activities subsided in the countryside and the Kuomintang took control over the larger coastal cities and central China, Stuart went to Nanking in October 1928 to make peace with the erstwhile revolutionary leadership. He was accompanied by Liu T'ing-fang, and he stayed in H. H. Kung's "big barn of a foreign house." He was introduced to "practically every man of first importance in the new government," including Kung's relatives, T. V. Soong and Madame and General Chiang Kai-shek. These ties were to last to the end of his work in China. Stuart also contacted Sun Fo, Sun Yat-sen's son, who later became head of the Legislative Yuan and also a member of Yenching's board of managers. He received assurances from Chiang Mon-lin, minister of education, and Wang Ch'ung-hui, minister of justice, that Nanking's policy vis-à-vis the Christian schools would be fair and square and would provide no difficulty for those ready to cooperate.[16]

Stuart's deepening attachment to these Kuomintang leaders led him to take sides in the conflict between the Nationalists and the Communists. In the wake of the December Ninth movement he acknowledged the "growing sentiment especially among younger intellectuals in favor of social and economic reforms through violent revolutionary methods." Communism was the "concrete pattern most appealing and available."[17] Until then he had demonstrated support for student patriotic protests with the solicitude of a father. But underlying that sympathy was his belief that the students would outgrow their radical ideas and come to the realization that the path to national salvation lay not in revolution. To deny legitimacy to the Nationalist system of education and reform programs, and especially to the Kuomintang government itself, would force still another rethinking of Yenching's basic purposes. This constant rethinking was extremely wearying. At times he said as much.

Stuart's weariness interfered with his political judgment. He asserted in 1936 that "China has at long last found herself." He was more "optimistic over the promise of political stabilization and social reconstruction than at any previous period." His hopes were pinned on the figure of Chiang Kai-shek, whose "personality dramatized this whole development" and whose integrity and high qualities of leadership were beyond reproach.[18] Chiang Kai-shek's capture and detainment by one of his subordinates, Chang Hsüeh-liang, in the Sian Incident in December 1936, just after this broad endorsement, was a "rather grim joke" on Stuart, he admitted, but his chagrin did not last long. Within a few months he was again praising Chiang's inner strength and affirming the "improvableness in existing conditions." In 1940 Stuart referred to himself as having become "thoroughly a Chiang man" and willing to do any favor he could on Chiang's behalf.[19]

Stuart's writings on Chiang Kai-shek in the 1930s are infused with a religious language. The Yenching students' declining interest in religion was disappointing even to liberal missionary educators like Stuart, but the frustration may have been softened by the prospect of President Chiang's becoming a sincere Christian. Between 1927, when Chiang outwardly converted, and the mid 1930s, Stuart's writings ignored Chiang's religious experience. But after 1936, when Stuart and Philip Fu helped Nanking broaden its base of support among military leaders in North China, Chiang's Christian connections assumed a new importance. On the eve of the Japanese occupation of North China many observers became highly critical of Chiang Kai-shek's leadership.[20] But Stuart vacillated, until in 1937 it appears he made a leap, dismissed the criticisms, and placed his complete faith in Chiang, the pious Christian. The fate of China, he wrote, now hung "tremulously in the balance" and depended on "spiritual rather than material forces." If Chiang's efforts at political unification could be completed and the "menace of communistic disturbances liquidated, if popular education and the newly emerging loyalties can be reinforced by spiritual ideals and energies sufficiently dynamic, the danger from the Japanese intrusion will be minimized."[21]

Chiang Kai-shek was indeed a pietistic individual. He read and quoted the Bible, conducted regular worship, employed a personal chaplain, and would occasionally talk about his religious life with foreigners, including Stuart. But there is also some indication that Chiang's religious conversion was a show for foreign missionaries, who in turn might help to shape Western policy in Chiang's direction. These two interpretations of course need not be mutually exclusive. The biographies of Chiang usually mention the general's relationship to the Christian faith, especially his marrying the Methodist Sung Mei-ling in 1927, but not all of them discuss his conversion. One biography ignores the Christian experience completely, and others simply do not assign to that experience the importance that Stuart did in the late 1930s.[22]

Soon after the Sian Incident Stuart visited Chiang in Nanking and the Chinese leader confided how distressed he was. He had "tried for eight years to eliminate communism" and was within "two weeks of the goal (only waiting for the river to be frozen over so that his men could cross)," when the "folly of 'that boy' [Marshall Chang Hsüeh-liang] snatched victory out of his grasp." Chiang quoted the "words of Jesus about a demon having been cast out of a man only to have the vacancy filled by seven worse ones, to show how his efforts to get rid of communism had been foiled."[23] During the visit Stuart also had an intimate talk with Madame Chiang in which she "told me things about their married life . . . never mentioned to anyone before." She had married Chiang "in order to help modernize and uplift his thinking," had steadily tried to improve him, "but with so little result," and was "uncertain as to what policy he would adopt vis-à-vis the Japanese." Stuart assured her of his "sympathy and daily prayer" and hoped the general had a "policy in mind that would justify itself as the situation developed." In view of the total situation Stuart felt the surest hope was to "trust to General Chiang for a solution, which if less forthright than the members of his family, students and radical patriots generally would desire, was perhaps more in accord with the Chinese genius and less apt to bring disaster." Stuart's assessment of political realities in the unfolding crisis of 1937 was clouded by his preoccupation with Chiang's piety. Whatever the general's shortcomings, he was, in Stuart's words, a "great man, growing constantly in moral character, in wisdom, and in unselfish devotion to the country."[24]

In 1939 Stuart perceived a growing popularity for Chiang and attributed this success to the "courage, clear-thinking, and utterly unselfish devotion," rooted in the conversion experience.[25] A year later, after visiting Chungking, Stuart recorded another lengthy conversation with Madame Chiang. His own appointment with Chiang had been delayed because the Generalissimo was at prayer. Madame Chiang reported that during their morning Bible study and prayer they had asked themselves "what after all they were doing for Christ." She had been studying photographs of her husband at different stages to see if she could "detect any spiritual growth in his face." She refrained from any conclusion, however, because she was "afraid that her eagerness to discover this unfitted her for forming a judgment." Stuart thought "his face seemed to . . . have softened and to reflect in its whole expression a gentleness as well as strength which again was an evidence of the inner life." Madame Chiang asked Stuart if he could "recommend any really good devotional literature in Chinese," as she felt "very sorely the lack of materials for him." Through her many years of contact with Yenching, and especially the family of Liu T'ing-fang, had she never heard of the publications of the Life Fellowship! She was bluffing, and Stuart must have known it. Stuart's report on his visit concluded, "This intimate account of the private life of two people . . . is recorded for the encouragement of those interested in the missionary enterprise."[26]

Stuart's attachment to Chiang after the war coincided with the further erosion of his sympathy for student politics at Yenching. It was a time when hatred of Chiang, in Stuart's words, had become almost universal among politically conscious citizens.[27] He became embittered over the prospect of the university being weakened from within by student strikes and from without by the Communist forces. He feared the anti-American agitation in 1946 and 1947 might undo Yenching's financial connections with New York.[28] In June 1948 he publicly addressed the students of China, who were then demonstrating against American policy (30,000 in the city of Kunming alone). He chastized them for seriously damaging the "traditional cordiality between the United States and China." And he insisted that the economic reconstruction of Japan in no way threatened China but merely guaranteed the protection against Japan going communist. Like an angry father to naughty children he added:

If those of you who agitate or who participate in the agitation against the United States on the question of Japan disagree with what I have said, then you must be prepared to face the consequences of your actions. If in your hearts you know that I am right, and still continue in your agitation for other and secret purposes, then I say to you that it is time you examined your consciences. If by dishonest means you are attempting to accomplish some clandestine purpose, you are not only damaging the United States, you are also damaging your own country.[29]

His threats were idle. He was out of touch.

Stuart felt entitled to make such a harsh judgment because of his "affection for student groups. If my life has not proven that, then it has been a total failure." He had "confidence that the students of China will not knowingly lend themselves to evil purposes or betray the trust which has been placed in them by their country."[30] But he was also angry at their "utter complacency" over the influence of Soviet Russia: "America has given billions of financial aid to China; Russia has stolen billions. America has never taken one inch of Chinese territory; Russia occupies Dairen and Port Arthur in defiance of treaties. America sends relief; Russia not a penny or a pound of flour. Why is there never anything but anger with America!"[31] In his official correspondence with Washington, Stuart lamented how the Russian behavior in Outer

Mongolia, Inner Mongolia, and the Northeast (Manchuria), aroused "nothing but airy skepticism as to the facts or mute indifference. It is a strange psychosis but one that must be reckoned with especially if—as has usually been the case—what the students are thinking now is an index of what the nation as a whole will soon be thinking."[32] Deep personal affection continued to infuse Stuart's relationship with many Yenching alumni, but the old idealism that had bound him to students in the past was eclipsed in the late 1940s by clear movements in opposite political directions.

Stuart was groping. On December 17, 1948, he had a long talk with Hu Shih, who had just arrived in Nanking at the request of Chiang Kai-shek to become the new premier. Hu declined but considered serving as head of Chiang's new "brain trust." He told Stuart that communism was so "implacable and intolerant, so diabolically thorough in its indoctrination, and so ruthless in enforcing its totalitarian control even in China, that Chiang Kai-shek should be supported." For Chiang alone had been "uncompromising in resisting it . . . and almost alone among the KMT leaders has been free from taint of avarice or other typical vices of Chinese officialdom." In tears Hu asked Stuart what he should do. Stuart wondered if Hu could lead in another New Thought movement or literary revolution on the issues of freedom and democracy as he had done with brilliant success thirty odd years before. Hu "bitterly regretted not having used his talents in this field since VJ day [1945] rather than selfishly returning, as he had, to more congenial academic activities."[33] What a sad and tragic exchange, former presidents of two prominent universities in North China, once the heroes of student patriots, now cut off and isolated, about to leave China and never to return. Their dreams of national salvation through education had all but vanished.

Other Yenching Westerners found themselves defending the Kuomintang leadership out of fear that the revolutionary movement might destroy their work. Grace Boynton, who knew Madame Chiang Kai-shek through Wellesley connections, once claimed she had no political sense at all. This was disingenuous on her part, for she was frequently given to political statements and was quite sensitive to the strength of Yenching student antagonism against the Kuomintang leadership especially in the 1940s. After the Communists had gained the upper hand in the civil war in North China she continued, though somewhat reluctantly, to endorse Chiang Kai-shek. She wrote in April

1948, "I can't get up any excitement at all about the political inequities which are arousing the students . . . and so I scribble in their mass meetings," which she did attend nevertheless. "At what point," she asked herself, "will my detachment end and my emotions become involved as theirs are? Is detachment God's mercy to me or is it blind selfishness? I ask, but I do not seem to need an answer." Always deferential to Stuart's positions on political matters, she reaffirmed her "faith in the Chiang Kai-sheks" and confessed she was "simple-minded enough to cling to Leighton's view of them as two people who do the best any human beings could do and suffer outrageous criticism for not being able to achieve the millennium in China after the war with Japan and during the struggle with the Communists." She pinned her "faith to individuals who seem worthy of trust, like Leighton and [General George C.] Marshall; I do not feel qualified to rage at them when they prove not to be all-wise and ever-successful."[34]

Lucius and Lillian Porter's letters to their children in the late 1940s reveal an even more spirited defense of the Nationalists during the civil war. Posing as a "strong supporter of the present government, in spite of the corruption in spots," Porter said he could not "conceive of any group in China that could take over control and maintain as much peace and order as is now maintained over most of China." When Representative Walter Judd of Minnesota, Chiang's most vocal spokesman in Washington, passed through China in November 1947, Porter concluded it was a good thing to have this "brilliant talker and keen thinker" in Congress, and agreed with Judd that any attempt to "replace the present Nanking control for some other would involve unimaginable suffering for the masses of the people." In May 1948 Porter recommended his children read Frieda Utley's *Last China in China,* a popular defense of Chiang Kai-shek at the time, as a "careful and . . . accurate account of conditions in China."

Like many liberals in the West the Porters had passed through a period of enchantment with the Soviet Union in the 1930s, but by the 1940s they had become unreservedly anti-Communist. Lucius Porter accused the Communists of having "only a negative policy of continually causing trouble," and of showing "nowhere any capacity to maintain order or offer relief to the regions they control." He concluded that the Communist alternative was "fundamentally opposed to the sense of personal, human values and freedom," and to the "sense of individual worth, human equality and concern for other persons that characterizes the Christian faith." He was so hostile that he failed to see that Yenching students condemned the Nationalist government precisely in these terms. Impervious to the hopes that filled students in their anticipation of the revolution, Lillian Porter saw nothing but doom. "Poor China!" she wrote in November 1948, "we have hoped against hope that she would surprise us all, as she had done so many times in the past, and suddenly straighten out and give her people peace, but I fear the Kuomintang is too much concerned in getting for itself what it can before the end comes. No one can foresee what the future of our beloved Yenching is to be."[35]

Other Westerners at Yenching did not necessarily concur with Boynton's and the Porters' assessment of the Nationalists. Randolph and Louise Sailer were well known for their more radical sympathies. So too with Ralph and Nancy Lapwood of the London Missionary Society who were among those Westerners welcomed the longest at Yenching after the Communist takeover.

Yenching Westerners held a unilinear concept of progress that rejected the idea that the political power of the Kuomintang government would have to be destroyed before a meaningful restructuring of society could take place. They repeated over and over again the need to be constructive and positive. They believed in the improvability of almost any existing order. It was an optimism that simply failed to comprehend the severity of the spiraling inflation, the corruption in government, the piecemeal nature of reformist projects, and the impotence of the Kuomintang leadership. They had been sojourners in China for decades, but they still projected onto the Chinese scene the optimism of the apparent success of gradual social reform within the recent American experience. This optimism was a major tenet of liberal Protestant theology, but it became a rootless transplant in Chinese soil. For thirty years these missionary educators had longed for the day when leading Chinese would be "more ready to take steps themselves toward saving their countrymen, rather than relying upon outside help."[36] But Porter, writing thus in January 1948, was so hostile to revolutionary social change that he failed to see that in practical terms only the Communists were fulfilling that wish.

In 1946 Harold Isaacs noted in his reports from China that this faith in the Kuomintang leadership was shared by many Westerners. It was rooted in an image of Chiang Kai-shek, which may be a bit overdrawn but captures nevertheless the unreality of their optimism. In these Westerners' eyes Chiang had emerged from the war with a "fine and misty portrait" as a "heroic leader . . . dedicated unto the death to the task of national unity, self-defense, fruitful growth, and modern progress." Here was the "towering and peerless and wise and long suffering and indispensable man of goodwill, the personification of Chinese virtue." Sometimes there was "slight acknowledgment for such . . . difficulties as the pervasive corruption and venality of his regime, the rapacity of his followers and henchmen, the absence of the most elementary democracy, the hounding of liberals and students, the imprisonment and execution of political opponents." But invariably, Chiang Kai-shek was absolved of any responsibility for these shortcomings. Rather he was surrounded by a "cabal of evil men . . . who go their nefarious ways balking his higher purposes." But he remained himself the "unique and irreplaceable leader, the chief and even the only unifying force in the land, the professing and practicing democrat who wants only to lead his people along the path of freedom and righteousness."[37] Stuart and other missionary educators at Yenching helped shape this "fine and misty portrait."

It is difficult to generalize about the political attitudes of the Chinese faculty in the 1940s. Some of the younger members, largely graduates of Yenching like Yen Ching-yüeh ('28), Chao Ch'eng-hsin ('30), Weng Tu-chien ('34), Kao Ming-k'ai ('35), and Hou Jen-chih ('36), were more in tune with the December Ninth spirit than the May Fourth spirit. In the years right after the war with Japan they performed responsibly as young faculty members, but they were largely disabused of any hope in gradual reform and the Kuomintang leadership. Yen and his wife, Lei Chieh-ch'iung, had worked intermittently with the Nanking government in the mid 1930s, but after the war they had concluded that it was "almost impossible for anyone with ideals and high moral standards to work inside the government set-up."[38] Age was not the only determinant of disaffection. Two older members of the faculty, Ku Chieh-kang and Chang Tung-sun, had been known among the students since the late 1920s for their radical sympathies. With the younger faculty they would soon help the university make the transition to the new order after 1949.

Another group of Chinese faculty was more cautious, though they were never as enthusiastic about the Kuomintang leadership as some of the prominent missionary educators. If they had doubts about the role of education in national salvation or about the viability of the current political order, they manifested their doubts by cynicism and withdrawal rather than by active opposition. In any case they were hardly radical. One faculty member told Grace Boynton in 1948 that he saw only violence and chaos for the future and feared the Reds would reduce educated people to begging and force them to dress in special clothing. A small group of rightists on the faculty even prepared poison to use in case they found it necessary, which fortunately they did not.[39] Chao Tzu-ch'en admitted after the revolution that the "thought of physical martyr-dom plagued the secret places of my mind."[40] Ts'ai Yi-o (Stephen O. Ts'ai) and Mei Yi-pao were also hostile to revolutionary politics throughout most of their careers at Yenching, though they were by no means unmindful of the huge problems of the Nationalist leadership. They had borne major administrative responsibilities for Yenching since the late 1920s, through the refugee years in Chengtu, down to the eve of the revolution. Ts'ai left Yenching in May 1948 to head up the student food program administered by the American funded China Relief Mission in Shanghai, and Mei left Yenching just before the turnover, neither of them to return to the campus.[41]

Chinese feelings about the Western connection at Yenching were closely tied to the question of the viability of the Nationalist political order. Stuart candidly admitted that as long as the unfavorable situation of rampant inflation, political corruption, and prolonged civil war continued, the United States would "remain the most convenient universal scapegoat; we will be accused simultaneously of having given too much and too little, of interfering too much and too little, of strengthening the moderates and the reactionaries, and of not letting the Chinese settle matters in their own way."[42] Lu Chih-wei and Chang Tung-sun concluded in March 1948, that American military and economic aid could not help China. More outspoken were the sociologist Lei Chieh-ch'iung and the historian Teng Chih-ch'eng, who argued that the aid amounted to outside intervention, and only prolonged the civil war.[43] By the spring of 1948 no Chinese faculty member openly defended American military and economic aid to the Nationalist government. But Lu Chih-wei still defended the continuation of the American influence on campus to which he attributed the university's high academic standards. Lu distinguished between those parts of American culture, such as the churches, which supported efforts like Yenching, and the fashions (Mei-kuo feng-ch'i) of American society, which only corrupted Chinese youth. Lu was aware of how unpopular pro-American statements were among student leaders at the time, but he asserted nevertheless that China needed the spirit of Christianity to offset the growing new power of the Communists.[44]

In short, by the late 1940s one finds a continuum of positions at Yenching on the Kuomintang leadership. Standing far to the right were some of the trustees like Henry R. Luce, head of Time-Life, Inc., member of the board since 1945 and son of Henry W. Luce, Yenching's first vice-president of financial affairs. Stuart also defended Chaing Kai-shek while he was president of Yenching and later when he became the American ambassador to China, though at times Stuart could be highly critical. Less supportive of Chiang were most Western members of the Yenching faculty and some of the more liberal trustees, such as Rufus Jones of the American Friends Service Committee. Even a few members of the board of managers, though they had been leaders in the various Republican governments for years, were more liberally inclined. For example, Yen Hui-ch'ing, the most senior member of the board, was involved in last minute negotiations with the Communists in the spring of 1949 and later supported the new government. As with Boynton and Porter, some faculty members were loyal to the Nationalist government until the eve of the revolutionary takeover but then quickly shifted positions once they had lived a few weeks under the new order.

More ambiguous perhaps than any other group were most of the Chinese faculty, whose commitments to liberal arts had necessarily translated into a definite, though uneasy, loyalty to the political order of the Republican governments that supported Yenching. But by the late 1940s events were forcing these Chinese to favor the Communist alternative to national salvation, though they were not unaware of the consequences for their own lives. Still further to the left were most, but not all, of the Yenching students. With fewer vested interests in the current state of affairs, they became largely disillusioned with both the Kuomintang leadership and the Western connection. In a sense liberal arts had failed in its purposes to find a middle way between the two political alternatives of the Nationalists and the Communists.

The Harvard-Yenching Institute

The one area of Yenching life which was furthest removed from the vicissitudes of Nationalist politics was the Harvard-Yenching Institute. Yenching's association with Harvard through the institute certainly helped boost the university's reputation in Chinese circles, and the name of the institute itself has helped familiarize students in the West with the university. Incorporated in 1928 under the statutes of the Commonwealth of Massachusetts, the institute has continued operation for almost half a century. The purposes of the institute were fully in concert with those of the Life Fellowship. And it may not just be coincidence that the three secretaries (as distinguished from the research staff itself) for the institute at Yenching from the late 1920s to the early 1940s, were early members of Life Fellowship, Liu T'ing-fang, Lucius Porter, and Hung Yeh. One of the institute's trustees was Eric M. North, who served on the board for almost four decades, 1928–66 (vice-chairman 1954–66), and was for a long time president of the American Bible Society. For them religion and scholarship converged.

Support for the institute from the Yenching side was many sided. One was the legacy of respect for scholarship in premodern China. Another was the belief that education, and research as part of higher education, was a part of national salvation. Still another source of support was the belief that scholarship would help the university transcend the barriers of nationalism, not only between China and the West—a relatively easy task given the basic American orientation of the university in the first place—but also the much more difficult barrier between China and Japan. The institute was less successful in transcending ideological and political differences after the revolution. Some who cooperated closely as scholars in the institute in the late 1930s, like Lu Chih-wei, Nieh Chung-ch'i, Hou Jen-chih, Weng Tu-chien, Ch'i Ssu-ho, and others, later would become bitter rivals in the administrative struggles in the highly charged atmosphere of thought reform in the early 1950s.

Early in his work in China Stuart had seen himself as a scholar. At Yenching he saw himself as a facilitator of others' scholarship. In her lengthy unpublished novel of the Yenching experience, "The Source of Springs," Grace Boynton chose not to describe Stuart's work as the building of a university, but rather a research institute, presumably the Harvard-Yenching Institute. What higher honor, the novel suggests, than to associate Stuart's efforts directly with one of the world's most prestigious universities and with the impartial search for knowledge. When the revolution forced the institution to sever its ties with the United States, Boynton lamented the passing of the time "when there were two-souled Chinese as well as two-souled Westerners, and when there had been communication between races and cultures which soon vanished and will not be seen again in our time. With it vanished Seaton's [Stuart's] dream of all his Institute was to contribute to world understanding and world peace."[45] Others, of course, would not share Boynton's sanguinity, and would doubt the ultimate value of scholarship.[46] Nevertheless the institute has established both a model and an ongoing institutional framework which have in the end influenced much that we in the West know about East Asia. And it reflects the internationalist spirit of the multitude of professional organizations, world around, that continue to thrive in all areas of scholarship.

Stuart had been in touch with the Hall estate trustees since the early 1920s, but substantial grants were not immediately forthcoming. In 1925 Wallace B. Donham, dean of the Harvard Graduate School of Business Administration and chairman of a fund-raising committee for the university, was also actively pursuing these funds. (Donham later served as a trustee of the institute from 1928 to 1954 and as chairman of the board from 1934 to 1954.) He was told of Hall's stipulations and was urged by Arthur Davis, one of the estate's trustees, to contact Stuart who was in New York at the time. With Davis' suggestion in mind Donham spent hours in conversation with Stuart in 1926 and submitted a proposal to finance an institute that would provide "facilities for research, instruction, and publication in the field of Chinese culture" with centers at Yenching and Harvard. The common task was to "encourage Oriental studies in China under the stimulus of American interest and critical methods." The task would be accomplished with the "assistance of Western scholars and educational resources of Harvard University," and it would carry the additional objective of "training Chinese and other students to assist in the dissemination and preservation of Chinese culture."[47]

Deeply impressed with the proposal, the Hall trustees granted the original US $60,000 requested, and the institute (known in its first years as the Harvard-Peking Institute) came into being. Encouraged by this propitious beginning, Stuart pressed on, and in 1928 Yenching itself was awarded endowment funds from the estate totaling US $1,500,000. One million was given directly to the university for its own use and $500,000 was to be held in trust by the Harvard-Yenching Institute to strengthen Chinese studies in the college. Other Christian colleges in China also benefited in similar ways from these early negotiations and proposals in 1928 and were awarded smaller amounts of money: Lingnan, $700,000; Nanking, $300,000; West China Union, $200,000; Shantung Christian, $150,000; and Fukien Christian, $50,000.[48]

The money awarded by the institute to the college at Yenching was channeled in two ways, through the graduate program known as the Research School of Chinese Studies (Kuo-hsüeh yen-chiu so) and through the undergraduate curriculum. In Peking the institute began publication of the *Yenching Journal of Chinese Studies* (*Yen-ching hsüeh-pao*), a semiannual, with only slight interruption during the war with Japan, from 1927 to 1951. Accompanying the journal was the publication of a separate monograph series. This series varied widely in its scope of publication and helped give exposure to promising scholars inside and outside the institute.[49] The institute also pioneered in archeological investigations led by Jung Keng of the Chinese department and Ku Chieh-kang of the department of history. In 1930 it began production of the Harvard-Yenching Sinological Index Series, carried out largely under the direction of Hung Yeh. These indices to important volumes of classical literature were prepared using a system in which a numerical value was assigned to each character in terms of the type and number of strokes. By 1946 Hung had overseen the production of indices to sixty-four major works which have become indispensable tools to sinological research ever since.[50]

Another major project of the institute at Yenching was to invite young Western scholars interested in East Asia to spend a year or so at the university and in Peking to gain research and language experience. Among them were such well-known Western sinologists as Joseph G. Needham, Harlee Glessner Creel, James R. Ware, Charles S. Gardner, Francis W. Cleaves, Edward A. Kracke, Jr., James R. Hightower, Knight Biggerstaff, Derk Bodde, George Taylor, Arthur Wright, Wm. Theodore deBary, Owen Lattimore, Laurence C. S. Sickman, and others.[51]

In 1940 Hung Yeh, longtime executive secretary, proposed that the institute at Yenching be the first to offer the Ph.D. degree, in any field, in China, but the ensuing war with Japan and then the civil war put an end to the idea.[52] Another use of the unrestricted funds from the institute was the building of the large research library for Chinese studies. Yenching's library holdings in the first years were mostly in English and contained in a few wooden boxes. In 1925 the total number of Chinese and Western volumes was still less than 10,000. By 1929 the Chinese collection had increased to 140,000 volumes, and by 1933 to 220,411 volumes (with 36,744 Western language works).[53] By 1940 it contained most of the collected writings of the Ch'ing dynasty and 2,003 local gazetteer titles in more than 20,021 ts'e. For its part in the university's efforts to blunt the pervasive anti-Japanese hostility, the institute compiled a "Bibliography of Orientological Contributions in One Hundred and Seventy-five Japanese Periodicals with Indices" in February 1940, under the direction of Torii Ryūzō. At the same time the library increased its Japanese holdings to 1,854 titles.[54]

The enthusiastic spirit of Yenching campus life was also evident in the institute. Its annual reports from the late 1920s are filled with lists of research and publication activities, both those completed and those planned for in the future, while full time scholars in the institute, furthermore, normally taught two courses within the university and took a serious interest in undergraduate education.

Many scholars of the institute were distinguished sinologists and were significant enough as historical figures to be included in Howard K. Boorman's *Biographical Dictionary of Republican China*.[55] The first is Ch'en Yüan, first director of the institute at Yenching, 1928–30, later president of the Catholic Fu Jen University and after 1952 Peking Normal University. Ch'en's research covered the historical investigation of religious groups in China, including the Jews and especially the early Jesuits, but he also did pioneering work in the indexing of the *Ssu-ku ch'üan-shu* and important Buddhist sutras. A second figure is Jung Keng, successor to Ch'en as director of the institute and editor of the journal, who is best known for his work on Chinese bronzes, calligraphy, and early painting.[56] Among those mentioned previously were Ku Chieh-kang, historian and folklorist, and Hung Yeh, who was best known for his work with the sinological index series.[57] Hsü Ti-shan was another famous personality connected with the institute. He was a Yenching alumnus (1921) and member of the Life Fellowship and he was known for his research in Taoist and Buddhist philosophy and on the Opium War, 1839–42, and perhaps best of all for his writings in fiction.[58] Feng Yu-lan, professor of philosophy at neighboring Tsinghua University, should also be included in this list because he did lecture at Yenching in the mid 1920s and for several years maintained a lecturer status within the institute. He is best known for his history of Chinese philosophy. Others could be mentioned.

Another long list could be made of famous scholars and writers in China who were not employees of the institute but maintained direct relations with it for shorter periods of time or were connected indirectly through the department of Chinese. The following list, also included in the Boorman dictionary, is suggestive: Ch'ien Mu, Ch'ien Hsüan-t'ung, Chou Tso-jen, Wen I-to, Chu Tzu-ch'ing, Chang Erh-t'ien, Po Shou-yi[59] and three Yenching alumni, Hsiung Fo-hsi, the playwright, Hsieh Wan-ying, the poet, and Yü P'ing-po. Their connections with the university varied, but all of them brought great prestige to the institute.

On the undergraduate side the institute encouraged students, in Stuart's words, to "overcome their deficiency in reading and writing classical Chinese" and bring them more closely in touch with the "literary heritage of their own country."[60] In Hung's words, Yenching's course offerings in Chinese studies "will deliberately encourage a number of these young people to look back into China's past and to rediscover and conserve those permanent values in her cultural heritage that are not incompatible with her modern requirements."[61] But there were difficulties in being both modern and more rooted to the Chinese past. Those who were inclined to a modern career, say in the sciences, seemed to care little for China's past and the larger purposes of the institute. On the other hand, those who as undergraduates specialized in Chinese studies, were often deficient, Stuart claimed, in non-Chinese subjects and thus faced considerable difficulty in gaining admission to graduate study programs, abroad, and even at Yenching. The standards were high all around. There were, however, notable exceptions who ably combined both these worlds. For example, Teng Ssu-yü, a research fellow at the institute, 1936–37, had turned in an undergraduate thesis in 1932 on a history of the Chinese examination system (*Chung-kuo k'ao-shih chih-tu shih*), a vast scholarly undertaking that was immediately published.[62] Other Yenching undergraduates went on to become well known sinologists in the West and are distinguished by their publications in English alone. In American colleges and universities, for example, even undergraduate specialists in Chinese studies may be familiar with the works of Teng and his Yenching colleagues, such as Fang Chao-ying ('28), Shih Yu-chung (Vincent Shih, '30), Cheng Te-k'un ('31), Yang Ch'ing-k'un ('33), Fei Hsiao-t'ung ('33, M.A.), Ch'ü T'ung-tsu ('34), Liu Tzu-chien (James T. C. Liu, '41), Hsü Chung-yüeh (Immanuel C. Y. Hsü, '46), and Yü Ying-shih (ex '51).

The institute also sponsored the *Shih-hsüeh nien-pao* (Historical annual) and the *Wen-hsüeh nien-pao* (Literary annual), both published by the students and staff in their respective departments. One ambitious project which attempted to fulfill both the modern and traditional purposes was the proposed undergraduate program in linguistics. It was headed by Lu Chih-wei, who in the late 1930s was involved in linguistics research. Working with Lu were Jung Keng, contributing his knowledge of morphology of the Chinese language, and two junior colleagues, Wang Ching-yu and Kao Ming-k'ai, working respectively in phonology and grammar, while Lu worked on the vernacular and the psychology of language. No evidence can be found to indicate how well the project succeeded, but it was another instance of the experimental atmosphere of the institute generally.[63]

The institute's program at Harvard lagged behind that at Yenching, and yet it has become historically important in the development of East Asian studies in the United States. Prior to the mid 1930s no center for such studies had existed in any of the major American universities, in contrast to European universities at the time. The goal of the institute was to correct this deficiency and to start with Harvard. It invited Paul Pelliot, the emminent French sinologist, to become the center's first director. Pelliot did in fact lecture at Harvard in 1928–29 and worked with Hung and Porter, also at Harvard that year, in shaping directions in research and teaching. But the new center did not take definite shape until after the arrival in 1934 of Serge Elisseeff, Pelliot's younger colleague who was a Japanologist (the first Western graduate from Tokyo Imperial University) but was also trained in classical Chinese studies. Elisseeff served as the director until 1957, while teaching at the same time as professor of Far Eastern languages. Under Elisseeff's leadership the institute made great strides: in 1937 it established the department of Far East languages, the first of this kind in the United States; it began to build the Harvard-Yenching library, under the leadership of Alfred Kaiming Chiu, starting with Harvard's own limited collection and creating over four decades one of the most usable collections of East Asian literature in the West; and the *Harvard Journal of Asiatic Studies* began publication in 1936 with an accompanying monograph series. With this kind of support from the institute Harvard had become by the late 1940s the leading center for East Asian studies in the United States.

When the ties between China and the United States were severed in 1950 the Harvard-Yenching Institute was forced to end its support of programs in China, especially Yenching, and shifted its attention to the sister colleges in Japan, Korea, Taiwan, and Hong Kong. In each of these areas coordinating councils were set up by the institute's new director, Edwin O. Reischauer (a son of missionary parents in Japan), to help administer the "growth and advancement" of East Asian studies in East Asia itself. Between 1954 and 1968 more than 150 East Asian scholars, most of them spending a year or more, studied at Harvard under the visiting scholars program; fellowships were given to Asian graduate students interested in East Asian studies; the Harvard-Yenching library broadened its collection of materials to include documents on contemporary East Asia; and publications continued to thrive. Over the years, in addition to the journal, monographs in the Harvard-Yenching Institute Studies and the Scripta Mongolica series, as well as language textbooks and dictionaries, were published.[64] The furthering of "intercultural understanding" between China and America, which was the central purpose of Stuart and his colleagues from the beginning, has surely found one of its most enduring expressions in the history of the Harvard-Yenching Institute.

7

Revolutionary Politics and Yenching Cosmopolitanism

The day [Monday, December 13, 1948] was dull and overcast . . . Our gates were guarded by both students and members of the faculty, but they were still open, and a steady stream of refugees tugging bundles, was coming in . . . Late on Wednesday, we learned that Communist troops were outside our gates and so we knew the change-over had taken place . . . [The next day] Lucius Porter was on twenty-four hour duty at the Yenching West Gate where he was in telephone communication with all parts of the campus . . . He ordered the gate unbarred and found a very young political cadre accompanied by two soldiers. The cadre was unarmed, but the guards were fairly draped with weapons. The first question asked was most disarming. "Has Yenching been hit during the fighting?" No. Then "Does Yenching need anything?"

Chancellor [Lu Chih-wei spoke] to us on the Thursday we were "liberated." He warned us that we are now making a much greater change than has been made by revolutions, or by falling dynasties in China's history . . . Then there was the meeting in Bashford on December 17 when our "liberators" sent a member of their political team of cadres to address the assembled University community. The auditorium was crammed, for there were servants, and work people like gatemen and janitors, as well as students and us teachers . . . It was obvious that the speaker [a former student at the American Board's Middle School in Paotingfu] was ill at ease. He had probably never completed the work in our Middle School, and here he was talking to learned university students and their tremendously learned professors! So he was sweating profusely and began rather stumblingly. But . . . he soon recovered his self-confidence and gave us a glowing picture of our future, along with a proper pep talk about the virtues of our new masters. He was received with cordial applause, but the audience was not as thrilled as I had expected us to be. The young man bowed, and went away followed by the two guards.[1]

Thus began Yenching's experience with the turnover from the old order to the new order, as recorded in Grace Boynton's diary.

The Political Context

The revolution was greeted with enthusiasm on the Yenching campus. For most it was not the beginning of the bitter end but the occasion for new hope. Revolution promised to rebuild China, not bit by grudging bit, but in bold and sweeping ways. A month after the turnover Chao Tzu-ch'en noted that the whole faculty and student body of Yenching were joyfully facing the reality of their "liberation," and he argued that every "thoughtful Christian in China" should regard the "impending and swift defeat of the Nationalists with a deep sense of gratitude to God."[2] A few months later President Lu Chih-wei claimed that to "most of us conscientious Chinese" the revolution was "not China's dark hour, but rather a new dawn." A bit sardonically he wrote to the trustees, "You will forgive us if we do not become despondent because the foreign policy of our old government did not land us where the masses of the Chinese people hoped to be."[3]

The New Democracy and Russian Influence. If the revolution brought hope to Yenching patriots, it also produced anxiety. They quickly understood that China's foreign policy would shift radically toward the Soviet Union, with far-reaching consequences for the life of the university. The question plaguing their minds was how far would the changes go. Could Yenching as an institution, even with drastic modifications, still continue to exist independently? In retrospect it may appear that the closing of the institution was a foregone conclusion of revolutionary politics, but it did not appear that way to the Yenching faculty at the time. To understand their position it is necessary to explore what Mao Tse-tung meant by New Democratic politics, which were in effect at the time of the turnover, and the nature of Soviet influence from 1949 to 1952.

"On New Democracy," was the title of a long essay Mao wrote in January 1940, as he was thinking about the future of China after Japan's defeat and settlement of the civil war with the Nationalists. Socialism, to be sure, was the ultimate goal of the Communist Revolution, but before it could be realized, China would have to pass through a democratic stage, called the New Democracy. How long this stage would last was uncertain, but reportedly Mao himself stated as late as 1949 that it might last for some time.[4] Different from the old democracy associated with the "European-American form of capitalist republic under bourgeois dictatorship," the New Democracy, Mao wrote, would also be "different from the socialist republic of the type of the Soviet Union."[5] The essay states that China under the New Democracy would be in alliance with Russia, and that those "cultural organizations run directly by the imperialists" and their "shameless Chinese toadies" would have no place. But the essay also called for assimilating "whatever we find useful today, not only from contemporary foreign socialist or new-democratic cultures, but also from the older cultures of foreign countries, such as those of the capitalist countries in their age of enlightenment." That assimilation, like the eating of food, should be "separated into nutriment to be absorbed and waste matter to be discarded; we should never swallow anything whole or absorb it uncritically." His suggestion was that the danger might not be just in keeping institutions such as Yenching but in adopting policies from the outside which might uncritically eradicate them.[6] The essay certainly portended great changes. But Yenching administrators were confident they were not shameless toadies and anticipated that the university still had a place in the new order.

As the Communists swept over China from north to south, the New Democratic politics were put into effect. On June 30, 1949, Mao commemorated the twenty-eighth anniversary of the Chinese Communist Party in an essay entitled "On the People's Democratic Dictatorship." In it he outlined China's foreign policy in terms of "leaning to one side," seemingly destroying the possibility that the new government might consider establishing relations with the United States, a possibility that was evident in various statements Mao had made in the intervening years, some as late as June of 1949.[7] Leaning to one side meant that "all Chinese without exception must lean either to the side of imperialism or to the side of socialism. Sitting on the fence will not do, nor is there a third road."[8] Another clue to the meaning of New Democratic politics was the "Common Program of the Chinese People's Political Consultative Conference," adopted September 29, 1949. Article 3 in the document called for the abolishment of "all the prerogatives of imperialist countries in China"; Article 11 stated the new government would unite "first of all with the Soviet Union"; three articles, 18, 41, and 45, emphasized the theme of serving the people. Again these documents would indicate that a drastic reorganization was in store for Yenching University. And yet neither indicated that Yenching would necessarily be closed.[9]

By the summer of 1949 all the English language newspapers in North China ceased publication. The only news available through the Chinese newspapers and local radio broadcasts parroted the official line and condemned American attempts to strengthen Japan, the Marshall Plan, continued American support of the Nationalist government in the United Nations, and discussions of a Pacific Pact to be built with South Korea, Taiwan, and the Philippines (discussions in which Stuart had been involved before leaving China).[10] The Chinese media were also angry over the publication by Washington of the White Paper in August 1949, which it portrayed as an open confession of American aggressive intentions toward China. One hundred and twenty-four Yenching faculty and staff quickly dissociated themselves from Stuart's role as the last American ambassador and issued a denunciation of the State Department document on August 23, 1949.[11] One student of the anti-American trend in 1949, herself a Yenching alumna, has estimated that over 90 percent of the international news in major Peking newspapers was taken directly from Russian sources.[12]

The year 1950 brought further expressions of hostility toward the West and the establishment of closer ties with the Soviet Union. In January the West compound of the American consulate in Peking was taken over and all diplomatic personnel were forcibly removed. These acts came hard upon the arrest three months before of American Consul Angus Ward in Mukden and outraged Westerners as a violation of diplomatic protocol.[13] In February Mao Tse-tung and Chou En-lai ended their lengthy visit in Moscow and returned to Peking with the thirty-year Sino-Soviet Treaty of Friendship, Alliance, and Mutual Assistance. February and March also saw the conclusion of a series of economic agreements providing for: the return of the Chinese Changchun Railway, Port Arthur, and Russian property in Dairen to China; long term credits for China amounting to US $300,000,000; telegraphic, telephone, and postal agreements; and arrangements for Sino-Soviet cooperation in aviation and the development of oil and nonferrous resources, especially in Sinkiang.[14]

The question remains, did Russian influence and the New Democratic politics, as of February 1950 when Mao returned from Moscow, make Yenching's dissolution a foregone conclusion? Or was there some justification for Yenching faculty to hope the university might survive in the new order? The Treaty of Friendship, one notices immediately, was defensive in nature and directed against Japan. In this respect it bears a striking resemblance to the Sino-Soviet Treaty signed in 1945 with the Nationalist government. The new element, admittedly, was the possibility of American collaboration "directly or indirectly in acts of aggression," but the fear remained focused on Japan. Russia may have gained some leverage in Peking through the promise of economic aid. And yet this aid was extremely small, equivalent to about one dime per capita per year and only a pittance compared to the size of the task of economic reconstruction. One scholar has observed that in "cash terms, Russian aid financed only about two percent of the Chinese investment program in the 1950's, and China received only about one eighth of Russia's total aid outflow, less than Poland or East Germany received, and only marginally more than tiny Mongolia."[15] Heavy dependence on Soviet aid for industrial purposes did not begin until 1953.[16]

Before the signing of the treaty in February some observers wondered if the Soviet Union was really the "guide and friend to China that the Communists claimed her to be." If the Russian stock was high by then it was because Marxists were the first to "tackle the problems Chiang Kai-shek had evaded," the only ones with a "clear doctrine and precise principles in the midst of confusion," and the Soviet Union was the first major power to establish equal relations. Robert Guillain of Le Monde, writing thus in 1949 and 1950, was convinced Russia was not "pulling the hidden strings in China," and that Mao was not Stalin's vassal.[17] Michael Lindsay, who had taught at Yenching in the late 1930s, spent four years with the Communists during the war, and returned to China in 1949, argued the Chinese were pro-Russian only because "Russian theory fits Chinese experience."[18] These skilled observers strongly rejected the idea that Mao would become the Far Eastern Tito, an assertion that Mao himself had made repeatedly. But they also thought that China would not become a Soviet satellite like other countries in Eastern Europe. Benjamin Schwartz has argued that Stalin himself may not have wanted to make China into a satellite. If Titoism spurred Stalin to follow a policy of suppression in Eastern Europe, it seems to have driven him in the direction of "caution and an unprecedented forbearance" in the case of China.[19] Politics in Eastern Europe, in short, may provide a highly misleading analogy in understanding the nature of Russian influence in China in the earliest years of the revolution.

In any case the Yenching faculty refused to conclude that Soviet influence or the New Democratic politics as of 1949 and 1950 meant the end of the university. Any readiness to dismiss their analysis as illusory may partake as much of fraudulent hindsight as a careful examination of the political and international scene at the time. Other major developments in China's foreign policy in the twenty-year period after the revolution, such as the Sino-Soviet impasse and the surprising ease of rapprochement between Washington and Peking in the 1970s, would lead one to be suspicious of attempts to explain China's international behavior only in terms of ideology and Soviet influence.

The Korean War. Developments in the Korean War rather than the turnover in December 1948 may be as significant a watershed in marking the beginning of Yenching's institutional demise. The war began in June 1950, but it did not have serious effect on Yenching until November, after General Douglas MacArthur had ordered American troops to cross north of the 38th parallel in Korea (October 7) and after American and Chinese troops had clashed in North Korea near the Chinese border. Prior to October 1950 the new government had given repeated assurances to Yenching that it would be allowed to continue, but after November they came to an end. With those reassurances in mind President Lu expressed optimism on June 28, 1950, three days after the outbreak of the Korean War, about the possibility of Stuart returning to Yenching to teach.[20] And on September 5 he informed Grace Boynton that her reentry permit had been extended to December 15 and was in the "keep of the university." (Not until November was the possibility of her reentry reconsidered.) Lu's first mention of international complications to the trustees was on October 28, 1950.[21]

In November 1950 official Chinese hostility toward Yenching escalated in the form of the Resist America Aid Korea movement (K'ang-Mei yüan–Ch'ao yün-tung). The movement spread to the Yenching campus and completely disrupted academic routine. It caused alarm among all Westerners connected with Yenching. And yet they were inclined to see it not just as a propaganda campaign but also as a legitimate response to the threats of attack as reflected in General MacArthur's words and behavior at the time. The civil war between the Communists and Nationalists was not yet over, and the sending in of the American 7th Fleet in the Taiwan Straits in late June 1950 and Mac-

Arthur's and the American Congress's deepening commitments to Chiang Kai-shek were seen by Yenching faculty and students as outside intervention. The Taiwan impasse was the focus of much anti-American hostility at Yenching and in the Chinese media generally. American led efforts in October to destroy the power of the North Korean government, which served as a kind of buffer to the new government in China, were seen as steps toward the further escalation of hostilities with China and were compared to the stages through which Japan had gained control of China before, through Korea, Manchuria, and then North China.[22]

The correlation of Yenching's demise with the Korean War is evident in administrative and financial developments. On September 1, 1950, more than two months after the outbreak of the war, the ministry of education requested President Lu to reorganize the board of managers as the proper liaison between the university and the government. As late as October 19 Yenching received US $34,000 from the government for its new engineering school with no hint that Yenching's independent status was in jeopardy. (The Nationalist government had made yearly grants to Yenching since the mid 1930s.) Still later, on October 28, Chou En-lai personally reassured President Lu that Yenching would be allowed to receive aid from abroad just as "water from a robber's spring can be used for irrigation."[23] The trustees didn't seem to mind Chou's derogatory reference to them, and on January 2, 1951, after much of the American press had portrayed China as the enemy of American national security and way of life, the trustees approved the budget of US $84,476 for the semester ending June 30, 1950, and fully expected to remit the funds to Peking.[24]

Yenching's loss of financial ties with the West was precipitated not by the Communist government nor by the trustees, but by the American government. On December 17 Washington froze all the Communist Chinese assets in the United States and made it unlawful for any American organization to remit funds to China without a special license. The trustees immediately applied for the special license but with no success. On January 3 the Yenching faculty held an extraordinary meeting to discuss Yenching's status, and the majority supported nationalization. As late as January 25, 1951, the trustees voted to continue funds to Yenching.[25] The university was formally taken over by the ministry of education on February 12 at a large meeting attended by Ma Hsü-lun of the ministry.[26] Had the faculty not decided to become nationalized in

January 1951 the university might well have died simply from the lack of funds.

My intent here is not to minimize the force of anti-American sentiment held by the revolutionary leadership in shaping foreign and domestic policies prior to the Korean War. Rather it is to underscore the idea that the closing of Yenching University must be seen in the context of American actions during the Korean War that were overtly hostile to China.

The Transfer of Power. As had been true before in Yenching's history, the transfer of power on the national scene during the turnover was closely reflected in administrative changes within the university. Those changes occurred in roughly three phases, beginning respectively with the Communist victories in the Yenching area in December 1948, the formation of the new government of the People's Republic of China in October 1949, and the Resist America Aid Korea Campaign of November 1950. The shift may be seen, furthermore, in terms of transfers of authority away from Westerners to Chinese, and from mission boards (represented by the trustees in New York) to the ministry of education in Peking.

In the first year after the turnover the government guidelines affecting university organization were vaguely expressed as protecting all public and private schools, encouraging all personnel in these institutions to remain at their posts, and protecting the lives and property of foreign nationals.[27] The purpose was to win over the intellectuals with a minimum of resistance and enlist their support in the consolidation of revolutionary power. Most Yenching personnel readily obliged. They were convinced that opposition would be futile and that the new order offered them meaningful opportunities for work. By April 1949 President Lu Chih-wei recognized that the new situation required a new ideology and that old patterns would have to be modified to meet the local needs. No longer would Yenching be a part of a "nationwide Christian education enterprise" existing alongside the "government enterprise."[28] Surprisingly, the trustees concurred in Lu's assessment.[29] Before the summer of 1949 Yenching faculty, led by Yen Ching-yüeh in sociology and Weng Tu-chien in history, launched their own study movement.[30] It was also facilitated by the absence of reprisals against the intellectuals by the new leadership and by the inspiring example of the cadres and the soldiers in the liberating armies.[31]

After the turnover the board of managers lost their usefulness more rapidly than the trustees. One reason was the financial indispensability of the New York board. For two full years Yenching still operated largely on American money. The managers' eclipse also reflected Lu Chih-wei's irritation with the board. By February 1949 Lu wielded great administrative power by virtue of his endorsement from the revolutionary leadership and the trustees. The managers' last meeting, with Stuart attending, was held in February 1949 in Shanghai just three months before the Communist seizure of that city.[32] Lu noted how some members of the board were regarded as "persona non grata if not outright war criminals," and he asked the trustees to concede, "You know as well as we do that the board of managers never did what it was expected to do."[33] For more than a year Lu simply tolerated the anomalous position of the managers until the government requested him to reestablish a new local board of control. He was spared from working through this embarrassing matter by the university's nationalization in February 1951. Lu's irritation with the board may be a bit misplaced, for there is some evidence to suggest that at least three longtime and prominent members of the board, Yen Hui-ch'ing, Ch'üan Shao-wen, and Chou Yi-ch'un, supported accommodation in ways not that dissimilar to his own.[34]

In this first phase in the transfer of power the changes in faculty composition were minimal. Only two recognized Marxist intellectuals, Chien Po-tsan in history and Shen Chih-yüan in economics, were added before October 1949. Chien had joined the Communist party in the mid 1930s and served at Yenching in 1949 as an editor of the *Yen-ching hsüeh-pao* and acting chairman of the history department.[35] Shen was a Russian returned student who had taught at Tsinan University before the revolution. He was so heavily involved in publishing and political activities that he spent little time on the campus. His influence in university affairs appeared to be minimal.[36] Other faculty were added in 1949, but they did not represent increased revolutionary influence in university affairs.

Culminating the first phase in the transition, nine Yenching faculty were invited to participate in the Chinese People's Political Consultative Conference, which met September 21, 1949, and ratified the Common Program that established the administrative guidelines for the new government. Those invited, in addition to Chien and Shen, were Chao Tzu-ch'en in religion, Chang Tung-sun in philosophy, Yen Ching-yüeh and Lei Chieh-ch'iung in sociology, Lin Han-ta, a new professor of education from Hangchow University, Ma Ssu-ts'ung, a new addition in music, and Lu Chih-wei, as a specially invited member. Also Chao Ch'eng-hsin in sociology and Weng Tu-chien in history, both Yenching alumni, were invited to the conference as auditors. According to Lu, Yenching had more members participating in the conference than any other educational institution in China.[37] Yen Hui-ch'ing of the board of managers was an elected member of the conference.[38]

The second phase in the tranfer of power began with the formation of the new national government in October 1949. During this phase, which lasted about a year, the government more directly shaped educational policy through: the increased activities of the newly formed ministry of education; the emergence of new revolutionary groups in the university; and the university's participation in the government-initiated campaign in political study. Yenching administrators were old hands at complying with government guidelines, and one finds no indication in reports and correspondence that their compliance with the new government met with any resistance. Organizationally the ministry was under the Government Administrative Council, headed by Chou En-lai, and directed by the Committee of Cultural and Educational Affairs, headed by Kuo Mo-jo and represented at Yenching by Chien Po-tsan.[39] The new minister of education, Ma Hsü-lun, a philologist who had taught at Peking National University, and President Lu apparently communicated directly, but the real asset for Yenching was the fact that the vice-minister of education was Wei Chüeh (Sidney K. Wei), a Lingnan University graduate who had served as minister of education in 1927 and who was an old classmate of Lu's.[40] (Wei had overseen Yenching's registration efforts in 1927.) The ministry issued guidelines which launched the political study campaign and approved Yenching's general curriculum. It also approved Yenching's continuing ties with the trustees in New York and prodded Lu to establish a new board of managers. Its most significant role from Yenching's perspective was reassuring the administrators that the university would have a place in the system of higher education under the New Democracy.

Among the important new organizations formed were the Yenching Communist Party Branch (Chung-kung Yen-ta chih-pu), the Educational Worker's Union (Chiao kung-hui), and the New Democratic Youth League (Hsin-min-chu ch'i ch'ing-nien t'uan). Figures on party affiliations at Yenching before the turnover have not been found, but it appears very few were actually members. One notable exception was Yang Ju-chi who had worked at Yenching since 1931 first as a clerk and later as an assistant in the president's office. Yang quickly assumed a new prominence in university affairs and was remembered by the Westerners who knew him for his efforts in easing their transition to the new order and eventual departure from China.[41] In June 1949, six months after the turnover, one public announcement was posted showing only two women students as party members and ten candidates for party membership, with about twice that number among the men students. The "lower staff" included three members and three candidates, but no membership or applicants for it were found among the senior faculty and staff.[42]

With the organization of the new government, a drive was begun to recruit more members into the party. In November a party branch (chih-pu) was formally organized, and two months later a central branch (tsung chih-pu) was formed with Lin Shou-chin, whose identity is obscure, as the secretary. By February 1950 the Yenching Party Branch reported a membership of 73 persons.[43] During the first months the new branch was preoccupied with political education, but its role in the campaign appeared largely auxiliary in nature. One published report of the branch's meeting indicated it spent more time in self-criticism, pointing out the need to oppose formalism, to work more closely with the student government, and to pay more attention to the needs of students, than in providing leadership in the campaign.[44]

Another important group in effecting change was the Educational Workers' Union, which was an umbrella organization that gradually overshadowed the president's office in administrative affairs. It was formally organized in January 1950, more than a year after the turnover. Its first chairman was Yen Ching-yüeh, a nonparty member, but strongly represented on the executive committee were members of the local party branch.[45] Within a month the union included all the salaried staff, faculty, administrative personnel, clerks, secretaries, accountants, technicians, librarians, maintenance personnel, servants, gardeners, and workers in the power plant. Union affiliation, according to Ralph Lapwood, raised the workers to new levels of consciousness. Prior to the turnover, his servant, Lao Jen (now salaried), would have scoffed at the idea of a voice in policy making. But after joining the union he and other workers learned to read, participated in discussions, and gradually accepted the idea that they were part of the vanguard in the revolution.[46]

With the purpose of helping in the management of university affairs, the union began its work by organizing study groups, welfare programs and health drives, and gradually expanded its role to the sponsorship of larger campaigns, notably the Resist America Aid Korea campaign.[47] Its influence in university life culminated in the Three Anti campaign against waste, corruption, and bureaucracy in the winter and spring of 1952. The union demanded the full participation of the membership, however costly it was in time. Lapwood estimated that one election of the union's nineteen member executive committee consumed more than 4,000 man-hours of deliberation. In the final vote union members were presented with a list of nineteen candidates and could register their choice by ticking off the names of those they approved and striking out the names of those they disapproved. All those presented by the union representatives were elected, most with over 90 percent of the vote.[48]

Despite the increase in party and union influence, the trustees forwarded money to the field until the American embargo in December 1950. Some donors had become angry with the board, charging "You are training Chinese to kill Americans," but trustee secretary Robert McMullen reassured Lu Chih-wei they would do all they could to keep Yenching financially independent and that they had large reserves which could be drawn on if necessary. The trustees were aware of serious outside pressures affecting the "educational and Christian purposes for which Yenching exists." But they placed their confidence in President Lu and recognized that "academic freedom must be evaluated in the perspective of the world situation."[49]

A third organization that facilitated Yenching's transition to the new order was the New Democratic Youth League. Active recruitment began on the Yenching campus in the fall of 1949. With historical roots in the 1920s, the youth league had served as an important adjunct to the party and assumed an especially vital role after 1946 when it was linked to the broadened appeal of the New Democracy. In April 1949 the league held a national conference in Peking, adopting a constitution and working program, and it began an extensive drive to gain new members. Recruitment into the league at Yenching occurred simultaneously with the political education campaign. In October membership in the Yenching branch was reported at twenty-five, but at the climax of the campaign in November, membership shot up to more than 200.[50]

Parallel to the formation of these three new organizations in the fall of 1949 was the program of political study (*cheng-chih hsüeh-hsi*). New courses were introduced in which each week students and faculty met jointly for a two hour lecture, known as the *ta-k'o,* followed by discussion sessions in small groups formed in each of the various departments, with a student serving as chairman and a faculty member always present. All students were required to take Historical Materialism and Social Evolution the first semester and Principles of the New Democracy the second semester, each for three hours credit. In addition all students in the arts and social sciences were required to take six hours of Political Economy, which overlapped with existing courses in international relations and foreign trade. Students in the natural sciences were freed from this latter requirement to pursue their more practical study. In the second semester of academic year 1949–50, the faculty organized their own regular sessions to better prepare themselves for their work with the students. Randolph Sailer estimated that the preparations, lectures, and discussions took ten to twelve hours of the students' and teachers' time each week.[51] This intensive program of political education was carried out largely by people within the university. Yenching professors, notably Yenching graduates themselves such as Yen Ching-yüeh, Kao Ming-k'ai, and Chao Ch'eng-hsin, were featured as the major interpreters of such concepts as the relationship between political and professional education, the mass and worker points of view, class struggle, and the differences between the socialist (Russian) and the New Democratic (Chinese) revolutions.[52]

Given the government direction of political study, which had been introduced into schools all over China, it is not surprising to see occasional references made in the testimonies of students to new found admiration for Stalin and the Soviet Union. But conspicuously lacking was any specific attack on the university as such. Generally the faculty and the administration were considered as patrons of the whole campaign. The newly instilled revolutionary consciousness was intended to permeate all areas of life, but political study was not supposed to replace professional study (yeh-wu hsüeh-hsi).[53] The major enemies in the attack, labeled as feudalism, imperialism, and capitalism, were identified with forces outside the university. President Lu, in fact, enthusiastically endorsed the campaign and went out of his way—he could have remained silent as he did on other occasions—to explain it to the trustees in New York. Assuming that Yenching was "not free to educate social miscreants," Lu argued that only with political education could the students "change their mode of living" in the revolutionary society. "Where orthodox Christianity has failed," Lu hoped the "New Democracy might bring us along to a vantage point where we can see the man

Jesus." Teachers who felt their work was jeopardized by political education, he pointed out, were not necessarily those who had mastered their
subjects under the old government. He reassured the trustees that academic freedom was not yet an issue, and the campaign, however costly
in time, had used up less than 1 percent of the budget.[54]

New Democratic politics apparently did not mean limitless political
indoctrination, nor did they necessarily portend the end of Yenching's
usefulness in the new design of higher education. Political study for
academic year 1950–51, before the Resist America Aid Korea campaign,
was decreased in scope and intensity. Only the freshman and nonscience
sophomores had to engage in it. The directives from the ministry of
education in Peking urged all other students to concentrate on work in
the classroom and laboratories.[55] Furthermore, despite the broad sympathy of Yenching students for the new order, their selection of courses,
even two years after the turnover reflected much continuity with the
pattern in the Republican years. (Figures in parentheses are for 1936.)
Thus in the fall of 1950 journalism, one of Yenching's most famous
departments, accounted for 8.8 percent (8.0) of course enrollments and
economics 11.5 percent (12.3). There was a percentage decline in Chinese, 2.4 percent (3.3) and an increase in Western languages, 10.3
percent (6.1). History enrollments declined, 2.3 percent (5.8), and
sociology dropped sharply to 2.9 percent (9.8). The enrollments in the
school of religion stayed about the same, 2.4 percent (2.5). The highest
enrollments, 20.0 percent, were in engineering (mechanical, chemical,
and civil), and accounted for a large share of the increase in total
enrollments.[56] To be sure, the course content differed somewhat from
before. Western languages in 1936, for example, included many courses
in literature, whereas by 1950 the emphasis was on language study. New
materials were written in the social sciences, incorporating Marxist analysis. But even here there was considerable continuity.

The third and last stage of Yenching's accommodation began with the
Resist America Aid Korea campaign in November 1950. The major
change effected was the complete replacement of the American trustees'
role by the ministry of education. With no meaningful private support
from within China, the university was now at the mercy of the government. By November the United States stepped up its support for the
Nationalist government, while fighting between Chinese and American
soldiers in Korea dominated the media on both sides. China and the
United States were at war, and the hopes of any continued cooperation

seemed at an end. Significantly the Resist America campaign merged with other campaigns and continued for more than two years. Common themes of the campaigns were the rooting out of any remaining "worship America" or "fear America" sentiments. The Korean War fired patriotic sentiment to an unprecedented level.[57]

During this campaign privacy and individual freedom were sharply reduced, beginning with the crowding of all faculty and staff into available housing. Before, only those with associate professor rank or above were provided for. These moves meant great personal sacrifice, but the noise, disturbances, petty irritations, and close physical contact, Lu Chih-wei philosophically noted, were all part of the process of reeducation.[58] Professors for the first time were forced to join the May Day parade in 1951. They had to run in the streets to keep up with their contingents filing past the reviewing stand in the huge T'ien-an-men square, stripping themselves symbolically of their "above politics" positions of previous years.

It was not until after the Resist America campaign that Yenching professors became seriously involved in land reform. As the Communists consolidated their power in the late 1940s and early 1950s in the rural areas they invited students and intellectuals to join work teams that went into the villages to implement land reform. Their work involved organizing the poorer peasants, struggling against the rich peasants and landlords, and ultimately redistributing the land and other village resources among all members in the village. These intellectuals had a contribution to make in applying their educational skills to the land reform process. But the work team experience also had the effect of educating them to the ways of rural living and the political programs of the new leadershp. Hou Jen-chih joined a work team in South China in April, while Lu Chih-wei went to Szechuan for six weeks in May. Others followed in the summer and fall.[59] The placing of intellectual and technical skills at the disposal of the Chinese government had long been an ideal at Yenching, but this concept of service after the turnover had to be carried out within the framework of revolutionary politics.[60]

With the launching of the Three Anti campaign in December 1951 it seemed only a matter of time until Yenching would be completely dissolved. In the small groups organized along departmental lines, each individual was asked to analyze his thoughts and behavior regarding waste, corruption, and bureaucracy, engage in self-criticism, and confess his faults. The climax came with the large mass meetings for struggle during which the worst offenders were exposed, denounced, sometimes forced to kneel, and not allowed to say anything on their own behalf.[61] Throughout the campaign the faculty were kept ignorant as to how long the campaign would last. For the first time in Yenching history no attempt was made to make up the loss in study time, and only the most "essential" courses were resumed. The big question in the minds of the faculty was the future of the university. The possibility of amalgamation with other institutions had been discussed since the fall of 1951, but just what role Yenching or individual faculty members might have in the combined arrangement remained uncertain. Even with nationalization Yenching had been allowed to retain a distinct identity as an institution, but after February 1952 the question of identity had paled in comparison to the question of whether or not Yenching would have any role to play at all.

The Question of Accommodation. In discussing the various ways Chinese and Westerners have responded to the revolution, the term fellow traveling quickly comes to mind. The term itself has been applied more often to the Soviet Union, especially in the 1930s, and in the West it has acquired a perjorative connotation. Those who are inclined to see good in the Chinese revolution have felt pressured to preface their statements with disclaimers to being soft on communism. Even the word accommodation in the context of revolution has sometimes carried a negative connotation. The price of this ideological bias has been high. Many writers on the missionary educators' experience in China at the time of the turnover have simply refused to take these years of transition seriously.[62] But only by overcoming these semantic difficulties and openly addressing the issue of the intellectuals' sympathy for the revolution can we understand Yenching's experience in the new order.

Fellow traveling arises in part out of the disillusionment with Western society. As a concept it includes both those who participate in the revolution and those who give their support at a distance, but it usually does not include already confirmed Marxists or party members. This disillusionment, in David Caute's comprehensive study on the subject, may be seen as a postscript to the Enlightenment. Those societies, in Caute's words, which

. . . nailed "Liberty, Equality, Fraternity," to their mastheads failed to live up to these ideals: the once-progressive doctrine of *laissez-faire* and enlightened self-interest resulted in poverty, unemployment and inexcusable inequities of wealth and opportunity. Freedom came to mean exploitation, treating the worker as a wealth-producing object. Nations which valued liberty at home trampled colonial peoples underfoot . . . Education, knowledge, and culture remained minority privileges, while art, appalled by its environment, turned its back on life.[63]

Troubled by the growth in the late nineteenth centery of the view of life which depicted man as "no more free than a slave crawling east across the deck of a ship traveling west," fellow travelers wanted to recapture the optimism of the Enlightenment.[64]

In exploring Yenching's accommodation to revolution one immediately confronts the problem of sources. Those documents produced under duress should be treated with skepticism, but they should not be dismissed out of hand. The attitudes expressed in them, though often overstated, are nevertheless corroborated by accounts of observers at the time. The record of the missionary educators is available through their diaries, letters, and published writings. President Lu Chih-wei's extensive correspondence with the trustees is also available. The personal writings of the Chinese faculty are more scarce, as prudence alone would encourage their silence in the last years of the Kuomintang rule and the years since the turnover. The personal writings of Yenching students are even more limited. What we do have on the Chinese side are conversations recorded in the writings of the missionaries. There are also newspaper reports, but as with most of the press in China then, these accounts are highly stylized and follow closely the accepted political line. Finally, there are the confessions of the faculty and students. Though they are obviously influenced by the will to survive in the new order, they should be treated with some seriousness. The language is different but the questions they raise bear some similarity to those of the Life Fellowship thirty years before. Those questions are convincing even if their answers to them are less so.[65]

The differences between the accommodating experiences in the Chinese Revolution and those in the Russian Revolution seem significant. Russian and non-Russian intellectuals have been castigated for their myopic and overenthusiastic endorsement of the Bolshevik Revolution, because in doing so, in Caute's words, they "deepened the despair of the non-official Soviet intelligentsia during the years of persecution and terror. In their darkest hours they heard themselves condemned by their own kind, by foreigners who shared their own idealistic traditions and whose immunity from imprisonment or death was due solely to the accident of nationality."[66] But the Chinese experience, though certainly crushing to intellectual freedom, has not entailed the extent of brutality found in the Russian experience.[67] The loss of intellectual freedom may appear to be less of a sacrifice than we would be inclined to admit in the West. The exposure to Enlightenment values, even among the most Westernized Chinese at Yenching, was relatively limited and recent. Their attraction to Christianity, as we have seen, was to a large extent in terms of service and self-sacrifice, an attraction which resonated with certain Confucian (as well as Buddhist and Taoist) predispositions in defining the individual's relationship to society. The battle waged against individualism after the turnover has been a variation on a familiar theme. The losses were real to them, to be sure, but they were greatly softened by the gains in China's recovery of national dignity, after her century long experience of humiliation. Their enthusiasm reflected the pervading disillusionment with Western society from their earliest contacts with the West, a disillusionment which has perhaps increased in the years after the turnover as the Chinese experiment with the Soviet model has also soured. It remains to be seen just how much their hopes in the Chinese Revolution may be misplaced. Despite thought campaigns, labor camps, leader worship, and ceaseless propaganda, it is not yet clear that the god of the Chinese revolution has failed in the way that it has with the Russian Revolution.[68] The criteria for judging success or failure here remain a great divide between human experiences in China and the West, past and present.

Any assessment of accommodation at Yenching necessarily remains tentative. More certain, however, is the number of Yenching personnel at the time of the turnover who left and who stayed. Those who left fell roughly into two categories. The first included those who had departed prior to the consolidation of Communist power, whenever that occurred in the various parts of the country. Among them were: a handful of Western and Chinese faculty residing at the time on campus; a larger group, mostly alumni, who were studying or living abroad at the time; and alumni who retreated with the Nationalist government before the Communist advance and took up residence mostly in Hong Kong, Taiwan, and the United States. It does not include the several hundred students who left campus prior to the turnover and went south to be with their families during the interregnum. These students, for the most part, soon accommodated to the new order wherever they happened to be in China.[69] Some Yenching personnel, notably Wu Wen-tsao (sociology) and Hsieh Ping-hsin (literature), who were with the Chinese

Diplomatic Mission in Tokyo at the time of the turnover, returned to China to work. In November 1949 the New York Branch of the Yenching Alumni Association, along with twenty-one other Chinese cultural and student bodies and representing some 3,600 Chinese citizens, issued a statement indicating their willingness to return and work for the new government.[70] It is not clear just how many of the Yenching alumni residing abroad in 1949 decided to return.

Precise figures on the number of Yenching Chinese residing abroad in December 1948 are hard to put together. One list, "Yenching Alumni in the U.S.A. and Canada, May 1945," included 267 names of which 58 were non-Chinese.[71] A "Directory, 1972" was compiled by the Yenching Alumni Association, Inc., U.S.A., and listed over 400 Chinese names. But the affiliation with the university was not indicated, and some names on the list were not alumni but were associated with Yenching through marriage, blood relationship, and friendship.[72] In 1967 the Yenching Alumni Association of Hong Kong published a list of over 240 names but again the affiliation with the university was not always clear.[73] Efforts to get an alumni list for Taiwan in 1969 were unsuccessful, but one alumna estimated approximately 60 Yenching Chinese were residing on the island at the time.[74] Other clusters of Yenching alumni have resided in larger cities scattered around the world.[75]

As an estimate more than 3,000 students actually graduated from Yenching between 1917 and 1949. Of these perhaps three fourths were still alive in 1949. And of the living, roughly six hundred chose either to remain abroad or flee the revolution, leaving, as a calculated guess, a ratio of about three to one between those who stayed and those who left China. One should not extract from this calculation the idea that those who stayed were necessarily happy with their position. Given the breakdown of the communication and transportation systems and the virtual absence of financial means for many Yenching Chinese to leave, one might argue they hardly had a choice. But ambivalence, to the extent it did exist, was not unique among those who stayed. One finds it existing as well among alumni who left and have felt isolated from the drama of China's revolutionary experience.[76]

The second category includes those who broke their ties with Yenching after the turnover. It included a larger group of faculty, mostly Western, who trickled out of China over the next two years. Before their departure, though, they had made some efforts at accommodation. In their eyes Yenching's chances of preserving some measure of independence lasted until February 1951, when the university was nationalized.

But by far the vast majority of Yenching Chinese, faculty and students, accommodated one way or another. Their affiliation with the institution ended finally in September 1952 when they scattered to other places of work. Whether or not they could have left China after 1952, had they desired, is not clear.[77]

The Students

One can hardly escape the conclusion that the majority of Yenching students sincerely endorsed the revolution and its vast implications for their lives.[78] When they felt impotent and when they felt humiliated by China's impotence they had contempt for the central government. But after the turnover as the new government had every prospect of achieving control over all of China and of solving the twin ills of internal decay and external threat, most students gladly brought themselves into line.

The first occasion for expressing their new patriotic enthusiasm was the turnover itself when the students welcomed the Red Army and mixed with the soldiers of liberation.[79] A month later in January 1949 twenty-eight Yenching student members of the singing group, the kao-ch'ang hui, along with Ralph Lapwood, were invited by representatives of the Red Army to join them in propaganda work at the ironworks factory fifteen miles west of Peking. Trading singing, dancing, and dramatic performances with the soldiers' propaganda team in front of the workers, the Yenching students were put to shame. In Lapwood's words the soldiers sang with "great vigor but no tune," danced with "great skill and abandon," and produced a play that "spoke to the audience." But the students' songs sounded "half hearted," the dances looked "sophisticated and stilted," and their play seemed "inadequately thought out and rehearsed." The Yenching students were so embarrassed they spent hours afterwards in grueling self-criticism. Yenching returned the invitation, and a week later the soldiers put on a big show at Bashford Hall with real explosions that broke thirteen windows.[80]

Revolution making did not come off smoothly nor did it always meet the expectations of student enthusiasts. One young cadre appeared on campus in January 1949 and urged the students to make preparations for helping in the liberation of Peking, which was expected any day. They were promised a hand in keeping order, protecting property, and explaining the new policies to the city dwellers. But the takeover of Peking was delayed, and the students "champed at the bit for a month" before the opportunity at last arrived. And then they were limited to explaining policies. Nor was it in the East suburbs but in the "humble suburbs" outside the West Gate nearer the Yenching campus. Nevertheless 500 of them fell in line with raised spirits, enduring twenty degree weather, sleeping in the unheated classrooms of Peking Normal University, practicing propaganda plays, singing songs, making speeches, and in the evenings engaging in self-criticism and planning for the next day's activities.[81]

In the spring of 1949 about eighty Yenching students joined the Communist offensive southward. Just before leaving, two women students with "glowing eyes, misfit uniforms, and happy as dedicated souls," stopped to say farewell to Grace Boynton, and the following day the whole university turned out for the big farewell with speeches, songs, cheers, and tears.[82] During the fall semester the Yenching branch of the Sino-Soviet Friendship Association was formed in time for commemorating the October Revolution. With Lu Chih-wei as co-chairman and 650 students, faculty, and workers as members, the branch celebrated Stalin's birthday on December 21.[83] In January 1950 Yenching students joined land reform efforts, first in small voluntary groups over the winter vacation. Before long all of the 200 plus students who were enrolled in the social sciences were asked to help with work teams around the country where land reform had not yet been carried out. In one case students stayed on thirty-five days until the reform in one village was completed. President Lu expressed full approval of their involvement and agreed to help the students make up missed classes.[84] Yenching students also joined in celebrating the signing of the Sino-Soviet Friendship Treaty on February 17, 1950.

After about a year and a half of intensive political activity, the students were told to concentrate on their studies. When they returned to the campus in September 1950, political study was at the lowest level in a year. But this relative calm was interrupted by developments in the Korean War. China's entry into the war in October and November stimulated a new outburst of patriotic feeling. During the second week in November classes were suspended, while the students, staff, faculty, and workers intensively studied the events of the war. The following week they fanned out into surrounding villages with dramatic stunts, songs, dances, private interviews, public talks, posters, and literature to inform the common people. Letters were written and packages of toilet articles were sent to Chinese and Korean soldiers fighting on the front. It was a time of great anxiety on campus. Bliss Wiant recalled that for the first time in two years since the turnover the hostility to Western personnel prevented him from conducting classes. The speech of American Ambassador Warren Austin on November 28, 1950, to the United Nations General Assembly listed Yenching University as a model of Chinese American friendship, and it was followed by a wave of protest on campus. The following day Wu Hsiu-ch'üan, Peking's delegate to Lake Success, gave Peking's interpretation of American Chinese relations and the war. Copies of his speech circulated widely on campus.[85]

When the government appealed for volunteer soldiers to fight on the Korean front, most Yenching students responded, according to Ralph Lapwood. But the selection process was very strict. No one in the sciences, no fourth year students, no one in weak health, no one from single-child families, and no one whose parents refused approval could be considered. After extensive interviews only twelve were finally accepted. They were extended an elaborate farewell by the Yenching community as heroes of the whole university. After the Resist America campaign began, political excitement on campus remained high until the dissolution of the university in September 1952.[86]

Just as the command of English had been the hallmark of Yenching cosmopolitanism before the turnover, the refusal to use it afterwards became one sure way to affirm revolutionary patriotism. Its widespread usage in the Republican years may have been an indication of the lack of national self-confidence. Stuart had conceded in the mid 1930s that English was a "device of the devil" and that students were "willing to study anything so long as it was in English." But little was done then to deter Yenching from holding its preeminent position as a place for mastering English.[87] The experience of revolution raised doubts in Yenching minds about their Western orientation as reflected in their use of English. In 1949 Chao Tzu-ch'en, one of the most gifted of all Yenching Chinese in spoken and written English, reportedly was loath to speak it. And within a year after the turnover Louise Sailer reported that nowhere could one hear English spoken, except in the dwindling number of classes taught by foreigners. By then no public meetings were held in English, nor was any attempt made to conduct university gatherings bilingually. All notices on the bulletin boards and all letters mailed in China were addressed only in Chinese. Professors also began writing textbooks in Chinese for courses that had none.[88] This trend in usage did not necessarily conflict with increased enrollments in English noted previously, for Yenching had been encouraged by the new ministry of education to continue training in English to meet the need for foreign laguage experts. Russian was not studied seriously at Yenching until late 1951.[89]

Changed dress styles reflected the new consciousness of being Chinese. Ruinous inflation in the late 1940s had reduced most student wardrobes to the bare minimum, but they became even smaller after the turnover. For the women students permanents and long hair were out, while straight boyish bobs were in. Western dresses gave way to slacks and short Chinese jackets, usually in dark colors. Men students substituted trousers and sweaters and short American army coats for their prewar long gowns and Western style suits. Women now dressed for comfort and convenience, and one seldom saw a silk gown or a pair of high-heeled shoes. Students with larger wardrobes faced difficulty finding a market to sell their foreign style clothes.[90]

Physical exercise also dramatized the new spirit on campus. Since the early decades of the twentieth century the YMCA in China had created a respect for physical exercise in urban centers. At Yenching some progress had been made through the department of physical education and the efforts of Lucius Porter to get the students to engage in physical exercise and competitive sports. During the Japanese occupation physical fitness was connected with resistance, and 90 percent of the Yenching students, according to one estimate, regularly took part in voluntary games.[91] Thus the introduction by the revolutionary leadership of physical jerks to radio instructions every morning on campus was in a sense the culmination of a longer trend at Yenching. And yet the cultist aspects were entirely new. By the summer of 1951 Yenching students had adopted the 50–1–8 system, meaning 50 hours of study a week, one hour of exercise a day, and eight hours of sleep a night. Swimming in the Yenching lake and at the Summer Palace near the campus became popular as never before. By 1952 the students were given paid group vacations as part of the new emphasis on outdoor activity.[92]

Most Yenching students approached political study eagerly, and yet patriotic enthusiasm did not mean complete identification with the revolution. Personal testimonies, for what they are worth, from some eight students were reproduced in the January and February issues (1950) of the *Hsin Yen-ching* and showed a new awareness of class backgrounds.

Those from upper class families testified to an increased knowledge in social development and to salvation from pessimistic, subjective, and reactionary thinking. They spoke of being freed from individualistic heroism and from superiority feelings over the masses. Characteristically the testimonies concluded with resolutions to further combat individualism and to devote themselves to serving the people.[93]

But a survey of student attitudes in November 1949 qualifies this apparent success. The survey was composed of ten questions which were sent out to 1,000 students. Eight hundred responded and the results were published in the *Hsin Yen-ching*. The first question presented the position of a pre-medical student who believed in serving the people but resented interference in his busy study schedule. Fourteen percent agreed with his objection, 7 percent were uncertain, and 76 percent disagreed. Question four was about a student who recognized the benefits of studying Marxism-Leninism but objected to discussion in small groups as a waste of time. Eleven percent agreed with him, 9 percent were uncertain, and 74 percent disagreed. The position taken in question six was to defend the intellectuals for not wanting to do physical work. After all, did not Mao Tse-tung and Liu Shao-ch'i work more with their minds than with their hands? Thirty-six and two tenths percent agreed with this position, 12.7 percent were uncertain, and 44.6 percent disagreed. Question nine asked the respondent if it was all right to want sometime to go to America. Only 4.7 percent thought so, 12.5 percent were uncertain, and 78 percent thought it not all right. The large number agreeing with the objections raised in question six indicate that the students felt free to express their opinions. Surprisingly, the desire to go to America had almost disappeared within a year after the turnover.[94] Despite some student reservations, the political education campaign was unmistakably getting results.

Political education was conducted mostly in small groups. Some recalcitrant cases were brought out into the open for public criticism. One occurred in November 1949 and involved the student, Liang Ssu-huan, who was charged with laziness, immorality, and bad influence, as well as counterrevoluntionary connections. Liang's case was so serious that five faculty members were asked to preside over the large public gathering. Liang apparently was a skilled debater and successfully resisted public humiliation. But in the end he was sent to reform through labor at the nearby town of Ching Ho where "work in the fields, combined with study and self-analysis, was turning a crowd of secret agents into hard-working and straightforward citizens." What a striking reversal of roles for this rural community from Yenching's heyday of rural philanthropy![95]

Christian cosmopolitanism had been a vital force in many areas of university life at the beginning. But its ability to stem antireligious and anti-Western nationalism in the three years after the turnover was hardly any more successful than the attempt to blunt anti-Japanese nationalism in the early 1930s. In the rehearsals for the annual Christmas performance of Handel's *Messiah* in October 1949, students were still receiving credit for singing. But radical members of the chorus requested Bliss Wiant, the choir director, to devote the first half hour to practicing songs honoring Mao Tse-tung. When that failed, they scheduled rehearsals of their own patriotic music close to the regular rehearsal hour, hoping to discourage others and get them to drop out. Again they had little success. After the turnover the famous oratorio took on a different meaning for some. After hearing it performed in December 1948 Ralph Lapwood was struck by the contrast between the "newly arrived People's Army, absolutely indigenous and drawing its strength directly from the peasants, and our sophisticated and Westernized students singing a European oratorio in English." Wiant had directed the premier performance of this oratorio in China in 1928 and he directed his last in December 1950 in the heat of the Resist America Aid Korea campaign. It was not an easy time to do it. The *Messiah* was sung one more time, Christmas 1951 with a choir of sixty members and 1,300 attending. For the first time in more than twenty years it was sung in Chinese.[96]

The Yenta Christian Fellowship, with about 200 members at the time of the turnover and representing roughly one fifth of the student body, experienced an increased vitality according to one member, as it tried to "bear a Christian witness in the midst of these rapidly changing conditions."[97] In July 1951 the group sponsored a two week conference on the theme of Christianity and Patriotism. The leadership for the 150 people attending was shared by recent graduates of the school of religion and members of the Jesus Family (Yeh-su chia), a small sect in China which practiced communal living and believed in the abolishment of private property. Located in some 100 communities, largely in Shantung province, this totally indigenous group voluntarily provided teams of medical workers to help in the mass construction of the Huai River project. This small sect quickly caught the attention of Christians at

Yenching because it suggested one way of practicing Christian idealism in the new order. Representatives of the sect were invited to the campus several times and, in Ralph Lapwood's words, provided hope for Christianity in the future.[98]

The ability to meet the demands of Christian cosmopolitanism and patriotic loyalty at the same time became increasingly difficult as religious freedom gradually crumbled in the face of the fierce demand for ideological conformity. Religious converts were discouraged, discriminated against, or barred from membership in the youth league and the party.[99] Many Christians took stands on political issues which in time meant denouncing the whole connection with the missionary enterprise. To be sure there were strong pressures on them to take these stands. But until the Resist America campaign at least they could have remained silent. Lucy Burtt, the English Quaker who was a leader in the Christian fellowship in the first months after the turnover, recognized the pressures to "completely and uncritically" identify with the Communist policy. But the young people, had to "go forward in creative action." Those with more experience saw "weaknesses and possible dangers" in the current changes, but they went along anyway in the hope of discovering what "God has to teach us in the present social upheaval." Clarification of the essentials of the Christian faith in the Chinese context remained a never ending challenge.[100]

One student told Grace Boynton she no longer believed in God but had found a new one, the Chinese people. Another influential Christian student, Chang Ching-yu, openly endorsed the Communist ideology.[101] One Christian friend of the Lapwoods was forced underground in 1948 for his radical beliefs. There he found it hard to counter the arguments of the revolutionary cadre but harder still to meet the challenge of their lives. "As a Christian," he testified, "I had believed for years that a man must surrender himself, give himself for others, forget personal pride, and face . . . in the service of mankind." But these cadre had "given themselves more wholeheartedly than I, had achieved more than I, had more energy and drive, better teamwork, and a clearer plan of living." All that he had sought in Christianity, "purpose, energy, joy, comradeship, self-giving," he now found in the spirit of the revolution. In addition he had the added satisfaction of knowing that he was putting his "whole energy into work which is of direct and immediate value to the Chinese people."[102] These testimonies did not necessarily represent all members of the Yenta Christian Fellowship. Those who may have differed with the current political line were silent for obvious reasons.

The stress on service and self-sacrifice in the earlier religious experiences of the Chinese members of the Life Fellowship provides a clue to the enthusiastic endorsement of the revolution among Christians. Those themes were only half-heartedly realized in Yenching's prerevolutionary setting, but with the turnover they took on a new meaning. The attitude of many Yenching Christians toward revolution was seen by Randolph Sailer as a mass religious experience. He said he had seen "conversions . . . testimony of former sin and present release and enlightenment." Sin, defined as class interest and bias, only blocked the conversion of more students. New converts were loath to give the "sinners a fair break and the benefit of the doubt" but equally eager to forgive them after conversion. There were practical effects too such as the breaking of bad habits, biting of fingernails, and so on. Sailer noted the presence of many skeptics who were bewildered at the rate of conversions, but he also noted that the converts included the sane and well-balanced. The believers challenged the unbelievers to produce comparable results.[103]

The Western Faculty

The turnover was no less a turning point for Westerners at Yenching. They had been through political turmoil before under the warlords and the Japanese occupation, but they had survived. Even in the worst cases of suffering in the Japanese prison camps these Westerners (and their Chinese colleagues) believed the Japanese would be defeated. But with the turnover the Westerners concluded the Communists were here to stay. Any thought of reestablishing the status quo before the civil war did not issue from the field but rather from twisted American politics. Hope was not light at the end of the tunnel but the possibility of adjustment and survival in the new order.

If ever there were mixed feelings and ambiguities in Sino-American relations at Yenching from the Westerners' point of view, it was now. Single-mindedness among them was gone. Doubts informed all thought and inquiry. Individuals were driven back to fundamentals, and one notes how often those who stayed on explained their experiences in terms of the religious faith. On the eve of takeover only mission board appointees were there representing the Western side.

Stuart must have spoken for many when he recalled after his return to the United States, an internal conflict in his personal sentiments regarding the two parties. In the Kuomintang were many friends of long standing, but since its rise to power it had "tolerated among its officials of all grades graft and greed, idleness and inefficiency, nepotism and factional rivalries—all the evils in short of the corrupt bureaucracy it had overthrown." As the Nationalist defenses crumbled before the Communist advance, Stuart noted sadly that the Kuomintang government, "benefiting from substantial American aid," was the body in whose principles and aims "we thoroughly believed." In painful contrast the Communist party was "free from private graft," while its "officers and men lived very much together, simply and industriously, severely disciplined, thoroughly indoctrinated." The Communists thus gave the appearance of being a "dynamic movement fostering among millions those qualities of which China had stood so palpably in need." These were the qualities which "Christian missions and other cultural forces had been slowly inculcating among so pitifully few." But with equal emotion Stuart was angered at the thought of the Communist party's "repressive techniques for absolute control of thought," and its "callous disregard for individual human rights." He "shuddered to think of the inescapable consequences to the Christian Movement . . . to educational institutions like Yenching, and to all of the fruitful cultural relations" with America.[104]

Stuart stayed on as the American ambassador more than a month after the liberation of Nanking in June 1949 to observe Communist intentions. If they were averse to discussing relationships with the United States then "we could form our policy accordingly.[105] He left China in August 1949. The internal conflict in his mind may have been settled in favor of the Nationalists with the appearance of the biting New China News Agency editorial, "Farewell Leighton Stuart." Stuart embodied the liberals' ambivalence on revolution, approving the end in most cases but rejecting the means. Till the end of the war with Japan, Yenching's Western community had spoken largely with one voice. But cold war currents, beginning with the civil war, forced a growing separation. Stuart would line up on the side condemning the revolution with Western definitions of freedom, worth, and rights. Ralph Lapwood would himself undergo the severe test of thought reform and still defend the revolution's attack on individualism.[106]

The turnover marked the gradual dispersion of the Western community at Yenching. Six longtime staff members shared Stuart's fears about the Communists and left campus prior to liberation in December 1948.[107] Other Westerners trickled out over the next four years. By the summer of 1951, hostility toward the United States was so strong in North China that all but two or three Protestant missionaries had left Peking. The Western faculty at Yenching had dwindled to five. Presbyterian Sam Dean, who some thought would have the best chance of staying because of his practical skills in engineering, left in the summer of 1952 but only after experiencing great personal trauma in the Three Anti thought reform campaign.[108] The last to leave was the Lapwood family in August 1952. Prior to the Korean War the major issue had been readjustment. After that it was survival.

After the turnover even those who were previously disinclined to political debate began to see political connections in their work and their lives. Bliss Wiant, treasurer, reversed the prevailing sympathy among the missionary educators by denouncing Chiang Kai-shek as the "one obstacle to peace. If Chiang Kai-shek had only gotten out of the way a long time ago, all this would have been avoided."[109] The crumbling of earlier hopes, Wiant soon recognized, was caused by the missionaries themselves and the American government whose "sins . . . have now come to plague us." He thought it was "entirely within the rights of the governing powers to eliminate all foreigners if they so desire," especially those supporting the "patterns which the American government followed in years past."[110]

Again the Korean War was a turning point. The students in Wiant's music history course challenged him for the first time in September 1950 on his ideological premises. He seized the initiative, he recalled, and asked them about Marx's teaching on music, to which they had no answer. Twelve students enrolled. But the class stopped meeting after the two week observance of the Resist America campaign in November. Soon after the American embargo in December, Chou En-lai, according to Wiant, personally assured him of a safe departure. The visa, however, did not come through until after both he and his wife, Mildred, had been denounced in posters and signs plastered around the campus, though they were spared the humiliation of a public denunciation (*k'ung-su hui*). All the charges, Wiant conceded, had an element of truth. The first was listening to Voice of America broadcasts. When foreigners were ordered to turn in their radios at the police station in Peking, Wiant readily complied. (Before his departure from China months later he was reimbursed in US dollars more than twice the original cost of the radio.) The second charge was assuring the Chinese faculty that American troops would not cross the thirty-eighth parallel in Korea. A third charge was trying to buy the hearts of the Chinese students with gifts of apples and candy purchased with money sent from Stuart in Washington, D.C., as late as Christmas 1950. A fourth charge was his purchasing of hundreds of Chinese art objects and musical instruments. Wiant was allowed to take these items with him, but instead of selling them, he used them over the next twenty years in his talks to religious, educational, and civic groups in the United States.[111]

On the eve of liberation Wiant had seen Yenching's "social service" continuing in the new order. Revolution then, provided "unparalleled opportunity" for experiments in Christian love. But two years later in the face of bitter anti-American hostility Wiant was able to speak of Yenching's role only in terms of the remnants of the "international Christian spirit at work in society."[112]

Lucius Porter transferred his support to the new order with remarkable rapidity, considering the endorsement he had given to the Nationalist government only a few months before. The turnover in 1948 reminded him of previous political takeovers, the warlord years, the Kuomintang victory in 1927—"how the populace welcomed them then! —and the day when Japanese 'baby tanks' came rumbling by Yenching gates. And then the recovery of the campus after VJ day!" With characteristic optimism he wrote, "And now we wait, rather calmly when all is noted, for the next overturn, confident that there is about our educational work and our Christian spirit something that will outlast and eventually overcome all these conflicts and hatreds." Confident of "getting along with new rulers and theories of life," he felt ready for a "fresh adventure in Christian living." He felt he could have a "personal share in the great, worldwide experiment for peace and goodwill among men."[113]

The Porters hoped the United States would sever completely its ties to Chiang Kai-shek and not follow the Nationalist retreat to Canton or Formosa. They described the new officials as being "very reasonable in their revolutionary activities, allowing what more logical peoples would forbid," and they found student enthusiasm for the new government "really thrilling." Their fears of Soviet influence were allayed somewhat when it became "clear . . . that at present the leaders are much more concerned with the Chinese people, their welfare, and upbuilding, than about any international relations." Before their departure from China in

July 1949 they reflected on their forty-one years in China, which had often been "strange and surrounded by many uncertainties and misgivings," but had turned out to be "exceedingly interesting, happy, and fruitful."[114]

Prior to Yenching's liberation, Grace Boynton had feared the revolutionary leadership as the enemies of democracy. The prospect of Communist victory in 1948 left her with a sense of diminishing usefulness and a loss of religious vitality. Previously Stuart had been able to allay any recurring doubts about herself and the missionary cause. But his last attempts in October 1948, while visiting the campus, only left her with a "strong sense of the limitations of the Yenching scene." She reflected then on past hopes that Peking might remain untouched but concluded that no change would only mean famine for the people. She was reminded that as "Assyria of old came to harry and made a clean sweep of rottenness, so now, again, rottenness must be savagely purged." The purging she regarded as inevitable and in some ways salutary. But would the new regime have any place for her? She was getting older and felt physically low. She feared the "terror and hardship," but she feared more the "severance of the Yenching bond."[115]

At the urging of the administration Boynton had left her cottage in the village of Haitien near the campus just prior to the turnover and moved into campus housing. But she returned to her village residence the summer of 1949 to accommodate on her own terms. She dismissed gratuitous advice from younger Western colleagues on how to cope with the revolutionary scene as "teaching grandmother to suck eggs," and she derived a well-deserved pride in the simplicity of her living quarters. She had no running water, central heating, or electricity. Her opportunity to cope firsthand with the revolution came when an officer of the liberation army, Comrade Wang, took over part of her small home in the summer and fall of 1949. She was disturbed by rumors of sexual promiscuity in the army, but even more so at the "fearful din" of the soldiers' music. At one point she offered them some of her own Victor Herbert albums preferring the strains of "kiss me, kiss me, again" to the clashing cymbals and squealing voices of the "mountain of Chinese opera records." The nudity of young comrades swarming around the tub of hot water in the courtyard for their baths also irritated her maiden lady instincts, but in the end she was pleased to have a "hand in cleaning up the Army of liberation." They used her soap without asking, but she responded with a motherly satisfaction, seeing her "drying yard full of boy's underwear, and khaki pants all getting sweetened in the hot August sun." By then radio broadcasts depicting America as an imperialistic enemy were echoed by children and adults. While walking in the village one evening she heard an adult voice sourly intone, "There go those Americans," but she took comfort in a child's voice piping up, "Oh that's just our Pao chiao-shih."[116]

Boynton good-heartedly went along with political study and read the speeches of Mao, Lenin, and Stalin, and a lot of other "Russian material," rationalizing to herself, "I who abominate politics and discussions must now try to pay attention to both." She recognized the self-criticism sessions (*chien-t'ao*) as an "excellent way to combat Chinese insistence upon face, with which the ideal of Christian humility has been struggling for years." These sessions reminded her of the "Oxford group techniques" used by small groups in the Yenta Christian Fellowship since the 1930s. Her endorsement of the new order was by no means unqualified. On the sly she read George Orwell's *Animal Farm,* feeling like a "naughty school child . . . tasting the sweets of stolen pleasure." She also deplored the replacement of decadent Christianity with the idols of Mao and Stalin.[117]

Grace Boynton's transition to the new order was aided greatly by her twenty-year friendship with Yang Kang (Yang Ping), who had studied English literature at Yenching, graduating in 1931, and who had attained prominence in the 1940s as the literary editor of the prestigious *Ta kung-pao* (Tientsin) and later as an assistant to Chou En-lai in the foreign ministry. In the mid 1930s Boynton had cared for Yang Kang's only daughter, Pao Tzu, while Yang worked underground for the Communists. Yang was featured as the heroine in the only novel Boynton ever published.[118] In 1944 American foreign service officers valued Yang as a contact with the intellectual community. John Service noted her considerable reputation among Chinese intellectuals and stated most emphatically she was not a Communist. Yang was then known for her belief that constructive American help and influence would promote political growth in China and result in a democratic coalition among the contending parties.[119] In March 1949 Boynton met Yang dressed in blue cotton clothing, thin, tired, and bothered with constant sore throat. She remembered the last meeting more than two years before at Radcliffe College in Cambridge where Yang was studying on a fellowship and was dressed "very stylish" complete with foreign clothes, an elaborate hair-do, and lipstick. Boynton's instinctive response was to ask if she could do anything for her child, as Yang had frequently referred to herself. But the revolutionary countered by returning the question. In a flash the American realized that, now, the power to give belonged to the Chinese. "My day of benevolence was over."[120]

Over the first year after the turnover they met several times, Boynton giving away some of her warmer clothing, but Yang bestowing the greater favor in easing Boynton's departure from China. Their last meeting in January 1950 began with a dinner at the home of Yen Ching-yüeh and Lei Chieh-ch'iung and ended with conversation deep into the night. It was the final affirmation of the "strong bond between the missionary and the communist." Yang settled on the bed with her cigarette, "her one indulgence," across from Boynton on the couch where she used her "indulgence . . . a hot water bottle." They had agreed not to spend the precious hours arguing, but clashes inevitably arose. At one point Boynton shot out some remark about the "great and oppressive regimentation and control," to which Yang retorted, "Well, I think Wall Street has some very fine ways of regimentation and control." When Boynton asked what she should say to the American people upon returning to the States, the cadre suggested the only thing was to slap them in their faces. The missionary replied that most of her New England relatives were conservative Republicans who might not get the intended message.

Grace Boynton was impressed with the utter simplicity of Yang Ping's life—sleeping in a dormitory, working twelve hours a day, eating only grain and vegetables, possessing only one change of underwear, owning no property, and carrying no money. But she was also irritated when Yang refused her offers of a fur coverlet, a hot drink made with bouillon cubes, cocoa and milk ("I am Chinese, I drink hot water"), and a poached egg for breakfast. Ideology did not have to pervade human relationships to such an extent. Nevertheless she confessed that American missionaries "ought to be glad that our special protection and our privileges are at last lifted off our backs." The cadre responded, "That's very moving because it is sincere, but how many missionaries feel like that?" Yang Kang returned the next morning to Peking with a sore throat. Grace Boynton, who left China a few weeks later because of eye trouble, never heard from her again.[121]

In a few months the eye difficulty cleared up and November 1950 found Grace Boynton heading back to China on board the *President Madison,* fully expecting to disembark at Tientsin sometime in early

December. But the Korean War intervened. During the stopover in Hong Kong in December Yenching alumni and friends told her of the anti-American campaign in Peking. Her frustration plainly evident, she reflected on hopes precariously built during her short experience in the revolution. She noted bitterly that people at Yenching who "owe their entire professional training to Leighton have been making speeches in public denouncing him as a spy and an enemy of the Chinese people." This was true for not just one person but a whole group! "So much for our hope that Chinese intellectuals would refuse regimentation! Perhaps in the end," she wrote, "the Chinese genius for individualism will assert itself, but at present there is no fight in anyone I have met or heard of outside of Formosa." Flailing, she asked, "So, is Formosa a hope after all?" She conceded that pressure for such psychological enslavement had arisen only after her departure from China in February, but now it was clear "there is no fight in anybody trained in Christianity and democracy!" Unconvincingly she contrasted their will power with Yang Kang's; it was like "wet paper to shining steel."[122]

As in the past Boynton again sought release from these frustrations in her religious faith. But new elements of fear, picked up it appears during her brief interlude back in America, were evident. She despaired over being "torn up by the roots," the "world situation," the "taut stern faces of men in uniform [the American soldiers in Japan returning from the Korean front]," and the "woe in the hearts of Chinese I have been teaching for thirty years." She taught a few months at Kobe College in Japan after failing reentry into China, and there she picked up the American hysteria over Chinese involvement in the war, recording in her diary without comment a radio message on the necessity of taking a stand in Korea in order to prevent fighting over Seattle, Detroit, or Shanghai. Eye trouble again forced her to leave the mission field, and she returned to America where she lived until her death in 1970.[123]

The letters of Randolph and Louise Sailer in 1949 and 1950 generally report favorably on the new order. There is skepticism but no touch of resentment. It was all right, they conceded, for foreigners to "stand around for awhile" in applying for various permits, as Chinese had stood before. Press censorship, however frustrating, was seen as a powerful means of education, not unlike the press of a very enthusiastic religious group elsewhere. When American newsmen were choked off in 1949, the Sailers urged them and American liberals generally to be more "philosophical about being cold-shouldered." But they recognized the tactical nature of Communist policies in the early stages and expected very great changes over the long run.[124]

Reluctantly they left China in the summer of 1950. Back in the United States Randolph Sailer encouraged the trustees not to withhold funds from the field. In November 1950, as the fighting between American and Chinese soldiers broke out in Korea, support for Yenching among the university's American supporters waned. The Campus Fund Committee at Princeton (Sailer's alma mater) held up a contribution already collected, pending the investigation of reports that students at Yenching were making hand grenades. Sailer refused to go along with the building anti-Chinese hysteria. He urged the trustees to continue support until there was adequate reason to believe the Chinese faculty had "abandoned their faith and ideals." Such evidence, he warned, was not "quickly or easily gathered. Deduction from political acts is not a method we would wish to apply to fellow-Christians in America." Later when the Yenching trustees, who formed a united board with the trustees of other China colleges, wanted to build a new college in Taiwan, Sailer resisted. He dissociated himself from the effort because he saw "political implications all around."[125]

Among the established missionary educators, Ralph and Nancy Lapwood of the London Missionary Society, were the last to leave Yenching. Their book *Through the Chinese Revolution* (London, 1954) provides the most extensive account available of Yenching after the turnover. It is especially valuable because Ralph Lapwood participated actively in the changeover down to his departure from China in the summer of 1952. In the 1930s the Lapwoods had cooperated with Chiang Kai-shek's New Life Movement, until their friend, Rewi Alley, pointed out that "far from solving the problems of corruption" the movement was itself a "demonstration of the hypocrisy which sheltered corruption."[126] Their tenure at Yenching, beginning in 1936, was interrupted by three years work, 1939–42, with the Chinese Industrial Cooperatives, which came under the sponsorship of the Nationalist government, and then another three years absence, 1945–48, in London. But they returned to Yenching in August 1948 fully expecting to continue teaching there indefinitely.

The Lapwoods' account of the revolution is generally favorable though they were not unmindful of harsh realities. They thought that Sam Dean's denunciation was based on "trumped-up charges of being an American spy." They were equally candid in regarding Lu Chih-wei,

Chao Tzu-ch'en, and Chang Tung-sun as scapegoats during the Three Anti campaign. But more often they gave the Communist leadership the benefit of the doubt. They too saw similarities between the continuous self-criticism sessions and the Oxford group techniques of the Student Christian Movement in England.[127] The infringements on religious freedom were seen mostly as the result of mistakes made by prejudiced or inexperienced officials. Revolutions, they argued, always involved elements of ruthlessness and could not succeed unless "long suppressed emotions and desires of the mass of people" were released. After his trying months in thought reform, Ralph Lapwood still concluded that the enemies of revolution would seize on these mistakes and excesses but that "friends will try to see them against the background of the tremendous good that is being achieved as the people are set free."[128]

The Lapwoods' experience is an illuminating testament to a willingness to reshape the cosmopolitan affirmation to the revolution. It was a valiant effort, but after three years their close Chinese friends advised them to leave. Fearful that Sam Dean's experience might become their own, they agreed. In 1956 both Ralph Lapwood and Randolph Sailer were invited to visit China as guests of the state. Sailer was unable to go then, but Lapwood went and returned again for another visit in 1964. Sailer visited in 1973. Both were able to visit Yenching personalities who had played a prominent role in the university's last years.[129]

After leaving China in August 1949 John Leighton Stuart inclined more and more toward a hard line on the revolution. Relativity, the hallmark of his presidency at Yenching, soon disappeared. Chiang Kai-shek, the Christian, had lost the war and legitimacy in China. At one point in June, just before his departure from China, Stuart, still the diplomat, had apparently set aside his objections to the Communist leadership and tried to use his position as the ambassador to establish contact with Mao Tse-tung and begin a redefinition of Sino-American relations. But Washington refused, and Stuart, obviously at war within himself, fell back into anti-Communist rhetoric, which according to Randolph Sailer was a "body blow to Yenching and American liberalism."[130] Soon after Stuart left China, his friends before the revolution denounced him and openly declared him as their enemy. He felt betrayed and deceived. "You are fully aware," he wrote Mary Ferguson of the United Board for Christian Higher Education in China in

November 1949, "that at first I was myself taken in to some extent by the Chinese Communist leaders before they came into power. And it was a long time before I fully realized the controlling influence of the Bolshevist element in their belief which is necessarily aggressive and ruthless."[131] Later in 1956 he did not think the mainland of China was irrevocably lost. Who can say, he wrote, that the "communist regime is in China to stay?" Communist ideology was "alien to China's political philosophy," and Communist practices were "violent, indifferent to human rights, and oppressive." He came to believe the Chinese had only contempt for the rights and interests of other nations, having gone so far as to "invade several neighboring states and to make war on the United Nations." He had "faith that somehow . . . this Russian satellite will have run its course and will be forced to relax its grip."[132] In November 1957 he endorsed Tunghai University on Taiwan and Chung Chi College in Hong Kong as being of "vital importance in the struggle for men's minds and hearts in East and Southeast Asia."[133] Stuart's description of official Chinese behavior was historically misleading. By the time he left China in the summer of 1949 he had chosen the highly emotional and inflexible view of China that became implanted in the cold war ideology in the West.

No matter how much Westerners may have been willing to adjust, developments in China, especially those associated with the Korean War, had destroyed their hope of accommodation. They had decried the narrow nationalism of their missionary colleagues in the past who identified Christianity with American culture and politics. But now many of them became equally irate when nationalism pressured their Chinese colleagues to embrace revolutionary ideology and denounce contacts with the West. In the early years of the new order they had resisted seeing adjustments in simplistic terms. Missionary zeal still glowed, but it did not rule out self-criticism. Over the years each new outburst of nationalism, from the Anti-Christian movement in 1922, to the December Ninth movement in 1935, to the turnover in 1948, had been met with characteristic flexibility. These antiforeign outbursts would momentarily destroy self-confidence, but their recovery was usually swift. On the eve of the revolution they still believed that Christian internationalism could be sustained even in revolution. But the Resist America Aid Korea and the Three Anti campaigns destroyed that confidence. Past hopes soon appeared false, and bitterness, in some cases, was the result. They went home. They were no longer welcome in the nativist atmosphere marked by revolutionary fervor. But their hopes were also threatened by another nativism, this one born out of a growing sickness at home.

The Chinese Faculty

The revolution forced far more painful choices upon the Chinese faculty than upon the students, who because of age had less of a stake in the old order, or the Westerners, who had the option of returning home. These Chinese leaders had faced the pressures of antiforeign nationalism before, but what had once been only a movement was now a political organization with every likelihood of staying in power. Liberal Protestant cosmopolitanism was gradually displaced by a revolutionary proletarian internationalism which raised up the Soviet Union and the culture of the masses as the new focus of loyalty, replacing America and the intimate Yenching community. The effect on the life of the institution was far-reaching.

Again, the assessment of the faculty's political sentiments is difficult. Randolph Sailer, echoing other Westerners who experienced the turnover at Yenching, expressed himself at length to the trustees on this question. He said that some American supporters might wish the Christian institutions in China had produced "men and women who would see the world situation . . . from the American viewpoint." But what Yenching actually produced was a "group of deeply patriotic Chinese citizens eager to sacrifice for what they see as their duty" and "sensitive to bargaining away any of their patriotism in return for American-supported education." Even before the American embargo Sailer suggested the Chinese faculty might prefer to strike out on its own as a government institution.[134] Most faculty, he argued, believed that China had chosen her road of political development, that they could make a positive contribution by cooperating with the party, and that they had no more thought of "active subversion than we do toward our government." They resented, furthermore, "American efforts to stir people of their kind against the government," and they deplored the "American tendency to evaluate China only as an enemy or potential friend against Russia." Sailer pointed out there was freedom of silence and claimed that Lu Chih-wei leaned over "backwards against talking opportunistically." After all, Lu and Chao Tzu-ch'en six years before had almost died in Japanese prisons rather than foreswear friendship with America.[135]

In the Three Anti campaign in the winter and spring of 1951–52, most of the 111 faculty who participated managed within a few weeks to present acceptable self-criticisms in their small groups. Their confessions exude varying degrees of self-criticism, but they all express a common revulsion of the American connection. Ch'u Shang-lin, chairman of physics and associate dean of studies, submitted one self-criticism denouncing his overconcern with face, self-protecting individualism, a purely academic attitude which had led him to become a tool of others, personal ambition to become a famous physicist, and unprincipled cordiality and the desire to please everybody, which were methods of self-protection in the old society. Later, under student pressure, he castigated himself even more strongly, saying that in his earlier self-criticism he had not really hated the faults confessed nor realized the full "hatefulness of my personal ambition and my blind worship of American capitalist ways." Now he wanted to "beat down that selfish 'I' and that foreign idol . . . to uproot the old shameful ways and make a new start," and become a people's teacher.[136] Chao Ch'eng-hsin of sociology confessed that for his ambition to become an international scholar, he had gathered information on Chinese politics and the economy and sent it abroad—an act he now realized "betrayed the fatherland for one's own fame and benefit." This he now "terribly deplored with an aching heart." Soon after, both Ch'u and Chao were elected to the executive committee of the union. Ts'ai Liu-sheng (1928) in chemistry, criticized himself for submitting papers for publication in the United States and encouraging his students to study there as the "concrete expression of non-differentiation between the enemy and friends and an act tantamount to guiding a tiger to his prey." Others turned in their golden keys and other academic medals, which had "dragged them into the mud" of working for "selfish interest, reputation, position and nothing else so that they would be made complete tools and slaves of the United States." Some faculty even criticized themselves for sending their wristwatches to the United States for repair.[137]

By March 1952 two groups had emerged whose criticisms were found unacceptable and whose cases were taken to the large mass meetings. In the first were senior faculty who had carried middle level administrative responsibilities and who had previously been anti-Communist. Included in it were such figures as Nieh Chung-chi, of the Harvard-Yenching Institute; Ch'i Ssu-ho, history; Shen Nai-chang, psychology; and Ch'en Fang-chih (Agnes Chen), political science, the latter being charged with ordering "reactionary" books from the United States as late as 1951.[138] The second more important group, however, was the trio of Chang Tung-sun, publicly denounced February 29, Chao Tzu-ch'en on March 10, and Lu Chih-wei on March 11. By summer's end there were about ten figures whose criticisms were still regarded as unacceptable.

Chao and Lu, more than anyone else at Yenching after the turnover, embodied the visions of the Life Fellowship which had shaped the pattern of Sino-Western relations in the university. Lu's role in the Life Fellowship did not equal that of Chao's and yet both epitomized the cosmopolitan ideal at Yenching. Both had come from non-Christian families, converted to Christianity as young boys, and studied abroad. They were above all cultural mediators, the Chinese counterparts to the missionary educators. Their experiences in thought reform acutely reveal the dilemma Westernized Chinese faced in the heat of revolutionary nationalism. So long as Chao could remain as dean of the school of religion and Lu as the president, one might say that Yenching as an institution was still alive. But when both were denounced in public and removed from their positions, Yenching's role in Sino-Western relations was practically at an end.

Their experiences in thought reform over three and a half years after the turnover followed roughly the pattern of the university's general accommodation discussed above. In the first two stages, between the turnover and the Resist America Aid Korea campaign, both Chao and Lu revealed very little if any opposition to the politics of the New Democracy. Quite the contrary, they were convinced that, however drastic the changes might be, the university would still have a place in the new order. Certainly when Yenching was nationalized in February 1951 in the wake of the Resist America campaign their hopes must have been greatly weakened, and yet even then both men refused to be silent. New Democratic politics, as they affected private institutions such as Yenching, came to an end sometime in 1951. Perhaps it was by the time of nationalization, forced by the turn of events in the Korean War. Perhaps it was evident to some when Yenching professors were forced to engage in extended periods of land reform in the spring and to run through the streets of Peking in the May Day demonstrations. Or maybe it was later in the fall when the first rumblings of the Three Anti campaign were heard. Whenever the precise time, by the fall 1951 it was evident that Yenching's existence would soon come to an end.

On November 3, 1951, the ministry of education called a conference to approve a plan for readjusting the engineering colleges in China. In that plan the affected departments at Yenching would be incorporated into Tsinghua, which in turn would become the major polytechnic school for North China. Soon after that, plans were drawn up (as revealed in April 1952) to merge the programs in the arts, social sciences, and natural sciences of Yenching, Tsinghua, and other colleges, into the new Peking University, which would become the major center for general studies in North China. In those adjustments the Yenching campus would become the site of the new Peking University, but the name of Yenching would be dropped.[139] By the time these major changes were completed the number of institutions of higher education in China would drop from a high of 65 in 1950 to 7, and all the names of the mission-related and private Chinese institutions would also be dropped. It seems clear that thought reform in the Three Anti campaign was intended to prepare students and professors for these changes in store. Anyone assenting, voluntarily or not, to the line that was to emerge would hardly be in a position to offer any resistance.

Chao's and Lu's role in that campaign, as distinct from their role in university life hitherto, was reversed. Before, they had endorsed the various campaigns and even led out in the beginning of the Three Anti campaign; but soon they became the objects of the attack. Before, the politics of the New Democracy seemed not incompatible with major tenets of faith of the Life Fellowship; but in the Three Anti campaign any attempt to merge the two became merely a charade in which anything they said would only be used against them until they were discredited in the eyes of their colleagues and students. Some might be inclined to see in the following account of Chao's and Lu's experiences merely the working out of the foregone conclusion of Yenching's demise. But neither Chao nor Lu saw it that way.

Chao had been a severe critic in the 1930s of Wu Lei-ch'uan's attempts to hammer out a revolutionary theology. Ironically by the late 1940s he developed a rationale not that dissimilar to Wu's. Even a few weeks before liberation of the Yenching campus, Chao endorsed the prospect of revolution. Resisting pressures to move the school of religion, Chao anticipated in November 1948 the "purifying" effect of the turnover and spoke of the need for a basic reorientation. "I believe it is high time," he wrote then, "to understand Marxism and even to see affinities between Christianity and some of the Marxist ideas."[140] Soon after, Chao spoke of creating a native theology related to "Chinese culture and Marxian dynamic immanentism," a "triangular affair" requiring "audacity of thought." Chinese churches, he lamented, had contained "so little heresy . . . so little creative thinking, so little originality."[141]

One senses that Chao's early endorsement reflected a certain guilt he felt about his and the church's previous reliance on foreign support. The revolution, he argued, was "man's challenge to Christianity," but "God's judgment on flabby churches."[142] He and his colleagues in the school of religion had no counter-arguments to offer to the charges that Christianity for so long had been "connected with imperialistic and bourgeois aspirations" and had bred "irresponsible liberalism, lukewarmness toward the revolution, aloofness and idol worship." He admitted the church had become "high-sounding, an attempt to build a castle in the air upon 'the lie of exalted ideas,' " and had fostered "atomic individualism which takes pleasure in snug corners of impractical idiosyncrasies." He was angered by the failure of the church in the past to renounce openly such people as the "Chiangs, Kungs, Sungs [all prominent in Yenching's past] as the Judases of the Christian faith."[143]

Two years after the turnover Chao was still defending the revolution and the appropriateness of accommodation. In December 1950, at the peak of Sino-American hostility in the Korean War he supported the Resist America campaign.[144] A year later at the beginning of the Three Anti campaign he opened a meeting of students and faculty by denouncing Yenching's past in most bitter terms. John Leighton Stuart, he charged, was a "United States secret agent, an anti-Soviet Union, anti-Communist, and anti-Chinese reactionary, and therefore a deadly enemy of the Chinese people. He is a sugar-coated pill of poison and a bayonet in a cotton roll." Symbol of "American traditional friendship in China," Stuart had brought many Chinese into his fold. Through "education and religion he spread the love-America worship-America poison." Chao wrote of himself, "I am an old man but I am confident that if an old man is determined to reform his thought, he can. I do not want to be left behind. Although I cannot gallop like a wild horse, I want to progress step by step like a camel towards reformation."[145]

Chao's confession was filled with desperation. At the beginning of the Three Anti campaign he must have seen that Yenching and his lifelong witness to Christian cosmopolitanism would soon come to an end. Always a leader, he must have feared there would be no place for him. And yet he did not want to leave China, nor did he wish to keep silent. In March 1952 Chao was publicly denounced in front of the whole Yenching community. By then the campaign against Western influence had become little more than a political device to prepare the whole campus for Yenching's inevitable demise. His "crimes" included his connections with the World Council of Churches, from which he resigned his vice-presidency in July 1951 but only after its executive committee had labeled North Korea as the aggressor in the Korean War.[146] The discrediting of Chao's past connections with Western personalities was one means of destroying any lingering loyalty Yenching Chinese might have felt for liberal arts and the Western connection. His efforts to write acceptable self-criticisms were repeatedly rejected. The authorities suspended all his clerical privileges, took away his offices within the North China Diocese of the Anglican Church, and requested the house of bishops to remove his holy orders. As late as September 1952 Chao had still failed to pass the censoring committee at Yenching.[147]

Even after such a thorough public denunciation Chao refused to accept silence and continued to defend the new order. When challenged by critics in the West as to why the Chinese church spoke only the words of the Chinese government, Chao responded, "No act or policy of the government led by the Communist Party and Chairman Mao . . . is in opposition to the highest ethical teachings and to Christian teaching." When asked about the lack of freedom, Chao replied in 1956, that he and the church had more freedom than ever before, that he had not had freedom in the former Yenching setting where he was paid by American money, conducting a school on behalf of Americans, not suitable for China, and holding a chair endowed by American gifts under the stated condition of defending the faith. Now, he insisted, it was "altogether different. I eat the Chinese people's rice, the rice of my own family. . . . I am not under compulsion to put a horse's mouth on a cow's head in order to occupy a professional chair. Now I, as well as all Chinese Christians, have complete freedom of religious belief." Hurling back the charge, Chao added, "One's individual freedom, the freedom of a small number, nominal freedom, is not enough. Freedom must go from bottom to top, it must be the freedom of all the people."[148]

Chao's treatment could be used as evidence to argue that fellow traveling in the Chinese revolution was unavailing. We will likely never know how Chao himself would respond, were it possible to discuss the matter with him outside of China.[149] It appears that thought reform may have been like a religious experience, and he might prefer to see the adjustments as desirable and necessary, given his deep patriotism since boyhood. Perhaps the costs were more than offset by the rewards of identifying with the success of the revolution. In a sense Chao's experience in the Three Anti campaign was a variation on earlier themes in his conversion experience more than forty years before.

On the eve of the turnover Lu Chih-wei had already considered the possibility of funds being cut off from New York. No doubt he preferred to see the flow of American dollars continue, but he did not seem overly anxious. He pointed out to the trustees that for months in a Japanese prison he had subsisted on about ten ounces of millet per day, and he was sure the new government would guarantee at least twenty-two ounces.[150] Lu was critical of the few colleagues who had left before the turnover and could not help thinking in "moments of weakness," that a person's cowardice would be proven by whether or not he eventually landed in America. Lu also feared they might try to persuade the trustees to establish another refugee Yenching somewhere south of the battle line or even in Taiwan.[151]

Rarely outspoken on religious matters prior to the turnover Lu noticeably increased his public defense of religion. The revolution helped purify the faith and brought to an end the view of "missions and the educational institutions as the final bulwark of civilization against barbarism." Christian love now had a new role to play, namely to serve as the mediator, if not synthesizer, between the conflicting ideologies of revolutionary China and America. But Yenching's contribution in the resolution of that conflict required the continued Western presence on campus. Maintaining the spirit of international friendship through the presence of mission appointees, in Lu's words, was the "best proof of what Yenching stands for." In a more personal way Lu admitted how much he relied on the support of those Westerners. They in turn uniformly praised him for his ability to guide the university through these difficult years.[152]

"American charity," Lu conceded, helped Yenching maintain relative independence in accommodating to the new order. It was his duty to see that foreign aid be put to "proper use, without betraying in the least the purpose of such funds," and without avoiding his "duty to the Chinese people and the Chinese government." He refused to sign a declaration against American aggression in Taiwan in late summer 1950, fearing to a "small extent" that such an action might unnecessarily jeopardize funds from abroad. Lu's in-between position became untenable with the outbreak of the Korean War and China's emerging role in it.[153] After the American embargo Lu endorsed Yenching's nationalization as the only possible solution, but even then the stirrings of patriotic fervor on the campus did not make him anti-American. He was able in February 1951 to admit the danger of "American imperialist cultural aggression," but he could not hate Americans just because "I never hate anybody or any class." A scholar's training had taught him not to rave at people, meaning, he admitted, that he was still backward in political ideas. Willing to recognize Stuart's "collaboration with the reactionary influences," he insisted nonetheless that to "be fair, Leighton Stuart thirty years ago was not entirely a secret agent accomplice of the State Department." His sarcasm went further. He recalled an instance from the 1930s when as acting chancellor he had dismissed the dean of women for getting on his nerves. But he was soon pressured to accept her return. Now he suddenly realized his great failure, because yielding to such pressure showed how overly influenced he was at the time by the American idea of women's rights.[154]

Understandably the trustees were concerned very much with religious freedom. They constantly pressed the field for reassurance on these matters which Lu and others seemed ready to provide. And yet the trend of events was decidedly in the opposite direction. A year after the turnover Lu still reassured them these freedoms were the "sine qua non for our very existence." But, he argued, such grand ideals did not provide guiding principles to meet concrete issues. The line was hard to draw. Lu doubted the occasion would ever arise when "we Christian educators" could all "point our fingers to one particular point or decision and say, 'Here is the limit.' " The issue gradually blurred under the pressure of political events. "Whatever we could bear under the old militaristic regime, we should be able to stand under the new regime," Lu wrote. He was as inclined to criticize those who failed to accommodate as those who forced the accommodation. The difficulty is "with ourselves, or with me as an individual Christian." If Yenching people failed, it would not be on account of "external pressures but for the lack of faith and self-criticism which is indeed our universal and life long problem."[155]

The issue of academic freedom was also fuzzy. Lu soon accepted the assault from the government. It was difficult for the faculty (more so for Chinese than Westerners, Lu thought) to understand that learning could no longer serve as a means of escape from political life. One could not go on being "neutral or indifferent or try to withdraw into a closet or alcove." Such a view was "so incongruent with the old gentlemanly standard of the scholar . . . that one may feel he is being rubbed in from all sides."[156] If academic freedom, as understood in the old Yenching, was still an issue after nationalization in February 1951, it would have been difficult to express it publicly. In any case Lu's correspondence with the trustees ended October 1950. In the beginning of the Three Anti campaign in September 1951 Lu took the lead at Yenching by denouncing John Leighton Stuart, just as the presidents of Peita, Tsinghua, and Nankai led attacks on their respective presidents (Hu Shih, Mei Yi-ch'i, and Chang Po-ling, all of them close associates in liberal arts higher education from the early 1920s).[157] After January 1, 1952, Mao Tse-tung exhorted the cadres to "put on a big show with flags and drums, as sudden and severe as the thunder, as all-pervading as the wind," and Lu became the major object of attack.[158]

In February a large exhibition was set up by the austerity inspection committee (Chieh-yüeh chien-ch'a wei-yüan hui), showing Yenching's role in American cultural imperialism. Among the items incriminating Lu were entries from Bliss Wiant's diaries, which showed that Lu had received word from the trustees in New York communicating their complete understanding on developments at Yenching (March 13, 1949) and that Wiant regretted Lu was only in education and not in politics where his influence would be more beneficial to Americans (July 17, 1949). They also showed that Lu had sent a telegram to Stuart expressing sympathy over an accident suffered by Stuart's younger brother (December 2, 1949), that Lu had said that China would allow Korea to remain divided (November 11, 1950), and that Yenching would remain private.[159] The entries in Wiant's diaries hardly indicated complicity in American imperialism.

The publicity given to the exhibition signaled drastic changes, but no one seemed to know just how or when the campaign would end. People seemed so frightened in their uncertainty and so pressured that any remaining trust soon disappeared. All the assurances of the New Democracy were at an end. Many students and faculty came forth to bring their charges against Lu. The witch hunt began in earnest. Wu Hsinghua, assistant professor of Western literature, began his accusation by recounting the high esteem he had held for Lu as a patriot, scholar, and administrator. But his esteem was destroyed when Lu allegedly had told

Wu that China's attempts to repel American forces in North Korea in November 1950 were doomed to failure. Lu's position was discredited by the brilliant victories of the Chinese volunteer armies driving the Americans South and forcing Wu to change his "fear America thoughts." Now Wu confessed that Lu had "persistently carried out the imperialist policy of aggression," advocating the "so-called international understanding, the Sino-American friendship, humanity . . . in short, the Tito line." To such a position, Wu shouted, "Comrades! What kind of a stand is this? Has such a man the least quality of being considered a patriotic Chinese?" Wu's exaggeration seemed to know no limit. "We bitterly hate the imperialist elements, but we more bitterly hate those who have lost their stand as Chinese and kneel down to lick the boots of the enemy."[160] The paroxysms of xenophobic nationalism seemed to hit the more recent converts hardest.

Hou Jen-chih stepped forward with accusations even more slanderous. The language of Hou's attack on Lu was highly personal, and yet one senses he was playing out a role in a sordid ritual, ultimately impersonal in nature. As the newly elected head of the Educators' Union Hou's charges appeared decisive. Previously his relationship with Lu had been amicable, but now he seemed bent on destroying any lingering respect for the president. Some of the charges appeared to be without foundation, for example: that Lu had told Mei Yi-pao to move Yenching south before liberation; that Lu had launched a frantic assault on the principles of the New Democracy; that Lu regarded his appointment as president in 1949 by the trustees as a great honor; that Lu had opposed the more progressive faculty members like Yen Ching-yüeh, Lei Chieh-chiung, Chao Ch'eng-hsin, and Kao Ming-k'ai, while relying on the "reactionary clique" in his attempts to forestall change; and that Lu opposed government directives on curriculum changes.[161]

Most hurtful was the denunciation by his daughter, Lu Yao-hua, a graduate student in biology at Yenching.[162] As with Wu and Hou, Lu Yao-hua, also must have faced fearsome pressures. The style of her accusation was not altogether unfamiliar at Yenching. Her behavior appears as an extreme expression of emotions that had gripped Yenching students who felt they had to compensate for their associations with the missionary enterprise. Her statement of accusation reflects long family debates about the difficulties of accommodation, especially after the Korean War. It suggests, furthermore, that Lu's previous statements on the Christian faith, academic freedom, patriotism, and revolution were sincere. But accommodations adequate for 1950 were found wanting in 1952. Any suggestion of cooperation with America was now treasonous. In the first years after the turnover Lu Yao-hua had seen her father as a progressive and was proud of his close contacts with the revolutionary leadership. But the Korean War again formed the watershed. Lu's suggestion that the family might have to evacuate to the countryside instilled doubts in her mind about the strength of the fatherland. His questions caused her, she charged, to "even fear America" and to "doubt the reports of the *People's Daily*."

Lu Yao-hua had helped her father write his first self-criticism which he delivered publicly in February 1952. She had also served as a recorder of that meeting and was confident, watching the participants hand in their "900 plus slips" to the stage, that the gathering would be found to be too leftish. But more information on her father the following day destroyed her confidence, she said. She had thought him to have backbone and the dignity of the race, but she now saw him as a "claw of imperialism" and a "Christian with no political sympathy for the Communist Party." Love for her father had overcome doubts in her mind before, but now she declared, "Even if this love is true, it is definitely insignificant as compared with the love among the broad masses." His love was "not love but deceit. . . . Why must I be deceived by you and revolt against the people?" Chinese volunteers had suffered great "cold and hunger and made valorous sacrifice" in Korea. Now Lu Yao-hua decided to wage a bitter struggle against her father like the "volunteers on the front." For having "poisoned many youth" and "politically obscured their vision of the future . . . no Chinese will ever pardon you." She concluded her remarks by resolving not to permit the "remnant influence of American imperialism to exist in the land of China, in the vicinity of the capital, or by the side of Chairman Mao Tse-tung."[163]

Following his daughter's denunciation, Lu Chih-wei made one more attempt at self-criticism on March 11, his contrition and compliance almost complete. He now confessed he had fallen into Stuart's "snare willingly and thus harmed a great number of students," and had "passively attacked" the policies of the New Democracy while trying to "keep the old tradition at Yenching." His previous stand had been "pro-American and therefore anti-Communist and anti-people," and he had "subconsciously feared that the Americans would return and hoped therefore to hand back Yenching in its entirety." He thanked the masses for helping him "open the iron door and see . . . the dark side of my thought." It was only right the "people hated me bitterly. I confess my crimes. I want to refute my past and to become a new man."[164] His spirit was crushed. The cold war ideology had become no less deeply implanted in China.

Prior to this campaign Lu had chosen to express his accommodation openly, but after the final round, in contrast to Chao, he chose silence. For all the emotional suffering involved in the Three Anti campaign, Lu, Chao, and Chang, were still allowed to live in their homes with their families and were regularly paid their salaries. They were never imprisoned, but for a while at least they were isolated. The Lapwoods discreetly avoided seeing Lu, though their son Peter talked with him several times over the garden fence in the course of the summer. At summer's end Lu was appointed to a research position in the Academy of Sciences.[165]

In August 1952 the Chinese faculty at Yenching were told to await the announcement detailing the reorganization of higher education in North China. In September the reallocation of the faculty took place. Lists were circulated indicating the wishes of the ministry of education, and each was given two to three days to consider. No one refused to comply, though some, who were sent to such far away places as Manchuria, reportedly expressed some reluctance to go. About half were asked to leave the campus, while the other half were allowed to stay and find their places in the new system of education.[166]

Curiously, the school of religion, formed thirty-seven years before and older than the college itself, was allowed to continue its separate existence, though it was financed completely by the government. Chao Tzu-ch'en, who held out the longest of the Yenching faculty in adjusting his confession, was removed from the deanship of the school, but he was still allowed to teach. The school moved to a dormitory complex on the former Peita campus and a few years later was combined with eleven other seminaries and renamed the Yenching Union Theological Seminary.[167]

8

Conclusion

On its own terms Yenching was both a success and a failure. It was the realization of a cosmopolitan ideal rooted in both the Protestant missionary enterprise and Chinese soil. The dream of amicable Sino-Western relations was translated into annual budgets, college degrees, and a magnificent university campus. By the early 1920s Yenching appeared to be a solidly conceived institution, and the prospects for its continuing existence were good. As late as the 1940s when the political order that sustained Yenching was on the verge of collapse, Yenching's status was still high. In September 1948, on the eve of the Communist takeover, applications to the freshman class were over 4,000, the highest in the history of the university. If ever there was a transcending of the cultural differences that separate East and West in the twentieth century, it may have been at Yenching.

The Yenching story, however, was not an unqualified success. Strong as the intercultural connection may have been and much as the university appeared to meet real needs, Yenching was vulnerable to attack, first from religious fundamentalism in the West, more seriously from militant Chinese nationalism, and finally from the strains of international politics in the Korean War. Yenching succeeded in the early years by fostering the hope of national salvation (*chiu-kuo*), from international disorder and external humiliation, but as that hope faded the university was in difficulty. National salvation, and the role of education and Christian social reform within it, remained an ever elusive goal throughout the Republican years. The earning of degrees, the setting up and staffing of schools, and the infusion of the skills and idealism of Yenching students into Chinese society and the government turned out not to be enough.

In the relative stability of the Western democracies in the late nineteenth and early twentieth centuries, social reform and education appeared to be effective. But in the Chinese context where such stability did not exist the hope of gradual social change soon disappeared. The transplant of Western solutions to the problems of social change bore quick fruit in the 1910s. But in the context of demands for more comprehensive solutions and patriotic impatience, social reform was reduced to philanthropy, and liberal arts education was in danger of becoming more a means to high social status than to social service. Even the boldest of these gradualist efforts, the rural reconstruction programs of the 1930s of which Yenching was a part, seemed to generate only the most slender threads of hope.

Yenching voices would speak of comprehensive solutions, but they were unconnected to any program for creating power to implement them and thus remained largely voices of protest. The social gospel promised social justice, but the means of delivery were never clearly spelled out. The Christian formulas for national salvation did produce new social patterns, a new vision of society, new tasks to perform like teaching, and the training of skills for carrying out those tasks. But these tasks involved only a small segment of society and had little effect on the reshaping of a new political order. The names of leading Christians, including Chiang Kai-shek, became associated with the ineffectiveness, corruption, and dependence upon the West. Out of obedience to God Christians were enjoined not to participate in the violent destruction of the established order, however flawed it might be. Yenching followers, furthermore, were unable to tap the one resource which Chinese patriots increasingly identified as the means to national salvation, namely the mobilization of the masses in the countryside.

In this sense, the urban success of Christian higher education may have been self-defeating, as well-intentioned reformers and patriots were themselves converted to Western ways that only increased their separation from the masses. Had the Yenching Christians not been patriots, this separation would have been less crucial. But from the conversion experiences of the older Chinese faculty in the 1910s to the behavior of members of the Yenta Christian Fellowship in the takeover period, patriotism was a dominant theme. As the Chinese members of the Life Fellowship repeatedly said, personal salvation could not be divorced from social reconstruction and national salvation.

Marxism provided the major critique of the Yenching experiment. In their appeal the early Marxist study groups were similar to the Life Fellowship. But Marxism took hold in ways that liberal Christianity could not because it provided the framework for translating the patriotic awakening into powerful organizations. More than any other set of ideas, Marxism addressed the questions of political power, while the Chinese Communists created the structures for a whole new set of vertical and horizontal linkages in society that would provide the foundation for a new order. The movements spawned in that framework touched the lives of the Yenching community from the earliest years, but only a few Yenching students actively participated prior to the Communist turnover. Those that did, through underground work, guerilla resistance to the Japanese, and uniting with the revolutionary movement in the late 1940s, found access to the wellsprings of power. After the turnover others found access through political study, the youth league, the party, and most of all through their jobs. National salvation was at hand, and they were a direct part of it. From the beginning Stuart and other members of the Life Fellowship had recognized how clearly revolutionary ideology held the rival appeal. After the 1920s one only heard of Christians becoming Marxists, not Marxists becoming Christians.

In addition to the politics of national salvation, Yenching was strongly affected by the politics of diplomacy. The onus that Yenching suffered through its associations with the foreign presence established through gunboat diplomacy in the nineteenth century was somewhat offset by the impressive efforts to establish racial equality through the organization of the university. On occasion the foreign connection was turned to an advantage, as for example Yenching's four years of protection by Western extraterritoriality during the war with Japan. But the irritation was never completely gone, and it was later fanned by the Communist government to unprecedented levels in 1950 during the Korean War when Yenching Chinese believed that American-led armies would invade China.

Yenching leaders also had to confront the growth of Japanese military influence. For thirty years anti-Japanese nationalism fired student discontent that severely disrupted university life. After 1937 some Yenching students and faculty fled to Western China and eventually set up another campus there during the rest of the war years. When the war ended the university made a strong comeback on the Haitien campus near Peking, but the toll exacted by the war remained a heavy one. The war with Japan also set the stage for the civil conflict between the Nationalists and the Communists that brought further disruptions.

The diplomacy of Russia also affected Yenching's existence. The aid and advice given by the Soviet Union to Sun Yat-sen in the early 1920s when the United States had turned its back on him and the Russian influence in shaping the revolutionary movement in China helped shape the trends in student thinking throughout the history of the university. After 1949 the increase of Russian influence in Chinese politics was associated with the closing of Yenching.

American influence and diplomacy were perhaps the most decisive of all the outside forces. Yenching was funded largely with American money, and American influence pervaded the Republican system of education that formalized Yenching's liberal arts curriculum and degree requirements. The American tie with China was strengthened during the war with Japan. But after the war this tie became a liability, as the students came to resent the American aid to Chiang Kai-shek, whose leadership by the late 1940s they had almost completely rejected. Stuart's personal loyalty to Chiang and his efforts as the American ambassador to strengthen the Nationalist government only hurt the Yenching cause. American policy toward the new government in 1949 and 1950 and American behavior in the Korean War must also be seen as an integral part of the wartime psychology that surrounded the dissolution of the university.

An appreciation of these political and diplomatic realities makes intercultural history that focuses only on ideas and personalities appear to be too limited a framework. The separation of ideas and politics may have seemed possible for a short while in the earliest years of the Republican period, years for which the almost uncritical acceptance of Western ideas in the New Culture movement was a culmination. But this curiosity was soon replaced by the awareness that the West's role in the destruction of the old order was above all a political act. As the Republican years progressed this awareness was transformed into a passionate search for a new set of values and structures of society that would restore order and dignity to China. A patriotism that could embrace the cosmopolitan ideal was soon challenged by a more militant and narrow nationalism. This politicization of ideas and loyalties was true not only for the students and faculty at Yenching but also for a whole generation of writers in China, who in their younger years were extreme individualists and romantics and seemingly unconcerned with politics but who by the late 1920s were unable to ignore the political fact of China's continuing indignity and disorder. Lamentable as this trend may be in Western (and Chinese) circles where art, literature, and education may be seen to be free from politics, this tie became one of the dominant facts of life from then on and helps explain the intellectuals' receptivity to the Communist Revolution in 1949, even as they knew that their own positions in society would be drastically affected. The failure to recognize this politicization of thought prior to the revolution is a major stumbling block in understanding how those Chinese personalities who were the main tie in intercultural relations could endorse a political system that was hostile to the continuation of those relations.

But in acknowledging the politics of Sino-Western relations, one should not equate cultural (or intercultural) history with political developments. In the end Chinese nationalism and the Communist Revolution and the Korean War did coalesce into an insurmountable barrier to Yenching's continued existence. Alone, however, either Chinese nationalism or revolutionary politics may not have ended Yenching's existence. Each forced dramatic changes to be sure, but even the board of trustees was willing to go along with those changes as late as January 1951. Revolutionary ideologies seriously modified the cosmopolitan ideal, but they did not necessarily destroy it. Diplomacy may well have been the decisive factor in Yenching's demise. If so, then the political forces that brought Yenching to an end may have been as much Western as Chinese.

It may not be possible to find all the meaningful variables to explain Yenching's existence or demise. But it does seem clear they were not all foretold in the events preceding its founding, nor are they to be explained only in terms of Chinese xenophobia, whatever that may be, or Western expansionism. The end of Christian missions in China and of Chinese experiments in liberal arts education is decisive enough to suggest that the currents of history that brought Yenching personalities together in the late 1910s may never occur again. But as cultural history the Yenching story also suggests there was nothing innately un-Chinese or un-Western about amicable Sino-Western relations.

Notes
Bibliography
Glossary
Index

AC   Administrative Correspondence of Yenching University, United Board for Christian Higher Education in Asia, 475 Riverside Drive, New York

         HSG   Howard S. Galt

         JLS   John Leighton Stuart

         LTF   Liu T'ing-fang

         UB   Correspondence with the United Board, 1945–58

AP   Administrative Papers of Yenching University, United Board

         BM   Minutes of the Board of Managers

         BT   Minutes of the Board of Trustees

         D   Directories and Bulletins

         HYI   Harvard-Yenching Institute

         R   Reports of presidents, deans, and departments

CLYSM   *Chen-li yü sheng-ming*

HYC   *Hsin Yen-ching*

PC   Private papers and correspondence collected by the author

         GMB   Grace Morrison Boynton (HL, on deposit at the Houghton Library, Harvard University)

         LLP   Lucius and Lillian Porter

         MBS   Margaret Bailey Speer

         RNL   Ralph and Nancy Lapwood, provided by Grace Boynton

         SFB   Stella Fisher Burgess

PSYTI   *Pei-p'ing ssu-li Yen-ching ta-hsüeh*

SM   *Sheng-ming*

YCHW   *Yen-ching hsin-wen*

YTCK   *Yen-ta chou-k'an*

YTYK   *Yen-ta yüeh-k'an*

YTYS   *Yen-ta yu-sheng*

Notes

1. Introduction

1. For one persuasive argument on the twentieth-century significance of Sino-Western Relations, see John K. Fairbank, "Assignment for the '70's," *American Historical Review*, 74.3:862 (February 1969).

2. Akira Iriye, a pioneer in the study of intercultural history, emphasizes the East Asian side of the relationship while combining the roles of both images and diplomacy in shaping those relations. See his *Across the Pacific: An Inner History of American–East Asian Relations* (New York, Harcourt, Brace and Jovanovich, 1967) and *The Cold War in Asia: A Historical Introduction* (Englewood Cliffs, N.J., Prentice Hall, 1974).

3. For a more extensive survey of the scholarly literature see Edward D. Graham, "Early American–East Asian Relations," in Ernest R. May and James C. Thomson, eds., *American–East Asian Relations: A Survey* (Cambridge, Harvard University Press, 1972), 3–18.

4. Y. C. Wang, *Chinese Intellectuals and the West, 1872–1949* (Chapel Hill, N.C., 1966), 377.

5. See James C. Thomson, Jr., *While China Faced West: American Reformers in Nationalist China, 1928–37* (Cambridge, Harvard University Press, 1969).

6. For a stimulating essay on cultural imperialism see Arthur Schlesinger, Jr., "The Missionary Enterprise and Theories of Imperialism," in John K. Fairbank, ed., *The Missionary Enterprise in China and America* (Cambridge, Harvard University Press, 1974), 336–373. For an annotated survey of Chinese studies on Sino-Western relations, see Albert Feurwerker and S. Cheng, *Chinese Communist Studies of Modern Chinese History* (Cambridge, Harvard University Press, 1961), 39–47.

252

Notes to pages 4–12

7. Jonathan Spence, *The China Helpers: Western Advisers in China, 1620–1960* (London, The Bodley Head, 1969).

8. Joseph Needham, *The Past in China's Present: A Cultural, Social, and Philosophical Background for Contemporary China* (London, Arts and Sciences in China, 1960), reprinted in *Far East Reporter* (March 1973), 37; Mark Selden, *The Yenan Way in Revolutionary China* (Cambridge, Harvard University Press, 1971), *viii.*

9. Michael Oksenberg, ed., *China's Developmental Experience* (New York, Academy of Political Science and Columbia University, 1973), preface.

10. Lewis A. Maverick, *China: A Model for Europe* (San Antonio, Texas, Paul Anderson Co., 1946).

11. Spence, *The China Helpers,* 293.

12. Arnold Toynbee, ed., *Half the World: The History and Culture of China and Japan* (New York, Holt, Rinehart and Winston, 1973), 11.

13. Fairbank, *The Missionary Eneterprise,* 2.

14. As quoted in Schlesinger, *The Missionary Enterprise,* 372.

15. C. K. Yang, *Religion in Chinese Society* (Berkeley, University of California Press, 1961), 6.

16. Richard C. Bush, Jr., *Religion in Communist China* (New York, Abingdon Press, 1970), 15–37; Carleton B. Lacy, "Protestant Missions in Communist China," Ph.D. diss., Yale University, 1953, chaps. 1–3.

17. Wm. Theodore deBary, ed., *Self and Society in Ming Thought* (New York, Columbia University Press, 1970), 18. For clarity on this point I am indebted to Charles Hayford. I recall discussing it with him at length during walks in the city of Taipei in 1968 when I began reading the religious literature published by Yenching Chinese.

18. William James, *The Varieties of Religious Experience* (New York, Modern Library 1902), 15.

19. Paul Varg, *Missionaries, Chinese, and Diplomats* (Princeton, Princeton University Press, 1958), 319–320.

20. Wolfram Eberhard, *Guilt and Sin in Traditional China* (Berkeley, University of California Press, 1967).

21. See D. Vaughan Rees, *The "Jesus Family" in Communist China* (London, Paternoster Press, 1959).

22. Endō Shūsaku, *The Golden Country,* trans. Francis Mathy (Rutland, Vermont, Charles E. Tuttle Co., 1970), 64. For a scholarly interpretation of Lord Inoue's judgment, see George Elison, *Deus Destroyed: The Image of Christianity in Early Modern Japan* (Cambridge, Harvard University Press, 1973).

23. Paul A. Cohen, *China and Christianity: The Missionary Movement and the Growth of Chinese Antiforeignism, 1860–1870* (Cambridge, Harvard University Press, 1963), 264–265.

24. Kenneth S. Latourette, *A History of Christian Missions in China* (London, Society for Promoting Christian Knowledge, 1929), 107, 129, 158, 182. William Hung estimated the number of Catholic Christians in China in 1837 to be 220,000; in 1850, 330,000; in 1881, 470,000; in 1911, 1,363,000; and in

1920, 1,971,180. See his "Contribution of the Western Church" in Milton Stauffer, ed., *China Her Own Interpreter* (New York, 1927), 86–87.

25. Varg, *Missionaries, Chinese, and Diplomats,* 89, 249.

26. Fairbank, *The Missionary Enterprise,* 1–19.

2. The Search for an Exportable Christianity

1. See Frederic Wakeman, Jr., "The Price of Automony: Intellectuals in Ming and Ch'ing Politics," *Daedalus* (Spring 1972), 55–67; Kuo Cheng-chao, "Ch'ing-mo min-chu hsüeh-hui huo-tung ti fen-hsi," paper delivered at the Sino-American Joint Research Workshop in Taipei, February 26, 1969; Mary Rankin, *Early Chinese Revolutionaries: Radical Intellectuals in Shanghai and Chekiang, 1902–1911* (Cambridge, Harvard University Press, 1971), passim.

2. Howard Boorman, ed., *Biographical Dictionary of Republican China* (New York, Columbia University Press, 1968), II, 229, 347; Hsiao Kung-ch'üan, "Economic Modernization: K'ang Yu-wei's Ideas in Historical Perspective," *Monumenta Serica* 27:39 (1968); Donald Treadgold, *The West in Russia and China: China 1582–1949* (New York, Cambridge University Press, 1972), 61, 64, 112.

3. Maurice Meisner, *Li Ta-chao and the Origins of Chinese Marxism* (Cambridge, Harvard University Press, 1967), 72; Boorman, II, 330.

4. Li Jung-fang was another important member of the Life Fellowship, preceding Liu T'ing-fang on the Yenching faculty and outliving most of his colleagues in the group. But he was less a shaper of events in both the study group and the university. Li and Chao Tzu-ch'en were the only two Chinese among the early members mentioned here who experienced thought reform after 1949.

5. There were analogous religious groups among Chinese converts in late Ming China. One was known as the Truth Society (Chen-shih she), similar in title to the Chen-li she, founded by Wu Lei-ch'uan in 1923 in Peking. Another group in the Ming period was the Sheng-shui hui, or Holy Water Society. See Arthur W. Hummel, ed., *Eminent Chinese of the Ch'ing Period, 1644–1912* (Washington, D.C., 1943), I, 894.

6. Hu Hsüeh-ch'eng, "Hsüan-yen" (Announcements), (November 20, 1919), *SM,* 1.1:i-ii; Liu T'ing-fang, "Sheng-ming yüeh-k'an—cheng-tao-t'uan—pen-ch'i t'e-hao" (This special issue of Life monthly and Apologetic group), *SM,* 2.7:7 (March 1922). Hu was a YMCA secretary in Peking and the first managing editor of the *Life Journal.*

7. Hu, "Hsüan-yen," p. ii; Frank J. Rawlinson et al., *The Chinese Church: The National Christian Conference* (Shanghai, 1922), 427.

8. Milton T. Stauffer, ed., *The Christian Occupation of China* (Shanghai, 1922), 455.

9. Yamamoto Sumiko, *Chūgoku Kirisuto-kyō shi ken-kyū* (Tokyo, 1972), 69.

10. Ernst Wolff, *Chou Tso-jen* (New York, 1971), 13–15.

11. Liu T'ing-fang, "Sheng-ming" (Life), *SM,* 1.1:10–11.

12. Two such lists for example are the twenty-one members published in *SM,* 1.4: back cover (November 15, 1920), and the list of sixty-five members, most of them Yenching faculty, published (October 1932) in *CLYSM,* 7.2:1; meet-

ings of the Life Fellowship are occasionally mentioned in Lucius Porter's line-a-day diaries throughout the 1920s; also see Yu Ch'ien, "Sheng-ming she ti-yi tz'u t'ui-hsiu hui chi-lüeh" (A report of the first retreat of the Life Fellowship), *SM,* 5.4:61–64.

13. Alice H. Gregg, *China and Educational Autonomy* (Syracuse, 1946), 213–214; Stauffer, *Christian Occupation,* appendix, p. civ; for rates of increase in Catholic converts see Kenneth Scott Latourette, "Christian Missions as Mediators of Western Civilization" in Jessie G. Lutz, ed., *Christian Missions in China, Evangelists of What?* (Boston, 1965), 83; and William Hung, "The Contribution of the Christian Church" in Milton Stauffer, ed., *China Her Own Interpreter* (New York, 1927), 86–87.

14. Kenneth Scott Latourette, *A History of Christian Missions in China* (London, 1929), 623.

15. Hsiao Kung-ch'üan, "Economic Modernization . . ." *Monumenta Serica,* 38 (1968); Latourette, *History of Christian Missions in China,* 567–569.

16. James A. Field, Jr., "Near East Notes and Far East Queries," in John K. Fairbank, ed., *The Missionary Enterprise in China and America* (Cambridge, Harvard University Press, 1974), 23–55.

17. Latourette, *Christian Missions in China,* 567–569.

18. Ibid., 854–586; see also Valentine Rabe, "Evangelical Logistics: Mission Support and Resources to 1920," and Clifton J. Phillips, "The Student Volunteer Movement and Its Role in China Missions, 1886–1920," in Fairbank, *The Missionary Enterprise,* 56–109.

19. Shirley S. Garrett, *Social Reformers in Urban China: The Chinese Y.M.C.A., 1895–1926* (Cambridge, Harvard University Press, 1970).

20. John S. Burgess, "Quarterly Report, First Quarter, 1913, April 8, 1913," submitted to the International Committee of the YMCA, PC:SFB; Garrett, *Social Reformers,* chaps. 2 and 3.

21. Sidney D. Gamble, assisted by John Stewart Burgess, *Peking: A Social Survey* (New York, George H. Doran Co., 1921), 99–101.

22. Burgess, "Quarterly Report," PC:SFB.

23. *Christian China* (published by the Chinese Student Christian Association in New York) 6.7:423–424 (May–June 1920).

24. Latourette, *Christian Missions in China,* 589; Hsü Pao-ch'ien, "Erh-shih nien lai chih hsin-tao ching-yen" (My religious experience of twenty years), *CLYSM,* 8.2:79 (April 1934); Garrett, *Social Reformers,* chap. 5.

25. Latourette, *Christian Missions in China,* 590.

26. Garrett, *Social Reformers,* 128.

27. This impression is gained simply by looking through the *Who's Who in China,* published in Shanghai by the *China Weekly Review,* for the years 1925, 1931, and 1936.

28. David Z. T. Yui, in *Nationalist China,* Foreign Policy Association Pamphlet, no. 54 (New York, 1924), 15.

29. The diary of Lucius Porter shows that for the month of February 1920 he spoke six different times at various YMCA meetings. Stuart worked closely with the YMCA in Nanking in the early 1910s, and Burgess originally came to

China as a YMCA foreign secretary. All the prominent Chinese members of the Life Fellowship who studied in America were leaders in YMCA activities wherever they were and also joined the Chinese Student Christian Association.

30. John Leighton Stuart, "Autobiographical Notes," ms., p. 11, PC:GMB; Stuart, *Fifty Years in China* (New York, Random House, 1954), 43. The first five chapters of the published memoirs are based largely on these unpublished notes, which were written in 1942 while Stuart was interned in Peking by the Japanese. The notes are unedited and include information on Stuart's life and Yenching University not used in the published version. These notes were originally intended as source material for the writer Hsieh Ping-hsin (Wan-ying), whom Stuart had first asked to write his biography. When she informed Stuart she preferred to translate an English version, Stuart then asked Grace Boynton to perform the task. Hsieh to Stuart, January 28, 1948, and Stuart to Boynton, February 2, 1948, PC:GMB. Boynton chose not to write a biography but a fictionalized account of Stuart. Her novel, "The Source of Springs," PC:GMB (HL), was completed in 1965 but has not been published. Before her death in 1970 Boynton turned the Autobiographical Notes and many other valuable papers on Yenching over to me.

31. Latourette, *Christian Missions in China,* 589; *The Chinese Yearbook* (Nanking, 1936), 1542.

32. This huge volume was published by the China Continuation Committee in Shanghai, 1922.

33. See for example the articles by Yü Chia-chü and Ch'en Ch'i-t'ien, in Chang Ch'in-shih, ed., *Kuo-nei chin shih-nien lai chih tsung-chiao ssu-ch'ao* (Peking, 1927), 305–338, 342–365.

34. The YMCA has been a part of the larger cultural and academic exchange between China and the West. Such organizations as the Chinese Social and Political Science Association (Chung-kuo cheng-chih hsüeh-hui) and the China Foundation for the Promotion of Education and Culture (Chung-hua chiao-yü wen-hua chi-chin tung-shih hui) were often staffed with YMCA related personalities. See W. W. Yen (Yen Hui-ch'ing), "China Foundation for the Promotion of Education and Culture," *Chinese Social and Political Science Review,* 12.2:426–430 (1928), for the YMCA connections of this organization. Yen himself was a paradigm: distinguished diplomat and government official, YMCA activist, and member of the Yenching board of managers for more than twenty-five years.

35. See *Jen-wu yüeh-k'an,* 1.2 (June 15, 1936), which contains five articles on Stuart; each of the four Yenching University Alumni Bulletins, the first three, 1963, 1965, 1967, published in Hong Kong as the *Yen-ta hsiao-yu t'ung-hsün,* and the last, 1973, published in Palo Alto as the *Yen-ta hsiao-k'an,* are filled with many fond reminiscences of Stuart by colleagues and admiring alumni.

36. The introduction in both the English and Chinese versions, largely praising of Stuart though not without some qualification, was written by Hu Shih, and the Chinese inscription of the Chinese version was done by Chiang Mon-lin. Both Hu and Chiang, were former presidents of Peking National University and two of Stuart's long-time colleagues in Peking.

37. Grace M. Boynton, "Biographical Sketch of Dr. Stuart," *Yen-ta yu-sheng,* 2.9 (June 24, 1936); Stuart, *Fifty Years,* 9–13.

38. Stuart, *Fifty Years,* 16.

39. Ibid., 16–17.

40. Stuart, "Autobiographical Notes," 5, PC:GMB (HL).

41. Stuart, *Fifty Years,* 28–30.

42. Ibid., 9–48.

43. Stuart, "Autobiographical Notes," 18, PC:GMB (HL).

44. Stuart, *Fifty Years,* 27.

45. Stuart, "Autobiographical Notes," 18–19, PC:GMB (HL).

46. Ibid.

47. Stuart, *Fifty Years,* 41–42.

48. Galt, "Yenching University," 83; Dwight Edwards, *Yenching University* (New York, 1959), 87–88.

49. Stuart, "Autobiographical Notes," 14, PC:GMB.

50. Edwards, *Yenching University,* 88.

51. *Far East Times of Tientsin and Peking,* July 3, 1926.

52. The Shanghai *Ta-kung pao* wrote: "He is universally liked by everyone who knows him or of him," while the Tientsin *Ta-kung pao* claimed that Stuart understood the "true wishes of the Chinese people in the growth and the shaping of the new China." The Shanghai *Wen-hui pao* antcipated that Stuart's efforts to help settle the civil war would be "respected by both those in the government and those in the opposition." Even a Communist spokesman told the Reuters News Agency that Stuart's appointment was "Greatly welcomed by the Chinese Communists." For these and other newspaper references to Stuart see items for July 11–12, 1946, Yenching University file, AC:UB.

53. Van Ogden Vogt, "In Memorium," September 10, 1958, PC:LLP.

54. Hu Shih to Elizabeth Kirkpatrick, September 7, 1958, PC:LLP.

55. Lucius Porter, *China's Challenge to Christianity* (New York, Missionary Education Movement, 1924), 30–34, 72–78, 82–94.

56. "Biographical Note," *Yale Divinity News* (September 1955), PC:LLP.

57. Beloit *Daily News,* April 30, 1953.

58. "Biographical Note," PC:LLP.

59. "Biographical Note," PC:LLP.

60. Van Ogden Vogt, "In Memoriam," PC:LLP.

61. "Biographical Note," PC:LLP.

62. Leters of Henry Porter, October–November 1900, as quoted in S. C. Miller, "Ends and Means: Missionary Justification of Force in Nineteenth Century China," in Fairbank, *The Missionary Enterprise,* 271, 274.

63. Porter to Chang Hsin-hai, July 14, 1958, PC:LLP.

64. S. C. Miller, "Ends and Means," 276–277.

65. Interview with Mildred Raible and Dorothy MacArthur, daughters of Howard Galt, Marlboro, Vermont, April 11, 1968.

66. Galt, "Yenching University," 46–55, AP; Edwards, *Yenching University,* 70.

67. "Oriental and Occidental Elements in China's Modern Educational System," *Chinese Social and Political Science Review*, 13.1:18 (January 1929).

68. Raible and MacArthur interview, April 11, 1968.

69. Mildred Raible to author, March 31, 1968; Wendell Galt, a son, has let me examine the second volume.

70. Letter of Sheffield to Judson Smith, February 26 and March 26, 1901, as cited in S. C. Miller, "Ends and Means," 274.

71. Raible and MacArthur interview, April 11, 1968.

72. Stuart, *Fifty Years*, 76.

73. Stella Burgess to me, March 11, 1968. Stella Burgess occasionally co-authored articles on China with her husband, but more often she translated poetry for publication. See *Survey*, 58:441 (August 1, 1927); *Atlantic Monthly*, 150:193 (August 1927); and *Christian Century*, 44:1385 (November 24, 1927), 42:470 (April 9, 1927), 41:1263 (October 2, 1924), 42:566 (April 30, 1925). She also published two collections of her own poetry, *A Peking Caravan* (Peking, 1924), and *Toward the Summit* (New York, Women's Press, 1948).

74. *The National Cyclopedia of American Biography* (New York, 1954), 39:423–24. Burgess was a frequent contributor of articles on China to *Survey Magazine, Survey Graphic,* and the *Christian Century*.

75. Garrett, *Social Reformers*, 111, 117, 126, 134–37, 171.

76. Chang Hung-chün interview, Taipei, January 25, 1969.

77. Stella Burgess wrote that her husband was an "early mentor" of Yen and "installed a fuse" with the question "In the 1,000 character movement you are laying pipes, yes. But what water is to run through them? What are your ideas on citizenship, responsibility . . . what goes with privilege, etc.?" Burgess' method with Yen as with all his Chinese contacts, was the so-called "John the Baptist method . . . He must increase, I must decrease." Stella Burgess to author, March 11, 1968.

78. Chang Hung-chün interview, January 25, 1969.

79. Leonard S. Hsü, "The Teaching of Sociology in China," *Chinese Social and Political Science Review*, 12:373–389 (July 1927).

80. Burgess (Columbia University Press, 1928), 7–8. See also Lucius Porter, *China's Challenge*, 32.

81. John S. Burgess, "China's Social Challenge, II, Beginnings of Social Investigation," *Survey*, 42 (October 13, 1917).

82. The forward to Gamble's and Burgess' study was written by G. Sherwood Eddy and suggests further the role of missionary figures in Chinese social work. The book was dedicated to the "missionaries whose work has made this study possible."

83. *Cyclopedia of American Biography*, 39:424.

84. Howard S. Galt, "Yenching University: Its Sources and Its History," ms., 34, 1939, AP. The best account of the period of negotiations and of the constituent schools is Galt's study, 1–78.

85. As quoted in Galt, "Yenching University," 28, AP.

86. Ibid., 30–31. D. Z. Sheffield, president of the North China College and mentor to Howard Galt translated many textbooks into Chinese. See Robert

Paterno, "Devello Z. Sheffield and the Founding of the North China College" in Liu Kwang-Ching, ed., *American Missionaries in China* (Cambridge, Harvard University Press, 1966), 42–84.

87. As quoted in Galt, "Yenching University," 34–35, 40, 45–46, 76, AP.

88. Stuart, "Autobiographical Notes," 13–14, PC:GMB (HL).

89. Galt, "Yenching University," 67, 89, AP.

90. Stuart, "Autobiographical Notes," 14; Stuart, *Fifty Years,* 53.

91. On the historical background of the new campus site, see Hung Yeh, *Ho Shen and Shu-ch'un-yüan: An Episode in the Past of the Yenching Campus,* pamphlet issued by Yenching University (Peiping, 1934).

92. Galt, "Yenching University," 173, AP.

93. B. A. Garside, *One Increasing Purpose: The Life of Henry Winters Luce* (New York, 1948), 179–180.

94. Edwards, *Yenching University,* 221.

95. Henry Killam Murphy, "An Architectural Renaissance in China," *Asia* 38.6:468–475 (June 1928).

96. Edwards, *Yenching University,* 224. The design of the buildings followed the general pattern of a rectangular base with massive pillars and beams supporting an overhanging, curved roof, decorated with animals on the ends of the ridges and on the corner ribs. The ornate treatment of the pillars, beams, and cornices, in the words of Howard Galt, provide one with the first impression "not only of beauty, but of splendor, bordering upon luxury." Within the limitations of the architectural style emphasis was placed upon simplicity, utility, and efficiency. Though the roofs curved as in the palace buildings of the Forbidden City, they were much lighter and more permanent because they were constructed with stamped cement tiles which could be fitted tightly together, an improvement over the thick layer of mud plaster sprouting grasses, weeds and small trees of traditional Chinese rooftops. Moreover, reinforced concrete trusses were used in place of wooden beams, and the intricate system of brackets in the cornices was cast from cement instead of laboriously fit wooden pieces. Galt, "Yenching University," 161, AP.

97. John Leighton Stuart, "The Chinese Mind and the Gospel," *International Review of Missions,* 548, 557 (October 1917). J. B. Tayler, an English member of the Life Fellowship, states that the "student in China is more readily moved by the appeal for social service than by any other." See his "China's Industrial Future: Can She Develop a Distinctive Order?" *World Tomorrow,* 6.2:339 (November 1923).

98. See Paul Varg, *Missionaries, Chinese, and Diplomats* (Princeton, 1958), chaps. 5 and 6; also see Latourette, *Christian Missions in China,* chaps. 25–26, 29–30.

99. As quoted in Varg, *Missionaries, Chinese, and Diplomats,* 68.

100. *Educational Review* [Shanghai], 15.4:331 (October 1932).

101. Jessie Gregory Lutz, *China and the Christian Colleges, 1850–1950* (Ithaca, Cornell University Press, 1971), chaps. 5 and 6.

102. Burgess, "China's Social Challenge, II," *Survey,* 41.

103. Galt's statement is found in Frank Rawlinson, ed., *The Chinese Church: The National Christian Conference* (Shanghai, 1922), 382.

104. Stuart, "The Chinese Mind," *International Review of Missions,* 559; Porter, *China's Challenge,* 101–107.

105. John Dillenberger and Claude Welch, *Protestant Christianity, Interpreted through Its Development* (New York, Charles Scribner's Sons, 1954), 224.

106. Stuart to editor of *Princeton Theological Review* (December 13, 1921), AC:JLS.

107. "Extracts from Princeton Review," ms., n.d., c.1922, AC:JLS; Stuart, "Autobiographical Notes," 18, PC:GMB (HL); Stuart, *Fifty Years,* 58.

108. Burgess, "China's Social Challenge, IV, The Christian Movement and Social Welfare," *Survey,* 633–637 (September 7, 1918); Pu Chi-shih (Burgess), "Chi-tu-chiao ti hsin-yang yü she-hui chin-pu" (Christian hope and social progress), *SM,* 1.2 (September 1, 1920); Irwin Scheiner, *Christian Converts and Social Protest in Meiji Japan* (Berkeley, University of California Press, 1970), chaps. 5, 6, and 7.

109. Stuart, "Chinese Mind," 552. J. E. Baker, longtime YMCA associate, friend of Yenching educators, and transportation adviser to the Chinese governments in the Republican years, stated his views on the social utility of Christianity in China in 1920 as follows: the Chinese people are too selfish to raise of their common striving for a lofty ideal, namely Christianity. The sense of personal allegiance to Jesus Christ instilled within the convert a feeling of compulsion. If the Chinese people converted to Christianity they too could overcome themselves above a certain level of social and industrial progress. But Westerners were able to overcome their selfishness and achieve unlimited progress because their selfishness and raise the national confidence to the point where China could once again "build Great Walls and dig Grand Canals." John Earl Baker, "Christianity and the Material Advance of China," *Chinese Recorder,* 51.12:826–836 (December 1920).

110. Stuart, "The Chinese Mind," *International Review of Missions,* 558–559; Porter, *China's Challenge,* chaps. 4 and 6; Burgess, "China's Social Challenge, IV," *Survey,* 637.

111. Galt, in Rawlinson, *The Chinese Church,* 382.

112. Edgar Snow, *Journey to the Beginning* (New York, 1958), 131.

113. As reproduced in a memorial statement written at the time of Stella Burgess' death in 1974 and sent to me by her son, David W. Burgess.

114. For an excellent account of the living pleasures for people with leisure in Peking in the 1930s, see George Kates, *The Years That Were Fat* (Cambridge, MIT Press, 1952).

115. Several better known examples of death and suffering in the lives of the prominent Western members of the Life Fellowship were the wife and mother of John Leighton Stuart in the mid 1920s, a childhood death in the Porter family, and serious illnesses for both the Burgess and Galt families. It must also be remembered that this optimism prevailed among them even after many had passed through severe physical deprivation during their Japanese internment.

116. Porter, "China Today," *SM*, 2.7:2–5 (March 1922). Also see Porter, *China's Challenge*, 91–107, for a similar diagnosis of China's problems.

117. Other contributors to this issue of *World Tomorrow*, 6.2 (November 1923) besides Porter, were Tyler Dennett, the historian, Henry Hodgkin, the English Quaker missionary who kept close ties with Yenching, and J. B. Tayler.

118. Dillenberger and Welch, *Protestant Christianity*, 234–238.

119. Yenching faculty wives organized needlework craft shops among the indigent Manchu communities surrounding the campus and set up part-time education classes, mothers' clubs, and instruction in household management. In addition a "Community Chest" with an annual budget between LC $1,300 and $2,000 was founded in 1926 to help finance programs of "relief for the destitute people of the community" and a "charity school for the children of the poor." Basil Learmonth, the English doctor on campus, ran a medical dispensary which treated more than 10,000 patients in 1931. See Galt, "Yenching University," 381–391, AP.

120. Chow Tse-tsung, *The May Fourth Movement* (Cambridge, Harvard University Press, 1964), chap. 9; Meisner, *Li Ta-chao*, 107–108.

121. Jonathan Spence, *To Change China: Western Advisers in China 1620–1960* (Boston, 1969), introduction.

122. Porter, *China's Challenge*, 222–223.

123. Lucius Porter, "Books Apropos" (review of Henry Hodgkin's *China in the Family of Nations* and Bertrand Russell's *The Problem of China*) in *World Tomorrow*, 6.2:347 (November 1923).

124. Lucius Porter, "Spiritual Exchanges in China," *SM*, 5.9:10–11, 15 (June 1925).

125. Stuart, "Autobiographical Notes," 28–29, 31, AP, parts of which are reproduced in *Fifty Years*, 73–74.

126. Stuart, "Autobiographical Notes," 28, 31 AP; Stuart, *Fifty Years*, 74.

127. John Stewart Burgess, "China's Social Challenge, I, An Opportunity for American Social Workers," *Survey*, 501, 503 (September 8, 1917).

128. Porter, *China's Challenge*, 40.

129. As recently as 1890 Protestant missionaries in China explicitly condemned these Jesuit policies of accommodation. See *Records of the General Conference of the Protestant Missionaries of China* (Shanghai, 1890), 631–660. At one point in the conference discussion Gilbert Reid took issue with the general condemnation of ancestor worship, quoting W.A.P. Martin for support, whereupon J. Hudson Taylor of the China Inland Mission asked all those who wished to raise a protest with Martin's position to rise. The conference proceedings record "almost the whole audience did so," ibid., 659.

130. Donald Treadgold, *The West in Russia and China: China 1582–1949* (New York, 1972), II, 9–22; also see George Dunne, *Generation of Giants* (South Bend, Notre Dame University Press, 1962), chaps. 3–5.

131. Stuart, "The Chinese Mind," *International Review of Missions*, 557–558; Stuart, *Fifty Years*, 100–105.

132. For an analysis of anti-Christian thought in China in the late Ming and

early Ch'ing, see George H. C. Wong, "The Anti-Christian Movement in Late Ming and Early Ch'ing," *Tsinghua hsüeh-pao*, 3.1:187–220 (May 1962).

133. Dunne, *Generation of Giants*, 30, 38, 116; Treadgold, *The West in Russia and China*, II, 30.

134. John Leighton Stuart, "The Outlook for Missionary Colleges," *Educational Review*, 12.1:59 (January 1921).

135. Edwards, *Yenching University*, 144; Lucius Porter diary, 1919–21, and 1923–24, passim; Stella F. Burgess to author, March 9, 1968.

136. See also Mei Yi-pao, "Tu-wei chiao-shou ti tsung-chiao kuan" (The religious outlook of Professor Dewey), *CLYSM*, 5.2 (December 1, 1930).

137. John Dewey, "Address, Annual Meeting of Chih-li-Shansi Christian Education Association, Peking," *Educational Review*, 12.2:106–107 (April 20, 1920). See also John Dewey, *Lectures in China, 1919–1920* (Honolulu, University of Hawaii Press, 1973), trans. and ed. Robert W. Clopton and Tsuin-chen Ou.

138. Stuart, "Outlook for Missionary Colleges," *Educational Review*, 61–62.

139. Burgess, "China's Social Challenge, I," *Survey*, 502 (September 8, 1917).

140. John Leighton Stuart to friends, written in Nanking, June 16, 1919, AC:JLS. Similar statements can also be found in Stuart, "President's Report to the Managers," June 1922, 3–4, AP; Stuart, "The Crisis in Christian Higher Education," *Chinese Recorder*, 4–5 (October 1928), as reprinted in AC:JLS; Stuart, "Christian Colleges in China," *International Review of Missions*, 13.50:245–246 (April 1924).

3. The Chinese Rationale

1. Chow Tse-tsung, *The May Fourth Movement* (Cambridge, Harvard University Press, 1964), 320.

2. Hsü Pao-ch'ien, "Erh-shih nien lai hsin-tao ching-yen tzu-shu" (My religious experience of twenty years) *CYLSM*, 8.4:180 (June 1934); Lucius Porter diary, March 14, 1920, PC:LLP; John Leighton Stuart, "Where Should the Emphasis Be?" *Chinese Recorder*, 51.5:349–350 (May 1920).

3. Jerome B. Grieder, *Hu Shih and the Chinese Renaissance: Liberalism in the Chinese Revolution, 1917–1937* (Cambridge, Harvard University Press, 1970), 22, n. 36; *Educational Review*, 21.1:101–102 (January 1928). Hu Shih, "Chi-tu-chiao yü Chung-kuo" (Christianity and China), *SM*, 2.7 (March 1922). Hu recognized the appeal of Christian morality among intellectuals, but he denounced Christianity's superstitious and theological aspects. The superstition, he claimed, grew out of the interpretations of Jesus' ignorant followers, and the theology was nothing more than the quibblings of medieval monks and pedants of the Middle Ages. Unless Christianity divested itself of these two undesirable elements it would have little to offer China. Despite his own atheism, Hu strongly defended religious freedom.

4. Chou Tso-jen, "Jen ti wen-hsüeh" (Humanistic literature), *Hsin ch'ing-nien* (New youth), 5.6:575–584 (December 15, 1918).

5. Chou Tso-jen, "Wo tui-yü Chi-tu-chiao ti kan-hsiang" (My views on Christianity), *SM*, 1.7 (March 1922); Ernst Wolff, *Chou Tso-jen* (New York, Twayne Publishers, 1971), 61–62.

6. Ch'en Tu-hsiu, *Hsin ch'ing-nien*, 3.3:284 (May 1, 1917).

7. Ch'en Tu-hsiu, "Ch'ao-hsien tu-li yün-tung chih kan-hsiang" (Thoughts on the Korean independence movement) *Tu-hsiu wen-ts'un* (Hong Kong, 1965), 607–608.

8. Ch'en, "Chi-tu-chiao yü Chung-kuo-jen" (Christianity and the Chinese people), *Hsin ch'ing-nien*, 7.3:15–22 (February 1920). Ch'en's article may also be found in *Tu-hsiu wen-ts'un*, 417–430; in Chang Ch'in-shih, ed., *Kuo-nei chin-shih-nien lai chih tsung-chiao ssu-hsiang* (Peking, 1927), 37–50; and an abridged version in *SM*, 2.7 (March 1922) in both Chinese and English. An abridged English translation also appeared in the *Chinese Recorder*, 51.7:453–457 (July 1920); and in Jessie G. Lutz, ed., *Christian Missions in China, Evangelists of What?* (Boston, 1965), 47–50, as "Jesus, the Incarnation of Universal Love."

9. From the English translation of the *SM* version.

10. Ch'en Tu-hsiu, "Chi-tu-chiao yü Chi-tu chiao-hui" (Christianity and the Christian church), in Chang, *Kuo-nei chin-shih-nien*, 190–193. This article originally appeared in the Non-Christian Student Federation (Fei Chi-tu-chiao hsüeh-sheng t'ung-meng) publication, *Wo-men wei she-ma fan-tui Chi-tu-chiao hsüeh-sheng t'ung-meng* (Why we oppose the Christian student alliance; Shanghai, 1922).

11. Hsü Ch'ien, *Chi-tu-chiao chiu-kuo chu-yi k'an-hsing chih san* (Shanghai, 1920). See also the lengthy biographical sketch of Hsü in the Boorman, II, 118–122.

12. It is not clear what relationship Hsü Ch'ien may have had with members of the Life Fellowship. Hsü's family was from Kiangsu, but he spent many years in Hangchow, as did Wu Lei-ch'uan; both rose through the examination system, taught in provincial colleges in the last years of the Ch'ing dynasty (Hsü in Anhwei), and both converted to Christianity, Wu in 1914 and Hsü in 1915, with apparently similar motivations. See Joan Hsü (Hsü Ying), "George Chien Hsu, Year to Year Event," mimeographed, an English translation of Hsü Chang's, *Hsü kung chi-lung nien-p'u* (Hong Kong, 1940). Joan Hsü attended Yenching University, and Hsü himself contributed an article to the first issue of the *Sheng-ming* (November 20, 1919).

13. See Irwin Scheiner, *Christian Converts and Social Protest in Meiji Japan* (Berkeley, 1970), chaps. 1–4, for a similar point in the case of Japanese converts to Protestantism. In addition to the five figures studied here, others at Yenching could be singled out for discussion. Chou Tso-jen, Hsieh Wan-ying, Hsü Ti-shan, Hsü Shu-hsi, Wu Wen-tsao, Ku Chieh-kang, and Chang Tung-sun, to name a few, were perhaps even better known in China at the time. But the Chinese members of the Life Fellowship better represent the earlier purposes of the university. Two other Yenching luminaries, Lu Chih-wei and Mei Yi-pao (both chancellors in time), were also members of the Life Fellowship, but they arrived at Yenching somewhat later and neither wrote more than a few short

pieces for the *Sheng-ming* and *Chen-li yü sheng-ming*. Lu will be considered more extensively in the last chapter.

14. For information on Liu T'ing-fang's early life, I have relied on interviews with Liu T'ing-wei, his younger brother, in Taipei, June 8 and 11, 1969. Other sources are Boorman, II, 416–417; Chao Tzu-ch'en, "A Glimpse at One Chinese Christian Worker," *Chinese Recorder*, 54:744 (December 1923); *Who's Who in China* (Shanghai, China Weekly Review, 1931, 1936); and "Biographical Information Sheet," AC:LTF. Stuart's quote is from Stuart to Lewis, January 20, 1926, AC:JLS.

15. Liu T'ing-wei, interview, June 8 and 11, 1969.

16. John Leighton Stuart, "Autobiographical Notes," ms., 56, PC:GMB.

17. See the "Biographical Information Sheet"; Boorman, II, 416; and *Who's Who in China*, 1936, 162.

18. Stuart read Liu's pieces in the *T'ung-wen pao* (The Chinese Christian Intelligencer), which was published weekly in Shanghai by the Presbyterian Mission. A friend of mine in Bloomington found a few copies of this periodical at an auction sale in southern Indiana.

19. Stuart, "Autobiographical Notes," 47, PC:GMB.

20. Stuart to North, April 13, 1927, AC:JLS.

21. Stuart, "Autobiographical Notes," 47–48, PC:GMB.

22. Liu T'ing-wei, interview, June 11, 1969; Grace M. Boynton, interview, November 14, 1967.

23. Stuart to Lewis, January 20, 1926, AC:JLS. Chao Tzu-ch'en's biographical piece on Liu also mentions some of Liu's problems of temperament. Liu T'ing-wei referred to his older brother's "struggle oriented mentality."

24. "Biographical Information Sheet," AC:LTF; "Published Writings and Other Activities, 1932–1934," AP:R (School of Religion). The *Sung-chu sheng-shih* (Shanghai, 1936) was published by the Christian Literature Society (Chung-hua Chi-tu-chiao wen-she) and became the standard collection of Protestant hymns in Chinese. It was republished in 1952 in Hong Kong.

25. Ma Meng, interview, Hong Kong, February 3, 1969.

26. One of his last writings was the introduction to Wu Lei-ch'uan's *Mo Ti yü Yeh-su* (Shanghai, 1939).

27. Mei Yi-pao, interview, Iowa City, July 16, 1968.

28. "Of Merit in Gardens," n.d., c.1930, 9–12, PC:GMB. Mei was one of those who would visit Wu in the setting described by Boynton.

29. Pearl Buck described this anti-Western trend, even among Westernized students, in her introduction to Lin Yutang's *My Country and My People* (New York, Halcyon House, 1938), xi-xvi.

30. Wu Lei-ch'uan, "Hsin-yang Chi-tu-chiao erh-shih nien ti ching-yen" (My experience of belief in Christianity over twenty years), in Hsü Pao-ch'ien, ed., *Tsung-chiao ching-yen t'an* (Shanghai, 1934), 15.

31. Chao Tzu-ch'en, "Wu Lei-ch'uan hsien-sheng hsiao-chuan" (A biographical sketch of Mr. Wu Lei-ch'uan), *CLYSM*, 10.8:418 (January 1937); Wu, "Hsin-yang," in Hsü, *Tsung-chiao*, 15.

32. Wu, "Hsin-yang," in Hsü, *Tsung-chiao,* 15; Chao, "Wu Lei-ch'uan hsien-sheng," *CLYSM,* 483.

33. Wu Lei-ch'uan, "Wo so hsiang-wang ti hsüeh-hsiao sheng-huo" (The campus life I expect to find), *YTCK,* 4.5:85 (February 5, 1925); Chao, "Wu Lei-ch'uan hsien-sheng," *CLYSM,* 484–485; *Who's Who in China,* 1936, 262.

34. Wu Lei-ch'uan, "Wo ko-jen ti tsung-chiao ching-yen" (My personal religious experience), *SM,* 3.8:2 (April 1923).

35. Wu, "Hsin-yang" in Hsü, *Tsung-chiao,* 14, 16, 17, 19.

36. Wu Lei-ch'uan, "Chen-li chou-k'an fa-k'an tzu" (A few words on the publication of Chen-li chou-k'an), *Chen-li chou-k'an,* 1.1:1 (April 1, 1923); Wu, "Hsin-yang" in Hsü, *Tsung-chiao,* 19.

37. *PSYTI,* 1931, 265; *Who's Who in China,* 1936, 262; *Yenching News,* Chengtu edition, 2.16 (March 14, 1945).

38. Hung Yeh, interview, Cambridge, Massachusetts, June 12, 1968.

39. Mei Yi-pao, interview, Iowa City, July 16, 1968.

40. Hsü was an especially close friend of John and Stella Burgess. Burgess wrote a short biographical piece on Hsü, no title, n.d., c.1920, ms., PC:SFB, but most of the information for this biographical sketch will be taken from Hsü's own account, "Erh-shih nien lai hsin-tao ching-yen tzu-shu," which appeared in eight installments in the *CLYSM* in 1933 and 1934 when he was serving as editor-in-chief of the publication.

41. Burgess' biographical sketch of Hsü, 2, PC:SFB; Hsü, "Erh-shih nien," *CLYSM,* 7.7–8:27–28 (May–June 1933).

42. Hsü, "Erh-shih nien," *CLYSM,* 7.7–8:28–29.

43. Thomson's book (New York, 1908) was a collection of five lectures delivered at Wake Forest College.

44. Hsü, "Erh-shih nien," *CLYSM,* 7.7–8:30 and *CLYSM,* 8.1:28–30.

45. Hsü, "Erh-shih nien," *CLYSM,* 8.1:30; Hsia Tsi-an, *The Gate of Darkness: Studies on the Leftist Literary Movement in China* (Seattle, University of Washington Press, 1968), 15. Successive chairmen for this social club were from the Customs College and from Peking National University.

46. Hsü, "Erh-shih nien," *CLYSM,* 8.2:78–79.

47. Ibid., 81. Also see John Stewart Burgess, "P. C. Hsu—A Chinese Christian," *Christian Century,* 496 (April 19, 1944).

48. Hsü, "Erh-shih nien," *CLYSM,* 8.3:114, 117, 8.5:216–218, and 8.7:373–378.

49. Hsü, "Erh-shih nien," *CLYSM,* 8.4:181 (June 1934); Burgess, "P. C. Hsu," *Christian Century,* 496.

50. Hsü, "Erh-shih nien," *CLYSM,* 8.4:182–183. Volumes 9 and 11 of *CLYSM* carried extensive reports of Hsü's work in rural reconstruction during his two years of work at Li-chüan, including an article on why he left. See *CLYSM,* 9.2:67–85 (December 1935), 9.4:188–192 (June 1935), 9.7:381–392 (December 1935), 9.8:465–473 (January 1936), 11.3:144–152 (May 1937), and 11.4:113–231 (June 1937), the last issue published of *CLYSM.*

On Hsü's death, see Burgess, "P. C. Hsu," *Christian Century,* 494–497. Twelve years earlier Hsü had translated Hocking's *Rethinking Missions* (written for the Laymen's Foreign Mission Inquiry) as *Hsüan-chiao shih-yeh p'ing-yi* (Shang-hai, 1934).

51. Boorman, I, 148, is the most extensive account of Chao's professional life, and states that Chao was born in 1890. This is corroborated by Hashikawa Tokio, ed., *Chūgoku bunkakai jimbutsu sōkan* (Peking, 1940), 648. But all other sources, even those which treat extensively Chao's thought, such as, Yama-moto Sumiko and Ng Lee Ming (see below), and the various editors of *Who's Who in China,* including Max Perleberg, ed. (Hong Kong, 1953), disagree and put Chao's birthdate as 1888. Ng, who has written extensively on Chao, even puts the date at 1885, p. 96. The New York *Times,* May 25, 1952, states Chao was then 64, thus placing his birthdate in 1888. None of the Yenching faculty directories are of any help here, and Chao's own published writings do not provide this information. Four of Chao's most popular works, published ori-ginally by the Association Press (Ch'ing-nien hsieh-hui shu-chü) in Shanghai and republished after the Communist revolution by the Council of Christian Literature for Overseas Chinese (Chi-tu-chiao fu-ch'iao ch'u-pan-she) in Hong Kong are: *Yeh-su chuan* (Life of Jesus, 1935); *Chi-tu-chiao chin-chieh* (An interpretation of Christianity, 1947); *Sheng pao-luo chuan* (The life of St. Paul, 1948); and *Shen-hsüeh ssu-chiang* (Four talks on theology, 1948). In addition, Chao wrote more than a hundred articles and short pieces including more than a dozen for the *Chinese Recorder* for the benefit of Western au-diences. Most of the Chinese pieces appeared in the *Life Journal* and the *Truth and Life.* Ng Lee Ming's "Christianity and Social Change: The Case in China, 1920-1950" (Princeton Theological Seminary, Th.D., 1971), 268-274, provides a useful listing of Chao's writings.

52. Unless noted otherwise, the information on Chao's childhood and youth is taken from his "Wo ti tsung-chiao ching-yen," *SM,* 4.3:1-16 (November 1923). In 1934 Chao wrote another short autobiographical piece with the same title. That one appeared in Hsü Pao-ch'ien, ed., *Tsung-chiao ching-yen t'an* (Shanghai, 1934), 67-74. The earlier account is intimate in detail on family and childhood background and on his conversion experience. The latter piece is less personal. It is written in a more rational vein and was aimed at preventing any further backsliding among Christian youth in the 1930s, as are all the other articles in Hsü's collection.

53. *Who's Who in China,* 1936, 22.

54. Chao, "Wo ti tsung-chiao ching-yen," *SM,* 4.3:5.

55. Ibid., 6. Chao's later version in Hsü, *Tsung-chiao,* 68, omits this violent outburst and merely states that as a student he thought that China's religious tradition was sufficient and that China had no need to import Christianity from the outside.

56. Chao, "Wo ti tsung-chiao," *SM,* 4.3:79; Chao, "Wo ti tsung-chiao," in Hsü, *Tsung-chiao,* 68-69.

57. *Chi-tu-chiao che-hsüeh* (Christian philosophy) (Shanghai, 1925) was Chao's first attempt at a systematic interpretation of Christianity. It was written in the form of a dialogue among students and Westerners of varying points of view, with Chao entering the exchange at crucial points presenting his socially

oriented and humanistic interpretation of Christianity. For information on Chao's later life, see Boorman, I, 147-148 and the New York *Times,* May 25, 1952.

58. Chao, "Wo ti tsung-chiao," *SM,* 4.3:16.

59. See Chao Tzu-ch'en, *Yeh-su chuan,* 203. This book underwent five printings in China before the revolution, and one after that in 1965 in Hong Kong. The most comprehensive analysis of this work is Yamamoto Sumiko, *Chūgoku Kiristokyō shi kenkyū* (Tokyo, 1972), 201-229. For the changes in Chao's thought in the late 1940s, see Ng, "Christianity and Social Change," 162-169, and Francis P. Jones, *The Church in Communist China* (New York, Friendship Press, 1962), 98 ff.

60. "An Annotated, Partial List of the Publications of William Hung," *Harvard Journal of Asiatic Studies,* 24:7-16 (1962-63).

61. William Hung, interview, Cambridge, Massachusetts, June 18, 1968.

62. His trip and costs of education were paid for by a wealthy trustee of Ohio Wesleyan University, who was traveling around the world recruiting students for the college and observed Hung in the Methodist school in Foochow one day reciting on the Napoleonic Wars. Ibid. Hung wrote, *Get Acquainted, Mr. American, Mr. Jun Kuo Ren* (New York, 1921), a 22-page tract distributed in Protestant church circles in America. In it he presents a case for China's position in world affairs in pithy language geared to the American lay audience, while trying to break down common stereotypes of the Chinese people.

63. Hung, interview, Cambridge, Mass., June 18, 1968; Stuart to North, June 16, 1927, AC:JLS.

64. Hung's account, "Amazing Experiences of a Prisoner in the Hands of the Japanese," appeared in *Guidepost,* 38, ed. Norman Vincent Peale (New York, 1946). For Hung's later life, see Glen Baxter, "In Tribute," *Harvard Journal of Asiatic Studies,* 24 (1962-63).

65. For extensive biographical information on each of these three figures see Arthur Hummel, ed., *Eminent Chinese of the Ch'ing Period* (Washington, D.C., Government Printing Office, 1943), 316-319, 452-454, 894-895.

66. Liu T'ing-fang, "Chung-kuo Chi-tu-t'u ai-kuo wen-t'i ti p'ing-yi" (Chinese Christians and the question of patriotism) *SM,* 4.9-10:2-3, 5 (June 1924).

67. Among the eighteen testimonies included in Hsü's collection, nine of them, including Hsü, Chao, and Wu, were related to Yenching University as students or teachers at one time or another. See Hsü, *Tsung-chiao,* 119-120.

68. See Wu's testimony in Hsü's *Tsung-chiao,* 16.

69. See Chao's testimony in Hsü's *Tsung-chiao,* 74. One can hardly overemphasize the importance of hope as a factor in religious experience. One of Wu Lei-ch'uan's books written a quarter century after his original conversion *Chi-tu-t'u ti hsi-wang* (Shanghai, 1940), was based on this theme. See also Hsü Pao-ch'ien, "Youth's Challenge to Youth" in Stauffer, ed., *China Her Own Interpreter,* 163. Chao Tzu-ch'en portrayed Jesus above all in terms of the practical problems facing the Chinese people. See Chao, *Yeh-su chuan,* introduction and chaps. 11-14; see also Yamamoto's analysis of Chao's interpretation of Jesus, in *Chūgoku Kirisutokyō,* 213-222.

70. The YMCA monthly, *Ch'ing-nien chin-pu*, had a circulation of 7,000 in 1921, but after the Anti-Christian movement it failed to penetrate very far into non-Christian circles. See Milton Stauffer, ed., *The Christian Occupation of China*, 455.

71. Hsü, *Tsung-chiao*, 1–2.

72. Wolfram Eberhard, *Guilt and Sin in Traditional China* (Berkeley, University of California Press, 1967).

73. See Wu's testimony in Hsü's *Tsung-chiao*, 17.

74. Chao, *Chi-tu-chiao che-süeh*, 158, as translated in Ng Lee Ming, "Christianity and Social Change," 103–104.

75. Wm. Theodore deBary ed., *Self and Society in Ming Thought*, 12–18, 145–150, 224–225.

76. Wu testimony in Hsü, *Tsung-chiao*, 18.

77. Chao, *Chi-tu-chiao che-hsüeh*, 156–157, as translated in Ng, "Christianity and Social Change," 103.

78. Hsü, *Tsung-chiao*, 2. Wu Lei-ch'uan, *Chi-tu-chiao yü Chung-kuo wen-hua* (Shanghai, 1936), 6; Yamamoto Sumiko, *Chūgoku Kirisutokyō*, 139–146. Imitating Jesus was at the heart of their commitment to the Christian faith. Whole articles in the Life Fellowship publications would discuss the importance of imitation and Jesus as a moral exemplar. See for example the articles by Wu Lei-ch'uan, *CLYSM*, 1.8:221–225 (September 1926), and by Chao Tzu-ch'en, *CLYSM*, 2.13:395–439 (1927) and 8.5 (October 1934).

79. Chao, *Yeh-su chuan*, introduction; Yamamoto, *Chūgoku Kirisutokyō*, 218.

80. As cited in Wm. Theodore deBary, ed., *Sources of Chinese Tradition* (New York, Columbia University Press, 1960), 834–835.

81. Hsü Pao-ch'ien, "Hsin-ssu-ch'ao yü Chi-tu-chiao (The new thought tide and Christianity), *SM*, 1.2 (September 1, 1920).

82. Hsü Pao-ch'ien, "Fan chi-tu-chiao yün-tung yü wu-jen ying-ts'ai chih fang-chi" (Strategies for adapting to the Anti-Christian movement), *SM*, 6.5:1–6 (March 1926); Hsü, *Ethical Realism in Neo-Confucian Thought* (Peiping, Yenching University, 1933), iv.

83. Hsü, *Ethical Realism*, v.

84. Chao Tzu-ch'en, "The Appeal of Christianity to the Chinese Mind," *Chinese Recorder*, 49:371 (1918); Chao, *Chi-tu-chiao che-hsüeh*, 108.

85. Chao, "Can Christianity Be the Basis of Social Reconstruction in China?" *Chinese Recorder*, 53.5:313 (May 1922).

86. Liu T'ing-fang, "The Contribution of the Christian Colleges," for the Chinese Association for Higher Education (Shanghai, 1924), AC:LTF.

87. Hung, "The Chinese Picture of Life," *Asia*, 31.9:586 (September 1931).

88. Hsü, "Erh-shih nien," *CLYSM*, 7.7–8:28 (May–June 1933).

89. Joseph Levenson, *Modern China and Its Confucian Past* (Berkeley, University of California Press, 1958), 174. Levenson argues that communism appealed to Chinese intellectuals where Christianity failed, because acceptance of this Western ideology "guaranteed that the pre-Communist West, the West which had impinged on China, was as firmly rejected by its own critics as by the most hidebound Chinese traditionalist. A Chinese who wishes to be con-

fident . . . of the equivalence of China and the West . . . need not fall back on a desperate traditionalism, since anti-traditionalism, under communist aegis, would serve his purpose. Instead of being the laggard, following in Western footsteps, a communist China, with Russia, could seem at the head of the queue." Ibid., 176.

90. Hsü, "Erh-shih nien," *CLYSM*, 7.7–8:29 (May–June 1933); also Hsü, *Ethical Realism*, i; Wu Lei-ch'uan, *Chi-tu-chiao yü Chung-kuo wen-hua*, 6–7; Liu T'ing-fang, "The Contribution of Christian Colleges and Universities to the Church in China," 2, AC:LTF; Chao Tzu-ch'en, "Can Christianity Be the Basis of Social Reconstruction in China?", 318.

91. Wu testimony in Hsü, *Tsung-chiao*, 17. For a discussion of Chao's broad interpretations on the nature of God, see Ng, "Christianity and Social Change," 131–133.

92. Wu, "Chung-kuo ch'ing-nien pu-tang hsiao-fa Yeh-su ma?" (The appropriateness of Chinese youth imitating Jesus), *CLYSM*, 1.8:221–222. Jesus' historical role within the context of Jewish national salvation was discussed extensively. See for example, Wu Lei-ch'uan, *Chi-tu-chiao yü Chung-kuo wen-hua*, chap. 4, and his *Mo Ti yü Yeh-su* (Shanghai, 1940), chap. 4; see also Chao Tzu-ch'en, *Yeh-su chuan*, chaps. 1, 5, and 14.

93. Chao, *Chi-tu-chiao che-hsüeh*, 255–269, as discussed in Ng, "Christianity and Social Change," 107–108.

94. Hsü testimony in Hsü, *Tsung-chiao*, 49–50.

95. Wu, *Chi-tu-chiao*, 6, 63; and Wu, *Mo Ti*, 113.

96. Boorman, I, 184; Yamamoto, *Chūgoku Kirisutokyō*, 205–210.

97. Liu T'ing-fang, "Yeh-su Chi-tu—pao-shou—fan-tui—sheng-ming" (Jesus Christ: conservative, radical, or giver of life), *SM*, 1.4 (November 15, 1920); also see Ng, "Christianity and Social Change," 136–137, for Chao's discussion of the "abundant life."

98. Chao, "Fu-yin ti hsiao chu-chieh" (An explanation of the social gospel) *CLYSM*, 8.8:418 (January 1935).

99. The list of articles in the *Sheng-ming* defending the internationalist position is very long. Some of those appearing in the *SM*, not to mention the *CLYSM*, are 1.2:1–5 (September 1921), 3.1:1–5 (September 1922), 4.8:1–5 (April 1924), 4.9–10:1–8 (June 1924), and 5.4:1–3 (January 1925).

100. Hsü, *Ethical Realism*, 164.

101. Liu, "Contributions," 5–6, and "Commencement Address at Yenching University, 1925," AC:LTF.

102. Chao, *Chi-tu-chiao che-hsüeh*, 288, as cited in Ng, "Christianity and Social Change," 98.

103. Liu T'ing-fang, "Chung-kuo Chi-tu-t'u ai-kuo wen-t'i ti p'ing-yi," *SM*, 4.9–10:5–7 (June 1924).

104. Chao, "Wo ti tsung-chiao ching-yen," *SM*, 4.3:13 (November 1923).

105. Hung, interview, June 12, 1968.

106. Wu's description of the qualities of behavior that would mark the social revolution was quite similar to that of the Communists at the same time. In his latest book *Mo Ti yü Yeh-su* (1940), 141–149, he spoke of the conditions for

those who wished to help in the establishment of the "Kingdom of Heaven": repentence, discipline, courage, struggle, firm resolve, throwing off of the old, and sacrificing all for the people. Christians joining in the revolution would have to become more martial in spirit. Struggle and violence were unavoidable. See also his *Chi-tu-t'u ti hsi-wang,* 41, and his testimony in Hsü, *Tsung-chiao,* 19.

107. Wu testimony, Hsü, *Tsung-chiao,* 17; Chao Tzu-ch'en, "The Chinese Church Realizes Itself," *Chinese Recorder,* 58:302 (1927).

108. Hung, "The Chinese Picture of Life," 564.

109. Wu Lei-ch'uan, "Wo so hsiang-wang ti hsüeh-hsiao sheng-huo," *YTCK,* 85:4–8 (February 5, 1925).

110. Liu T'ing-fang, "Education for Democracy," *Princeton-Peking Gazette,* April 1927, AP.

111. See the articles by Chou Tso-jen and Chang Tung-sun in *SM,* 2.7 (March 1922).

4. Organizing a Bicultural University

1. John Israel, *Student Nationalism in China, 1927–1937* (Stanford, Stanford University Press, 1966), 5.

2. Stuart to the finance committee of the board of trustees, April 21, 1921, AC:JLS.

3. Hsia Tsi-an, *The Gate of Darkness: Studies in the Leftist Literary Movement in China* (Seattle, University of Washington Press, 1968).

4. See Yamamoto Tatsuro and Yamamoto Sumiko, "The Anti-Christian Movement in China, 1922–1927," *Far Eastern Quarterly,* 12.2:133–148 (February 1953); and Yamamoto Sumiko, *Chūgoku Kirisutokyō shi kenkyū* (Tokyo, 1972), 96–115. Other sources on the Anti-Christian movement are Jessie G. Lutz, *China and the Christian Colleges, 1850–1950* (Ithaca, Cornell University Press, 1971), 215–270; Kiang Wen-han, *The Chinese Student Movement* (New York, King's Crown Press, 1948), chap. 3; T. C. Wang, *The Youth Movement in China* (New York, New Republic, 1927), chap. 11; and Kenneth Scott Latourette, *History of Christian Missions in China* (London, 1929), chap. 27. From these studies the question arises as to the source of Chinese antiforeignism. Is there, for example something innately xenophobic in being Chinese? One scholar, Tsiang T'ing-fu, has linked traditional xenophobia with neo-Confucianism, but he does so only in passing. The link needs to be explored further. See Tsiang, "China and European Expansion," in Immanuel C. Y. Hsu, *Readings in Modern Chinese History* (New York, Oxford University Press, 1971), 130.

5. Liu T'ing-fang, "Huan-ying" (Welcome) *SM,* 2.7 (March 1922). The Non-Christian Student Federation was begun in Shanghai and its manifesto was printed in both Chinese and English in *SM,* 2.7 (March 1922); also see Chang Ch'in-shih, ed., *Kuo-nei chin-shih-nien,* 187–189.

6. The best source on the Movement for the Restoration of Educational Rights is Cyrus Peake, *Nationalism and Education in Modern China* (New York, Columbia University Press, 1932), 72–159. Also see Alice Gregg, *China and*

Educational Autonomy (Syracuse, Syracuse University Press, 1946), chap. 8; and Kiang Wen-han, *Chinese Student Movement,* 87–95.

7. Yü Chia-chü, "Chiao-hui chiao-yü wen-t'i" (The question of Christian education) in Chang, *Kuo-nei chin-shih-nien,* 305–338; Ch'en Ch'i-t'ien, "Wo-men chu-chang shou-hui chiao-yü ch'üan ti li-yu yü pan-fa" (The rationale and methods for our support of the restoration of educational rights), in Chang, *Kuo-nei chin-shih-nien,* 342–365. Ch'en continued to write on education for many years after the decline of the movement. See, for example, his *Tsui-chin sha-nien Chung-kuo chiao-yü shih* (A history of Chinese education over the last thirty years; Taipei, 1962).

8. Wu Lei-ch'uan cited the higher figures in "Hu-an yü Chung-kuo Chi-tu-chiao ch'ien-t'u" (The Shanghai incident and the future of Christianity), *SM,* 5.5 (June 1925); for an extensive account of the effects on mission institutions see Dorothy Borg, *American Policy and the Chinese Revolution, 1925–1928* (New York, The MacMillan Co., 1947), 20–45; and Jessie Lutz, *China and the Christian Colleges,* 246–254.

9. "Christian Schools under the Nationalistic Government," *Educational Review,* 19.2:141, 160 (April 1927).

10. Lutz, *China and the Christian Colleges,* 255–270.

11. For a joint declaration by professors at Peita, see "Chu-chang hsin-chiao tzu-yu hsüan-yen" (An announcement supporting religious freedom) in Chang, *Kuo-nei chin-shih-nien,* 199. See also Liang Ch'i-ch'ao, "P'ing fei tsung-chiao t'ung-meng" (A criticism of the non-religious alliance) in Chang, *Kuo-nei chin-shih-nien,* 260–271. Chou Nien-tzu, who attended Yenching in the mid-1930s, was a granddaughter of Liang Ch'i-ch'ao and recalled the Liang family's vigorous defense of the Christian schools as the best place for students to receive a moral education. Interview, Milton, Mass., May 5, 1968.

12. H. C. Tsao, "The Present Situation of Education in China," *Educational Review,* 20.4:374 (October 1928).

13. Stuart to North, April 10, 1927, AC:JLS; Alice Gregg, *China and Educational Autonomy,* 86–92; "Minutes of the Faculty Organization," September 12, 1923, and "President's Report to the Board of Trustees," January 1925, 2–4, AP:R.

14. Ssu-t'u Lei-teng (John Leighton Stuart), "Chi-tu-chiao chiao-yü wen-t'i" (The question of Christian education), *SM* 5.4:9 (January 1925); "Declaration of the Yenching Faculty, June 3, 1925," *SM,* 5.9:67 (June 1925). For the declaration of the Chinese faculty, see "Yenching ta-hsüeh Chung-kuo chiao-chih-yüan ch'üan-t'i hsüan-yen" (An announcement of the Yenching Chinese faculty), *SM,* 5.9:48 (June 1925).

15. Lucius Porter, "Cry of the Chinese Heart," *SM,* 5.9:1–2 (June 1925), in the English section; Porter diary, June 4, 1925, PC:LLP.

16. Stuart to the trustees, April 22, 1926, AC:JLS; *Yenching University: A Few Facts and Figures* (Peiping, 1929), 5, AP:R. For another assessment by Stuart see his "Crisis in Christian Higher Education," *Chinese Recorder,* 59 (October 1928), reprint in AC:JLS. For Howard Galt's views on the Anti-Christian movement and mission school education in China, see his "Oriental

and Occidental Elements in China's Modern Educational System," pt. III, *Chinese Social and Political Science Review,* 13.1:22–24 (January 1929).

17. This exchange between Stuart and MacMurray is in the State Department Records Relating to Internal Affairs of China, 1910–27, 893/00.7378, in the National Archives in Washington, D.C. On March 18 MacMurray fired back a reply accusing one of the Yenching signatories of erroneously quoting him to be an initiator of the Western ultimatum to the Chinese. See MacMurray to Stuart, Peking, March 18, 1926.

18. Interview, Grace M. Boynton, November 14, 1967, and Elizabeth Kirkpatrick (Porter's oldest daughter), August 28, 1969. See also Porter's diary for July 1927. One journalist's account of the escape is Vincent Sheean, *Personal History* (New York, 1934), 256. Porter and Sheean met frequently in July 1927.

19. For these exchanges see "Editorial," Peking and Tientsin *Times,* February 3–5, 1926; *North China Standard,* Peking, May 6, 1927. Copies were found in the Tientsin Consular Archives in the National Archives in Washington.

20. Minute, Board of Trustees, April 6 and 14, 1927, AP:BT. The cable from the field was dated April 9, 1927.

21. Stuart to the finance committee of the board of trustees, April 21, 1921, AC:JLS.

22. "Pei-ching chiao-yü-pu pu-kao ti shih-liu hao" (The sixteen points of the announcement of the Peking board of education) and "Ssu-li hsüeh-hsiao kui-ch'eng" (Regulations for private colleges; November 1926) were reproduced in Chang Ch'in-shih, ed., *Kuo-nei chin-shih-nien lai chih tsung-chiao ssu-ch'ao* (Peking, 1927), 370–373. English translations of both these regulations were carried in the *Educational Review,* 18.1:99–101 (January 1926) and 19.2:163–180 (April 1927), respectively.

23. Stuart, "Current Religious Issues as Faced at Yenching University," *Educational Review,* 23.1:42–44 (January 1931).

24. "Chung-kuo-jen ts'ung Ou-Mei Chi-tu-chiao kuo-chia so-te chih Chi-tu-chiao ying-hsiang" (The impressions of Christianity that the Chinese people have gained from Western Christian nations), *SM,* 2.7:1–6 (March 1922); Liu T'ing-fang, "Fan-tui tsung-chiao ti yün-tung" (The anti-religious movement), *SM,* 2.9:2–5 (June 1922); Yamamoto Sumiko, "Chūgoku no Kirisuto kyōdai jiritsu undō ni tsuite" (The independence movement of the Chinese Christian church), *Kindai Chūgoku Kenkyū,* 1:287 (September 1958).

25. Wu Lei-ch'uan, *Chi-tu-chiao yü Chung-kuo wen-hua,* 10; Wu, "Chiao-hui hsüeh-hsiao tang ju-ho ying-fu shih-chü" (How Christian schools should regard the current situation), *CLYSM,* 2.3:52 (February 15, 1927).

26. Hsü Pao-ch'ien, "Er-shih nien lai hsin-tao ching-yen tzu-shu," *CLYSM,* 8.4:182 (June 1934).

27. Liu T'ing-fang, "Fei Chi-tu-chiao hsüeh-sheng t'ung-meng" (The non-Christian student alliance), *SM,* 2.7:11 (March 1922); Liu, "To the Members of the General Board, the Three Councils, Regional Associations, and other Members of the China Christian Education Association," printed (n.d., c. summer 1925), 6–7, AC:LTF.

28. Wu Lei-ch'uan, "Hu-an yü Chung-kuo Chi-tu-chiao ch'ien-t'u," *SM,*

272

5.5:18 (June 1925). For a similar statement in English, see Hsü Pao-ch'ien, "Youth's Challenge to Youth" in Milton Stauffer, ed., *China, Her Own Interpreter* (New York, 1927), 159–168.

29. Wu Lei-ch'uan, *Chi-tu-t'u ti hsi-wang*, 4–5; Liu T'ing-fang, "Chi-tu-chiao yü Chung-kuo kuo-min hsing" (Christianity and the Chinese national character), *SM* 5.9:4–15 (June 1925). For an account on how the charge of denationalization affected student converts at the time, see the testimony by the granddaughter of Tseng Kuo-fan, a Yenching graduate, Tseng Pao-sun, "Wo ti tsung-chiao ching-yen t'an" (My religious experience), in Hsü, ed., *Tsung-chiao ching-yen t'an* (Shanghai, 1934), 60.

30. "Chung-kuo-jen ts'ung Ou-Mei," *SM*, 4.

31. Wu Lei-ch'uan, "Lun Chung-kuo Chi-tu-t'u tui-yü kuo-chia ying-fu ti tse-jen" (The responsibilities Chinese Christians should have toward the nation), *SM*, 5.5:5 (February 1925).

32. Liu T'ing-fang, "Chi-tu-chiao yü Chung-kuo kuo-min hsing," *SM*, 11.

33. Liu T'ing-fang, "Chung-kuo Chi-tu-t'u ai-kuo wen-t'i ti p'ing-yi," *SM*, 4.9–10:5 (June 1924). Liu's article was carried in two installments, the first part appearing in *SM*, 4.8:1–5 (April 1924).

34. Liu, "Chi-tu-chiao yü Chung-kuo kuo-min hsing," *SM*, 12–15.

35. Wu Lei-ch'uan, "Lun Chung-kuo Chi-tu-t'u tui-yü kuo-chia," *SM*, 6–7; Liu T'ing-fang, "Wu-hu wu-sha" (The cry of May Thirtieth), *CLYSM*, 1.4:91–92 (May 1926); Hsü Pao-ch'ien, "Pien-chi-che yen" (A word from the editors), *CLYSM*, 3.1:2–3 (c. January 1928).

36. Lu to McMullen, September 1, 1950, Lu Chih-wei file, AC:UB.

37. Whatever their professional and personal affiliations were, the trustees were as sound in body and spirit as they were secure in their wealth. More than two thirds of them lived to be over seventy, and four of the seventeen listed in 1945 lived into their nineties.

38. Copies of the original 1889 charter of Peking University and the ammendation of 1915 and the revisions of 1923 and 1928 can be found in AP:BT.

39. Article II, sec. 1, Article III, sec. 3, and Article VII, AP:BT.

40. Article III, sec. 5, and Article IV, sec. 1, AP:BT.

41. The Peking University board of managers in 1892, for example, consisted of eleven members, six representing mission boards (four of them Methodist and two non-Methodist), three representing the foreign legations (including Charles Denby, U.S. Minister, and J. H. Ferguson, Netherlands Minister), and two from nonmission and nonlegation sources (including Robert Hart, Inspector-General of the Chinese Maritime Customs, and W. A. P. Martin, president of the Imperial Tung Wen College). Howard Galt, "Yenching University," 4, AP.

42. Stuart to Garside, June 25, 1934, AC:JLS.

43. Lu to McMullen, April 13, September 1, and October 12, 1950, AC:UB.

44. Stuart to North, July 5, 1927, AC:JLS.

45. The trustees oversaw the property of the university, which was valued at US $2,224,000 in 1951.

46. Minute, Board of Trustees, December 9, 1927, AP:BT.

47. Ibid.

48. Wu Lei-ch'uan, "Chiao-hui hsüeh-hsiao li-an yi-hou" (After the church schools register), SM, 6.2:1–3 (October 1925).

49. Galt, "Yenching University," 201, AP.

50. PSYTI, 1–6 (1931); PSYTI, 3–11 (1937).

51. Minute, Board of Managers, September 23 and October 1, 1928, AP:BM.

52. Liu T'ing-fang, "Chiao-hui ta-hsüeh pan-hsüeh chih k'un-nan" (The difficulties of managing church schools) YTYS, 2.9:27 (June 1936).

53. The three American denominations, Congregational, Presbyterian, and Methodist, contributed $100,000 each, while the London Missionary Society contributed $50,000.

54. Dwight Edwards, Yenching University, 105; Minute, Board of Trustees, July 6, 1918, AP:BT.

55. Minute, Board of Trustees, February 17, 1936, AP:BT.

56. Edwards, Yenching University, 170.

57. Galt, "Yenching University," 213–215, 391, AP; Edwards, Yenching University, 228–230; see also James C. Thomson, Jr., While China Faced West (Cambridge, Harvard University Press, 1969), chap. 6.

58. "President's Report," 1920, 12, AP:R; Philip Fu, interview, February 1 and May 1, 1968; Stuart, "Autobiographical Notes," 49, PC:GMB.

59. Stuart, Fifty Years, 122.

60. In addition to working for Stuart, Fu also worked in the 1930s for the Chinese Cultural and Economic Institute (Chung-kuo wen-hua ching-chi hsieh-hui), from which he received a part-time salary. Criticism of Stuart's close relationship to Fu continued into the ambassadorial years. After Stuart left China in 1949 he suffered a severe stroke, from which he never completely recovered. For almost fifteen years of convalescence Fu, much like a son, took care of Stuart until his death in 1964.

61. Stuart to Haines, September 26, 1924, AC:JLS; Stuart to Luce, November 8, 1926, AC:JLS; Edwards, Yenching University, 127; Fu, interview, May 1, 1968; Stuart, Fifty Years, 125.

62. T'ien Hsing-chih, interview, Hong Kong, February 11, 1969 (T'ien was secretary to this campaign); Galt, "Yenching University," 219, AP; Edwards, Yenching University, 229.

63. PSYTI, 188 (1937); Minute, Board of Trustees, February 17, 1936, AP:BT; Galt, "Yenching University," 218, AP.

64. Wannamaker to Stuart, June 1, 1929, AC:JLS.

65. Stuart to Garside, October 18, 1929, AC:JLS; Edwards, Yenching University, 229.

66. Wannamaker to Stuart, June 1, 1929, AC:JLS.

67. Minute, Board of Trustees, April 14, 1930, AP:BT. The committee was composed of Stuart, Dwight Edwards, Roger Greene of the Peking Union Medical College, and C. R. Bennett of the National City Bank of New York in Peking.

68. Stuart to Garside, n.d., c. August 1930, AC:JLS.

69. Stuart to Garside, August 5 and November 10, 1930, AC:JLS.

70. Garside to Stuart, January 7, 1931; and Stuart to Garside, February 6, and 19, 1931; Stuart to Hague, April 3, 1932; and Stuart to McBrier, May 9, 1932, AC:JLS.

71. Edwards, *Yenching University,* 175.

72. Minute, Board of Trustees, December 7, 1933, AP:BT.

73. Ts'ai Yi-o (Stephen Tsai) to the trustees, as reproduced in a minute of the Board of Trustees, March 3, 1931, AP:BT.

74. Garside to Galt, August 23, 1930, AC:HSG.

75. Minute, Board of Trustees, June 19, 1929, AP:BT.

76. Stuart to McBrier, December 10, 1930, AC:JLS.

77. Minute, Board of Trustees, April 14, 1932, December 29, 1933, April 6, 1934, and April 9, 1935, AP:BT; Sailer to McBrier, March 22, 1947, Sailer file, AC:UB.

78. Government regulations in 1928 eliminated the position of associate professor and resulted in an increase in the number of full professors over the next two years. Furthermore no Western faculty members were ever listed as graduate or student assistants, while by 1930 twenty-four Chinese were listed in these categories. Two other categories used were part-time lecturer and honorary appointments, ranging from the rank of lecturer to professor. The part-time category was for Chinese faculty from neighboring institutions, especially Tsinghua, and in 1930 accounted for thirty or almost half of the Chinese faculty with the rank of lecturer or above. Many Westerners were employed as honorary teachers, a category which in 1924 accounted for almost one fourth of their total figure. This arrangement allowed the university to make use of the wives of male faculty members, YMCA workers, staff of the PUMC, and other Western dignitaries like Robert E. Park and I. A. Richards, who were invited as visiting professors for a year. See Galt, "Yenching University," 297, AP; *PSYTI,* 265-279 (1931); *Directory of Students and Faculty, 1930-1931* (Peiping, 1930), 3-10, AP:D.

79. See the various directories of faculty from 1924 to 1937, AP:D; Minute, Board of Trustees, September 30, 1947, AP:BT; "Proposed Budget for Yenching University for 1950-51," 12, Bliss Wiant file, AC:UB.

80. Stuart to North, August 27, 1926, AC:JLS.

81. *Statistical Report of Christian Colleges and Universities in China* (Shanghai), no. 26 (1928) and no. 28 (1930).

82. Galt report to trustees, November 21, 1929, AC:HSG.

83. Minute, Board of Trustees, April 11, 1922, AP:BT.

84. Liu T'ing-wei, interview, June 11, 1969, Taipei; also Grace M. Boynton, interview, November 14, 1967.

85. Boynton, interview, November 14, 1967.

86. Contributors to *Christian China,* publication of the Chinese Student Christian Association, included many not usually associated with Christianity in China, such as Tsiang T'ing-fu (who served as the association's president in 1920-21), Hu Shih, and Chao Yüan-jen.

87. *PSYTI,* 265-279 (1931).

88. Interviews with Grace Boynton, April 3, 1968, and Liu T'ing-wei, June 11, 1969; Lucius Porter diary, July 6 and 7, 1921, PC:LLP.

89. I am indebted to Peter Buck for this information presented in a report to CHAOS (Committee to Hazard the Application of Organization Theory to Sinology), Harvard University, November 1969.

90. *Educational Review*, 17.4:176–177 (April 1925) and 18.4:306 (April 1926).

91. Liu T'ing-fang, "The Problems of Chinese Christian Leadership: A Preliminary Psychological Study," *International Review of Missions*, 11:42:221 (April 22, 1922); Stuart, "Autobiographical Notes," 16.

92. North to Stuart, May 12, 1921, and Stuart to North, June 17, 1921, AC:JLS.

93. Minute, Board of Trustees, January 27, and July 17, 1923, December 20, 1926, July 15, 1927, March 13, 1928, AC:BT.

94. Minute, Board of Managers, March 1, 1930, AP:BM; Memo on salary schedules for university appointed Western faculty, November 5, 1929, AC: HSG; Garside to Stuart, May 28, 1931, AC:JLS.

95. *Hsiu-cheng chiao-chih-yüan tai-yü t-ung-tse* (Revised regulations on faculty treatment; Peiping, 1935), 4–6 (Chinese), 5–7 (English), AP:R. Galt, "Yenching University," 300–303, AP. Some conflict arose between Westerners and Chinese over the annuity plan for which each faculty member was asked to pay 5 percent of his annual salary, while the university provided an equal amount. Some Chinese members of the faculty were reluctant to invest that much for use by the Sun Life Insurance Company of Montreal when the same amount invested in China could have produced greater dividends.

96. Porter to children, September 14, 1947, PC:LLP; Grace Boynton diary, April 6, 1947 and March 13, 1949, PC:GMB; Lucy Burtt correspondence March 14, 1951, PC:GMB.

97. Stuart to North, January 2, 1925, AC:JLS.

98. Galt to Garside, Febraury 7, 1929, AC:HSG.

99. The archives of the United Board for Christian Higher Education in Asia at 475 Riverside Drive, New York, include many photographs of faculty housing at Yenching, as well as lists designating where faculty members lived.

100. Liu T'ing-fang, "Chiao-hui ta-hsüeh pan-hsüeh chih k'un-nan," *YTYS*, 2.9:19 (June 1936).

101. Ibid., 20–21. At the end of his article Liu inserted a section subtitled "Ssu-t'u lei-teng—k'un-nan chih cheng-fu che" (John Leighton Stuart—the Conqueror of Difficulties), indicating how much Liu distinguished between Stuart and other missionary educators. Ibid., 27–28.

102. Galt, "Yenching University," 116–117, 246, 254.

103. "President's Report to the Board of Managers," June 6, 1918, AP:BM; Directories of faculty and students, 1924–25 and 1930–31, AP:D; minute, board of trustees, May 11, 1923, AP:BT; *PSYTI* (1931), 332–338, and (1937), 188–189; "Proposed University Budget for 1950–51," Bliss Wiant file, AC:UB, 1930–31, AP:D.

104. *Annual Reports of the President and Deans for 1926–1927* (Peking, 1927), 2, AP:R.

105. *PSYTI,* 319–326 (1931).

106. *Annual Report of the President and Deans, 1924–1925* (Peking, 1925), 19, AP:R; "President's Report," June 1921, 8, AP:R; "Yen-ching ta-hsüeh tsung-chiao hsüeh-yüan t'ui-hsiu-hui t'ao-lun hui-chi-lu" (A record of the discussions of the Yenching School of Religion retreat), *CLYSM,* 5.14:16–19 (December 9, 1929).

107. Minute, Board of Trustees, April 10, 1928, AP:BT.

108. "Selected Minutes of the Appraisal Committee," ms., no. 889, Laymen's Foreign Mission Inquiry, April 5, 1932, 5–8 (Missionary Research Library).

109. *PSYTI,* 342–356 (1931).

110. "Report of the School of Religion to the Board of Managers," 1930–31, 1, AP:R.

111. As quoted in Galt, "Yenching University," 249–250, AP.

112. "President Stuart's First Annual Report to the Board of Managers of Peking University," June 11, 1920, 9, AP:R.

113. "President's Report," June 1922, 3, AP:R.

114. Galt, "Yenching University," 117–119, 140, AP. The administrative papers, AP:R, of Yenching University include lengthy reports from the agriculture department throughout the 1920s. Agriculture and the problems of rural China were also discussed in the writings of the Life Fellowship. See for example the whole issue of *SM,* 4.4–5 (January 1924) and the complete issue of *Chen-li yü sheng-ming,* 8.6 (November 1934).

115. Galt, "Yenching University," 119, 241, AP. Born in Ireland (1860), Bailie began work in China in 1890 with the Presbyterian Mission in Soochow. In 1898 he went to Peking as an English instructor at the Imperial University. A veteran of the Boxer siege, he became involved later in famine relief projects and developed a passion for introducing Western technology into China, which the bureau of Yenching was designed to facilitate. Stuart endorsed the project, but the trustees turned him down. Bailie, then, turned his attention to organizing industrial schools, known as Bailie Schools, beginning in Shanghai. These efforts later merged with the Industrial Cooperative (INDUSCO) efforts of the late 1930s. See Victoria W. Bailie, *Bailie's Activities in China: The Account of the Life and Work of Professor Joseph Bailie In and For China, 1890–1935* (Palo Alto, 1964).

116. "President Stuart's First Annual Report," June 1920, 8, AP:R.

117. "Second Annual Report of the President," June 1921, 5, AP:R; Galt, "Yenching University," 120, 121, AP; *Educational Review,* 15.3:229 (July 1923); Minute, Board of Trustees, January 9, 1946, AP:BT.

118. Galt, "Yenching University," 231, AP; *Yenching University Alumni Directory* (Peiping, December 1931), II, 12, AP:D.

119. Galt, "Yenching University," 280–286, AP; *PSYTI,* 185 (1937); Edgar Snow's *Red Star over China* (New York, Random House, 1938) was based on his extensive visit to Communist areas in 1936. Valuable help was given him by

Yenching students in the department of journalism where he had been teaching for two years.

120. *Yenching University Alumni Directory*, II, 109. Post-graduate work in China was done in research institutes such as the Academia Sinica (Chung-yang yen-chiu yüan) and the National Academy of Peiping (Pei-p'ing yen-chiu yüan).

121. "Annual Report of the Yenching University Christian Fellowship, 1927–1928," as cited in Galt, "Yenching University," 357, AP; Kiang Wen-han, "Christian Work in Government Schools," *Chinese Recorder*, 67.5:265 (May 1936); Wu Yao-tsung, "Christian Forces and Educated Youth," *Chinese Recorder*, 67.3:147 (March 1936).

122. Wei Chao-ch'i, "Wo tse-yang yu fan-tui Chi-tu-chiao erh hsin Chi-tu" (Why I stopped being an anti-Christian and believed in Christ), in Hsü Pao-chi'ien, ed., *Tsung-chiao*, 93–100. The late 1920s saw a considerable reaction against the stridency of revolutionary change. Li An-che, a writer and later professor of sociology and social work at Yenching, translated into English for the benefit of the Western faculty, some correspondence between the writer Lu Hsun and youth expressing this reaction; see the correspondence in *Yü Ssu*, 4.17 (April 1928), English translation, PC:SFB.

123. Interviews with T'an Jen-chiu, Hong Kong, February 2, 1969; Yeh Ch'u-sheng, Taipei, May 30, 1969; Li Man-kuei, Taipei, June 5, 1969; and Chang T'ing-che (Wen-li), Taipei, June 9, 1969.

124. Hsü Pao-ch'ien, "Yen-ta Chi-tu-chiao t'uan-ch'i" (The Yenta Christian fellowship), *CLYSM*, 3.16:7–11 (January 1929); Wu Lei-ch'uan, "Yen-ching Chi-tu-chiao t'uan-ch'i ti ch'eng-li yü Chung-kuo chiao-hui ti kai-tsao" (The establishment of the Yenta Christian fellowship and the reform of the Chinese church), *CLYSM*, 1.10:285–288 (October 1926); "Annual Report of the Yenching University Christian Fellowship, 1927–1928," as cited in Galt, "Yenching University," 357, AP; "The Yenching University Christian Fellowship, 1933–1934," 3, AP:R; "Yen-ta Chi-tu-chiao t'uan-ch'i nien-pao, 1937–1938" (The Yenta Christian fellowship annual, 1937–1938), 5, AP:R.

125. Ralph Lapwood to friends, November 15, 1950, PC:RNL.

126. Elizabeth Rugh Price, "When the President Plays," *Jen-wu yüeh-k'an*, 1.2:132 (June 15, 1936). Some of the women faculty were critical of the way Stuart handled the merger and then the administration of the combined men's and women's colleges. Margaret Speer called it a swallowing up of the women's college. Speer, interview, Philadelphia, January 31, 1968; Grace Boynton to me, December 10, 1969.

127. "Tzu-chih ta-kang" (An outline of organization), *PSYTI*, 7 (1931).

128. Mei Yi-pao, interview, July 16, 1968.

129. Galt to Garside, July 1, 1930, AC:HSG.

130. Minute, Board of Managers, March 1, 1929, AP:BM. Unfortunately I have been unable to locate copies of the Chinese language weekly faculty bulletin, *Yenching ta-hsüeh hsiao-k'an*, 1927–37, compiled until 1933 by Wu Lei-ch'uan. More than any other this publication might illuminate administrative

issues from the Chinese perspective. Complete holdings are at the Peking National University; see *Ch'üan-kuo Chung-wen ch'i-kan lien-ho mu-lu, 1833–1949* (The consolidated index of Chinese language periodical literature in China; Peking, 1961), 1242.

131. Stuart to Garside, July 25, 1927, and October 25, 1928, AC:JLS.

132. Wu Lei-ch'uan, "Yü hsien-tai ch'ing-nien shang-liang chiu-kuo ti wen-t'i" (The problem of discussing national salvation with contemporary youth), *CLYSM*, 1.11:311–314 (November 15, 1926).

133. Wu, "Chung-kuo ch'ing-nien pu-tang hsiao-fa Yeh-su ma?" *CLYSM*, 1.8:224–225 (September 30, 1926). See also Hsü Pao-ch'ien, "Hsiu-yang pu wang nu-li, nu-li pu wang hsiu-yang" (In self-cultivation do not forget striving and in striving do not forget self-cultivation), *CLYSM*, 2.13:410–412 (November 1927).

134. Ma Meng, interview, Hong Kong, February 8, 1926; Wu Lei-ch'uan (trans. Liu T'ing-fang) to Stuart, February 18, 1930, AC:JLS; Stuart to Farley, September 17, 1932, AC:JLS.

135. Galt to Stuart, March 14, 1930, AC:HSG.

136. Minute, Board of Managers, May 15 and June 20, 1931, May 1934, AP:BM.

137. *Yenching News*, November 16, 1940, AP; Minute, Board of Trustees, May 10, 1945, AP:BT.

138. Porter to children, June 19 and July 27, 1948, PC:LLP.

139. Stuart to Corbett, August 5 and 26, 1946, and July 1947, Stuart file, AC:UB.

140. Minute, Board of Trustees, March 17, 1947, AP:BT; Minute of the faculty executive committee, May 7, 1947, AP:BM; Stuart to McMullen, July 5, 1947, Stuart file, AC:UB.

141. Stuart to McMullen, January 21, 1947 and July 23, 1948, Stuart file, AC:UB; Grace Boynton diary, October 8, 1948. PC:GMB.

142. Stuart to Corbett, August 5, 29, 1946, and Stuart to McMullen, March 9, 1949, Stuart file, AC:UB.

143. Grace Boynton diary, September 4, 1947; Lu Chih-wei, "Jen-wu chih" (An account of personalities), *YCHW* (June 2, 1947).

144. Minute, Board of Managers, February 26, 1949, AP:BM.

145. Minute, Board of Trustees, March 11, 1949, AP:BT.

146. Edwards, *Yenching University*, 418; Wiant to McMullen, April 3, 1949, Wiant file, AC:UB; Lapwood to friends, November 15, 1950, PC:RNL; Sailer to McMullen, October 24, 1950, Sailer file, AC:UB.

147. Stuart to McMullen, March 9, 1949, Stuart file, AC:UB.

148. *PSYTI* (1931), 6.

149. Edwards, *Yenching University*, 215.

150. Galt, "Yenching University," 184, AP.

5. The Radicalization of a Student Elite

1. For further discussion of the student movements in the Republican period see John Israel, *Student Nationalism in China, 1927–1937* (Stanford, Stanford

University Press, 1966); Jessie G. Lutz, *China and the Christian Colleges, 1850–1950* (Ithaca, Cornell University Press, 1971), chap. 9, which includes an analysis of Yenching students in the December Ninth movement; Y. C. Wang, *Chinese Intellectuals and the West, 1872–1949* (Chapel Hill, University of North Carolina Press, 1966); and Kiang Wen-han, *The Chinese Student Movement* (New York, King's Crown Press, 1948). Conspicuously lacking in Dwight Edwards' *Yenching University* (New York, 1959) is any serious attention given to student thought and protest. Howard S. Galt's manuscript history, by contrast, has extensive discussion of student origins, graduate careers, student thinking, student-faculty relations, chaps. 16–18. The best description of Yenching student behavior after 1949 is Ralph and Nancy Lapwood,, *Through the Chinese Revolution* (London, Spalding and Levy, 1954), chaps. 4, 6, 10, 14–17.

2. Statements and speeches of the "Formal Opening on the New Campus," December 16, 1929, AP:R.

3. *Ch'üan-kuo kao-teng chiao-yü t'ung-chi* (Statistics of Chinese higher education; Nanking, 1933), table 55, p. 38. Yenching's recruitment of students from all over China tended to break down strong provincial loyalties. In 1936 the student body included representatives from all 22 provinces, though more than half came from the four provinces of Hopei, Kwangtung, Kiangsu and Fukien. *PSYTI* (1937), 187. A more significant indicator was the high percentage that came from cities.

4. The figures are all in local currency. Minute, Board of Trustees, July 15, 1927, AP:BT; *PSYTI*, 24–25 (1931); and *PSYTI*, 43–44 (1937).

5. *YCHW*, December 29, 1947. Yenching's high tuition rates continued until almost two years after the Communist Revolution. Alice Boring to Grace Boynton, March 24, 1951, PC:GMB; Lu to McMullen, June 28, 1950, Lu Chih-wei file, AC:UB.

6. *Ch'üan-kuo kao-teng chiao-yü t'ung-chi*, table 18.

7. Cheng T'ing-ch'un, "My College Life in Yenching University," n.d., c. 1935, in file on "Student Life," AC; also see Hsü Chao-ying, "The Lean and Fat Years," *Yen-ta hsiao-k'an* (Palo Alto, 1973), 8–13.

8. Minute, Board of Trustees, April 13, 1923, AP:BT; Mrs. Maxwell Stewart, "Self Help for Students?" December 1928, AC:JLS.

9. Stuart to Garside, September 1, 1939, AC:JLS; *Yenching News*, no. 18, February 8, 1941, AP.

10. Edwards, *Yenching University*, 390.

11. "The Students of 1945–1946," ms., Yenching file, AC:UB.

12. *YCHW*, October 10, 1947; Alice Boring to Yenchinians, September 7, 1948, Yenching file, AC:UB; Lucius Porter to children, November 3, 1948, PC: LLP; Ralph and Nancy Lapwood, *Through the Chinese Revolution*, 57.

13. Fenn to Lu, December 16, 1946, Lu Chih-wei file, AC:UB.

14. Galt, "Yenching University," 314, AP.

15. Han Su-yin, *A Mortal Flower* (New York, G. P. Putnam, 1965), 262.

16. These figures are taken from the *China Christian Education Bulletin Statistics* (Shanghai), for each of the years mentioned.

17. Han Su-yin, *Mortal Flower*, 278–279.

280

Notes to pages 142–147

18. Ida Pruitt, interview, January 30, 1968, Philadelphia.
19. Stuart to Garside, June 5, 1936, AC:JLS.
20. See for example L. K. Tao, "Unemployment among Intellectual Workers in China," *Chinese Social and Political Science Review*, 13:251–261 (1929); see also a series of articles on problems in education in 1932 by Fu Ssu-nien, former chancellor of Peita, *Fu Ssu-nien hsüan-chi* (Taipei, 1967), V, 715–770.
21. Richard L. Jen (Jen Ling-hsün), Deliberate Unemployment," *Peiping Chronicle*, June 12, 1936; "Unemployed Graduates," *Peiping Chronicle*, May 29, 1935.
22. As quoted in Y. C. Wang, *Chinese Intellectuals*, 371.
23. *Fu Ssu-nien hsüan-chi*, V, 769.
24. Stuart, "Problems of Modern Education in China," ms., n.d., c. summer 1936, p. 20, AC:JLS.
25. Stuart to Garside, April 8, 1940, AC:JLS.
26. Mei Yi-pao, interview, July 16, 1968.
27. Liu T'ing-fang, "Chiao-hui ta-hsüeh pan-hsüeh chih k'un-nan" (The difficulties of managing church schools), *YTYS*, 2.9:27 (June 1936).
28. Chu Yu-kuang, "A Proposed Theory of Education for the Reconstruction of China," *Educational Review*, 24.4:334 (October 1932).
29. Presbyterian North China Mission, Yenching University, 1938–1939 Report, 8–9, AP:R.
30. Wu Yao-tsung, "Movements among Chinese Students," *China Christian Yearbook* (Shanghai, 1931), 259–262.
31. Kiang Wen-han, "Secularization of Christian Colleges," *Chinese Recorder*, 67.5:305 (May 1937).
32. John Israel, *Student Nationalism*, 186.
33. Liu T'ing-fang, "Re-adjustments of Christian Education Work in China Today in View of the Changing Social and Intellectual Conditions," *Chinese Recorder*, 61.8:485–491 (August 1930).
34. Stuart, convocation address, September 5, 1932, AC:JLS.
35. Olga Lang, *Chinese Family and Society* (New Haven, Yale University Press, 1946), 318–319, writes: "It seems that the students of missionary universities were less radical not only because they were on the average wealthier than students of government universities but also because they were subjected to ideological influences which deflected them from radical ideas." But the evidence at Yenching does not support this conclusion. Of the original eleven members of the Yen-ta k'ang-Jih hui (Resist Japan society), formed in 1936, seven were Christians. See *CLYSM*, 6.6:8 (April 1, 1932); Chang T'ieh-sheng, "Yung-chiu wang-pu-liao ti yi-chien shih" (An unforgettable story), *YTYS*, 2.9:40 (June 1936); Yeh Ch'u-sheng, interview, Taipei, May 30, 1969.
36. Margaret Speer to parents, March 28, 1936, PC:MBS.
37. Hsieh Wan-ying et al., "Yen-ching ta-hsüeh" (Yenching university), *SM*, 2.2:4–5 (September 15, 1921).
38. Liu T'ing-fang, "Chi-tu-chiao yü Chung-kuo kuo-min hsing" (Christianity and the Chinese national character), *SM*, 5.9:12 (June 1925); John Leighton

Stuart, "Problems of Modern Education in China," ms., n.d., c. June 1936, p. 16, AC:JLS; Han Su-yin, *Mortal Flower,* 369.

39. This information is derived from a survey over these years of the *Yen-ching hsin-wen,* Lucius and Lillian Porter's letter to their children, and Grace Boynton's diary for 1947 and 1948.

40. *YCHW,* November 17, 1936, and November 10, 1947.

41. Chou Nien-tzu (Nancy Chou Bennett) joined the march but was later embarrassed by it and regarded her decision to participate as immature, interview, May 5, 1968, Milton, Mass. The details on the December Ninth movement are from Augusta Wagner to Stuart, December 17, 1935, and Speer to parents, December 22, 1935, PC:MBS.

42. Speer to parents. January 5, 1936, PC:MBS.

43. Nym Wales, *Notes on the Chinese Student Movement,* mimeo. (Madison, Conn., 1959), 1–13, 112–120.

44. Galt, "Yenching University," 352–353.

45. *Yen-ching hsin-wen,* November 16, 1936.

46. The monthly, *Yen-ta yüeh-k'an,* began publication October 1927 and for the first year was edited and managed by the student-faculty Yenta Monthly Committee. The following year it was taken over by the student government until the end of its publication in 1934. Stuart graced the first issue with his words of hope that the publication could draw students, faculty, and administration together. Prominently featured as contributors for the first few years were Yenching notables, Hsieh Wan-ying (Ping Hsin), Hsiung Fo-hsi, and Hsü Ti-shan. Contributions ranged from poems to inquiries on "What a University Student Does" to scholarly pieces on sinology. The editors had originally intended the monthly to circulate outside the university. Publication was highly irregular. In its first years it stressed literary themes, but after April 1930 it became heavily political which is our primary interest here. Sixteen issues were available for this study. By contrast the weekly, *Yen-ta chou-k'an,* reflected more immediate student responses to events inside and outside the university. Like the monthly, though, the weekly suffered all the vicissitudes of yearly reelection of officers for the student government, and in the fourteen years of its existence from 1923 to 1936 it varied greatly in format, distribution, editorial policy, and frequency of publication. The ten issues I have seen cluster around the post December Ninth period. After 1936 the major publication reflecting student opinion is the journalism department's *Yen-ching hsin-wen,* sometimes published with an English version known as the *Yenching News.* More than forty issues of the *Yen-ching hsin-wen* are available for the late 1936 period and the late 1940s. In 1949 it was retitled as the *Hsin Yen-ching,* and there are issues available for the first year of the revolution and also a large issue in 1952 covering the Three Anti campaign.

47. Wei Ching-meng, interview, Taipei, January 7, 1969; T'an Jen-chiu, interview, Hong Kong, February 6, 1969; confidential report of John Leighton Stuart to the trustees, January 10, 1939, AC:JLS, Lucius Porter to children, March 28, 1948, PC:LLP.

48. Joseph R. Levenson, "Communist China in Time and Space: Roots and Rootlessness," *China Quarterly*, 39:5–6 (July–September 1969).

49. Wu Kung, "Yu ching-chi-shang kuan-ch'a hsien-tai she-hui wen-t'i fa-sheng ti yüan-yin" (The reasons for looking at contemporary social questions from an economic point of view), *YTYK*, 7.1–2:77 (December 1930): Wu Hsü-ts'an, "Ti-kuo chu-yi ti mo-lu" (The near end of imperialism), *YTYK*, 7.1–2: 95–103 (December 1930); Jen T'i, "Shih-chü ch'ien-t'u chih chang-wang" (The outlook for the present situation), *YTYK*, 9.3:1–10 (April 1933).

50. Chang Ch'ing-yeh, trans., "Hsien-tai chih-shih chieh-chi lun" (On the modern intelligentsia), *YTYK*, 8.2:73–87 (June 1931).

51. Mu Han, "Fei-ch'ang shih-ch'i chiao-yü" (Crisis education), *YTYK*, 6.10:3–4 (February 9, 1936).

52. Ch'u Shan, "Hsiang chiao-shou-men chin yi-yen" (A word to the professors), *YTCK*, 6.10:11 (February 9, 1936); Liang Yang, "Liu Chieh p'i-yao—nu-hua chiao-yü chi-shih" (The slander by Liu Chieh—evidence of slave education), ibid., 9.

53. Chün, "Nu-hua chiao-yü ch'ien-shih" (A brief explanation of slave education), ibid., 7–8.

54. Margaret Speer to parents, February 2, 1936, PC:MBS.

55. Richard L. Jen, "Deliberate Unemployment," *Peiping Chronicle*, June 12, 1936.

56. Chang Fei, "Chiao-shou ti pei-ai" (The tragedy of the professor), *YTCK*, 7.3:28–30 (May 16, 1936).

57. Mei Yi-pao, "Chi-nien wu-ssu" (Memorial to May Fourth), *YCHW*, April 28, 1947.

58. Yen Ching-yüeh, "Hsüeh-sheng yün-tung yü ch'ing-nien hsiu-yang" (The student movement and the cultivation of youth), *YCHW*, May 12, 1947).

59. Wu Chen, "Hsin wu-ssu yün-tung (The new May Fourth movement), *YCHW*, April 28, 1947; "Hsüeh-sheng hsiao-lun-t'an" (Student essays), *YCHW*, May 5, 1947.

60. Chou Hua, "Hu Shih and the May Fourth Movement," *YCHW*, translated in the *Chinese Press Review*, 608:3–4 (May 10, 1948), and cited in Jerome Grieder, *Hu Shih and the Chinese Renaissance*, 307–308. This charge by Yenching students in the *YCHW* is misleading. It is true that from his earliest days at Peking Nationalist University Hu opposed the revolutionary views of students. Later, as Chinese ambassador to the United States (1938–42) and as the chancellor of Peita after Japan's defeat, he strongly defended China's tie with the United States and opposed Russian influence in China. See *Foreign Relations of the United States, Far East: China, 1948* (Washington, D.C., 1973), VII, 52. But in the late 1940s Hu was also openly critical of the Kuomintang government and used his power and influence as chancellor to protect students from the Kuomintang police, even when he disagreed with their demonstrations and protest activities. See *Foreign Relations of the United States, Far East: China, 1947* (Washington, D.C., 1973), VII, 160, and (1948) VII, 180–181, 583–594, 665–666, 675–677.

61. Hsieh Ping-hsin (Wan-ying), "Wo ti hsüeh-sheng" (My students), *Kuan-yü nü-jen* (Hong Kong, 1968), 61–73.

62. Stephen Becker, *Season of the Stranger* (New York, Harper and Brothers, 1951), 97.

63. Hsieh Wan-ying et al., "Yen-ching ta-hsüeh" (Yenching university), *SM,* 2.2:7–8 (September 15, 1921).

64. Luella Miner, "Report of the Women's College," ms., June 11, 1921, AP:R.

65. *Alumni Directory* (Peiping, 1931) II, 112: Chang Fu-liang, "Agricultural Education and Country Life," *Educational Review,* 22.2:188–193 (April 1930).

66. Galt, "Yenching University," 385–386, AP; Cato Young (Yang K'ai-tao) et al., *Ching Ho: A Sociological Analysis* (Peiping, 1930), passim.

67. Stuart to Garside, February 25, 1935, AC:JLS; for a discussion of the North China Council for Rural Reconstruction, see Thomson, *While China Faced West,* chap. 6.

68. *Occasional News of the College of Public Affairs,* no. 1 (June 1934), no. 2 (October 1935), no. 3 (April 1935), AP:R; *Quarterly News of the College of Public Affairs,* no. 2 (February 1936), 2.1 (September 1936), AP:R; *Announcement of Courses, 1936–37: Yenching University Bulletin,* 21.10 (December 1936), AP:D.

69. Lawrence Schneider, *Ku Chieh-kang and China's New History* (Berkeley, University of California Press, 1971), 4, 126–127, 147–148.

70. Ku Sung, "Ssu" (Death), *YTCK,* 7.4:22–26 (May 30, 1936).

71. "Ling-sui ti chi-lu" (A record of some "fragments"), *YTCK,* 7.4:14–19 (February 9, 1936).

72. Lin Cho-yüan, "Hsiang-chien yün-tung neng chiu Chung-kuo ma?" (Can the rural reconstruction movement save China?), *YTCK,* 7.2:9 (May 16, 1936); Ch'en Hsin-feng, "Kuan-yü hsiang-chien yün-tung neng-fo chiu Chung-kuo" (On the question of whether or not the rural reconstruction movement can save China), *YTCK,* 7.3:12–14 (May 23, 1936); Wang Hou-fang, "Ssu-lu yi-t'iao" (A dead end road), *YTCK,* 7.4:10 (May 30, 1936).

73. William Band, physics professor at Yenching, and Claire Band left the university and spent two years in guerilla base areas and Yenan and published an account of their experiences, including descriptions of the problems students (including some from Yenching) faced in the countryside. See William and Claire Band, *Two Years with the Chinese Communists* (New Haven, Yale University Press, 1948).

74. *Accumulated List of Publications from the School of Public Affairs of Yenching University* (Peiping, 1932), AP:R; *News Bulletin of the College of Public Affairs, Yenching University,* 5.3 (June 1940), AP:R.

75. Stuart, *Fifty Years,* 79.

76. "Ching-ju Ssu-t'u hsiao-wu-chang liu-shih shou-ch'en" (Our best wishes to president Stuart on his sixtieth birthday), *YTYS,* 2.9:16 (June 1936).

77. Grace Boynton diary, June 1, 1947.

78. Lutz, *China and the Christian Colleges,* 170.

79. Grace Boynton diary, July 15, 1948, and October 30, 1949; Lapwood, *Through the Chinese Revolution,* 156; see also the Hong Kong alumni's *Yen-ta hsiao-yu t'ung-hsün* (December 1963, January 1965, and October 1967), passim, and the Yenching Alumni Association (USA), *Yen-ta hsiao-k'an* (March 1973), passim.

80. Hsieh Wan-ying et al., "Yen-ching ta-hsüeh," *SM,* 2.2:8 (September 15, 1921).

81. Galt, "Yenching University," 330–331, AP.

82. *Yen-ching hsin-wen,* January 13, 1947; Grace Boynton diary, January 2, 1947. See also Thurston Griggs, *Americans in China: Some Chinese Views* (Washington, D.C., 1948), 10, 25–30, 38, 55; and items indexed under "Anti-American demonstrations and feelings" in *Foreign Relations of the United States,* volumes on China for 1946 and 1947.

83. Carleton Lacy, "Education for International Goodwill," *Educational Review,* 25.2:143–146 (April 1933); and "International Attitudes of Some Chinese Students," *Educational Review,* 26.1:61–84 (January 1934). Randolph Sailer of Yenching helped in the study.

84. "Our Tragic Experiences in Petition Demonstration of March 18, 1926," Yenching University, March 20, 1926, PC:MBS; Margaret Speer to father, April 5, 1936, PC:MBS; *YCHW,* February 23, 1948.

85. *YCHW,* March 29, 1948, and November 10, 1948.

86. *YTYK,* 8.2:6–87, 105–110 (June 1931).

87. *YCHW,* December 8, 1947.

88. Hsü Pao-ch'ien, "Hsin-ssu-ch'ao yü Chi-tu-chiao" *SM,* 1.2:1 (September 1, 1920).

89. Chün, "Nu-hua chiao-yü," *YTCK,* 6.10:7–8 (February 9, 1936).

90. "Freshman Views of Yenching at the End of the Term," ms., March 15, 1947, Yenching file, AC:UB.

91. Augusta Wagner to Stuart, December 10, 1935, PC:MBS; Grace Boynton diary, April 6, 1947; Lucius Porter to children, July 12, 1948, PC:LLP.

92. Galt, "Yenching University," 188–189, AP; "Patriotic Week in Yenching University, November 30–December 6, 1931," ms., file on Student Life, AC; Yen-ta wei-yüan-hui (Yenta committee), "Kuo-nan t'ao-lun ta-kang" (Outline for the discussion of national difficulties), *CLYSM,* 6.3:6–9 (December 1, 1931); "Yen-ta ai-kuo yün-tung shih-ling" (Excerpts from the Yenta patriotic movement), *CLYSM,* 6.4 (January 1, 1932).

93. Wu Lei-ch'uan, "Shuo ch'ing-nien yün-tung" (The youth movement), *CLYSM,* 2.8:207–209 (May 1927); and "Yü hsien-tai ch'ing-nien shang-liang chiu-kuo ti wen-t'i," *CLYSM,* 1.11:311–312 (November 15, 1926).

94. Lu Chih-wei to Stuart, January 16, 1936, AC:JLS, as cited in Lutz, *China and the Christian Colleges,* 343; Ralph Lapwood letter to friends, November 15, 1950, PC:RNL; interviews with Grace Boynton, April 3, 1968 and Randolph Sailer, April 27, 1968.

95. *YCHW,* January 13, 1947.

96. Lucius Porter to children, November 10, 1947, and December 1, 1947, PC:LLP; *YCHW*, December 9, 1946, and January 13, 1947.

97. "To the Student Body of Yenching University," ms., January 1933, file on Student Life, AC.

98. Margaret Speer to parents, December 29, 1935, PC:MBS.

99. Stuart, "Autobiographical Notes," 41, PC:GMB.

100. "Address by Dr. Stuart, University Assembly," ms., April 14, 1936, AC:JLS.

101. Stuart, "The Problems of Modern Education in China," 8–9, AC:JLS.

102. Chang T'ieh-sheng, "Yung-chiu wang-pu-liao ti yi-chien shih," *YTYS*, 2.9:40 (June 1936).

103. Stuart, "The Future of Christian Colleges," *Chinese Recorder*, 48.2:76–78 (February 1937).

104. Stauffer, *China Her On Interpreter*, 92–93.

105. Liu T'ing-fang, "Chi-tu-chiao tsai Chung-kuo tao-ti shih ch'uan she-ma?" (What in fact has Christianity transmitted to China?), *CLYSM*, 6.1:11–15 (October 1931).

106. Hsü Pao-ch'ien, "Wo tse-yang chüeh-chih li-k'ai Li-ch'uan" (Why I decided to leave Li-ch'uan), *CLYSM*, 11.3:144–152 (May 1937). T'ien Hsing-chih (Gerald Tien) a Yenching graduate working at the Li-ch'uan project recalled how some of the youth resented Hsü's efforts, as an administrator, to persuade the youth to greater commitment and effort through religious services. Interview with T'ien, Hong Kong, February 11, 1969.

107. Mei Yi-pao, interview, July 16, 1968.

108. See Ch'en Hsin-feng, "Kuan-yü hsiang-chien yün-tung neng-fo chiu Chung-kuo," *YTCK*, 7.3:12–14 (May 23, 1936); Galt, "Yenching University," 387–394, AP.

109. Wu Lei-ch'uan, "Chi-tu-t'u ju-ho shih-hsing chiu-kuo ti kung-tso" (How Christians should carry out the work of national salvation), *CLYSM*, 6.5:15–19 (March 1932), and Wu Lei-ch'uan, "Chi-tu-chiao ying chu-yi huan-ch'i min-chung" (Christianity should pay attention to waking the masses), *CLYSM* 6.8:1–7 (June 1932).

110. "A Service Order for the Service of National Humiliation," tentative translation, no. 18 of the *Experimental Series of Chinese Christian Liturgy*, Liu T'ing-fang, ed., Yenching University School of Religion, PC:MBS.

111. The emerging outline of Wu's thought was quite similar to that of Wu Yao-tsung, also an early member of the Life Fellowship, who led the movement in the Protestant church, known as the Three Self movement, which led in the Christian accommodation to the revolutionary order in the late 1940s and early 1950s. These two men brought very different backgrounds and experiences to their redefinition of Christianity along revolutionary lines, and this makes the convergence of their thinking all the more convincing. Wu Yao-tsung, for example, was considerably younger, fluent in English and had been trained in New York at the Union Theological Seminary. In contrast to Wu Lei-ch'uan, he appeared cosmopolitan and westernized. As editor of YMCA publications

in the 1930s Wu Yao-tsung wrote the introduction to Wu Lei-ch'uan's *Chi-tu-chiao yü Chung-kuo wen-hua,* which appeared as no. 37 in the series published by the YMCA Press. Two extensive studies have been done on Wu Yao-tsung, one of them by Miriam Levering, "Wu Yao-tsung: An Intellectual Biography, 1923–1950," honors thesis, Wellesley College, 1966, and Ng Lee Ming, "Christianity and Social Change: The Casé of China, 1920–1950," Th.D. diss., Princeton University 1971, 174–235.

112. Wu Lei-ch'uan, "Chi-tu-chiao yü ko-ming" (Christianity and revolution), *CLYSM,* 5.4:1–5 (February 1931); Kiang Wen-han, *Chinese Student Movement,* 127–128.

113. Wu's understanding of the political meaning of Jesus' life and teaching is discussed at length in his *Chi-tu-chiao yü Chung-kuo wen-hua,* chap. 4.

114. Wu Lei-ch'uan, "Chi-tu-chiao yü ko-ming," 1–3; Wu, *Chi-tu-chiao yü Chung-kuo wen-hua,* 85.

115. Wu, "Chi-tu-chiao yü ko-ming," *CLYSM,* 5.

116. Wu, *Chi-tu-chiao yü Chung-kuo wen-hua,* 289–292; for further discussion of Wu's thinking on communism, see Yamamoto Sumiko, *Chūgoku Kirisutokyō shi kenkyū,* 258–265.

117. Wu, *Chi-tu-chiao yü Chung-kuo wen-hua,* 70–71, 86, 292.

118. Chao Tzu-ch'en, "Yeh-su wei Chi-tu, p'ing Wu Lei-ch'uan hsien-sheng chih Chi-tu-chiao yü Chung-kuo wen-hua" (Jesus as Christ; a criticism of Wu Lei-ch'uan's Christianity and Chinese culture), *CLYSM,* 10.7:412–413 (December 1936).

119. Chao Tzu-ch'en, "Christianity and the National Crisis," *Chinese Recorder,* 68.1:5–12 (January 1937).

120. Chao Tzu-ch'en, "The Future of the Church in Social and Economic Thought and Action," *Chinese Recorder,* 69:349 (1938).

121. Chao Tzu-ch'en, *Hsi-yü chi* (Shanghai, 1948), 52.

122. Hsü Pao-ch'ien, "Erh shih-nien lai," *CLYSM,* 8.4:183 (June 1934).

123. Wu Yao-tsung, "To Make Christianity Socially Dynamic," *Chinese Recorder,* 66:8 (1934), as cited in Ng, "Christianity and Social Change," 209.

124. Wu Lei-ch'uan, "Lun Chi-tu-chiao ti kung-yi yü jen-ai" (Justice and love in Christianity), *CLYSM,* 7.1:8 (October 1932).

6. The Cosmopolitan Ideal and Politics

1. Hsü Pao-ch'ien, "Erh-shih nien lai hsin-tao ching-yen tzu-shu," *CLYSM,* 8.4:81 (June 1934); interview with Ariga Tetsutarō, December 13, 1974, Kyoto, Japan. Ariga's personal files include his correspondence with the Yenching faculty, his reports submitted to the Japanese Ministry of Foreign Affairs, and several photographs of his visit on the Yenching campus.

2. "A page fram an International Correspondence," and "Kei Chung-kuo Chi-tu-t'u ch'ing-nien t'ung-chih-men ti yi-feng kung-k'ai ti hsin" (An open letter to our Chinese Christian comrades), *CLYSM,* 6.6:5–8 (April 1932). The six Yenching students who signed the cover letter to the student body were Kuan Sung-shan, Yeh Ch'u-sheng, Ch'en Kuan-sheng, T'an Hui-ying, Yeh Te-kuan, and Chang Kuan-lien.

3. Stuart to Garside, December 31, 1934, and February 20, 1935, AC:JLS.

4. Hsü Pao-ch'ien, "Pacifism and Nationalism," a letter to Mrs. Hipps, June 10, 1937, *Chinese Recorder,* 67.10:617 (October 1937). Hsü elaborated on the question of violence in Christian missions in China in "Christianity: A Religion of Love Spread by Force" in Roy J. McCorkel, ed., *Voices from the Younger Churches* (New York, 1939), 3–20, as reproduced in Jessie G. Lutz, ed., *Christian Missions in China: Evangelists of What?* (Boston, D.C. Heath, 1965), 60–66.

5. The question of the relationship between Christianity and the national crisis was one of the most commonly discussed problems in the pages of the *Chen-li yü sheng-ming,* throughout the 1930s. See, for example, *CLYSM,* 6.2:1–5, 6.3:1–5, 6.5:15–19; and 7.4:1–4. See also Kiang Wen-han, *The Chinese Student Movement,* 132–133. The Western faculty at Yenching expressed their anti-Japanese sentiment in a spoof they circulated as an "inexpensive holiday pasttime to whittle your own wheezes"; it was entitled "We're Japalled!" n.d., c. 1940, PC:GMB. Some choice phrases were "The spokesman displayed Japlomb when he predicted a great Japanese victory in the battle for Changsha; The four horsemen of the Japocalypse have been riding through China since the start of the war; Japologists make out that Japan is fighting China out of feelings of the purest brotherly love; He was a Japostle of anti-Communism; A Japparition haunts Mr. Wang Ching-wei; The Jappetite for conquest has diminished steadily since the Nomonhan Incident, in which Sure-Shot Saito shot down 382 Soviet planes in a single engagement; Mr. Wang Ching-wei's pronouncements are all Japplesauce."

6. Brank Fulton, "Notes on Dr. Stuart's Life" (personal interviews conducted in 1940 and 1941 and corrected by Stuart), 30–32, PC:GMB. Stuart's use of extraterritoriality during the war years is discussed in John Carter Vincent, *The Extraterritorial System in China: Final Phase,* Harvard East Asian Monographs, no. 30 (Cambridge, Harvard University Press, 1970), 35–37.

7. Fulton, "Notes on Dr. Stuart's Life," 31–32, PC:GMB.

8. Stuart memorandum to the trustees, February 23, 1939, AC:JLS.

9. Stuart's correspondence to B. A. Garside and his confidential memoranda to the trustees, May 7, July 15, July 30, 1939, and April 8, 1940, and April 28, 1941, AC:JLS.

10. Stuart's lengthy confidential reports to the trustees, January 10, February 21, July 3, and November 8, 1939; January 18, July 6, August 29, September 28, October 19, November 9, and 26, 1940; February 18, April 3, 28, and June 21, 1941, AC:JLS. See also Stuart to Cordell Hull, Secretary of State, February 22, 1939, and Stuart to Garside, August 17, 1939, regarding Stuart's explicit advice for American foreign policy and plans to talk with President Roosevelt, AC:JLS.

11. Stuart, "Autobiographical Notes," 30, PC:GMB; Stuart, *Fifty Years,* 134.

12. Stuart address to university assembly, September 11, 1941, AC:JLS.

13. Stuart, "China Enters the Nationalist Era," *Christian Century,* 54:111 (January 27, 1937).

14. See Noam Chomsky's essay on A. J. Muste's interpretations of the war

with Japan in *American Power and the New Mandarins* (New York, 1967), 159–220.

15. Fulton, "Notes on Dr. Stuart's Life," 22, PC:GMB.

16. Stuart memorandum to the trustees, October 25, 1928, AC:JLS.

17. Stuart memorandum to the trustees, January 28, 1937, 7, AC:JLS.

18. Stuart, "China Enters the Nationalist Era," *Christian Century,* 54:109–111 (1937).

19. Stuart to Hutchinson, December 18, 1937, AC:JLS; John Leighton Stuart, "General Chiang Kai-shek—An Appreciation," *Democracy,* 1.2:55–56 (May 15, 1937); and Fulton, "Notes on Dr. Stuart's Life," 30, PC:GMB.

20. Thomson, *While China Faced West,* 23–25.

21. Stuart, "China Enters the Nationalist Era," 111.

22. Among the biographies consulted were: Hollington K. Tong, *Chiang Kai-shek: Soldier and Statesman* (London, 1938), 186–189; General and Madame Chiang Kai-shek, *General Chiang Kai-shek: The Account of the Fortnight in Sian When the Fate of China Hung in the Balance,* with a foreward by John Leighton Stuart (New York, 1938), *v-viii,* 40–45, 169; Chang Hsin-hai, *Chiang Kai-shek: Asia's Man of Destiny* (Garden City, 1944), 185–186, 223–224; Sven Anders Hedin, *Chiang Kai-shek: Marshal of China* (New York, 1940), 80–91. In the late 1930s and early 1940s when China eagerly sought greater American aid, Chiang Kai-shek discussed his religious life openly and publicly. See, for example, "My Religious Faith," April 16, 1938; "Message to the Christians in America," February 20, 1939; "Appreciation of the Y.M.C.A.," July 28, 1939; "Spiritual Ramparts and Weapons," March 12, 1940, as compiled in English by the Chinese Ministry of Information, *The Collected Wartime Messages of Generalissimo Chiang Kai-shek, 1937–1945,* 2 vols. (New York, 1945). His religious life was also documented in a diary reportedly kept during his kidnaping experiences in Sian, December 1936. It was published as *Hsi-an pan-yüeh chi* (Nanking, 1937). An interesting tract portraying Chiang as a pious Christian is by Chiang himself, *I Bear My Witness.* Only five pages long, it was published by the Methodist Church in 1937. The tract is a "testimony sent to a Methodist conference, upon [Chiang's] release from Sian." Very simple and direct in style, it claims Chiang had been a Christian for several years and was a "constant reader of the Bible."

23. Stuart memo to the trustees, January 28, 1937, 4, AC:JLS. Stuart reported attending an evening gathering, which included Chiang Kai-shek, his wife, and relatives. At the gathering the Young Marshall turned out, in Stuart's words, to be the "life of the party."

24. Ibid., 6–7.

25. Stuart memo to the trustees, July 30, 1939, AC:JLS.

26. Stuart, "The Religious Life of General and Madame Chiang Kai-shek," ms., May 17, 1940, AC:JLS.

27. *Foreign Relations of the United States, 1948, Far East: China* (Washington, D.C., 1973), VII, 674.

28. Robert McMullen to Stuart, January 6, 1947, Stuart file, AC:UB.

29. *United States Relations with China* (Washington, D.C., 1949), 870.

30. Ibid., 871.

31. Grace Boynton diary, June 1948, PC:GMB.

32. Stuart to Secretary of State, June 29, 1948; *Foreign Relations of the United States, 1948, China,* VII, 329.

33. Stuart to Secretary of State, December 21, 1948; *Foreign Relations of the United States, 1948, China,* VII, 675, 676; *United States Relations with China,* 898–899.

34. Grace Boynton diary, January 8, 1947, April 10, and September (date unclear) 1948, PC:GMB.

35. Lucius Porter to children, November 10, 11, 1947, and January 6, May 31, and November 20, 1948, PC:LLP.

36. Ibid., November 17, 1947, and September 27, 1948.

37. Harold R. Isaacs, *No Peace for Asia* (New York, Macmillan, 1947), 47.

38. For reports on Chinese intellectuals' views of the Nationalist leadership see Otto van der Sprenkel, ed., *New China: Three Voices* (London, 1950), which also included accounts by Robert Gullain and Michael Lindsay; Derk Bodde, *Peking Diary* (New York, Fawcett, 1950); Robert J. Lifton, *Thought Reform and the Psychology of Totalism: A Study of "Brainwashing" in China* (New York, W. W. Norton, 1963); and the various reports in *Foreign Relations of the United States, Far East: China,* for the years 1946, 1947, and 1948. The quote on Yen and Lei is from Lucius Porter to children, November 10, 1947, PC:LLP.

39. Grace Boynton diary, November 22 and December 9, 1948.

40. Chao Tzu-ch'en, "Red Peiping after Six Months," *Christian Century,* 66.2:1066 (September 14, 1949).

41. Edwards, *Yenching University, viii-ix;* Grace Boynton diary, March 27, 1949; Ts'ai to author, April 26, 1973.

42. Lu Chih-wei, *YCHW,* December 8, 1947. See also the discussion on negotiations and American aid by Lu Chih-wei and Chang Tung-sun, *YCHW,* March 1, 1948.

43. These views were also expressed by Lei Chieh-ch'iung, Teng Chih-ch'eng, and Wu Han, *YCHW,* March 1, 1948.

44. *YCHW,* December 8, 1947.

45. Grace Boynton, "Source of Springs," ms., 1965, p. 112. A copy of Boynton's novel is deposited at the Houghton Library of Harvard University.

46. For a sampling of humorous and skeptical views on the worth of scholarship by famous personalities, see Rhoda Thomas, comp., *International Thesaurus of Quotations* (New York, 1970), 337, 560–562.

47. Edwards, *Yenching University,* 174. Brief accounts of the Harvard-Yenching Institute can be found in Edwards, 171–177, 274–277, and Howard Galt, "Yenching University," 265–276, AP.

48. Edwards, *Yenching University,* 176.

49. Annual Report for the Harvard-Yenching Institute, 1940–41, 7, AP:HYI.

50. *Harvard-Yenching Institute: Purposes and Programs, 1928–1968* (Cam-

bridge, Harvard-Yenching Institute, 1968), 4. For a description of Hung's method of indexing, see his "Indexing Chinese Books," *Chinese Social and Political Science Review,* 15.1:48–61 (April 1931).

51. *Yenching University Directory, 1930–31* (October 30, 1930) 12.14:23; Glen W. Baxter to me, April 25, 1972.

52. William Hung, "Suggestions for a Harvard-Yenching Institute Five Year Plan for Graduate Teaching and Research at Yenching University," ms., February 10, 1940, AP:HYI. Hung's report outlines the difficulties of setting up a Ph.D. program that would meet the requirements of the ministry of education in China and at the same time be academically respectable in the West. He wrote, "There is the problem of two requirements that a Chinese doctor in Chinese studies will need to meet; in addition to the scientific mastery of a research field, he will need to demonstrate a reasonably good Chinese calligraphy and style of composition, good enough, at any rate, not to disgrace the ancient and honourable appellation of *po-shih* or 'doctor,' otherwise, he will be marked by the students as *yang po-shih* or 'outlandish doctor.' One is the result of scientific discipline which can be transplanted in China; the other is that of long literary and artistic discipline under a number of skilled masters, which is at the present moment not easy, and for American students not as necessary, to transport to an American university." Ibid., 7.

53. Wu Lei-ch'uan, *Yen-ching ta-hsüeh t'u-shu-kuan kai-k'uang* (Peiping, 1933), 4.

54. Annual reports of the Harvard-Yenching Institute, 1939–40, 6–7, and 1940–41, 10, AP:HYI.

55. This list of scholars and the one in the next paragraph is taken from the various directories for Yenching University between 1927 and 1939, AP:D.

56. Jung Keng was not included in the Boorman biographical dictionary, but his eminence as a sinologist is suggested by his long list of publications in the *Catalog of the Chinese Collection, Hoover Institution* (Stanford, Stanford University Press, 1969), VII, 595–596.

57. Boorman's failure to include Hung in the biographical dictionary disappointed Hung. In an interview with the author Hung pointed out there had been others in their time who were not fully appreciated, men such as Jesus, Socrates, and Confucius. A partial listing of Hung's scholarly work, in addition to the sinological index series, was published in the *Harvard Journal of Asiatic Studies,* 24:7–16 (1962–63).

58. Hsü Ti-shan was an active writer for the *Chen-li yü sheng-ming.* He published a series of essays on the history of anti-Christianity in China, entitled "Fan Chi-tu-chiao ti Chung-kuo," which appeared in *CLYSM,* 2.1, 2.3, 2.4, 2.5, 2.6, 2.7, 2.8, 2.9 (1927).

59. For Po's writings see the *Chinese Collection,* X, 81.

60. Stuart's report to the Harvard-Yenching Institute, 1940–41, p. 3, AP:HYI.

61. Hung, "Suggestions," 6.

62. In addition to his study of the examination system Teng Ssu-yü has published widely on many topics in Chinese history. Among the better known works are *An Annotated Bibliography of Selected Chinese Reference Works* with

Knight Biggerstaff (Cambridge, Harvard University Press, 1950, 1971); co-author with John K. Fairbank, *China's Response to the West* (Cambridge, Harvard University Press, 1960); and *The Taiping Rebellion and the Western Powers* (New York, Oxford, 1971).

63. Annual Reports of the Harvard-Yenching Institute, 1939–1940, 2–3, and 1940–41, 3, AP:HYI. For a listing of Lu Chih-wei's scholarly publications in the *Yen-ching hsüeh-pao* see the Annual Report, 1940–1941, 6, AP:HYI, and the *Chinese Collection, Hoover Institution*, IX, 169.

64. *Harvard-Yenching Institute: Purposes and Programs, 1928–1968*, 7–11; Glen W. Baxter to me, April 25, 1972.

7. Revolutionary Politics and Yenching Cosmopolitanism

1. Boynton diary, December 20 and 23, 1948.

2. Chao, "Days of Rejoicing in China," *Christian Century*, 66.9:265 (March 2, 1949), written January 27, 1949).

3. Lu to McMullen, April 5, 1949, Lu Chih-wei file, AC:UB.

4. Otto van der Sprenkel, ed., *New China: Three Views* (New York, John Day, 1951), 48.

5. Mao Tse-tung, *On New Democracy* (Peking, 1954), 21. The essay may also be found in *Selected Works of Mao Tse-tung* (Peking, 1969), IV, 339–384, and *Mao Tse-tung hsüan-chi* (Peking, 1964), 665–704.

6. Mao, *On New Democracy*, 44–55, 56, 75.

7. On June 15, 1949, Mao said, "We are willing to discuss with any foreign government the establishment of diplomatic relations on the basis of the principles of equality, mutual benefit and mutual respect for territorial integrity and sovereignty," a statement obviously directed toward the United States. *Selected Works*, IV, 408. A similar statement was made in April, *Selected Works*, IV, 397–400. See also John Leighton Stuart diary, June 26 and 28, 1949, and Seymour Topping, *Journey Between Two Chinas* (New York, Harper and Row, 1972), 83–87.

8. Mao, *Selected Works*, IV, 415.

9. Article 59 of the Common Program explicitly "protects law-abiding foreign nationals." See Albert P. Blaustein, *Fundamental Legal Documents of Communist China* (South Hackensack, N.J., F. B. Rothman, 1962), 53.

10. Stuart diary, February 11, 1949. In his last years as ambassador Stuart was ambivalent on American policy toward the Communists. See Stuart, *Fifty Years*, 236, and Topping, *Journey Between Two Chinas*, 83–89. But his diplomatic dispatches for 1948 show a full-blown anticommunism. *Foreign Relations of the United States, 1948, Far East: China*, VII, 164–165, 167–168, 472–473, 522–523, and 635–636. On December 28, 1948, he wrote ominously, "Is there any possibility that Northern Korea constitutes an area in which a diplomatic offensive on our part might catch the Soviets off balance, with resultant repercussions not only in the Chinese Communist Party but throughout Asia? We realize serious risks and disadvantages would be involved. Nevertheless, we believe that it is essential without loss of time to regain initiatives in Asia by positive action which would be within the United Nations framework and

backed by the possbility, in extremes, of applying force. Otherwise we will suffer the full consequences of major diplomatic defeat in China with all its ultimate strategic implications in Asia." Ibid., 695.

11. *Jen-min jih-pao,* August 23, 1949. Soon after the Yenching faculty protest, Dr. Loucks of the Peking Union Medical College returned to Peking from a visit to the United States and reported to Yenching Westerners how quickly and pervasively the White Paper was interpreted as pro-Communist in the United States. See Boynton to Charlotte Boynton, September 19, 1949, PC:GMB (HL). For other denunciations of the White Paper in China see Mao, *Selected Works,* IV, 425-432, 433-439, and 441-445.

12. Chen, Wen-hui C., *Chinese Communist Anti-Americanism and the Resist-America Aid-Korea Campaign* (Maxwell Air Force Base, Alabama, 1955), 5.

13. Tsou Tang, *America's Failure in China, 1941-1950* (Chicago, University of Chicago Press, 1963), 516-519, stresses Mao's inflexibility, and yet Tsou's account makes it clear how Sino-American relations in 1949 also were strongly affected by domestic and foreign politics in America.

14. A convenient collection of these documents describing Sino-Russian Relations in 1950 can be found in van der Sprenkel, *New China,* appendix. Also see Robert North, *Moscow and the Chinese Communists* (Stanford, Stanford University Press, 1953), 266-269.

15. Dick Wilson, *Anatomy of China: An Introduction to One Quarter of Mankind* (New York, New American Library, 1966), 218.

16. See Chen Tien-fang (Ch'eng T'ien-fang), *A History of Sino-Russian Relations* (Washington, D.C., Public Affairs Press, 1951), 317-318; *People's Republic of China: An Economic Assessment* (Washington, D.C., Joint Economic Committee, Congress of the United States, 1972), 344-345.

17. Van der Sprenkel, *New China,* 74, 79, 114-115.

18. Ibid., 140-142.

19. Benjamin Schwartz, *Communism and China: Ideology in Flux* (Cambridge, Harvard University Press, 1968), 37, 55, and 85. According to Seymour Topping, Mao told the Eighth Meeting of the Central Committee in 1962 about the "struggle" involved in working out the treaty. Stalin reportedly signed the treaty after two months of hard negotiations, and his confidence in Mao began only in the "winter of 1950, during the Resist America Aid Korea Campaign. Stalin *then* believed we were not Yugoslavia and not Titoist," Topping, *Journey Between Two Chinas,* 89.

20. Lu to McMullen, June 28, September 1, October 12 and 28, 1950, Lu Chih-wei file, AC:UB.

21. Lu to Boynton, September 5 and October 28, 1950, PC:GMB; Lu to McMullen, October 28, 1950, AC:UB.

22. Two widely circulated documents in Peking at the time were the speech of Wu Hsiu-ch'uan at the United Nations Security Council, November 18, 1950, and the article, "Tse-yang jen-shih Mei-kuo" (How to know America), November 5, 1950. Both documents appear in the *Wei-ta k'ang-Mei yüan-Ch'ao yün-tung* (Peking, 1954), 47-65 and 674-684, respectively. Wu's speech may also be found in the *New York Times,* November 29, 1950, and the *United Na-*

tions Security Council Official Records (New York, 1951), 527th meeting, November 28, 1950, 2–26. For an authoritative analysis of Chinese views of the Korean War, see Allen Whiting, *China Crosses the Yalu: The Decision to Enter the Korean War* (New York, Columbia University Press, 1954).

23. Wiant to H. B. Seaman, October 19, 1950, Wiant file, AC:UB; Lu to McMullen, October 28, 1950, Lu file, AC:UB.

24. Minute, Board of trustees, January 2, 1951, AP:BT.

25. Ralph Lapwood to friends, January 3, 1951, PC:RNL; Wiant to McMullen, January 5, 1951, and H. B. Seaman to Wiant, January 25, 1951, Wiant file, AC:UB.

26. *New China News Agency,* February 12, 1951. Fu Jen University, the other major Christian college in Peking run by the Catholics, was nationalized October 12, 1950, four months before Yenching. One reason for government action at that time, it appears, was the refusal of its American board of control to abandon religious instruction and modify religious qualifications for admission. Fu Jen's position contrasted sharply with both Western and Chinese administrators at Yenching. *China Monthly Review,* 96–97 (November 1950), and 130–131 (December 1950); Richard C. Bush, Jr., *Religion in Communist China* (Nashville, Abingdon Press, Tennessee, 1970), 72–73, 75.

27. "Proclamation of the Chinese People's Liberation Army," April 25, 1949, *Selected Works,* IV, 397–400.

28. Lu to McMullen, April 5, 1959, Lu Chih-wei file, AC:UB.

29. Minute, Board of Trustees, May 9, 1950, AP:BT.

30. Boynton diary, July 25, 1949; and van der Sprenkel, *New China,* 15.

31. Van der Sprenkel, *New China,* 3–14, 64–70.

32. Minute, Board of Managers, February 13, 1949, AP:BM.

33. Lu to McMullen, April 13, 1950, Lu Chih-wei file, AC:UB.

34. Yen Hui-ch'ing was one of the four members of the "peace party" sent by acting president Li Tsung-jen to Peking and later Shih-chia-chuang in March 1949 to talk with Mao Tse-tung and Chou En-lai. He died in 1950. Stuart, *Fifty Years,* 221–222; and Perleberg, *Who's Who in Modern China,* 240–250. Ch'üan Shao-wen was an original signer of the "Message from Chinese Christians to Mission Boards Abroad," December 1949, and a founder of the post-revolutionary Three Self-Movement. See Wallace Merwin and Francis P. Jones, eds., *Documents of the Three Self Movement* (New York, National Council of Churches, 1963), 14–18. Chou Yi-ch'un left China for Hong Kong in 1949, but maintained contact with Yenching leaders. When the new government requested Lu Chih-wei to reform the board of managers, Lu was willing to reconsider Chou as a possible continuation from the old board; Lu to McMullen, October 12, 1950, Lu Chih-wei file, AC:UB.

35. For detailed information on Chien and Shen, see *Who's Who in Communist China* (Hong Kong, 1969), I, 142, and II, 559. Despite Chien's prominent political role in the early years he was later portrayed as a "flower vase" kept by the "reactionary clique" to "decorate the school." After nationalization of the university he became an editor of the *Yen-ching hsüeh-pao* and chairman of the history department when Ch'i Ssu-ho was absent during his work with

land reform. Chien later served as head of the history department at Peking University between 1954 and 1966 until he was branded as a "reactionary scholar tyrant" in December 1966 during the Cultural Revolution. Shen was heavily involved in local politics and actually spent only a few months on the Yenching campus. Later, in 1957, he too was denounced as a rightist and deprived of membership in the National People's Congress.

36. HYC, April 14, 1952.

37. Lu to McMullen, November 1, 1949, Lu Chih-wei file, AC:UB.

38. Perleberg, *Who's Who in Modern China,* 298.

39. Chung Shih, *Higher Education in Communist China* (Hong Kong, Union Research Institute, 1953), 17; *Who's Who in Modern China,* 327–332.

40. Lu to McMullen, November 1, 1949, Lu Chih-wei file, AC:UB.

41. Wiant to me, May 17, 1973; Randolph Sailer, an "interim report" on a visit to China, May 15, 1973.

42. Louise Sailer to Yenching Women's College Committee, July 13, 1949, Sailer file, AC:UB.

43. Other members of the branch committee were Chang Shih-lung, Hsieh Tao-yüan, and Yüan Ming; HYC, November 14, 1949, and February 15, 1950. The pre-October figures are from Louise Sailer to Yenching Women's College Committee, July 1949, Sailer file, AC:UB.

44. *HYC,* November 14, 1959.

45. Ibid., February 15 and 22, 1950.

46. Lapwood, *Through the Chinese Revolution,* 107–108.

47. *HYC,* November 7, 1949, and January 9, 1950.

48. Lapwood, *Through the Chinese Revolution,* 109–113.

49. McMullen to Lu, February 7, 1950, Lu Chih-wei file, AC:UB; Minute, Board of Trustees, May 8, 1950, AP:BT.

50. *HYC,* November 21, 1949, and December 7, 1949. For a general discussion of the youth league, see James P. Harrison, *The Long March to Power: A History of the Chinese Communist Party, 1921–1972* (New York, Praeger, 1972), 262–263, 404–405.

51. Kenneth Ch'en to Elisseeff, February 15, 1949, Yenching file; Lu to McMullen, November 1, 1949, Lu Chih-wei file; Louise Sailer to Yenching Women's College Committee, April 4, 1950, and Randolph Sailer to McMullen, November 13, 1950, Sailer file, AC:UB.

52. These points were expressed in various issues of the *Hsin Yen-ching,* for example, those by Kao Ming-k'ai, November 28, 1949, and by Yen Ching-yüeh, December 14 and 28, 1949.

53. Kao Ming-k'ai, "Cheng-chih hsüeh-hsi, yeh-wu hsüeh-hsi" (Political study and professional study), *HYC,* November 28, 1949.

54. Lu to McMullen, November 1, 1949, and June 28, 1950, Lu Chih-wei file, AC:UB.

55. Lu to McMullen, June 28, 1950, Lu Chih-wei file, and Randolph Sailer to McMullen, November 13, 1950, Sailer file, AC:UB.

56. "Yenching University: Incomplete Report on Student Enrollment," Sep-

tember 21, 1950, ms., PC:GMB; *Pei-p'ing ssu-li Yen-ching ta-hsüeh yi-lan* (1937), 185.

57. Hsiao Feng, "What Did the US Open Yenching University For," *Ta-kung pao* (Hong Kong), April 22, 1952, as translated in *Current Background,* published by the American Consulate in Hong Kong, no. 182, p. 20; Theodore T. H. Ch'en, *Thought Reform of the Chinese Intellectuals* (Hong Kong, University of Hong Kong Press, 1960), chaps. 7 and 8. In Ch'en's analysis only slight attention is given to the American involvement in the Korean War as a factor in provoking this vast outpouring of anti-American sentiment. And yet the extensive quotations he takes from the thought reform literature of the time reveal how central the war was in their thinking.

The argument that Western nations used religion to expand their political influence in China was, of course, an old one, but it was expressed with a new urgency after the outbreak of the Korean War. See "Chung-kuo Chi-tu-chiao tsai hsin Chung-kuo chien-she chung nu-li ti t'u-ching ti hsüan-yen" (An announcement on the struggle ahead for the Christian church in the new China), September 22, 1950, and Kuo Mo-Jo's report to the Administrative Council, December 29, 1950, *Wei-ta ti k'ang-Mei yüan-Ch'ao yün-tung* (Peking, 1954), 700 and 797–798. Also Lapwood to friends, April 21, May 2, and 10, 1951, PC:RNL; and Lapwood, *Through the Chinese Revolution,* 96–98, 135–138.

58. Lu to McMullen, June 28, 1950, Lu Chih-wei file, AC:UB.

59. Lapwood to friends, July 31, 1951, PC:RNL. The specialized skills of other Yenching faculty were also sought by the government, Liang Ssu-ch'eng, architect, Hou Jen-chih, geographer and city planner, Huang Wei-te, mechanical engineer in irrigation, and Tai Wen-sai, in the standardization of Chinese astronomical terminology. Lapwood, *Through the Chinese Revolution,* 98.

60. Almost thirty years before, Ch'en Tu-hsiu, after endorsing Christianity as one way of spreading the spirit of service and sacrifice, raised the question, namely "sacrifice for what and love for whom?" *Hsin ch'ing-nien,* March 22, 1922, in Chang, *Kuo-nei chin-shih nien lai chih tsung-chiao ssu-ch'ao,* 190–193. Ch'en's question remained ignored by most of the Yenching educators, but it received new attention after the revolutionary takeover. See Lo Cheng-ching, "K'an chiu Yen-ching wei shie fu-wu" (A look at who the old Yenching served), *HYC,* April 14, 1952, 5.

61. Lapwood, *Through the Chinese Revolution,* 165. So intense was this campaign that the math department, of which Lapwood was a member, once held more than twenty-six hours of meetings over a four-day period. Also see Lapwood to friends, March 16, 20, and June 29, 1952, PC:RNL.

62. Among the individual histories of the Christian colleges in China published by the United Board of Christian Higher Education in Asia in New York, the one on Yenching University by Dwight Edwards treats the statements and actions of the Chinese faculty and students after 1949 most seriously. The others tend to slight the Chinese side. See, for example, Roderick Scott, *Fukien Christian University* (1954), 102–123; W. B. Nance, *Soochow University* (1956), 133–134; Charles Hodge Corbett, *Shantung Christian University* (1955), 263–264; Mrs. Lawrence Thurston and Ruth M. Chester, *Ginling College* (1955),

143–146; and Mary Lamberton, *St. John's University, Shanghai* (1955), 249–250. The one comprehensive and scholarly study of the Christian colleges by Jessie Lutz, *China and the Christian Colleges, 1850–1950*, 444–484, provides an extensive discussion of the post-1949 period.

63. For a vivid account of prison experience by a young Western English teacher who arrived at Yenching just before Pearl Harbor, see Langdon Gilkey, *Shantung Compound: The Story of Men and Women under Pressure* (New York, Harper and Row, 1966).

64. David Caute, *The Fellow-Travellers: A Postscript to the Enlightenment* (New York, Macmillan, 1973), 6.

65. Ibid., 251. Two excellent studies of thought reform are Theodore H. E. Ch'en, *Thought Reform of the Chinese Intellectuals* (Hong Kong, 1960), which is based largely on the confessions published in Chinese periodicals in the 1950s; and Robert J. Lifton, *Thought Reform and the Psychology of Totalism: A Study of "Brainwashing" in China* (New York, 1961), which is based on Lifton's extensive interviews of Chinese and Westerners who fled to Hong Kong. Albert Biderman, has suggested a correlation between the widespread American revulsion of thought reform in China and the brainwashing of American prisoners of war in Korea. The term brainwashing, as embedded in the English language, has come to refer to any attempts by "Communist functionaries to . . . coerce, instruct, persuade, trick, train, delude, debilitate, frustrate, bribe, threaten, promise, flatter, degrade, starve, torture, isolate . . . and various other means of manipulating individuals . . . against one another for which our language has not yet evolved one word verbs." More generally it refers to any means of persuading "people to act in ways of which the user of the term disapproves." See Biderman, *March to Calumny: the Story of the American POWs in the Korean War* (New York, Macmillan, 1963), 141.

66. Caute, *Fellow-Travellers*, 13.

67. Even the story of Bao Ruo-wang (Jean Pasqualini) which is an account of long and extensive thought reform through labor, shows that prison experiences of political prisoners in China was apparently less harsh than in the Soviet Union generally. See Bao and Rudolph Chelminski, *Prisoners of Mao* (New York, Coward, McCann, and Geoghegan, 1973). For another inside account by two Americans, who also suffered as political prisoners, see Adele and Allyn Rickett, *Prisoners of Liberation* (New York, Cameron, 1957).

68. One recent collection of essays by American scholars on China which is largely free from cold war perceptions and appraises the Chinese revolution in the context of larger problems facing mankind in the twentieth century and even poses the question on what America might learn from China, is Michael Oksenberg, ed., *China's Developmental Experience* (New York, Academy of Political Science, 1973), esp. the essays by Oksenberg, Tsou, Sidel, Munro, Li, and Pfeffer.

69. Minute, Board of Managers, February 13, 1949, AP:BM.

70. Boynton to Charlotte Boynton, October 28, 1949, and January 4, 1950, PC:GMB (HL). For a later account of Hsieh Ping-hsin and Wu Wen-tsao, see Yang Ch'ing-k'un's report in *Shih-chih chien-pao*, 10 (April 1, 1972).

71. The file may be found under "Alumni," AC.

72. The 1972 list included alumni who may have previously been members of other alumni associations outside the United States. See *Yen-ta hsiao-k'an,* in Chinese and English (Palo Alto, Calif., March 1973), 70–77. An earlier list was also published by the Yenching University Alumni Association Inc., USA, in 1968 and showed approximately 280 Yenching-related people residing in the United States.

73. *Yen-ta hsiao-yu t'ung-hsün* (Hong Kong, 1967), 21. This list was published in 1968 as a separate directory, giving the year of graduation for the alumni, mailing address, and telephone number.

74. Interview with Yeh Ch'u-sheng, June 18, 1969, Taipei. For an account of alumni activities in Taiwan, focusing largely on the John Leighton Stuart Memorial Scholarship Fund, see *Yen-ta hsiao-yu t'ung-hsün* (1968), 68.

75. *Yen-ta hsiao-yu t'ung-hsün* (1963), 68–82, (1965), 33–37, and (1967), 23–25.

76. T'an Jen-chiu, interview, February 6, 1969.

77. Ma Ssu-ts'ung joined the Yenching faculty in music in 1949 and left China, after humiliation and injury by the Red Guards, during the Cultural Revolution. See *Who's Who in Communist China,* II, 504–505. See also *New York Times,* April 13 and May 28, 1967.

78. Stuart to McMullen, June 24, 1947, and March 9, 1949, Stuart file, AC:UB; Grace Boynton diary, April 10, 1948, and January 21, 1949; Randolph Sailer to McMullen, October 24, 1950, Sailer file, AC:UB; Lapwood to friends, February 29, 1952, PC:RNL; Lapwood, *Through the Chinese Revolution,* 167–171.

79. Lucy Burtt to friends, January 10, 1949, Yenching file, AC:UB; Grace Boynton to Charlotte Boynton, December 23, 1948, PC:GMB (HL); Lapwood, *Through the Chinese Revolution,* 43–54. For two popularized accounts of take-over at other universities see Stephen Becker, *The Season of the Stranger* (New York, 1954), chaps. 17 to 25, which is generally sympathetic to the revolution, and Maria Yen (Yen Kuei-lai), *The Umbrella Garden: A Picture of Student Life in Red China* (New York, Macmillan, 1954), chaps. 2 and 3, a hostile account.

80. Lapwood, *Through the Chinese Revolution,* 49–50; Lucius Porter letters, January 9, 1949, PC:LLP; Grace Boynton diary, January 8, 1949.

81. Lapwood, *Through the Chinese Revolution,* 48–49; Boynton diary, February 6, 1949.

82. Boynton diary, March 3, 1949.

83. News items on the Sino-Soviet Friendship Association in *HYC,* November 7, 1949, December 14 and 28, 1949, and February 22, 1950.

84. Huang Kuan, "T'u-kai t'ung-hsün" (Report on land reform), *HYC,* February 22, 1950; reports on student participation in land reform in *HYC,* January 25, February 8, 15, 1950; and Lapwood, *Through the Chinese Revolution,* 139.

85. Bliss Wiant to Henry B. Seaman, November 17, 1950, Wiant file, AC:UB;

interview with Wiant, November 16, 1972; Lapwood to friends, December 16, 1950, PC:RNL.

86. Ralph Lapwood reported that patriotic sentiment was so high that few, if any, listened to Voice of America broadcasts which were not jammed. Listening to them was as unpatriotic as listening to Hitler's broadcasts in wartime England. See Lapwood to friends, December 16, 1950, October 31, 1951, and August 16, 1952, PC:RNL; and Lapwood, *Through the Chinese Revolution*, 156, 175–183.

87. John Leighton Stuart, "The Problems of Modern Education in China," n.d., c. June 1936, ms., 14, AC:JLS.

88. Louise Sailer to Yenching Women's College Committee, April 4, 1950, Sailer file, AC:UB. By October 1951 Ralph Lapwood was using Chinese exclusively even with colleagues whose English was good. Also a vast effort was underway to write Chinese language textbooks in courses where none had existed. Ralph Lapwood to friends, no. 51–B3, n.d., c. October 1951, PC:RNL.

89. Lapwood to friends, May 5, 1952, PC:RNL; Grace Boynton noted in her diary that the Russian teacher in January 1950 was ridiculed by students, January 8, 1950.

90. Louise Sailer to Yenching Women's College Committee, April 4, 1950, Sailer file, AC:UB; Grace Boynton diary, June 30, 1949; *HYC*, November 28, 1949.

91. Stuart report to the trustees, October 9, 1939, AC:JLS.

92. Lapwood, *Through the Chinese Revolution*, 66–70.

93. "Tsung-chieh cheng-chih hsüeh-hsi" (Summing up political study), *HYC*, December 28, 1949, and January 4, 1950. See *HYC*, January 4, 11, 15, and 18, 1950, for the student testimonies.

94. *HYC*, November 28 and December 7, 1949.

95. Lapwood, *Through the Chinese Revolution*, 147; Grace Boynton diary, November 6 and 25, 1949.

96. Grace Boynton diary, October 31, 1949; interview with Bliss Wiant, November 16, 1972; Lapwood, *Through the Chinese Revolution*, 47, 200.

97. Lucy Burtt to friends, January 10, 1949, Yenching file, AC:UB.

98. Ralph Lapwood translates Yeh-su chia as the Jesus Homes, Lapwood to friends, July 31, 1951, PC:RNL. For other discussions of the Jesus Family, see Yamamoto Sumiko, *Chūgoku Kirisutokyō shi ken-kyū*, 82–94; Richard Bush, *Religion in Communist China*, 200; and a detailed eyewitness account by D. Vaughan Rees, *The "Jesus Family" in Communist China* (London, Paternoster Press, 1959).

99. Randolph Sailer to William Fenn, August 1949, Sailer file, AC:UB.

100. Lucy Burtt to friends, January 10, 1949.

101. Boynton diary, October 3 and 26, 1949.

102. Lapwood, *Through the Chinese Revolution*, 199–200. One prominent Protestant leader in Peking, Wang Ming-tao, regarded the revolution with great hostility and offers a sharp contrast to the way in which Yenching leaders tried to adapt their Christian beliefs into the revolutionary order. See Ng Lee Ming, "Christianity and Social Change: The Case in China, 1920–1950," chap. 2.

103. Randolph Sailer to William Fenn, August 1949, Sailer file, AC:UB. One woman student plunged into work at a center for thieves and prostitutes in the Heavenly Bridge district of Peking and testified how, for the first time, her eyes were opened to the way people really lived. Louise Sailer to Yenching Women's College Committee, July 13, 1949, Sailer file, AC:UB.

104. Stuart, *Fifty Years*, 242–243.

105. Ibid., 236; Boynton diary, August 20, 1949.

106. Stuart, *Fifty Years*, chaps. 14 and 15.

107. Bliss Wiant reported seven faculty members, Chinese and Western, left before fan-shen, Wiant to McMullen, December 6, 1948, Wiant file, AC:UB. But Grace Boynton indicated more had left. In addition to Dwight Edwards and Mary Cookingham mentioned in Wiant's correspondence, Boynton notes the departures of Philip de Vargas, school of religion, Ruth Stahl, dean of women, Thomas and Ruth Breece, English, and Hilda Hague, longtime secretary to Stuart since the 1929s. Boynton diary, November 28, and December 12, 1948.

108. Bliss Wiant and Mildred Wiant, interview, November 17, 1972; Boynton diary, January 21, 1950; copy of William Gilkey letter, May 24, 1952, PC:GMB.

109. Wiant to Evans, January 27, 1949, Wiant file, AC:UB.

110. Wiant to McMullen, April 3, 1949, Wiant file, AC:UB.

111. During the Resist America Campaign Westerners on campus were asked to buy war bonds. Wiant complied and bought two, worth US $16. One dramatic symbol of anti-American feeling was the removal of the bust of Bishop James Bashford, the Methodist leader who was instrumental in the founding of Yenching. For two years the bust had remained at one end of the ground floor in Bashford Hall, with Mao Tse-tung's bust at the other end. The Bashford Hall sign, Pei Kung Lou, was also taken down and burned in the courtyard. Despite the hostility and his growing isolation, Wiant, was still allowed to conduct a performance of the *Messiah* that Christmas, though not on campus but in the Episcopalian Church in Peking. Wiant interview, November 16, 1972.

112. This contrast may be seen by comparing Wiant's letters to McMullen, December 6, 1948, and December 11, 1950, Wiant file, AC:UB.

113. Porter to children, December 12, 1948, PC:LLP.

114. Ibid., January 30, 1949, March 13, 1949, April 24, 1949, May 11, 1949.

115. Grace Boynton diary, February 28, 1947, May 25, 1947, May 17, 1948. The full ambiguity of her feelings was expressed in the closing lines of a poem she wrote at the time:

Thou hast revealed to me the strong new life
Which is surging over this land
In the Red Armies of the Chinese youth.
There is in me a longing to believe in their goodness
And yet I will not bow to those who deny Thee and
    Thy freedom.

Ibid., September 28, 1947.

116. Ibid., July 29, 1949, September 26, 1949.

117. Ibid., January 31, July 25, August 11, 19, September 26, October 3, 17, November 6, 1949.

118. Perleberg, *Who's Who in Modern China*, 245; and Grace Boynton, *The River Garden of Pure Repose* (New York, 1952).

119. Service's dispatch was entitled "Hope of Chinese Liberals That America Can Save China by Forcing Democratic Reform," dated July 11, 1944. It was published in *The Amerasia Papers: A Clue to the Catastrophe of China* (Washington, D.C., Senate Judiciary Committee, 1970), I, 665. Boynton, who knew Yang well, had never regarded her, since their contact on the Yenching campus in the late 1920s, as a liberal. Rather she saw Yang as the revolutionary paradigm among students. Even during her study and writing in America in 1946 and 1947, Yang Ping did not stray from her revolutionary commitment. Yang to Boynton, February 12, September 3, October 27, 1945, and March 6, June 6, 1946, and April 12, 1948, PC:GMB.

120. Boynton diary, March 1, 1949.

121. Ibid., January 29, and November 11, 1949.

122. Boynton letters, November 20 and December 31, 1950, PC:GMB (HL).

123. Boynton to Russell Boynton, December 28, 1950, PC:GMB (HL).

124. Sailer to Fenn, August 1949, Sailer file, AC:UB.

125. Sailer to McMullen, November 22, 1952 and to Mary Ferguson, July 25, 1952, Sailer file, AC:UB.

126. Lapwood, *Through the Chinese Revolution*, 163.

127. Lapwood to friends, March 19 and December 29, 1951, PC:RNL.

128. Lapwood, *Through the Chinese Revolution*, 171-172, 197; Lapwood to friends, June 2, 1952, PC:RNL. William Gilkey, the recent American recruit to the Yenching faculty in music, also stayed on through the Three Anti campaign, but he suffered greatly for it. The struggle directed against him, though, was not conducted as part of the campaign on campus but rather at the public safety headquarters in downtown Peking. Gilkey reported in May 1952, after arriving in Hong Kong that he had been "horrified at even whispering for almost a year now," ever since the Peking police had arrested Adele and Allyn Rickett and Harriet Mills on July 25, 1951, and led them through the streets of Peking. Gilkey was accused more than six months later of serving as an American agent in league with the Ricketts. He dismissed these charges as completely false and resented greatly the long six-hour sessions of interrogations by the police. During his travail Gilkey, a pianist, apparently suffered spasms of the hand and for a while could not even write his own name. Copy of letter of William Gilkey, May 14, 1952, PC:GMB.

129. Ralph Lapwood, "Extracts from my China Diary, 1964," mimeographed, 1964, PC:RNL.

130. Sailer to author, June 8, 1973.

131. Stuart to Mary Ferguson, November 1, 1949, Stuart file, AC:UB. Boynton recorded the declining esteem for Stuart among faculty members, especially after the denunciation of the White Paper in August. Boynton diary, October 17 and 30, 1949.

132. John Leighton Stuart's introduction to Cheng Tien-fang's *History of*

Sino-Russian Relations. I have quoted extensively from this source, which bears strong resemblance to the last chapter in Stuart's memoirs, *Fifty Years*, to show that this hostile position toward the revolution was not just the result of Stanley Hornbeck's influence in Stuart's memoirs as suggested by Topping, *Journey Between Two Chinas*, 89.

133. See item dated November 1957, and Stuart to Fenn, November 25, 1947, Stuart file,AC:UB.

134 Sailer to McMullen, November 22, 1950, Sailer file, AC:UB.

135. Ibid., October 24. 1950.

136. Lapwood, *Through the Chinese Revolution*, 167–171; Lapwood to friends, February 29, 1952, PC:RNL.

137. "What Did the United States Open Yenching University For?" *Ta kung-pao* (Hong Kong) April 22, 1952, and "Ideological Struggle Reaches New High in Yenching," *Chin-pu jih-pao* (Tientsin) March 17, 1952, both in *Current Background*, no. 182.

138. See the attack by Hou Jen-chih, *HYC*, April 14, 1952; Lapwood to friends, May 5, 1952, AC:RNL.

139. *Jen-min jih-pao*, November 3, 1951, and April 16, 1952, as cited in Chung Shih, *Higher Education in Communist China*, 41–43.

140. T. C. Chao to "Y. C. and David," November 26, 1948, Yenching file, AC:UB.

141. Chao, "Days of Rejoicing in China," *Christian Century*, 66.9:266 (March 2, 1949); and "Christian Churches in Communist China," *Christianity in Crisis*, 9.11:85 (June 27, 1949).

142. Chao, "Christian Churches," *Christian Century*, 85.

143. Chao, "Days of Rejoicing," 266, and "Red Peiping after Six Months," *Christian Century*, 66:37:1066 (September 14, 1949).

144. *Wei-ta ti k'ang-Mei yüan-Ch'ao yün-tung*, 703–704.

145. *Ta-kung pao* (Hong Kong), December 12, 1951. An English translation of this report can be found in the Yenching file, AC:UB. At the same meeting Philip de Vargas, though Swiss, was accused of spreading the "poison for the aggressors with American dollars and through an American missionary organization"; Frank Price was denounced as an "agent in missionary disguise"; Professor Tsai Yung-ch'un confessed to his own sickness and having been led to the blind alley of "non-revolution and fear of struggle"; and Bliss Wiant, was accused of quoting the Biblical passage "Blessed are the persecuted for righteousness sake" in his efforts to "distort the situation of Christians in New China, slander the People's Government, and undermine the unity of the Chinese people." All resolved to "entirely reform the school."

146. *Jen-min jih-pao*, July 12, 1951.

147. *Documents of the Three Self Movement*, 70–71; and Lapwood to friends, September 26, 1952, PC:RNL.

148. *Documents of the Three Self Movement*, 138–139.

149. Randolph Sailer had a cordial visit with Chao in May 1973; Sailer, "interim report," May 15, 1973.

150. Lu to McMullen, December 9, 1948, Lu Chih-wei file, AC:UB.

151. Kenneth Ch'en to Serge Elisseeff, February 15, 1949, Yenching file, AC:UB; interview with Mei Yi-pao, July 16, 1968, Iowa City; and Dwight Edwards, *Yenching University,* vii–ix, 405.

152. Wiant to Seaman, November 17, 1950, and Sailer to McMullen, October 24, 1950, AC:UB; Lapwood to friends, December 29, 1951, PC:RNL; Boynton diary, March 13, June 30, and September 11, 1949.

153. Lu to McMullen, October 28, 1950, Lu Chih-wei file, AC:UB.

154. "United States Imperialist Cultural Aggression as Seen in Yenching University," *Hsin kuan-ch'a* (Peking, February 10, 1951), as translated in *Current Background,* no. 107.

155. Lu to McMullen, November 1, 1949, AC:UB.

156. Ibid.; Boynton diary, September 11, 1949.

157. *New China News Agency,* Peking, December 5, 1951; Lapwood to friends, December 29, 1951, PC:RNL.

158. Lapwood to friends, February 6, 1952, PC:RNL.

159. "Ti-kuo chu-yi fen-tzu Fan T'ien-hsang jih-chi chung ti Lu Chih-wei" (Lu Chih-wei in the diary of imperialist element, Bliss Wiant), *HYC,* April 14, 1952, 6; also James Endicott, "A Report on How American Imperialism Used Religion in China," *China Monthly Review,* June 1952.

160. Wu Hsing-hua, "Wo jen-shih le Lu Chih-wei shih tse-yang ti hsüeh-che" (The kind of scholar I now recognize Lu Chih-wei to be), *HYC,* April 14, 1952.

161. Hou Jen-chih, "Chieh-lu Lu Chih-wei fan-tung chi-t'uan ti tsui-hsing" (Expose the sins of the Lu Chih-wei reactionary clique), *HYC,* April 14, 1952.

162. Lu Yao-hua, "K'ung-su wo ti fu-ch'in—Lu Chih-wei" (I denounce my father, Lu Chih-wei), *HYC,* April 14, 1952.

163. Ibid.

164. "Lu Chih-wei ti chien-t'ao" (Lu Chih-wei's self criticism), *HYC,* April 14, 1952.

165. Lapwood letters, June 2, 1952; "Extracts from a letter to the Bliss Wiants from the Lapwoods," n.d., c. summer 1952, PC:GMB; Randolph Sailer, "Interim Report," May 15, 1973.

166. Lapwood to friends, June 29 and September 26, 1952, PC:RNL.

167. Edwards, *Yenching University,* 437–438.

Bibliography

The Amerasia Papers: A Clue to the Catastrophe of China. 2 vols. Washington, D.C., Committee on the Judiciary, United States Senate, January 26, 1970.

Arima, Tatsuo. *The Failure of Freedom: A Portrait of Modern Japanese Intellectuals.* Cambridge, Harvard University Press, 1969.

Bailie, Victoria W. *Bailie's Activities in China: The Account of the Life and Work of Professor Joseph Bailie in and for China, 1890–1935.* Palo Alto, Calif., Pacific Books, 1964.

Band, William and Claire. *Two Years with the Chinese Communists.* New Haven, Yale University Press, 1948.

Bao Ruo-wang (Jean Pasqualini) and Rudolph Chelminski. *Prisoner of Mao.* New York, Coward, McCann & Geoghegan, 1973.

Becker, Stephen. *The Season of the Stranger.* New York, Harper and Brothers, 1951.

Biderman, Albert. *March to Calumny: The Story of the American POWs in the Korean War.* New York, Macmillan, 1963.

Blaustein, Albert P. *Fundamental Legal Documents of Communist China.* South Hackensack, N. J., F. B. Rothman, 1962.

Bodde, Derk. *Peking Diary.* New York, Schuman, 1950.

Boorman, Howard, ed. *Biographical Dictionary of Republican China.* 4 vols. New York, Columbia University Press, 1967, 1970, 1971.

Borg, Dorothy. *American Policy and the Chinese Revolution, 1925–1928.* New

York, The Macmillan Co., 1947.

Boynton, Grace. *The River Garden of Pure Repose*. New York, McGraw Hill, 1952.

Bush, Richard C., Jr. *Religion in Communist China*. Nashville, Abingdon Press, 1970.

Caute, David. *The Fellow-Traveler: A Postscript to the Enlightenment*. New York, Macmillan, 1973.

Chang Ch'in-shih, 張欽士 ed. *Kuo-nei chin-shih-nien lai chih tsung-chiao ssu-ch'ao* 國內近十年來之宗教思潮 (Tides of religious thought in China over the last ten years). Peking, 1927.

Chao Tzu-ch'en 趙紫宸. *Yeh-su chuan* 耶穌傳 (The life of Jesus). Shanghai, 1935.

—— *Hsi yu chi* 繫獄記 (My experience in prison). Shanghai, 1948.

Chen-li chou-k'an 眞理週刊 (The truth weekly). Peking, 1923–26.

Chen-li yu sheng-ming 眞理與生命 (The truth and life). Peiping, 1926–37.

Ch'en, Theodore H. E. *Thought Reform of the Chinese Intellectuals*. Hong Kong, Hong Kong University Press, 1960.

Ch'en Tu-hsiu 陳獨秀. *Tu-hsiu wen-ts'un* 獨秀文存 (Collected essays of Ch'en Tu-hsiu). Hong Kong, 1965.

Chen, Wen-hui C. *Chinese Communist Anti-Americanism and the Resist-America Aid Korea Campaign*. Series 1, no. 4. Maxwell Air Force Base, Ala., Human Resources Research Institute, May 1955.

Cheng Tien-fong (Ch'eng T'ien-fang). *A History of Sino-Russian Relations*. Washington, D. C., Public Affairs Press, 1957.

China Christian Yearbook. Shanghai, Christian Literature Society, 1926, 1929, 1931.

China Monthly Review. Shanghai, 1949–53.

Chinese Recorder. Shanghai, 1874–1940.

Chinese Social and Political Science Review. Peking, 1916–40.

The Chinese Yearbook. Shanghai, 1935–36.

Christian Century. Chicago, The Christian Century Press.

Chow Tse-tsung. *The May Fourth Movement*. Cambridge, Mass., Harvard University Press, 1964.

Christian China. New York, Chinese Student Christian Association, 1910s and 1920s.

Ch'uan-kuo kao-teng chiao-yu t'ung-chi 全國高等教育統計 (Statistics on Chinese higher education). Nanking, Central Government Publications, 1931, 1933.

Chung Shih. *Higher Education in Communist China*. Hong Kong, Union Research Institute, 1953.

Current Background. Hong Kong, Press monitoring service of the American

Consulate, 1950–.

DeBary, Wm. Theodore, ed. *Self and Society in Ming Thought*. New York, Columbia University Press, 1970.

—— *Sources of Chinese Tradition*. New York, Columbia University Press, 1960.

Dewey, John. *Lectures in China, 1919–1920*, trans. and ed. Robert W. Clopton and Tswin-chen Ou. Honolulu, University Press of Hawaii, 1973.

Dillenberger, John, and Claude Welch. *Protestant Christianity, Interpreted Through Its Development*. New York, Scribner, 1954.

Dunne, George. *Generation of Giants: The Story of the Jesuits in China in the Last Decades of the Ming Dynasty*. South Bend, Indiana, Notre Dame University Press, 1962.

Educational Review. Shanghai, 1907–38.

Edwards, Dwight. *Yenching University*. New York, United Board for Christian Higher Education in Asia, 1959.

Fairbank, John K., ed. *The Missionary Enterprise in China and America*. Cambridge, Harvard University Press, 1974.

Foreign Relations of the United States, China volumes for years 1945, 1946, 1947, 1948. Washington, D.C., U.S. Government Printing Office.

Fraser, Stewart. *Chinese Communist Education*. Nashville, Tenn., Vanderbilt University Press, 1965.

Fu Ssu-nien 傅斯年. *Fu Ssu-nien hsüan-chi* 傅斯年選集 (Selected works of Fu Ssu-nien). 5 vols. Taipei, 1967.

Fulton, Brank. "Notes on Dr. Stuart's Life." Interviews during 1940–41, in GMB:PC.

Gamble, Sidney D. *Peking: A Social Survey*. New York, George H. Doran, 1921.

Garrett, Shirley S. *Social Reformers in Urban China: The Chinese Y.M.C.A., 1895–1926*. Cambridge, Harvard University Press, 1970.

Garside, B. A. *One Increasing Purpose: The Life of Henry Winters Luce*. New York, F. H. Revell, 1948.

Gilkey, Langdon Brown. *Shantung Compound: The Story of Men and Women under Pressure*. New York, Harper and Row, 1966.

Gregg, Alice H. *China and Educational Autonomy*. Syracuse, N.Y., Syracuse University Press, 1946.

Grieder, Jerome B. *Hu Shih and the Chinese Renaissance: Liberalism in the Chinese Revolution, 1917–1937*. Cambridge, Harvard University Press, 1970.

Griggs, Thurston. *Americans in China: Some Chinese Views*. Washington, D.C., Foundation for Foreign Affairs, 1948.

Han Su-yin. *A Mortal Flower*. New York, G. P. Putnam, 1965.

Harrison, James P. *The Long March to Power: A History of the Chinese Communist Party*. New York, Praeger Publishers, 1972.

Hashikawa Tokio 橋川時雄 ed. *Chūgoku bunka kai jimbutsu sōkan* 中國文化界人物總鑑 (Biographical dictionary of Chinese intellectuals). Peking, 1940.

Hsin ch'ing-nien 新青年 (The new youth). Peking and Shanghai, 1915-21.

Hsin Yen-ching 新燕京 (The new Yenching). Peking, 1949-52.

Hsü, Immanuel C. Y., ed. *Readings in Modern Chinese History*. New York, Oxford University Press, 1971.

Hsü Ch'ien 徐謙. *Chi-tu-chiao chiu-kuo chu-yi k'an-hsing chih san* 基督教救國主義刊行之三 (Three publications on Christian national salvation). Shanghai, 1920.

Hsü, Pao-ch'ien. *Ethical Realism in Neo-Confucian Thought*. Peiping, Yenching University, 1933.

—— *Tsung-chiao ching-yen t'an* 宗教經驗譚 (Discussions of religious experience). Shanghai, Ch'ing-nien hsieh-hui shu-chü, 1934.

Hummel, Arthur W., ed. *Eminent Chinese of the Ch'ing Period, 1644-1912*. 2 vols. Washington, D.C., U.S. Government Printing Office, 1943.

Hung Yeh. *Ho Shen and Shu-sh'un-yuan: An Episode in the Past of the Yenching Campus*. Peiping, Yenching University, 1934.

International Review of Missions. London, Continuation Committee of the World Missionary Conference, 1910–.

Isaacs, Harold R. *No Peace for Asia*. New York, Macmillan, 1947.

Israel, John. *Student Nationalism in China, 1927-1937*. Stanford, Stanford University Press, 1966.

James, William. *Varieties of Religious Experience*. New York, Modern Library, 1902.

Jen-wu yüeh-k'an 人物月刊 (Journal of personalities). Vol. 1. Peiping, 1936.

Jones, Francis P. *The Church in Communist China*. New York, Friendship Press, 1962.

Kates, George Norbert. *The Years That Were Fat*. New York, Harper, 1952.

Kiang Wen-han. *The Chinese Student Movement*. New York, King's Crown Press, 1948.

Kindai Chūgoku Kenkyū 近代中國研究 (Studies of modern Chinese). Tokyo, 1958–.

Lang, Olga. *Chinese Family and Society*. New Haven, Yale University Press, 1946.

Lapwood, Ralph and Nancy. *Through the Chinese Revolution*. London, Spalding and Levy, 1954.

Latourette, Kenneth Scott. *A History of Christian Missions in China*. London, Society for Promoting Christian Knowledge, 1929.

Levenson, Joseph. *Modern China and Its Confucian Past*. Garden City, N.Y., 1964. (Paperback version of *Confucian China and Its Modern Fate*. Berkeley, University of California Press, 1958.)

Lifton, Robert J. *Thought Reform and the Psychology of Totalism: A Study of "Brainwashing" in China*. New York, Norton, 1963.

Lin Yu-tang. *My Country and My People*. New York, Reynal & Hitchcock, 1935.

Liu Kwang-ching, ed. *American Missionaries in China*. Cambridge, Harvard University Press, 1966.

Lutz, Jessie. *China and the Christian Colleges, 1850–1950*. Ithaca, N.Y., Cornell University Press, 1971.

Lutz, Jessie G., ed. *Christian Missions in China: Evangelists of What?* Boston, D.C. Heath, 1965.

Mao Tse-tung. *On New Democracy*. Peking, Foreign Languages Press, 1954.
——— *Selected Works*. 4 vols. Peking, Foreign Languages Press, 1964.

Meisner, Maurice. *Li Ta-chao and the Origins of Chinese Marxism*. Cambridge, Harvard University Press, 1967.

Merwin, Wallace, and Francis P. Jones, eds. *Documents of the Three-Self Movement: Source Materials for the Study of the Protestant Church in Communist China*. New York, National Council of the Churches of Christ, 1963.

National Cyclopedia of American Biography. New York, James T. White, 1954.
Nationalist China. New York, Foreign Policy Association, 1931.

Ng, Lee Ming. "Christianity and Social Change: The Case in China, 1920–1950," Ph.D. dissertation, Princeton Theological Seminary, 1971.

North, Robert. *Moscow and the Chinese Communists*. Stanford, Stanford University Press, 1953.

Oksenberg, Michael, ed. *China's Developmental Experience*. New York, Praeger, 1973.

Peake, Cyrus. *Nationalism and Education in Modern China*. New York, Columbia University Press, 1932.

Pei-p'ing ssu-li Yen-ching ta-hsüeh yi-lan 北平私立燕京大學一覽 (Catalogue of Yenching University). Peiping, Yenching University, 1931, 1937.

People's Republic of China: An Economic Assessment. Washington, D.C., U.S. Government Printing Office, May 18, 1972.

Perleberg, Max. *Who's Who in Modern China.* Hong Kong, Ye Olde Printerie, 1954.

Porter, Lucius C. *China's Challenge to Christianity.* New York, Missionary Education Movement of the United States and Canada, 1924.

Price, R. F. *Education in Communist China.* New York, Praeger, 1972.

Rankin, Mary. *Early Chinese Revolutionaries: Radical Intellectuals in Shanghai and Chekiang, 1902–1911.* Cambridge, Harvard University Press, 1959.

Rawlinson, Frank, et al., eds. *The Chinese Church: The National Christian Conference.* Shanghai, Oriental Press, 1922.

Records of the General Conference of the Protestant Missionaries of China. Shanghai, American Presbyterian Mission Press, 1890.

Scheiner, Irwin. *Christian Converts and Social Protest in Meiji Japan.* Berkeley, University of California Press, 1970.

Schneider, Laurence A. *Ku Chieh-kang and China's New History: Nationalism and the Quest for Alternative Traditions.* Berkeley, University of California Press, 1971.

Schram, Stuart R. *The Political Thought of Mao Tse-tung.* New York, Frederick A. Praeger, 1963, 1969.

Schwartz, Benjamin. *Communism and China: Ideology in Flux.* Cambridge, Harvard University Press, 1968.

Sheean, Vincent. *Personal History.* New York, The Literary Guild, 1935.

Sheng-ming 生命 (The life journal). Peking, Sheng-ming she, 1919–26.

Snow, Edgar. *Journey to the Beginning.* New York, Random House, 1958.

Snow, Helen Foster. *Women in Modern China.* Hague, Mouton, 1967.

Stauffer, Milton T., ed. *The Christian Occupation of China.* Shanghai, China Continuation Committee, 1922.

———— *China Her Own Interpreter.* New York, Missionary Education Movement of the United States and Canada, 1927.

Stuart, John Leighton. *Fifty Years in China: The Memoirs of John Leighton Stuart, Missionary and Ambassador.* New York, Random House, 1954. (Stuart's memoirs were published in Chinese as *Ssu-t'u Lei-teng hui-yi lu* 司徒雷登回憶錄. Taipei, 1954.)

Sung-chu sheng-shih 頌主聖詩 (Hymns of universal praise). Shanghai, Chung-hua Chi-tu-chiao wen-she, 1936.

Thomson, James C., Jr. *While China Faced West: American Reformers in Nationalist China, 1928–37.* Cambridge, Harvard University Press, 1969.

Topping, Seymour. *Journey Between Two Chinas.* New York, Harper and Row,

1972.

Treadgold, Donald. *The West in Russia and China: China 1582–1949.* Vol. II. New York, Cambridge University Press, 1972.

Tsou Tang. *America's Failure in China, 1941–1950.* Chicago, University of Chicago Press, 1963.

United Nations Security Council Official Records. New York, United Nations, 1951.

United States Relations with China. Washington, D.C., U.S. Government Printing Office, 1949.

Varg, Paul. *Missionaries, Chinese and Diplomats.* Princeton, N.J., Princeton University Press, 1958.

Vincent, John Carter. *The Extraterritorial System in China.* Cambridge, Harvard University Press, 1970.

Wang, T. C. *The Youth Movement in China.* New York, New Republic, 1927.

Wang, Y. C. *Chinese Intellectuals and the West, 1872–1949.* Chapel Hill, N.C., North Carolina University Press, 1966.

Wei-ta ti k'ang-Mei yüan-Ch'ao yün-tung (The great Resist America Aid Korea movement). Peking, 1954.

Whiting, Allen S. *China Crosses the Yalu: The Decision to Enter the Korean War.* New York, Macmillan, 1960.

Who's Who in China. Shanghai, China Weekly Review Press, 1925, 1931, and 1936.

Who's Who in Communist China. 2 vols. Hong Kong, Union Research Institute, 1969.

Wu Lei-ch'uan 吳雷川. *Chi-tu-chiao yü Chung-kuo wen-hua* 基督教與中國文化 (Christianity and Chinese culture). Shanghai, 1936.

—— *Chi-tu-t'u ti hsi-wang* 基督徒的希望 (The Christian's hope). Shanghai, 1939.

—— *Mo-ti yü Yeh-su* 墨翟與耶穌 (Motzu and Jesus). Shanghai, 1940.

Yamamoto Sumiko 山本澄子. *Chūgoku Kirisutokyō shi kenkyū* 中國キリスト教史研究 (Studies on the history of Christianity in China). Tokyo, 1972.

Yang K'ai-tao (Cato Yang) et al. *Ching Ho: A Sociological Analysis.* Peiping, Yenching University, 1930.

Yen, Maria (Kuei-lai). *The Umbrella Garden: A Picture of Student Life in Red China.* New York, Macmillan, 1954.

Yen-ching ta-hsüeh hsiao-k'an 燕京大學校刊 (Yenching University Faculty Bulletin). Peiping, 1927–37.

Yen-ta chou-k'an 燕大週刊 (Yenta weekly). Peking, 1923–36.

Bibliography

Yen-ta hsiao-k'an 燕大校刊 (Yenta Alumni Bulletin). Palo Alto, Calif., Yenching Alumni Association, USA, 1973.

Yen-ta hsiao-yu t'ung-hsün 燕大校友通訊 (Yenta Alumni Bulletin). Hong Kong, Yenching University Alumni Association, 1963, 1965, 1967.

Yen-ta yu-sheng 燕大友聲 (Yenta Alumni News). Peiping, 1931–37.

Yen-ta yüeh-k'an 燕大月刊 (Yenta monthly). Peiping, 1927–34.

Glossary

Ariga Tetsutarō 有賀鉄太郎
ch'a-pu-tuo 差不多
Chang Chao-lin 張兆麐
Chang Ch'in-shih 張欽士
Chang Ch'ing-yeh 張清業
Chang Chün-mai 張君勱
Chang Erh-t'ien 張爾田
Chang Fei 張蜚
Chang Fu-liang 張福良
Chang Hsüeh-liang 張學良
Chang Hung-chün 張鴻鈞
Chang Kuan-lien 張官廉
Chang Po-ling 張伯苓
Chang T'ieh-sheng 張鐵笙
Chang T'ing-che (Wen-li) 張廷哲 (文理)
Chang Tsai 張載
Chang Tso-lin 張作霖
Chang Tung-sun 張東蓀
Chao Ch'eng-hsin 趙承信
Chen-li she 眞理社
Chen-shih she 眞實社
Ch'en Ch'i-t'ien (Gideon Ch'en) 陳其田
Ch'en Ch'i-t'ien 陳啟天
Ch'en Fang-chih (Agnus Chen) 陳芳芝
Ch'en Han-po 陳翰伯
Ch'en Hsin-feng 陳新桂
Ch'en Kuan-sheng 陳觀勝
Ch'en Yüan 陳垣
cheng-chih hsüeh-hsi 政治學習
Cheng-tao t'uan 證道團
Cheng Te-k'un 鄭德坤
Cheng T'ing-ch'un 鄭庭椿
Ch'eng-fu 成府
Ch'i Ssu-ho 齊思和
Chi-tu-chiao chiu-kuo chu-yi hui 基督會救國主義會
Chi-tu chiao hsieh-chin hui 基督教協進會
Chi-tu-chiao hsin-ssu-ch'ao 基督教新思潮
Chiang Monlin (Meng-lin) 蔣夢麐
Chiang-pei kao-teng hsüeh-t'ang 江北高等學堂

chiao-yü chiu-kuo 教育救國

Chieh-yüeh chien-ch'a wei-yüan hui 節約檢查委員會

Chien Po-tsan 翦伯贊

Ch'ien Hsüan-t'ung 錢玄同

Ch'ien Mu 錢穆

ch'ih chiao-t'u 吃教徒

chin-shih 進士

Ch'ing-chiang 清江

Ch'ing-ho 清河

chiu-kuo 救國

Ch'iu Jen-ch'u 邱軼初

Chou Nien-tz'u (Nancy Chou) 周念慈

Chou Tso-jen 周作人

Chou Tso-min 周作民

Chou Yi-ch'un (Y. T. Tsur) 周詒春

Chu Tzu-ch'ing 朱自清

Chu Yu-kuang 朱有光

Ch'u Shan 出山

Ch'ü Shih-ying 瞿世英

Ch'üan Shao-wen 全紹文

Chün 軍

Chung-hua Chi-tu-chiao wen-she 中華基督教文社

Chung-kung Yen-ta chih-pu 中公燕大支部

Chung-kuo chiao-yü kai-chin she 中國教育改進社

Chung-kuo wen-hua ching-chi hsieh-hui 中國文化經濟協會

Chung-yang yen-chiu yüan 中央研究院

chü-jen 舉人

Ch'ü T'ung-tsu 瞿同祖

fan-shen 翻身

fan-wan ti chi-tu t'u 飯碗的基督徒

fei-ch'ang shih-ch'i chiao-yü 非常時期教育

Fei Hsiao-t'ung 費孝通

fen-tou hsi-sheng chiu-kuo 奮鬥犧牲救國

Feng Yu-lan 馮友蘭

Feng Yü-hsiang 馮玉祥

Fu Ch'ing-po (Philip Fu) 傅涇波

Fu Ssu-nien 傅斯年

Hai-tien 海甸

han-chien 漢奸

han-lin 翰林

Hou Jen-chih 侯仁之

Hsiao kung-hui 校工會

hsiao-chang 校長

hsiao-wu-chang 校務長

hsieh-chu 協助

Hsieh-ho ta-hsüeh 協和大學

Hsieh Ping-hsin (Wan-ying) 謝冰心 (婉瑩)

Hsin-min chu chu-yi ch'ing-nien t'uan 新民主主義青年團

hsiu-ts'ai 秀才

hsiu-yang 修養

Hsiung Fo-hsi 熊佛西

Hsü Ch'ien 徐謙

Hsü Kuang-ch'i 徐光啟

Hsü Pao-ch'ien 徐寶謙

Hsü Shih-lien (Leonard S.) 許仕廉

Hsü Shu-hsi 徐淑希

Hsü Ti-shan 許地山

hsüeh-she 學社

hsüeh-sheng tzu-chih hui 學生自治會

Hu-chiang ta-hsüeh (University of Shanghai) 滬江大學

Hu Hsüeh-ch'eng 胡學誠

Hu Shih 胡適

hui-kai 悔改

Hui-wen ta-hsüeh 匯文大學

Hung Yeh 洪業

Ikeda Kiyoko 武田清子

jen-ko 人格

jen-ko chiu-kuo 人格救國

Jen Ling-hsün (Richard L. Jen) 任玲遜

Jen T'i 仁惕

jen-ts'ai chiu-kuo 人材救國
ju-yi 儒醫
Jung Keng 容庚
kao-ch'ang hui 高唱會
Kao Ming-k'ai 高名凱
Ku-an 固安
Ku Chieh-kang 顧頡剛
Ku Sung 孤松
Ku Wei-chün (Wellington Koo) 顧維鈞
Kuan Sung-shan 關頌姍
Kuang-hua ta-hsüeh 光華大學
kuei-tsu hsüeh-hsiao 貴族學校
K'uei-chia-ch'ang 盔甲廠
Kung P'u-sheng 龔普生
Kung Wei-hang (Kung P'eng) 龔維航
K'ung chiao-hui 孔教會
K'ung Hsiang-hsi (H. H. Kung) 孔祥熙
K'ung-su hui 控訴會
kuo-hsüeh yen-chiu so 國學研究所
kuo-min hsing 國民性
Kuo Mo-jo 郭沫若
Lang Jun Yüan 朗潤園
Lao Chang 老張
Lei Chieh-ch'iung 雷潔瓊
Li An-che (An-chai) 李安宅
Li Chih-tsao 李之藻
Li-ch'uan (Lichuan) 黎川
Li Jung-fang 李榮芳
Li Man-kuei 李滿桂
Li Min 李敏
Li Ta-chao 李大釗
Li Yüan-hung 黎元洪
Liang Ch'i-ch'ao 梁啟超
Liang Shih-ch'un 梁士純
Liang Yang 梁楊
Lin Cho-yüan 林卓園
Lin Shou-chin 林壽晋
Ling-nan ta-hsüeh 嶺南大學
Liu Chieh 劉節

Liu T'ing-fang 劉廷芳
Liu Tzu-chien (James T. C. Liu) 劉子建
Lu Chih-wei 陸志韋
Lu Hsün 魯迅
Lu Yao-hua 陸瑤華
Ma Hsü-lun 馬敍倫
Ma Meng 馬蒙
Ma Ssu-ts'ung 馬思聰
Mei-kuo hua 美國化
Mei Yi-ch'i 梅貽琦
Mei Yi-pao 梅貽寶
Mu Han 慕韓
Nieh Ch'ung-ch'i 聶崇歧
Pai Shou-yi 白壽彝
pan-fan 半番
pao 報
Pei-p'ing yen-chiu yüan 北平研究院
Peita 北大
pen-se 本色
P'ing-hsi pao 平西報
p'ing-min hsüeh-hsiao 平民學校
po-shih 博士
pu-tsu 不足
pu-tzu-ssu ti ching-shen 不自私的精神
Sakisaka Itsurō 向坂逸郎
she 社
she-hui shih-chin hui 社會實進會
Shen-pao 申報
she-li-che 設立者
Shen Chien-hung (James C. H. Shen) 沈劍虹
Shen Chih-yüan 沈志遠
Shen Nai-chang 沈廼璋
Sheng-ming 生命
Sheng-ming she 生命社
Sheng-shui hui 聖水會
Shih-hsüeh nien-pao 史學年報
shih-ming 使命
Shih Yu-chung (Vincent Shih) 施友忠

Shou-hui chiao-yü-ch'üan yün-tung
收回教育權運動

Shui-wu hsüeh-hsiao 稅務學校

Sun Ko (Fo) 孫科

Sung Che-yüan 宋哲元

Sung-chu sheng-shih 頌主聖詩

Ta kung-pao 大公報

ta-tzu-pao 大字報

tai-yü 待遇

Tanaka Tadao 田中忠夫

T'an Hui-ying 譚誨英

T'an Jen-chiu 譚紉就

tang-hua chiao-yü 黨化教育

T'ang Shao-yi 唐紹儀

T'ao Ch'ien 陶潛

te-chiu 得救

Te-chou 德州

Teng-chih-ch'eng 鄧之誠

Teng-shih-k'ou 燈市口

Teng Ssu-yü 鄧嗣禹

t'ien 天

Torii Ryūzō 鳥居龍藏

T'ien Hsing-chih (Gerald Tien)
田興智

Ts'ai Liu-sheng 蔡鎦生

Ts'ai Yi-eh (Stephen O.) 蔡一諤

Ts'ai Yüan-p'ei 蔡元培

ts'an-shih 參事

ts'e 冊

Tseng Pao-sun 曾寶蓀

Tsing-hua ta-hsüeh 清華大學

tsui 罪

tsui-e 罪惡

tsung-chiao ching-yen 宗教經驗

Tu Fu 杜甫

tu-shu chiu-kuo 讀書救國

Tuan Ch'i-jui 段祺瑞

t'uan 團

tung-shih-hui 董事會

Tung-t'ai-p'ing 東太平

Tung-wu ta-hsüeh 東吳大學

T'ung-wen pao 通問報

tuo-hsing 惰性

t'uo-shih-pu 託事部

tzu-ssu 自私

Wan-kuo kung-pao 萬國公報

Wang Ching-wei 汪精衛

Wang Ch'ung-hui 王寵惠

Wang Hou-feng 王厚風

Wang Yang-ming 王陽明

Wang Ju-mei (Huang Hua) 王汝梅

Wei-ai she 惟愛社

Wei Chao-ch'i 魏兆淇

Wei Ching-meng 魏景蒙

Wei Chüeh (Sidney K.) 韋愨

wei-jen fu-wu 爲人服務

Wei Shih-yi 魏士毅

Wen-hsüeh nien-pao 文學年報

Wen I-tuo 聞一多

Wen T'ien-hsiang 文天祥

Wo-fo-ssu 臥佛寺

Wu Cho-sheng 吳卓生

Wei-jen 委任

Wen-chow 溫州

Wu Hsing-hua 吳興華

Wu Hsiu-ch'üan 伍修權

Wu Hsü-ts'an 吳序燦

Wu Kung 武公

Wu Lei-ch'uan 吳雷川

Wu Wen-tsao 吳文藻

Wu Yao-tsung 吳耀宗

Yang Ch'ing-k'un (C. K. Yang)
楊慶堃

Yang Ju-chi 楊汝佶

Yang K'ai-tao (Cato Yang) 楊開道

Yang Kang (Yang Ping) 楊鋼
(楊繽)

yang-nu 洋奴

yang po-shih 洋博士

Yang T'ing-yün 楊廷筠

Yeh Ch'u-sheng 葉楚生

Yeh-su chia 耶穌家

Yeh Te-kuang 葉德光

yeh-wu hsüeh-hsi 業務學習

Yen-ching hsüeh-pao 燕京學報
Yen Ching-yüeh 嚴景耀
Yen Fu 嚴復
Yen Hui-ch'ing (W. W. Yen) 顏惠慶
Yen-ta k'ang-Jih hui 燕大抗日會
Yen-ta k'ang-Mei hui 燕大抗美會
yi-lai hsin-li 倚賴心理
yin chen-li te tzu-yu yi fu-wu 因眞
理得自由以服務
Yü Chia-chü 余家菊
Yü Hsia-ch'ing (Ya-ching) 虞洽卿
yü-k'o 預科
Yü P'ing-po 兪平伯
Yü Ying-shih 余英時
yün-tung 運動

Index

Index